The Augsburg Confession
– and the –
Apology of the Augsburg Confession
– with –
Key Historical Documents:

The Concordia Reader's Edition

Excerpted from the Book of Concord in *Concordia: The Lutheran Confessions*

Available from Concordia Publishing House
800-325-3040 or cph.org/concordia

Published 2020 Concordia Publishing House
3558 S. Jefferson Ave., St. Louis, MO 63118-3968
1-800-325-3040 • cph.org

The Richard C. Kessler Reformation Collection; Pitts Theology Library, Candler School of Theology, Emory University, pages 56, 63, 73, 81, 85, 89, 99, 113, 122, 127, 135, 140, 142, 145, 168 (bottom), 188, 192, 211, 223, 231.

Rev. Matthew C. Harrison, Private Collection, pages 11, 12, 18, 24, 25, 43, 58, 92, 143, 148, 168 (top).

The Complete Woodcuts of Albrecht Dürer, edited by Willi Kurth (New York: Arden Book Company, 1936, page 8.

The Smithey Collection of Reformation Works, Pritzlaff Memorial Library Rare Book Collection: Concordia Seminary Library, St. Louis, Missouri, page 17, 154, 177, 206, 226.

Manufactured in the United States of America

1 2 3 4 5 6 7 8 9 10 29 28 27 26 25 24 23 22 21 20

Table of Contents

Publisher's Introduction

The two most foundational statements of what the Lutheran Church believes, teaches, and confesses are the Augsburg Confession[1] and the Apology of the Augsburg Confession.[2] This book provides both of these documents, along with several other historical texts that are important for understanding the historical context of the preparation and presentation of the Augsburg Confession and the Apology. The supplemental texts include Martin Luther's *Exhortation to the Clergy Assembled at the Diet at Augsburg* (May 1530), John Eck's *404 Theses* (June 1530), and the Roman *Confutation of the Augsburg Confession* (August 1530).

The Lutherans who attended the Diet of Augsburg in 1530 had to leave Luther behind at the Coburg Castle because he was still in considerable danger. Coburg was the southernmost city of Electoral Saxony, so Luther was safe there. It was from Coburg that Luther prepared his Exhortation for the Lutheran princes and theologians, and chiefly for Philip Melanchthon, who was finalizing the text of the Augsburg Confession. Melanchthon took Luther's words very seriously; we can see Luther's influence in the Augsburg Confession. The Roman Catholic scholar who was directed to translate Luther's Exhortation into Latin for the Roman Catholic theologians in Augsburg told a friend, "It is a summary of all Lutheranism. If you want to know the whole Luther, you would better buy it."

Dramatically, right before the Diet began to meet, Luther's old nemesis John Eck launched a "sneak attack" and published and distributed to all those in Augsburg a document titled simply *404 Theses*. It was a scorched-earth attack on Luther and other reformers, offering up a mishmash of accusations, lies, half-truths, and obfuscations, all designed to lump Luther in with Ulrich Zwingli and other Reformed theologians and beyond them, even the most wild-eyed radicals of the Reformation. Eck's document forced the Lutherans to add to the Augsburg Confession a series of doctrinal statements clarifying what it was that they believed, taught, and confessed and what therefore they condemned. At first, the Augsburg Confession was intended only to be an explanation of what the Lutherans had reformed and corrected; these articles were put behind the doctrinal assertions.

The Augsburg Confession was read out loud and formally presented to Emperor Charles V on June 25, 1530. Charles V quickly ordered his court advisors and theologians to prepare a written refutation and response, titled "*Confutation of the Augsburg Confession*." Five drafts were rejected before finally, after six weeks, the emperor accepted their text. It was read aloud to the Lutherans, but they never were provided

1 "Confession" here means a public statement of doctrinal beliefs.

2 "Apology" here does not mean, "I'm sorry," but rather, "defense," from the Greek "apologia."

a copy, and ironically, it was never even published until 1573, in Latin, and not in German until 1808. But, fortunately, Lutheran stenographers accurately wrote the content down as it was being read. The Apology was published in May 1531 and is known as the "quarto"[3] edition. Though Melanchthon kept making changes to the Apology, this quarto edition was included in the Latin edition of the Book of Concord in 1584; thus, it is the official edition of the Apology of the Augsburg Confession. The later "octavo"[4] edition with Melanchthon's changes is not an official version of the Apology and, while useful for study, should not be used in translations of the Lutheran Church's Book of Concord.

The translation of the Augsburg Confession and the Apology of the Augsburg Confession (from their Latin versions), along with introductions, explanations, annotations, notes, and graphics, are from a special edition of the Book of Concord titled *Concordia: The Lutheran Confessions—A Reader's Edition of the Book of Concord.* The texts of the supplemental documents, along with their introductions, are reproduced from public domain sources, as noted at the beginning of each document and as indicated on the copyright page of this book.[5]

Anyone interested in the history of the Reformation will find this collection useful, but it will be particularly important for those who make the Augsburg Confession and its Apology their own confession of faith. Genuinely Lutheran Christians and churches take their place with generations of other Lutherans who, for nearly five hundred years, have taken their stand for the truth of Holy Scripture as it is so clearly, powerfully, and beautifully summarized and articulated in these statements of faith. We do so always for sake of the precious Good News of Jesus Christ, the Savior of sinners, the world's redeemer and only hope, by whom we are saved by grace alone, through faith alone, on account of Jesus Christ alone.

I will also speak of Your testimonies before kings and shall not be put to shame.

PSALM 119:46.

Rev. Paul T. McCain
Publisher, Concordia Publishing House
June 25, 2020
The 490th Anniversary of the
Presentation of the Augsburg Confession

---

3 A book size in which four pages are cut from a single sheet of paper.

4 A book size in which eight pages are cut from a single sheet of paper.

5 I would be remiss were I not to heartily recommend *The Augsburg Confession: A Collection of Sources with a Historical Introduction* by Johann Michael Reu. This is ideal for readers who want to go even more deeply into the history and context of the Augsburg Confession. It remains to this day, by far, the most comprehensive collection of sources pertaining to the development, presentation, and publication of the Augsburg Confession and subsequent history available in English. There is nothing else like it. It is available from Concordia Publishing House as an ebook. There are reprints of it available elsewhere, but be sure they are the entire, nearly 800-page edition.

THE CONFESSION OF FAITH

‹THE AUGSBURG CONFESSION›

which was submitted to
His Imperial Majesty Charles V at the
Imperial Meeting of Augsburg
in the Year 1530
‹by certain princes and cities›

*I will also speak of Your testimonies before kings
and shall not be put to shame.*

Psalm 119:46

The Wise Men Adore Christ

During the Imperial Meeting [Diet] of Augsburg, Lutheran princes confessed their faith boldly before the most powerful leaders of Europe. The powerful and mighty are always most wise when they bow in humble adoration before Christ.

Editor's Introduction to the Augsburg Confession

Against the gates of hell, with the grace and help of God.

—Layman Gregory Brück

On Saturday, June 25, 1530, at three o'clock in the afternoon, Dr. Christian Beyer stood, walked toward the Emperor of the Holy Roman Empire, Charles V, and began reading the Augsburg Confession in a loud and distinct voice. Through the open windows a hushed crowd outside in the courtyard hung on his every word, as did the two hundred or so people gathered in the hall. Beside Dr. Beyer stood Dr. Gregory Brück, holding a copy of the Augsburg Confession in Latin. The German princes around them stood up to indicate their support for the Confession. The emperor motioned for them to sit down.

When Dr. Beyer finished reading, Dr. Brück took the German copy of the Confession from him, handed both copies to the emperor, and said, "Most gracious Emperor, this is a Confession that will even prevail against the gates of hell, with the grace and help of God." Thus was the Augsburg Confession presented as a unique Confession of the truth of God's holy Word, distinct from Romanism on the one hand, and Reformed, Anabaptists, and radicals on the other. June 25, 1530, is a date every bit as important for Lutherans as is the more familiar date of October 31, 1517— the day on which Luther posted his Ninety-five Theses.

Events Leading to Augsburg

The presentation of the Augsburg Confession was a decisive moment, one long in coming. It is important to understand the history leading up to the Imperial Meeting at Augsburg. Nine years earlier, on April 18, 1521, at the Imperial Meeting in Worms, Charles had listened as Martin Luther refused to recant his teachings, saying, "I cannot and will not recant. I cannot do otherwise. Here I stand. God help me. Amen." Now Charles was watching as the most important rulers in his German territories confessed their faith openly and courageously in spite of the threats to their lives from both the government and the Church.

Martin Luther had been declared a criminal and a heretic; he was excommunicated and sentenced to death in April of 1521. By 1526, the Reformation had spread to the point that during an Imperial Meeting at Speyer, the Lutheran princes forced through a resolution that gave each of them the right to arrange religious matters in their respective territories—in any way he felt was best—until the emperor was able to have the pope call a General Council of the Church. So from 1526 to 1529, little changed in the Holy Roman Empire. As a result, most of Northern Germany became

Lutheran, along with many cities in Southern Germany. At the second Imperial Meeting in Speyer (1529), the princes loyal to Rome reversed the decision made three years earlier. The princes loyal to the Lutheran Reformation and other reforming movements fiercely protested this decision, issuing a formal *Protestio*. Thus the Lutherans, along with other reformers, were labeled *Protestants*. The name has stuck ever since.

Charles ordered all rulers within the Empire to go to Augsburg to attend the Imperial Meeting (also known as a *Reichstag* or a *Diet*). He wanted to settle, once and for all, the controversies in the churches throughout his Germany. The armies of the Turkish Empire were literally at the eastern gates of Charles's Empire. He wanted unity so that the Turkish threat could be met. He hoped that a combination of kindness, cajoling, and finally, threats, would stop the Lutheran movement and restore Romanism throughout the Empire. But things did not go as Charles had hoped.

The Schwabach, Marburg, and Torgau Articles

Lutheranism was only tolerated where it could not be eliminated by military force. Lutherans had no protection in German territories that were loyal to Rome. After the 1529 Diet of Speyer, Philip of Hesse sought to create a political federation for the mutual defense of those who had protested the autocratic action of Charles V. Philip of Hesse and Jacob Sturm united Saxony and Hesse with certain Southern German evangelical cities (with Ulm, Strasbourg, and Nürnberg as the nucleus). The coalition was created on April 22, 1529, in a secret agreement at Speyer. To clear the way for possible inclusion of the Swiss in the federation, Philip of Hesse planned to settle the dispute between Luther and Ulrich Zwingli at a meeting at Philip's castle in Marburg.

The Lutherans were concerned by Philip of Hesse's desire to put political unity ahead of doctrinal unity. After the Diet of Speyer, Philip Melanchthon (who had kept silent regarding differences between the German Lutherans and the Swiss) had a change of heart and tried to thwart the federation. Luther also opposed a federation without confessional unity. The Schwabach Articles were prepared by Luther and others sometime between July 25 and September 14 of that year.

The Marburg Colloquy took place October 2–4, 1529. Ulrich Zwingli and Martin Luther faced each other across a table for most of the meeting. The two groups identified much that they agreed about, yet the talks broke down. The disagreement had to do with the Lord's Supper. Zwingli was willing to settle for an "agreement to disagree" approach, but Luther insisted that Jesus' words "This is My body" mean "This *is* My body." In fact, he took a piece of chalk and wrote the words "This is My body" on the table itself (*Hoc est Corpus Meum*). Whenever Zwingli or the other Swiss Reformers tried to disagree with Luther about the reality of those words, Luther would lift the tablecloth and point to the words. The Marburg Articles therefore indicate "We are not agreed as to whether the true body and blood of Christ are bodily present in the bread and wine."

The Marburg Articles, along with the Schwabach Articles, provided a firm foundation for the writing of the Augsburg Confession. The seventeen Schwabach

Articles were first presented on October 16, 1529. They insisted on unity in doctrine as a prerequisite for any cooperation among the various Protestant groups in Germany.

Charles V persisted with his efforts to eliminate the religious controversies in his territories. He was facing pressure from the threat of a Turkish invasion from the East. He was also mindful that the pope might, at any time, strike an alliance with the ruler of France and attack his Empire from the West. The Empire was a coalition of relatively independent territories and free cities. The key rulers of the Empire were known as "electors," for they actually elected the emperor. (See chart, p. 287.) Charles depended on them both militarily and politically. He could not afford to alienate them. Charles was very devout and felt strongly that it was his duty to protect the Roman Church from the threat posed by the Lutherans and other Protestant reformers. He hoped that the meeting at Augsburg would settle all disputes.

The elector of Saxony, John the Steadfast, at first refused to attend the meeting in Augsburg. But Charles urged him to do so. Since Charles invited everyone attending to share their "opinions, thoughts, and notions," Elector John asked the Wittenberg theologians, led by Martin Luther, to prepare a statement of confession. Martin Luther, Philip Melanchthon, Justas Jonas, and John Bugenhagen met in Torgau and went to work immediately. Their document was given to Elector John at the Torgau Castle in March of 1530, and is therefore known as the Torgau Articles.

Philip Melanchthon (1497–1560)

Philip Melanchthon was asked by the Elector to write a comprehensive statement of faith. He did so without close consultation with Luther, but he relied heavily on the Schwabach, Marburg, and Torgau Articles—each of which was very much a product of Martin Luther. Luther indicated he approved of Melanchthon's work, though he pointed out that he would never have been able "to tread as lightly" as Melanchthon did.

The Gathering at Augsburg

On April 4, Elector John left Torgau with Martin Luther, Philip Melanchthon, Justas Jonas, and Veit Dietrich (a secretary to Luther). Ten days later, on Good Friday, they arrived at Coburg Castle. Luther and the Elector remained at Coburg while the others traveled on to Augsburg. There, Philip Melanchthon was given the responsibility of leading the Lutheran theologians. (However, the Elector had set up a special courier service to make sure letters between Luther and his colleagues would be sent and received quickly.) Elector John arrived in Augsburg on May 2.

The meeting began with a clear signal that the courageous Lutheran laymen were not about to concede to the emperor's demands, nor compromise their convictions. As Charles's royal procession approached Augsburg, it was met by a large delegation

Emperor Charles V (1500–58)

Charles V became Holy Roman Emperor on June 28, 1519, about two years after Martin Luther posted the Ninety-five Theses. For forty years Charles struggled against Lutheranism. This woodcut depicts him in Erlangen in 1532, two years after the Diet of Augsburg. In 1547 he captured Wittenberg. His knights wanted to desecrate Luther's grave. Charles explained that he made war against the living, not the dead. He relinquished his throne in 1558, having failed to exterminate Lutheranism in his lands. He died in a monastery in Spain, a lonely, broken man who had suffered emotionally, physically, and spiritually.

from the city, including the Lutheran princes. The pope's ambassador stood to give the whole assembly a special blessing from the pope. When the crowd knelt, Elector John and his fellow Lutheran princes refused to kneel. Charles and those with him made their way into the city and arrived at the cathedral, where a special Mass was held. The crowd noticed that again Elector John and Philip of Hesse refused to kneel and remained standing, with their heads covered, during the blessing.

Later that evening, Charles and his brother Ferdinand, the King of Austria, met privately with the Lutheran princes. They ordered them to forbid any Lutheran preaching in Augsburg during the meeting. They commanded them to attend the Corpus Christi festival the next day with the emperor. George, Margrave of Brandenburg, spoke boldly for the Lutherans. He refused to concede to Charles's demands, saying, "Before I let anyone take from me the Word of God and ask me to deny my God, I will kneel and let them strike off my head." The emperor, clearly taken aback by George's boldness, sputtered in broken German, "Not cut off head, dear prince. Not cut off head."

Writing the Augsburg Confession

The plan to present the Torgau Articles had to be scrapped when it was found out that a lengthy, slanderous attack on Luther had been prepared by John Eck—Luther's old nemesis. At Leipzig in 1519, it was Eck who had tried to brand Luther as a heretic. Now, he had secretly written a lengthy attack on Luther and his followers in a book titled *Four Hundred and Four Articles for the Diet in Augsburg*. It included quotations from Martin Luther's writings, as well as from other Protestant reformers.

The book was highly inaccurate and tried to equate the Lutherans with the teachings of Ulrich Zwingli and the most radical of all the reformers, known as the Anabaptists. Eck's goal was to identify Lutheranism with the most extreme reformers, some of whom denied the most basic doctrines of historic Christianity. In light of this development, the Lutherans were forced to prepare a new statement of faith and specifically distance themselves from Zwinglians, Anabaptists, and others.

The Augsburg Confession was intentionally crafted to present a gentle and peaceful response to the emperor. It was intended only to speak for Saxony. However, as various German leaders read it they indicated that they, too, wanted to sign their names and make it their Confession.

So on June 25, 1530, courageous Lutheran laymen confessed their faith and told the emperor and the Roman Church what they believed, taught, and confessed. They relied on the promise of God's Word, as contained in Psalm 119:46, "I will also speak of Your testimonies before kings and shall not be put to shame." The Augsburg Confession was presented as a statement of biblical truth and a proposal for true unity in the Christian faith. It has never been withdrawn.

The translation is from the 1584 Latin edition of the Book of Concord, which was the base text for the Augsburg Confession in the *Concordia Triglotta*. See the User's Guide on page xxvii for details about the use of brackets and symbols.

TIMELINE

1521 Luther excommunicated by papal bull *Decet Romanum Pontificem*; appears before Diet of Worms; refuses to recant

Anabaptist Thomas Münzer begins preaching against infant Baptism

1524 Peasants' War begins, led in part by Thomas Münzer

1525 George Blaurock is rebaptized by Conrad Grebel; marks formal beginning of Anabaptist movement

Luther marries Katharina von Bora, June 13

1526 Diet of Speyer grants German princes right to establish religion in their territory

1529 Luther publishes *Small Catechism* and *Large Catechism*

Following Second Diet of Speyer, term *Protestant* used to refer to those who agree with Luther

Schwabach Articles drafted, July–September

Luther, Melanchthon, and Zwingli meet for Marburg Colloquy; unable to agree on Lord's Supper; Marburg Articles drafted

Turks unsuccessfully lay siege to Vienna

1530 Torgau Articles drafted, March

Augsburg Confession presented to Charles V at Diet of Augsburg, June 25

1531 *Augsburg Confession* and *Apology* published, April–May; *Apology's* second edition published, September

Ulrich Zwingli dies on Swiss battlefield at Kappel am Albis

OUTLINE

Preface to Emperor Charles V

I. God

II. Original Sin

III. The Son of God

IV. Justification

V. The Ministry

VI. New Obedience

VII. The Church

VIII. What the Church Is

IX. Baptism

X. The Lord's Supper

XI. Confession

XII. Repentance

XIII. The Use of the Sacraments

XIV. Order in the Church

XV. Church Ceremonies

XVI. Civil Government

XVII. Christ's Return for Judgment

XVIII. Free Will

XIX. The Cause of Sin

XX. Good Works

XXI. Worship of the Saints

A Summary Statement

A Review of the Various Abuses That Have Been Corrected

XXII. Both Kinds in the Sacrament

XXIII. The Marriage of Priests

XXIV. The Mass

XXV. Confession

XXVI. The Distinction of Meats

XXVII. Monastic Vows

XXVIII. Church Authority

Conclusion

THE AUGSBURG CONFESSION

Preface

To Emperor Charles V

1 Most invincible Emperor, Caesar Aug-
ustus, most clement Lord: Your Imperial
Majesty has summoned a meeting of the
Empire here at Augsburg to consider taking
action against the Turk, discussing how best
to stand effectively against his fury and at-
tacks by means of military force. The Turk is
the most atrocious and ancient hereditary
enemy of the Christian name and religion.
2 This meeting is also to consider disagree-
ments in our holy religion, the Christian
faith, by hearing everyone's opinions and
judgments in each other's presence. They are
to be considered and evaluated among our-
selves in mutual charity, mercy, and kind-
3 ness. After the removal and correction of
things that either side has understood differ-
ently, these matters may be settled and
brought back to one simple truth and Chris-
4 tian concord. Then we may embrace and
maintain the future of one pure and true re-
ligion under one Christ, doing battle under
Him [Psalm 24:8], living in unity and con-
cord in the one Christian Church.

5 We, the undersigned elector and princes,
have been called to this gathering along
with other electors, princes, and estates in
obedient compliance with the Imperial
mandate. Therefore, we have promptly
come to Augsburg. We do not mean to boast
when we say this, but we were among the
first to be here.

6 At the very beginning of the meeting in
Augsburg, Your Imperial Majesty made a
proposal to the electors, princes, and other
estates of the Empire. Among other things,
you asked that the several estates of the Em-
pire—on the strength of the Imperial edict—
should submit their explanations, opinions,
and judgments in German and Latin. On the 7
following Wednesday, we informed Your Im-
perial Majesty that after due deliberation we
would present the articles of our Confession
in one week. Therefore, concerning this reli- 8
gious matter, we offer this Confession. It is
ours and our preachers'. It shows, from the
Holy Scriptures and God's pure Word, what
has been up to this time presented in our
lands, dukedoms, dominions, and cities, and
taught in our churches.

In keeping with your edict, the other 9
electors, princes, and estates of the Empire
may present similar writings, in Latin and
German, giving their opinions in this reli-
gious matter. We, and those princes previ- 10
ously mentioned, are prepared to discuss, in
a friendly manner, all possible ways and
means by which we may come together. We
will do this in the presence of your Imperial
Majesty, our most clement Lord. In this way,
dissensions may be put away without offen-
sive conflict. This can be done honorably,
with God's help, so that we may be brought
back to agreement and concord. As your 11
edict shows, we are all under one Christ and
do battle under Him [Exodus 15:3]. We
ought to confess the one Christ and do
everything according to God's truth. With
the most fervent prayers, this is what we ask
of God.

However, regarding the rest of the elec- 12
tors, princes, and estates, who form the other
side: no progress may be made, nor any result

achieved by this treatment of religious mat-
ters, as Your Imperial Majesty has wisely de-
termined that it should be dealt with and
treated, by mutual presentation of writings
and calm conferring together among our-
13 selves. We will at least leave with you a clear
testimony. We are not holding back from
anything that could bring about Christian
concord, such as could be effected with
14 God and a good conscience. Your Imperial
Majesty—and the other electors and estates
of the Empire, and all moved by sincere love
and zeal for religion, who will give an impar-
tial hearing to this matter—please graciously
offer to take notice of this and to understand
this from our Confession.

15 Your Imperial Majesty, has—not once
but often—graciously pointed something
out to the electors, princes, and estates of the
Empire. At the meeting of Speyer (1526), ac-
cording to the form of Your Imperial instruc-
tion and commission, this point was given
16 and prescribed. Your Imperial Majesty
caused it to be stated and publicly pro-
claimed that Your Majesty—in dealing with
this religious matter, for certain reasons that
were alleged in Your Majesty's name—was
not willing to decide and could not deter-
mine anything. But that Your Majesty would
diligently use Your Majesty's office with the
Roman Pontiff for the convening of a Gener-
17 al Council. The same matter was publicly set
forth at greater length a year ago at the last
18 meeting of the Empire, at Speyer. There Your
Imperial Majesty (through His Highness Fer-
dinand, King of Bohemia and Hungary, our
friend and clement Lord, as well as through
the Orator and Imperial Commissioners)
caused the following to be submitted among
other things: concerning the calling of a
council, Your Imperial Majesty had taken no-
tice of and has pondered, the resolution of
(a) Your Majesty's Representative in the Em-
pire, and of (b) the President and Imperial
Counselors, and (c) the Legates from other
Estates convened at Ratisbon. Your Imperial 19
Majesty also judged that it was helpful to
convene a Council. Your Imperial Majesty
did not doubt that the Roman pontiff could
be persuaded to hold a General Council. For
the matters between Your Imperial Majesty
and the Roman pontiff were nearing agree-
ment and Christian reconciliation. Your Im- 20
perial Majesty himself pointed out that he
would work to secure the said chief pontiff's
consent for convening a General Council, to-
gether with your Imperial Majesty, to be an-
nounced as soon as possible by letters that
were to be sent out.

Therefore, if the outcome should be that 21
the differences between us and the other
parties in this religious matter should not
be settled with friendliness and charity, then
here, before Your Imperial Majesty, we obe-
diently offer, in addition to what we have al-
ready done, to appear and defend our cause
in such a general, free Christian Council.
There has always been harmonious action
and agreement among the electors, princes,
and other estates to hold a Council, in all
the Imperial Meetings held during Your
Majesty's reign. Even before this time, we 22
have appealed this great and grave matter, to
the assembly of this General Council, and to
your Imperial Majesty, in an appropriate
manner. We still stand by this appeal, both 23
to your Imperial Majesty and to a Council.
We have no intention to abandon our ap-
peal, with this or any other document. This
would not be possible, unless the matter be-
tween us and the other side is settled with
friendliness and charity, resolved and
brought to Christian harmony, according to
the latest Imperial Citation. In regard to this 24
appeal we solemnly and publicly testify
here.

John the Steadfast of Saxony (1468–1532)

John the Steadfast, brother of Frederick the Wise and father of John Frederick the Magnanimous, was the leader of the Lutheran princes and cities who gathered for the Diet of Augsburg. He well deserved to be called "Steadfast." He boldly confessed the truth of God's Word and risked everything rather than compromise and lose the Gospel of Jesus Christ.

Gregory Brück (1485–1557)

Courageous Lutheran layman, counselor and aid to Frederick the Wise. He wrote the preface and the conclusion of the Augsburg Confession. He stood with Christian Beyer as he publicly read the Augsburg Confession (June 25, 1530). Then Brück handed the German and Latin copies to the Emperor.

CHIEF ARTICLES OF FAITH

ARTICLE I

God

Note: Martin Luther never intended to start a new church, but rather to purify the one, holy, catholic, and apostolic Church. The Augsburg Confession strongly affirms the doctrine of the Trinity confessed at the Council of Nicaea (325), and later affirmed by the Council of Constantinople (381). God is one divine essence in three distinct persons—Father, Son, and Holy Spirit. The Scriptures reveal this great mystery, confessed by all Christians.

During the Reformation, radical groups espoused various forms of earlier heresies. The Augsburg Confession condemns the ancient heresies concerning God. Article I proves that Lutheranism is deeply anchored in the historic doctrine of biblical Christianity. It embraces the faith of the Church through the ages and rejects all the errors the Church has rejected. (See also Ap I; SA I.)

1 Our churches teach with common con-
sent that the decree of the Council of Nicaea
about the unity of the divine essence and the
2 three persons is true. It is to be believed with-
out any doubt. God is one divine essence
who is eternal, without a body, without
parts, of infinite power, wisdom, and good-
ness. He is the maker and preserver of all
things, visible and invisible [Nehemiah 9:6].
3 Yet there are three persons, the Father, the
Son, and the Holy Spirit [Matthew 28:19].
These three persons are of the same essence
4 and power. Our churches use the term *person*
as the Fathers have used it. We use it to signi-
fy, not a part or quality in another, but that
which subsists of itself.

Our churches condemn all heresies 5
[Titus 3:10–11] that arose against this article,
such as the Manichaeans, who assumed that
there are two "principles," one Good and the
other Evil. They also condemn the Valentini-
ans, Arians, Eunomians, Muslims, and all
heresies such as these. Our churches also 6
condemn the Samosatenes, old and new, who
contend that God is but one person.
Through sophistry they impiously argue that
the Word and the Holy Spirit are not distinct
persons. They say that *Word* signifies a spo-
ken word, and *Spirit* signifies motion created
in things.

ARTICLE II

Original Sin

Note: Sin is much more than thinking, saying, and doing things that are wrong. It is a terminal disease. We are all conceived and born in sin; we inherit it from our first parents, Adam and Eve. The disease of sin can be overcome, but only by one medicine: the cleansing, healing, and forgiving blood of God's own Son. By rejecting Pelagian errors in Article II, the Augsburg Confession subtly refers to the Roman view of sin. The Roman Church taught and still teaches that concupiscence (the inborn inclination to sin) is not actually sin. By misdiagnosing our fatal illness, Rome leads people to believe they are able to cooperate with God's grace for salvation. Lutheranism rejects all teachings that imply we are responsible for or contribute to our salvation. (See also Ap II; SA III I; FC Ep I and SD I.)

Our churches teach that since the fall of 1
Adam [Romans 5:12], all who are naturally
born are born with sin [Psalm 51:5], that is,
without the fear of God, without trust in
God, and with the inclination to sin, called

2 concupiscence. Concupiscence is a disease and original vice that is truly sin. It damns and brings eternal death on those who are not born anew through Baptism and the Holy Spirit [John 3:5].

3 Our churches condemn the Pelagians and others who deny that original depravity is sin, thus obscuring the glory of Christ's merit and benefits. Pelagians argue that a person can be justified before God by his own strength and reason.

ARTICLE III
The Son of God

Note: The Augsburg Confession teaches the historic, biblical doctrine of Christ. Many early controversies about Christ's human and divine natures were resolved through careful study of God's Word, and are reflected in the Nicene Creed. Article III echoes that creed—our Lord Jesus Christ is one person having two natures: truly God and truly man. This is another mystery of the Christian faith that we receive with thanks, bowing before Christ in humble adoration. His incarnation in the womb of His virgin mother, Mary, was for our salvation. He is, and remains, for all eternity the God-man, the One who appeased, or propitiated, God's wrath against our sin and won for us eternal life. Even now He is present with us through His appointed means of grace—the Gospel and the Sacraments. He comes to strengthen, sustain, and support us, and to bring us safely to our heavenly home. (See also Ap III; SA II I; FC Ep VIII and SD VIII.)

1 Our churches teach that the Word, that is, the Son of God [John 1:14], assumed the human nature in the womb of the Blessed
2 Virgin Mary. So there are two natures—the divine and the human—inseparably joined in one person. There is one Christ, true God and true man, who was born of the Virgin Mary, truly suffered, was crucified, died, and
was buried. He did this to reconcile the Fa- 3
ther to us and to be a sacrifice, not only for original guilt, but also for all actual sins of mankind [John 1:29].

He also descended into hell, and truly 4
rose again on the third day. Afterward, He ascended into heaven to sit at the right hand of the Father. There He forever reigns and has
dominion over all creatures. He sanctifies 5
those who believe in Him, by sending the Holy Spirit into their hearts to rule, comfort, and make them alive. He defends them against the devil and the power of sin.

The same Christ will openly come again 6
to judge the living and the dead, and so forth, according to the Apostles' Creed.

ARTICLE IV
Justification

Note: There is a historic saying in Lutheranism that the Church stands or falls on the article of justification. To justify means "to declare righteous." God's sure and certain declaration that we are righteous in His eyes is possible only because of our Savior, Jesus Christ. Through His life, Jesus satisfied God's demand for perfect obedience. Through His sacrificial death, Jesus took God's wrath and atoned for the sins of the world. The Holy Spirit, through the means of grace, works in us saving faith, which personally apprehends what Christ has done for us. Our justification before God, therefore, is brought about by the One who lived, suffered, and died for our salvation. We cannot merit God's favor through our obedience; we cannot offer sacrifices to pay for our sins. But what we cannot do for ourselves, Christ has done for us. He is the solid Rock on which God builds His Church. On Him, and Him alone, we stand forgiven. (See also Ap IV; SA III XIII; FC Ep III and SD III.)

1 Our churches teach that people cannot
be justified before God by their own
2 strength, merits, or works. People are freely
justified for Christ's sake through faith,
when they believe that they are received into
favor and that their sins are forgiven for
Christ's sake. By His death, Christ made sat-
3 isfaction for our sins. God counts this faith
for righteousness in His sight (Romans 3 and
4 [3:21–26; 4:5]).

ARTICLE V
The Ministry

Note: How can what Christ did for us two thousand years ago—through His life, death, and resurrection—become effective in our lives today? During the Reformation, as also today, some imagined they would experience the Holy Spirit through their own reflections, by enjoying nature, or by ecstatic religious experiences. The comforting truth is that the Holy Spirit works through objective, external, sure, and certain means of grace, through which we receive justification by grace alone, through faith alone, on account of Christ alone. While the most direct concern of Article V is to confess the Holy Spirit's work through the means of grace, there is also in view, indirectly, the Office of the Ministry, which the German version of the Augsburg Confession calls "the Preaching Office" [*das Predigtamt*]. The Preaching Office is not instituted by man, but is established by God Himself. Article XIV discusses the necessity of the Church call. (See also SA III VII and X; Treatise.)

1 So that we may obtain this faith, the min-
istry of teaching the Gospel and administer-
ing the Sacraments was instituted. Through 2
the Word and Sacraments, as through instru-
ments, the Holy Spirit is given [John 20:22].
He works faith, when and where it pleases
God [John 3:8], in those who hear the good
news that God justifies those who believe 3
that they are received into grace for Christ's
sake. This happens not through our own
merits, but for Christ's sake.

Our churches condemn the Anabaptists 4
and others who think that through their own
preparations and works the Holy Spirit
comes to them without the external Word.

ARTICLE VI
New Obedience

Note: Lutherans are sometimes accused of denying that Christians should do good works. The article on new obedience follows on the heels of the articles on justification and the ministry, and clearly states that Lutherans do insist on good works. The faith given by the Holy Spirit is a living and active power in our lives, bearing the fruit of good works. We must do good works. God commands them. However, they do not save us. They are always the result of saving faith. This article refers to an Early Church Father as proof that this teaching is anchored in the Church's historic teaching and practice. (See also Ap V.)

Our churches teach that this faith is 1
bound to bring forth good fruit [Galatians
5:22–23]. It is necessary to do good works
commanded by God [Ephesians 2:10], be-
cause of God's will. We should not rely on
those works to merit justification before
God. The forgiveness of sins and justification 2
is received through faith. The voice of Christ
testifies, "So you also, when you have done all

that you were commanded, say, 'We are un-
worthy servants; we have only done what was
3 our duty'" (Luke 17:10). The Fathers teach
the same thing. Ambrose says, "It is ordained
of God that he who believes in Christ is
saved, freely receiving forgiveness of sins,
without works, through faith alone."

ARTICLE VII
The Church

Note: Article VII has been rightly called the evangelical Magna Carta of the Lutheran Church. It cuts through the clutter of man-made ceremonies that had accumulated by the sixteenth century, focuses on the very heart of the matter, and defines church with eloquent simplicity. Outward unity in the Church is shaped, defined, and normed by biblical truth (teaching), not the other way around. Church fellowship is common participation in the saving treasures of the Church: Christ's gifts, His Gospel, and His Sacraments. Not any "Gospel" will do, but only that Gospel which is purely taught alongside correctly administered Sacraments (as noted in the German version). (See also Ap VII and VIII; SA III XII.)

1 Our churches teach that one holy Church
is to remain forever. The Church is the con-
gregation of saints [Psalm 149:1] in which
the Gospel is purely taught and the Sacra-
2 ments are correctly administered. For the
true unity of the Church it is enough to agree
about the doctrine of the Gospel and the ad-
3 ministration of the Sacraments. It is not nec-
essary that human traditions, that is, rites or
ceremonies instituted by men, should be the
4 same everywhere. As Paul says, "One Lord,
one faith, one baptism, one God and Father
of all" (Ephesians 4:5–6).

ARTICLE VIII
What the Church Is

Note: This article elaborates on Article VII and makes it clear that the Church consists only of believers in Christ, those made holy by His mercy. Hypocrites are not in this sense any part of the Church. One may think of the term church in a broad and narrow sense. The Church, broadly speaking, is all those who assemble around Word and Sacrament. Narrowly speaking, the Church encompasses only believers. There are not two churches, one "visible," and one "invisible." Rather, we understand that here on the earth the Church is hidden because faith, or spiritual life, is "hidden with Christ in God" (Colossians 3:3). This hidden Church has public, visible marks, by which it is recognized with absolute certainty: Christ's Gospel and Sacraments, purely preached and administered. (See also Ap VII and VIII; SA III XII.)

Strictly speaking, the Church is the congre- 1
gation of saints and true believers. However,
because many hypocrites and evil persons are
mingled within them in this life [Matthew
13:24–30], it is lawful to use Sacraments ad-
ministered by evil men, according to the
saying of Christ, "The scribes and the Phar-
isees sit on Moses' seat" (Matthew 23:2).
Both the Sacraments and Word are effective 2
because of Christ's institution and command,
even if they are administered by evil men.

Our churches condemn the Donatists, 3
and others like them, who deny that it is law-
ful to use the ministry of evil men in the
Church, and who think that the ministry of
evil men is not useful and is ineffective.

ARTICLE IX

Baptism

Note: The Bible teaches that Baptism is a gift of God's grace by which He applies the benefits of Christ's life, death, and resurrection to us personally. Because all people are conceived and born in sin, we all need salvation. Because Baptism is God's way of bringing us salvation, infants should also be baptized. During the Reformation, as now, some Christian groups turned Baptism from God's saving activity into an act of Christian obedience. This view of Baptism arises from the denial of original sin and a semi-Pelagian view of salvation, whereby faith becomes the good work we contribute. This article concentrates on what God gives in this Sacrament. (See also Ap IX; SA III V; LC IV.)

1 Concerning Baptism, our churches teach that Baptism is necessary for salvation [Mark 16:16] and that God's grace is offered
2 through Baptism [Titus 3:4–7]. They teach that children are to be baptized [Acts 2:38–39]. Being offered to God through Baptism, they are received into God's grace.

3 Our churches condemn the Anabaptists, who reject the Baptism of children, and say that children are saved without Baptism.

ARTICLE X

The Lord's Supper

Note: By the time the Augsburg Confession was written, deep divisions had arisen among the various reformers concerning the Lord's Supper. The Lutherans were very careful to distance themselves from those who reject that the body and blood of Christ are in fact truly present in His Supper and distributed to all those who eat and drink. Transubstantiation, consubstantiation, or any other human speculation asks the wrong question: *how* is Christ present? Lutheranism has no theory or philosophical explanation of how Christ is present. Rather, Lutherans insist on answering the *what* of the Lord's Supper. We believe, teach, and confess that of the bread, Christ said, "This is My body," and of the wine, "This is My blood." These are given and shed "for the forgiveness of sins" (Matthew 26:26–28). We reject any teaching that is contrary to our Lord's Word. (See also Ap X; SA III VI; LC V; FC Ep VII and SD VII.)

Our churches teach that the body and 1
blood of Christ are truly present and distributed to those who eat the Lord's Supper
[1 Corinthians 10:16]. They reject those who 2
teach otherwise.

ARTICLE XI

Confession

Note: By the time of the Reformation, the practice of confessing sins privately and confidentially to a pastor had been a well-accepted church practice for more than a thousand years. Private Confession and Absolution was never something Lutherans wanted to get rid of. As time went on, the practice fell into disuse, but clearly Article XI assumes that private Confession and Absolution will take place in the Lutheran Church. The problem addressed by this article is that the Roman Church demanded every sin be recalled and confessed. Clearly, this is humanly impossible and makes our forgiveness dependent on our work. Such teaching is certainly dangerous to repentant consciences, which need firm assurance that Christ forgives all sin. (See also Ap XI; SA III VIII; Appendix B, Brief Exhortation to Confession.)

Our churches teach that private Absolution should be retained in the churches, 1

John Oecolampadius (1482–1531)

Ally of Zwingli who opposed Luther at the Marburg Colloquy (1529). Condemned in Article X of the Augsburg Confession.

Ulrich Zwingli (1484–1531)

Leader of the "Sacramentarians." The Romanists tried to lump all Protestants together. The Augsburg Confession was clear that Lutherans rejected the teachings of Zwingli and others like him. After Zwingli died in battle, John Calvin continued Zwingli's work, creating the Reformed churches.

although listing all sins is not necessary for
2 Confession. For, according to the Psalm, it is impossible. "Who can discern his errors?" (Psalm 19:12).

ARTICLE XII

Repentance

Note: The Roman teaching about repentance was the spark that ignited the Lutheran Reformation. When Luther learned his congregational members were buying indulgences, hoping to avert God's punishment for sins by paying money, he was incensed. Repentance is not about "paying off" God or making some satisfaction for our sin. Repentance is recognizing the reality of our sin and turning to God in faith for His mercy. God reveals our sin through His Law; He forgives our sin and restores us to a right relationship with Himself through His Gospel. While we affirm there is fruit of repentance, the focus of the Gospel must be clear: our sins are forgiven only because of Christ. Our lives in Christ are lives of repentance, returning again and again to the fount and source of all mercy, our Savior. Notice that this article rejects any teaching that implies our works of satisfaction are part of true repentance. Article XII strikes a fatal blow at the very heart of the Roman sacramental system. (See also Ap XII; SA III III; Appendix B, Brief Exhortation to Confession.)

Selling Indulgences

The pope (center) hands a commission to sell indulgences to a monk. Right: The purchase of an indulgence, with people being directed where to put their money. Left: A lame man asks for help, while others purchase their indulgences. Their names are being written on the indulgence receipt.

1 Our churches teach that there is forgive-
ness of sins for those who have fallen after
2 Baptism whenever they are converted. The
Church ought to impart Absolution to those
who return to repentance [Jeremiah 3:12].
3 Now, strictly speaking, repentance consists of
4 two parts. One part is contrition, that is, ter-
rors striking the conscience through the
5 knowledge of sin. The other part is faith,
which is born of the Gospel [Romans 10:17]
or the Absolution and believes that for
Christ's sake, sins are forgiven. It comforts
the conscience and delivers it from terror.
6 Then good works are bound to follow,
which are the fruit of repentance [Galatians
5:22–23].

7 Our churches condemn the Anabaptists,
who deny that those who have once been jus-
8 tified can lose the Holy Spirit. They also con-
demn those who argue that some may reach
such a state of perfection in this life that they
cannot sin.

9 The Novatians also are condemned, who
would not absolve those who had fallen after
Baptism, though they returned to repen-
tance.

10 Our churches also reject those who do
not teach that forgiveness of sins comes
through faith, but command us to merit
grace through satisfactions of our own.

They also reject those who teach that it is necessary to perform works of satisfaction, commanded by Church law, in order to remit eternal punishment or the punishment of purgatory.

ARTICLE XIII

The Use of the Sacraments

Note: God gives the Sacraments to His people for their forgiveness, life, and salvation, and this happens as they call forth trust and confidence in Christ, the Savior. By the sixteenth century, the Roman Church had developed a complicated sacramental system that had transformed the Sacraments into meritorious works performed by priests. This was especially evident in the Mass, where priests "sacrificed" Christ again and again on behalf of the living and the dead. The Bible, however, reveals the key to the Sacraments: the promises of God. God attaches His Word of promise to the element of the Sacrament—water, wine, or bread—and gives and strengthens the faith of those receiving them. (See also Ap XIII.)

Our churches teach that the Sacraments 1
were ordained, not only to be marks of pro-
fession among men, but even more, to be
signs and testimonies of God's will toward
us. They were instituted to awaken and con- 2
firm faith in those who use them. Therefore,
we must use the Sacraments in such a way
that faith, which believes the promises of-
fered and set forth through the Sacraments,
is increased [2 Thessalonians 1:3].

Therefore, they condemn those who 3
teach that the Sacraments justify simply by
the act of doing them. They condemn those
who do not teach that faith, which believes
that sins are forgiven, is required in the use of
the Sacraments.

ARTICLE XIV

Order in the Church

Note: When this article speaks of a rightly ordered call, it refers to the Church's historic practice of placing personally and theologically qualified men into the office of preaching and teaching the Gospel and administering the Sacraments. No one in the Church can take such authority for himself or bestow such authority on his own. The ministry is conferred by means of a formal, public, and official call from the Church.

At the time this article was presented, it was understood that a minister's first call is publicly ratified and confirmed by means of prayer and the laying on of hands, ordination, a practice that dates back to the time of the apostles. In the Lutheran Confessions, "ordination" is a term often used as shorthand for both the call and ordination. (See also Ap XIV; SA III X.)

Our churches teach that no one should publicly teach in the Church, or administer the Sacraments, without a rightly ordered call.

ARTICLE XV

Church Ceremonies

Note: Lutheranism embraces the good historic traditions of the Church, especially those of the Western Church. These include such things as following the pattern of the Church year, lectionary readings from the Bible, a liturgical order of worship, various festival days, vestments worn by clergy, and the use of candles, crucifixes, and other objects. As this article makes very clear, in the Lutheran Church, rites, decorations, or traditions are never used or followed to appease God's wrath or to earn the forgiveness of sins. Lutheranism removed from the Church useless and harmful traditions such as monastic vows and insisting on certain foods on certain days. (See also Ap XV; SA III XV; FC Ep X and SD X.)

1 Our churches teach that ceremonies ought to be observed that may be observed without sin. Also, ceremonies and other practices that are profitable for tranquility and good order in the Church (in particular, holy days, festivals, and the like) ought to be observed.

Yet, the people are taught that con- 2
sciences are not to be burdened as though
observing such things was necessary for sal-
vation [Colossians 2:16–17]. They are also 3
taught that human traditions instituted to
make atonement with God, to merit grace,
and to make satisfaction for sins are opposed
to the Gospel and the doctrine of faith. So 4
vows and traditions concerning meats and
days, and so forth, instituted to merit grace
and to make satisfaction for sins, are useless
and contrary to the Gospel.

ARTICLE XVI

Civil Government

Note: It was important for Lutherans to make clear they did not share the beliefs of the radical reformers of the sixteenth century. Some of these radicals rejected all forms of order and authority, in both Church and State, even rejecting their homes and families in order to be "super spiritual." This article points to the biblical doctrine of the two kingdoms, a way of speaking about God's care for us spiritually though the Church and temporally through the various orders in society: chiefly, home and government. Christians live out their various callings in life in service to God and their fellow humans, doing so in the stations, or situations, to which God has called them. (See also Ap XVI.)

Our churches teach that lawful civil regu- 1
lations are good works of God. They teach 2
that it is right for Christians to hold political office, to serve as judges, to judge matters by imperial laws and other existing laws, to impose just punishments, to engage in just wars, to serve as soldiers, to make legal contracts, to hold property, to take oaths when required by the magistrates, for a man to

marry a wife, or a woman to be given in mar-
riage [Romans 13; 1 Corinthians 7:2].
3 Our churches condemn the Anabaptists
who forbid these political offices to Chris-
4 tians. They also condemn those who do not
locate evangelical perfection in the fear of
God and in faith, but place it in forsaking po-
5 litical offices. For the Gospel teaches an eter-
nal righteousness of the heart (Romans
10:10). At the same time, it does not require
the destruction of the civil state or the fami-
ly. The Gospel very much requires that they
be preserved as God's ordinances and that
6 love be practiced in such ordinances. There-
fore, it is necessary for Christians to be obe-
7 dient to their rulers and laws. The only ex-
ception is when they are commanded to sin.
Then they ought to obey God rather than
men (Acts 5:29).

ARTICLE XVII

Christ's Return for Judgment

Note: This article affirms the biblical view of the end times. It pointedly rejects any speculation or opinion about believers ruling the world before the final resurrection of the dead. It also rejects all theories about a "millennial" earthly rule of Christ as contrary to God's Word. (See also Ap XVII.)

1 Our churches teach that at the end of the
world Christ will appear for judgment and
will raise all the dead [1 Thessalonians
2 4:13–5:2]. He will give the godly and elect
3 eternal life and everlasting joys, but He will
condemn ungodly people and the devils to be
tormented without end [Matthew 25:31–46].
4 Our churches condemn the Anabaptists,
who think that there will be an end to the
punishments of condemned men and devils.
5 Our churches also condemn those who
are spreading certain Jewish opinions, that
before the resurrection of the dead the
godly shall take possession of the kingdom
of the world, the ungodly being everywhere
suppressed.

ARTICLE XVIII

Free Will

Note: By the time of the Reformation, the Roman Church had fully developed a false and potentially damning doctrine, one that stated that a person is able, to some degree, to strive for and receive God's mercy. Article XVIII asserts Scripture's teaching that people, apart from God's grace, are wholly incapable of perceiving spiritual things. The longest quote from a Church Father in the Augsburg Confession occurs here. It demonstrates Lutheranism's continuity with the Church catholic—in contrast to Roman error on this doctrine. Augustine echoes the Bible's teaching that while we humans can perform acts of civil righteousness, which may be called "good," spiritually we are evil and enemies of God. However, in Christ, our loving God breaks down the wall of hostility separating us from Him. By His Spirit, through His Word, He gives us Christ's perfect righteousness as a gift. In external, worldly matters we do have the freedom to make decisions according to human reason, but this does not mean, apart from God's grace, that we have similar powers in matters of eternal life. (See also Ap XVIII; FC Ep II and SD II.)

Our churches teach that a person's will 1
has some freedom to choose civil righ-
teousness and to do things subject to reason.
It has no power, without the Holy Spirit, to 2
work the righteousness of God, that is, spiri-
tual righteousness. For "the natural person
does not accept the things of the Spirit of
God" (1 Corinthians 2:14). This righteous- 3

ness is worked in the heart when the Holy Spirit is received through the Word [Galatians 3:2–6].

4 This is what Augustine says in his *Hypognosticon*, Book III:

> We grant that all people have a free will. It is free as far as it has the judgment of reason. This does not mean that it is able, without God, either to begin, or at least to complete, anything that has to do with God. It is free only in works of this life, whether
> 5 good or evil. Good I call those works that spring from the good in nature, such as willing to labor in the field, to eat and drink, to have a friend, to clothe oneself, to build a house, to marry a wife, to raise cattle, to learn various useful arts, or whatsoever
> 6 good applies to this life. For all of these things depend on the providence of God. They are from Him
> 7 and exist through Him. Works that are willing to worship an idol, to commit murder, and so forth, I call evil.

8 Our churches condemn the Pelagians and others who teach that without the Holy Spirit, by natural power alone, we are able to love God above all things and do God's
9 commandments according to the letter. Although nature is able in a certain way to do the outward work (for it is able to keep the hands from theft and murder), yet it cannot produce the inward motions, such as the fear of God, trust in God, chastity, patience, and so on.

ARTICLE XIX

The Cause of Sin

Note: The blame for sin rests solely with the devil and with us, not with God. Apart from God's mercy in Christ, there is no hope for the wicked. Years after the Augsburg Confession was written, in order to accentuate the depth of mankind's sinful condition, some Lutherans would imply that sin is of the very essence of people. (See pp. 518–19.) The result of this faulty teaching is that God becomes responsible for, indeed the Creator of, sin. Sin is a deep corruption of that which God created, and is entirely mankind's fault. (See also Ap XIX; SA III I.)

Our churches teach that although God creates and preserves nature, the cause of sin is located in the will of the wicked, that is, the devil and ungodly people. Without God's help, this will turns itself away from God, as Christ says, "When he lies, he speaks out of his own character" (John 8:44).

ARTICLE XX

Good Works

Note: This is another key article in the Augsburg Confession. Article XX offers more details about faith and works than what was previously written. Lutherans insist on the biblical truth that our good works do not save us. So they are sometimes accused of opposing good works. This article sets forth the Bible's clear teaching that good works are the fruit of faith, not the cause of our salvation. The Lutheran hymn "Salvation unto Us Has Come" offers a short, powerful summary of these essential Gospel truths:

> Faith clings to Jesus' cross alone
> And rests in Him unceasing;
> And by its fruits true faith is known,
> with love and hope increasing.
> For faith alone can justify;
> Works serve our neighbor and supply
> The proof that faith is living.

(Paul Speratus, 1484–1531; tr. *The Lutheran Hymnal*, 1941, alt.)

Rome continues to insist that people are saved by God's grace, but not through faith alone. This teaching dangerously encourages people to believe they are able, even in some small way, to contribute toward their salvation. This diverts their focus from Christ and His merits to their own works. It also leads to despair, doubt, and uncertainty when people come to realize the enormity of their sin and wonder if in fact they have done "enough" to merit or deserve God's favor. After setting forth the proper biblical distinction between faith and good works, the Augsburg Confession asserts very clearly that our good works are necessary, not to merit grace, but because this is God's will for our lives. God's gift of saving faith enables us to do good works. (See also Ap XX; SA III XIII; FC Ep IV and SD IV.)

---

1 Our teachers are falsely accused of for-
2 bidding good works. Their published writ-
ings on the Ten Commandments, and other
similar writings, bear witness that they have
usefully taught about all estates and duties of
life. They have taught well what is pleasing
to God in every station and vocation in life.
3 Before now, preachers taught very little about
these things. They encouraged only childish
and needless works, such as particular holy
days, particular fasts, brotherhoods, pilgrim-
ages, services in honor of the saints, the use
of rosaries, monasticism, and such things.
4 Since our adversaries have been admonished
about these things, they are now unlearning
them. They do not preach these unhelpful
5 works as much as they used to. In the past,
there was only stunning silence about faith,
but now they are beginning to mention it.
6 They do not teach that we are justified only
by works. They join faith and works together,
and say that we are justified by faith and
7 works. This teaching is more tolerable than
the former one. It can offer more consolation
than their old teaching.

The doctrine about faith, which ought to 8
be the chief doctrine in the Church, has remained unknown for so long. Everyone has to admit that there was the deepest silence in their sermons concerning the righteousness of faith. They only taught about works in the churches. This is why our teachers teach the churches about faith in this way.

First, they teach that our works cannot 9
reconcile God to us or merit forgiveness of sins, grace, and justification. We obtain reconciliation only by faith when we believe that we are received into favor for Christ's sake. He alone has been set forth as the Mediator and Atoning Sacrifice (1 Timothy 2:5), in order that the Father may be reconciled
through Him. Therefore, whoever believes 10
that he merits grace by works despises the merit and grace of Christ [Galatians 5:4]. In so doing, he is seeking a way to God without Christ, by human strength, although Christ Himself said, "I am the way, and the truth, and the life" (John 14:6).

This doctrine about faith is presented 11
everywhere by Paul, "By grace you have been saved through faith. And this is not your own doing; it is the gift of God" (Ephesians 2:8).

If anyone wants to be tricky and say that 12
we have invented a new interpretation of
Paul, this entire matter is supported by the
testimony of the Fathers. Augustine defends 13
grace and the righteousness of faith in many
volumes against the merits of works. Am- 14
brose, in his book *The Calling of the Gentiles*,
and elsewhere, teaches the same thing. In *The Calling of the Gentiles* he says,

> Redemption by Christ's blood would be worth very little, and God's mercy would not surpass man's works, if justification, which is accomplished

> through grace, were due to prior merits. So justification would not be the free gift from a donor, but the reward due the laborer.

15 Spiritually inexperienced people despise
this teaching. However, God-fearing and
anxious consciences find by experience that
it brings the greatest consolation. Consciences cannot be set at rest through any
works, but only by faith, when they take the
sure ground that for Christ's sake they have a
16 gracious God. As Paul teaches, "since we have
been justified by faith, we have peace with
17 God" (Romans 5:1). This whole doctrine
must be related to the conflict of the terrified
conscience. It cannot be understood apart
18 from that conflict. Therefore, inexperienced
and irreverent people have poor judgment in
this matter because they dream that Christian righteousness is nothing but civil and
philosophical righteousness.

19 Until now consciences were plagued
with the doctrine of works. They did not
20 hear consolation from the Gospel. Some
people were driven by conscience into the
desert and into monasteries, hoping to
21 merit grace by a monastic life. Some people
came up with other works to merit grace
22 and make satisfaction for sins. That is why
the need was so great for teaching and renewing the doctrine of faith in Christ, so
that anxious consciences would not be
without consolation but would know that
grace, forgiveness of sins, and justification
are received by faith in Christ.

23 People are also warned that the term *faith*
does not mean simply a knowledge of a history, such as the ungodly and devil have
[James 2:19]. Rather, it means a faith that believes, not merely the history, but also the effect of the history. In other words, it believes
this article: the forgiveness of sins. We have
grace, righteousness, and forgiveness of sins
through Christ.

The person who knows that he has a Fa- 24
ther who is gracious to him through Christ
truly knows God [John 14:7]. He also knows
that God cares for him [1 Peter 5:7], and he
calls upon God [Romans 10:13]. In a word,
he is not without God, as are the heathen. For 25
devils and the ungodly are not able to believe
this article: the forgiveness of sins. Hence,
they hate God as an enemy [Romans 8:7] and
do not call Him [Romans 3:11–12] and ex-
pect no good from Him. Augustine also 26
warns his readers about the word *faith* and
teaches that the term is used in the Scriptures, not for the knowledge that is in the ungodly, but for the confidence that consoles
and encourages the terrified mind.

Furthermore, we teach that it is necessary 27
to do good works. This does not mean that
we merit grace by doing good works, but be-
cause it is God's will [Ephesians 2:10]. It is 28
only by faith, and nothing else, that forgive-
ness of sins is apprehended. The Holy Spirit 29
is received through faith, hearts are renewed
and given new affections, and then they are
able to bring forth good works. Ambrose 30
says: "Faith is the mother of a good will and
doing what is right." Without the Holy Spirit 31
people are full of ungodly desires. They are
too weak to do works that are good in God's
sight [John 15:5]. Besides, they are in the 32
power of the devil, who pushes human be-
ings into various sins, ungodly opinions, and
open crimes. We see this in the philosophers, 33
who, although they tried to live an honest life
could not succeed, but were defiled with
many open crimes. Such is human weakness, 34
without faith and without the Holy Spirit,
when governed only by human strength.

Therefore, it is easy to see that this doc- 35
trine is not to be accused of banning good

works. Instead, it is to be commended all the
more because it shows how we are enabled
36 to do good works. For without faith, human
nature cannot, in any way, do the works of
the First or Second Commandment [1 Corin-
37 thians 2:14]. Without faith, human nature
does not call upon God, nor expect anything
from Him, nor bear the cross [Matthew
16:24]. Instead, human nature seeks and
38 trusts in human help. So when there is no
faith and trust in God, all kinds of lusts and
human intentions rule in the heart [Genesis
39 6:5]. This is why Christ says, "Apart from Me
you can do nothing" (John 15:5). That is
40 why the Church sings: "Lacking Your divine
favor, there is nothing in man. Nothing in
him is harmless."

ARTICLE XXI

Worship of the Saints

Note: The Early Church had developed an appreciation for those who confessed, and sometimes died for, their faith. However, deep corruption had developed within the Church regarding the honor given to the saints, resulting in what could only be described as idolatrous worship. Those who have gone before us in the faith are to be honored, remembered, and imitated according to our various stations and callings in life. That is clear. However, it is clearly contrary to Scripture to teach that the saints are to be prayed to and invoked for aid. There is simply no command, no example, and no promise in Scripture indicating that we should pray to our departed brothers and sisters in Christ. (See also Ap XXI; SA II II.)

1 Our churches teach that the history of
saints may be set before us so that we may
follow the example of their faith and good
works, according to our calling. For example,
the emperor may follow the example of
David [2 Samuel] in making war to drive
away the Turk from his country. For both are
kings. But the Scriptures do not teach that we 2
are to call on the saints or to ask the saints for
help. Scripture sets before us the one Christ
as the Mediator, Atoning Sacrifice, High
Priest, and Intercessor [1 Timothy 2:5–6].
He is to be prayed to. He has promised that 3
He will hear our prayer [John 14:13]. This is
the worship that He approves above all other
worship, that He be called upon in all afflic-
tions. "If anyone does sin, we have an advo- 4
cate with the Father" (1 John 2:1).

[A Summary Statement]

This then is nearly a complete summary 1
of our teaching. As can be seen, there is
nothing that varies from the Scriptures, or
from the Church universal, or from the
Church of Rome, as known from its writ-
ers. Since this is the case, those who insist
that our teachers are to be regarded as
heretics are judging harshly. There is, how- 2
ever, disagreement on certain abuses that
have crept into the Church without rightful
authority. Even here, if there are some dif-
ferences, the bishops should bear with us
patiently because of the Confession we
have just reviewed. Even the Church's
canon law is not so severe that it demands
the same rites everywhere. Nor, for that 3
matter, have the rites of all churches ever
been the same. Although, in large part, the 4
ancient rites are diligently observed among
us. It is a false and hate-filled charge that
our churches have abolished all the cere-
monies instituted in ancient times. But the 5
abuses connected with the ordinary rites
have been a common source of complaint.
They have been corrected to some extent
since they could not be approved with a
good conscience.

A Review of the Various Abuses That Have Been Corrected

1 Our churches do not dissent from any ar-
ticle of the faith held by the Church catholic.
They only omit some of the newer abuses.
They have been erroneously accepted
through the corruption of the times, con-
trary to the intent of canon law. Therefore,
we pray that Your Imperial Majesty will gra-
ciously hear what has been changed and why
the people are not compelled to observe
those things that are abuses against their
2 conscience. Your Imperial Majesty should
not believe those who have tried to stir up
hatred against us by spreading strange lies
3 among the people. They have given rise to
this controversy by stirring up the minds of
good people. Now they are trying to increase
the controversy using the same methods.
4 Your Imperial Majesty will undoubtedly find
that the form of doctrine and ceremonies
among us are not as intolerable as these un-
5 godly and ill-intentioned men claim. Besides,
the truth cannot be gathered from common
6 rumors or the attacks of enemies. It can eas-
ily be judged that if the churches observed
ceremonies correctly, their dignity would be
maintained and reverence and piety would
increase among the people.

ARTICLE XXII

Both Kinds in the Sacrament

Note: Prior to the Reformation, the practice had developed of withholding the consecrated wine from the laity during the Lord's Supper. Only the consecrated bread was distributed to them. However, priests who celebrated Mass drank from the cup. Theories developed within the Church to help support this practice. One stated that the bread alone was enough for the laity, since Christ's body must also contain His blood. The practice of withholding the cup from the congregation was clearly contrary to Scripture and was an insult to God's royal priests—all those who trust in Christ for the forgiveness of sins. The Early Church Fathers spoke about *all* of God's people receiving both "kinds," or elements, of this Holy Meal. (See also Ap XXII; SA III VI; FC Ep VII and SD VII.)

The laity are given both kinds in the 1
Sacrament of the Lord's Supper because this
practice has the Lord's command, "Drink of
it, all of you" (Matthew 26:27). Christ has 2
clearly commanded that all should drink
from the cup.

And lest anyone misleadingly say that this 3
refers only to priests, in 1 Corinthians 11:27
Paul cites an example. From this it appears
that the whole congregation used both kinds.
This practice has remained in the Church 4
for a long time. It is not known when, or by
whom, or by whose authority, it was changed.
Cardinal Cusanus mentions the time when it
was approved. Cyprian in some places testi- 5
fies that the blood was given to the people.
Jerome testifies to the same thing when he 6
says, "The priests administer the Eucharist
and distribute the blood of Christ to the peo-
ple." Indeed, Pope Gelasius commands that 7
the Sacrament not be divided (dist. II., *De*
Consecratione, cap. Comperimus). Only a re- 8
cent custom has changed this.

It is clear that any custom introduced 9
against God's commandments is not to be al-
lowed, as Church law bears witness (dist. III.,
cap. Veritate, and the following chapters).
This custom has been received, not only 10
against the Scripture, but also against old
canon law and the example of the Church.
Therefore, if anyone preferred to use both 11
kinds in the Sacrament, they should not
have been compelled to do otherwise, as an

12 offense against their conscience. Because the
division of the Sacrament does not agree
with the ordinance of Christ, it is our custom
to omit the procession [with the host], which
has been used before.

ARTICLE XXIII

The Marriage of Priests

Note: Underlying the issue of forced priestly celibacy, as with other abuses arising in the Church, is the authority of the Church to command and forbid something not mentioned in Scripture. The Lutherans maintained that the Church has no authority from God to command what He has not commanded, nor to forbid what He has not forbidden. The Bible clearly teaches that the apostle Peter had a wife. This example should have served as convincing proof that priestly marriages were God pleasing. That there are men who are given the gift of chastity is affirmed, but the view that the Church can, and should, forbid all who wish to be priests from marrying is resoundingly rejected. Marriage is a gift from God to be received with thanksgiving both by laypeople and clergy. To suggest otherwise is to introduce a teaching of the evil one into the Church. (See also Ap XXIII; SA III XI.)

1 Complaints about unchaste priests are
2 common. Platina writes that it is for this rea-
son that Pope Pius is reported to have said
that although there are reasons why marriage
was taken away from priests, there are far
more important reasons why it should be
3 given back. Since our priests wanted to avoid
these open scandals, they married wives and
taught that it was lawful for them to enter
4 into marriage. First, because Paul says, "Be-
cause of the temptation to sexual immorali-
ty, each man should have his own wife" and
"It is better to marry than to be aflame with
passion" (1 Corinthians 7:2, 9b).
Second, Christ says, "Not everyone can 5
receive this saying" (Matthew 19:11), where
He teaches that not everyone is able to lead a
single life. God created human beings for
procreation (Genesis 1:28). It is not within a 6
person's power, without God giving a unique
gift, to change this creation. ‹For it is clear, as
many have confessed, that no good, honest,
chaste life, no Christian, sincere, upright con-
duct has resulted from the attempt to lead a
single life. Instead, a horrible, fearful unrest
and torment of conscience has been felt by
many until the end.› Therefore, those who 7
are not able to lead a single life ought to
marry. No human law, no vow, can destroy 8
God's commandment and ordinance. For 9
these reasons the priests teach that it is lawful
for them to marry wives.

It is clear that in the Ancient Church 10
priests were married men. For Paul says, "An 11
overseer must be the husband of one wife"
(1 Timothy 3:2). Four hundred years ago in 12
Germany, for the first time, priests were vio-
lently forced to lead a single life. They offered
such resistance that when the archbishop of
Mainz was about to publish the pope's decree
about celibacy, he was almost killed in a riot
by enraged priests. This matter was handled 13
so harshly that not only was marriage forbid-
den in the future, but existing marriages were
torn apart, contrary to all laws, both divine
and human. This was even contrary to canon
law itself, as made by not only popes, but also
by the most celebrated synods.

Seeing that man's nature is gradually 14
growing weaker as the world grows older, it is
good to be on guard to make sure no more
vices work their way into Germany.

Furthermore, God ordained marriage to 15
be a help against human weakness. Canon 16
law itself says that the old rigor ought to be

relaxed now and then, in these latter times, because of human weakness. We wish this
17 would also be done in this matter. We expect that at some point churches will lack pastors if marriage continues to be forbidden.
18 While God's commandment is in force, and the custom of the Church is well known, impure celibacy will cause many scandals, adulteries, and other crimes that deserve punishment from just rulers. In light of all this, it is incredibly cruel that the marriage of
19 priests is forbidden. God has commanded
20 that marriage be honored. Marriage is most highly honored in the laws of all well-ordered commonwealths, even among the hea-
21 then. But now men, even priests, are cruelly put to death, contrary to the intent of canon law, for no other reason than that they are
22 married. Paul, in 1 Timothy 4, says that a doctrine of demons forbids marriage (vv.
23 1–3). This is clearly seen by how laws against marriage are enforced with such penalties.
24 Since no human law can destroy God's command, neither can it be done by any vow.
25 So Cyprian advises women who do not keep the promise they made to remain chaste, that they should marry. He says (Book I, Epistle XI), "If they are unwilling or unable to persevere, it is better for them to marry than to fall into the fire by their lusts. They should certainly give no offense to their brothers and
26 sisters." And even canon law shows some leniency toward those who have taken vows before the proper age, as has been the case up to this point.

ARTICLE XXIV
The Mass

Note: This article clearly demonstrates Lutheranism's desire to continue—not to reject—the wholesome, beneficial, and historic worship practices of the Church. Lutheranism retained the traditional form of the Mass, that is, the service of Holy Communion. In many respects, the ceremonies and liturgy of the Lutheran Church were very similar to those of the Roman Church. The difference lay in Lutheranism's rejection of false teaching concerning the Mass: that somehow, and without faith, simply by attending and observing the spectacle of the Mass, people could merit the forgiveness of sins. Worst of all was Rome's teaching that a priest saying Mass is actually offering Christ in an unbloody manner to appease God and secure His favor. Masses became a source of considerable revenue for the Church, since people were encouraged to "sponsor" the saying of a Mass for their living—and dead—friends and relatives. All this is entirely contrary to Christ's institution of the Lord's Supper. He gave the Church this Sacrament as a gift and blessing, to be used in faith by the people of God. See excursus, p. 219. (See also Ap XXIV; SA III II; FC Ep X and SD X.)

Our churches are falsely accused of abol- 1
ishing the Mass. The Mass is held among us and celebrated with the highest reverence.
Nearly all the usual ceremonies are also pre- 2
served, except that the parts sung in Latin are interspersed here and there with German hymns. These have been added to teach the
people. For ceremonies are needed for this 3
reason alone, that the uneducated be taught
‹what they need to know about Christ›. Not 4
only has Paul commanded that a language understood by the people be used in church (1 Corinthians 14:2, 9), but human law has
also commanded it. All those able to do so 5
partake of the Sacrament together. This also increases the reverence and devotion of pub-
lic worship. No one is admitted to the Sacra- 6
ment without first being examined. The peo- 7
ple are also advised about the dignity and use of the Sacrament, about how it brings great

consolation to anxious consciences, so that
they too may learn to believe God and to ex-
8 pect and ask from Him all that is good. This
worship pleases God [Colossians 1:9–10].
Such use of the Sacrament nourishes true
9 devotion toward God. Therefore, it does
not appear that the Mass is more devoutly
celebrated among our adversaries than
among us.

10 It is clear that for a long time the most
public and serious complaint among all good
people is that the Mass has been made base
and profane by using it to gain filthy wealth
11 [1 Timothy 3:3]. Everyone knows how great
this abuse is in all the churches. They know
what sort of men say Masses for a fee or an
income, and how many celebrate these
12 Masses contrary to canon law. Paul severely
threatens those who use the Eucharist in an
unworthy manner, "Whoever eats the bread
or drinks the cup of the Lord in an unworthy
manner will be guilty of profaning the body
and blood of the Lord" (1 Corinthians
13 11:27). Therefore, when our priests were
warned about this sin, private Masses were
discontinued among us, since hardly any pri-
vate Masses were celebrated except for the
sake of filthy gain.

14 The bishops were not ignorant of these
abuses. If they had corrected them in time,
15 there would now be less discord. But until
now they have been responsible for many
16 corruptions seeping into the Church. Now,
when it is too late, they begin to complain
about the Church's troubles. This distur-
bance has been caused simply by those
abuses that were so open that they could no
17 longer be tolerated. There have been great
disagreements about the Mass, that is, the
18 Sacrament. Perhaps the world is being pun-
ished for profaning the Mass for such a
long time and for tolerating this in the
churches for so many centuries by the very
men who were both able and duty-bound
to correct this situation. It is written in the 19
Ten Commandments, "The LORD will not
hold him guiltless who takes His name in
vain" (Exodus 20:7). But since the world 20
began, nothing that God ever ordained
seems to have been so abused for filthy
wealth as the Mass.

An opinion was added that infinitely in- 21
creased private Masses. It states that Christ,
by His passion, made satisfaction for origi-
nal sin and instituted the Mass as an offering
for daily sins, both venial and mortal. From 22
this opinion has arisen the common belief
that the Mass takes away the sins of the liv-
ing and the dead simply by performing the
outward act. Then they began to argue 23
about whether one Mass said for many is
worth as much as special Masses for individ-
uals. This resulted in an infinite number of
Masses. ‹With this work, people wanted to
obtain from God all that they needed, and in
the meantime, trust in Christ and true wor-
ship were forgotten›.

Our teachers have warned that these 24
opinions depart from the Holy Scripture and
diminish the glory of the passion of Christ.
For Christ's passion was an offering and sat- 25
isfaction, not only for original guilt, but also
for all other sins, as it is written, "We have 26
been sanctified through the offering of the
body of Jesus Christ once for all" (Hebrews
10:10). Also, "By a single offering He has 27
perfected for all time those who are being
sanctified" (Hebrews 10:14). ‹It is an un-
heard-of innovation in the Church to teach
that by His death Christ has made satisfac-
tion only for original sin and not for all other
sin. So it is hoped that everybody will under-
stand that this error has been rebuked for
good reason.›

Scripture teaches that we are justified 28
before God, through faith in Christ, when

we believe that our sins are forgiven for
29 Christ's sake. Now if the Mass takes away
the sins of the living and the dead simply by
performing it, justification comes by doing
Masses, and not of faith. Scripture does not
allow this.

30 But Christ commands us, "Do this in re-
membrance of Me" (Luke 22:19). Therefore,
the Mass was instituted so that those who
use the Sacrament should remember, in
faith, the benefits they receive through
Christ and how their anxious consciences
31 are cheered and comforted. To remember
Christ is to remember His benefits. It means
to realize that they are truly offered to us.
32 It is not enough only to remember history.
(The Jewish people and the ungodly also re-
33 member this.) Therefore, the Mass is to be
used for administering the Sacrament to
those who need consolation. Ambrose says,
"Because I always sin, I always need to take
the medicine."

34 Because the Mass is for the purpose of
giving the Sacrament, we have Communion
every holy day, and if anyone desires the
Sacrament, we also offer it on other days,
when it is given to all who ask for it. This cus-
35 tom is not new in the Church. The Fathers
before Gregory make no mention of any pri-
vate Mass, but they speak a lot about the
36 common Mass, ‹Communion›. Chrysostom
says "that the priest stands daily at the altar,
inviting some to the Communion and keep-
37 ing back others." It appears from the ancient
council decisions that one person celebrated
the Mass from whom all the other presbyters
and deacons received the body of the Lord.
38 The records of the decisions of the Council
of Nicaea state, "Let the deacons, according
to their order, receive the Holy Communion
after the presbyters, from the bishop or from
39 a presbyter." Paul, in 1 Corinthians 11:33, has
this command in regard to Communion:
"wait for one another" so that there may be a
common participation.

Therefore, since the Mass among us fol- 40
lows the example of the Church, taken from
the Scripture and the Fathers, we are confi-
dent that it cannot be disapproved. This is
especially so because we keep the public cer-
emonies, which are for the most part similar
to those previously in use. Only the number
of Masses differs. Without a doubt, these
might be reduced in a helpful way, because
of very great and clear abuses. For in older 41
times, even in churches attended the most
often, the Mass was not celebrated every
day, as the *Tripartite History* (Book 9, chap.
33) testifies, "In Alexandria, every Wednes-
day and Friday the Scriptures are read, and
the doctors expound them, and all things
are done, except the solemn rite of Commu-
nion."

ARTICLE XXV

Confession

Note: The practice of private Confession and Absolution with one's pastor has fallen out of use in many Lutheran congregations. This was never Luther's intention. Neither was private Confession and Absolution abandoned during the first two centuries of Lutheran history. What the Lutheran Reformation corrected were the false teachings about Confession. Problems arose in the Church when teachings about Confession made "satisfactions" such a prominent part of it. When people were told to do certain activities (e.g., repeating the Hail Mary or doing acts of contrition) to "make up" for their sins, Christ's Gospel was overshadowed, if not completely hidden. Lutheranism, therefore, did away with the antibiblical teaching about satisfaction for sins and the requirement that people try to remember and confess each sin committed. (See also SA III VIII; Appendix B, Brief Exhortation to Confession.)

1 Confession in the churches is not abol-
ished among us. The body of the Lord is not
usually given to those who have not been ex-
amined [1 Corinthians 11:27–28] and ab-
2 solved. The people are very carefully taught
about faith in the Absolution. Before, there
3 was profound silence about faith. Our people
are taught that they should highly prize the
Absolution as being God's voice and pro-
4 nounced by God's command. The Power of
the Keys [Matthew 16:19] is set forth in its
beauty. They are reminded what great conso-
lation it brings to anxious consciences and
that God requires faith to believe such Abso-
lution as a voice sounding from heaven [e.g.,
John 12:28–30]. They are taught that such
faith in Christ truly obtains and receives the
5 forgiveness of sins. Before, satisfactions were
praised without restraint, but little was said
about faith, Christ's merit, and the righ-
teousness of faith. Therefore, on this point,
our churches are by no means to be blamed.
6 Even our adversaries have to concede the
point that our teachers have diligently taught
the doctrine of repentance and laid it open.

7 Our churches teach that naming every
sin is not necessary and that consciences
should not be burdened with worry about
naming every sin. It is impossible to recount
all sins, as Psalm 19:12 testifies: "Who can
8 discern his errors?" Also Jeremiah 17:9, "The
heart is deceitful above all things, and des-
9 perately sick; who can understand it?" If only
sins that can be named are forgiven, con-
sciences could never find peace. For many
10 sins cannot be seen or remembered. The an-
cient writers also testify that a listing of sins is
11 not necessary. For in the Decrees, Chrysos-
tom is quoted. He says,

> I do not say that you should make your sins known in public, nor that you should accuse yourself before others, but I would have you obey the prophet who says, "Make known your ways before God" [Psalm 37:5]. Therefore, confess your sins before God, the true Judge, with prayer. Tell your errors, not with the tongue, but with the memory of your conscience, and so forth.

And the Gloss (*Of Repentance*, Distinct. 12
V, *Cap. Consideret*) admits that Confession is
of human right only. Nevertheless, because 13
of the great benefit of Absolution, and be-
cause it is otherwise useful to the conscience,
Confession is retained among us.

ARTICLE XXVI

The Distinction of Meats

Note: Choosing not to eat particular foods, or any food at all, at particular times or on particular occasions is entirely a matter of Christian freedom. By the time of the Reformation, however, the Church had devised complex regulations commanding abstinence from certain foods on certain days. Church teaching misled people into believing that by following such regulations they merited God's grace and favor. Such a theory is entirely contrary to the Gospel, overturns the all-sufficient merit of Jesus Christ, and replaces Him with human works. Contrived laws such as these placed enormous burdens on the common people, who frequently considered themselves less spiritual than the monks and nuns who adhered to these dietary regulations very closely. Bodily discipline and working to curb one's sinful desires is entirely appropriate and necessary, but never is it to be suggested that such activities earn God's grace. In highlighting the issue of dietary restrictions, the Augsburg Confession once more repeats that Lutherans do not do away with good traditions and practices, such as the order of Bible readings in the Communion Service, but only such things as take away from the Gospel. (See also SA III XV.)

---

1 Not only the people, but also those teach-
ing in the churches, have generally been per-
suaded to believe in making distinctions be-
tween meats, and similar human traditions.
They believe these are useful works for mer-
iting grace and are able to make satisfaction
2 for sins. From this there developed the view
that new ceremonies, new orders, new holy
days, and new fastings were instituted daily.
Teachers in the Church required these works
as a necessary service to merit grace. They
greatly terrified people's consciences when
3 they left any of these things out. Because of
this viewpoint, the Church has suffered great
damage.

4 First, the chief part of the Gospel—the
doctrine of grace and of the righteousness of
faith—has been obscured by this view. The
Gospel should stand out as the most promi-
nent teaching in the Church, in order that
Christ's merit may be well known and faith,
which believes that sins are forgiven for
Christ's sake, be exalted far above works.
5 Therefore, Paul also lays the greatest stress on
this article, putting aside the Law and human
traditions, in order to show that Christian
righteousness is something other than such
works [Romans 14:17]. Christian righ-
teousness is the faith that believes that sins
6 are freely forgiven for Christ's sake. But this
doctrine of Paul has been almost completely
smothered by traditions, which have pro-
duced the opinion that we must merit grace
and righteousness by making distinctions in
7 meats and similar services. When repentance
was taught, there was no mention made of
faith. Only works of satisfaction were set
forth. And so repentance seemed to stand en-
tirely on these works.

Second, these traditions have hindered 8
God's commandments, because traditions
were placed far above God's command-
ments. Christianity was thought to stand
wholly on the observance of certain holy
days, rites, fasts, and vestments. These ob- 9
servances won the exalted title of the "spiri-
tual life" and the "perfect life." Meanwhile, 10
God's commandments, according to each
one's vocation, or calling, were without
honor. These works include a father raising
his children, a mother bearing children, a
prince governing the commonwealth—these
were considered to be worldly and thus im-
perfect works, far below the glittering obser-
vances of the Church. This error greatly tor- 11
mented people with devout consciences.
They grieved that they were held in an im-
perfect state of life, as in marriage, in the of-
fice of ruler, or in other civil services. They
admired the monks and others like them.
They falsely thought that these people's ob-
servances were more acceptable to God.

Third, traditions brought great danger to 12
consciences. It was impossible to keep all tra-
ditions, and yet people considered these ob-
servances to be necessary acts of worship.
Gerson writes that many fell into despair, 13
and that some even took their own lives, be-
cause they felt that they were not able to sat-
isfy the traditions. All the while, they had
never heard about the consoling righ-
teousness of faith and grace. We see that the 14
academics and theologians gather the tradi-
tions and seek ways to relieve and ease con-
sciences. They do not free consciences
enough, but sometimes entangle them even
more! The schools and sermons have been 15
so occupied with gathering these "tradi-
tions" that they do not even have enough
leisure time to touch on Scripture. They do

not pursue the far more useful doctrine of faith, the cross, hope, the dignity of secular affairs, and consolation for severely tested
16 consciences. Therefore, Gerson and some other theologians have complained sadly that because of all this striving after traditions, they were prevented from giving atten-
17 tion to a better kind of doctrine. Augustine forbids that people's consciences should be burdened. He prudently advises Januarius that he must know that they are to be observed as things neither commanded by God nor forbidden, for such are his words.

18 Therefore, our teachers must not be regarded as having taken up this matter rashly or from hatred of the bishops, as some falsely
19 suspect. There was a great need to warn the churches of these errors that arose from mis-
20 understanding the traditions. The Gospel compels us to insist on the doctrine of grace and the righteousness of faith in the churches. This cannot be understood if people think that they merit grace by observances of their own choice.

21 So our churches have taught that we cannot merit grace or be justified by observing human traditions. We must not think that such observances are necessary
22 acts of worship. Here we add testimonies of Scripture. Christ defends the apostles who had not observed the usual tradition (Matthew 15:3). This had to do with a matter that was not unlawful, but rather, neither commanded or forbidden. It was similar to the purifications of the Law. He said in Matthew 15:9, "In vain do they worship Me, teaching as doctrines the commandments of
23 men." Therefore, He does not require a useless human service. Shortly after, He adds, "It is not what goes into the mouth that defiles a person, but what comes out of the mouth; this defiles a person" (Matthew
24 15:11). So also Paul, in Romans 14:17, "The kingdom of God is not a matter of eating and drinking but of righteousness and peace and joy in the Holy Spirit," and in
Colossians 2:16, "Let no one pass judgment 25
on you in questions of food and drink, or
with regard to . . . a Sabbath." And again, "If 26
with Christ you died to the elemental spirits of the world, why, as if you were still alive in the world, do you submit to regulations—'Do not handle, Do not taste, Do not
touch'" [Colossians 2:20–21]. Peter says, 27
"Why are you putting God to the test by placing a yoke on the neck of the disciples that neither our fathers nor we have been able to bear? But we believe that we will be saved through the grace of the Lord Jesus,
just as they will" (Acts 15:10–11). Here 28
Peter forbids burdening consciences with
many rites, either from Moses or others. In 29
1 Timothy 4:1–3 Paul calls the prohibition of meats a teaching of demons. It is contrary to the Gospel to institute or do such works thinking that we merit grace through them, or as though Christianity could not exist without such service of God.

Our adversaries object by accusing our 30
teachers of being against discipline and the subduing of the flesh. Just the opposite is true, as can be learned from our teachers'
writings. They have always taught that 31
Christians are to bear the cross [Matthew
16:24] by enduring afflictions. This is gen- 32
uine and sincere subduing of the flesh [1 Peter 2:11], to be crucified with Christ
through various afflictions. Furthermore, 33
they teach that every Christian ought to train and subdue himself with bodily restraints, or bodily exercises and labors. Then neither overindulgence nor laziness may tempt him to sin. But they do not teach that we may merit grace or make sat-
isfaction for sins by such exercises. Such 34
outward discipline ought to be taught at all

35 times, not only on a few set days. Christ
commands, "Watch yourselves lest your
hearts be weighed down with dissipation
36 and drunkenness" (Luke 21:34). Also in
Matthew 17:21, "This kind never comes out
37 except by prayer and fasting." Paul also
says, "I discipline my body and keep it
38 under control" (1 Corinthians 9:27). Here he
clearly shows that he was keeping his body
under control, not to merit forgiveness of
sins by that discipline, but to keep his body in
subjection and prepared for spiritual things,
for carrying out the duties of his calling.
39 Therefore, we do not condemn fasting in it-
self [Isaiah 58:3–7], but the traditions that
require certain days and certain meats, with
peril of conscience, as though such works
were a necessary service.

40 Nevertheless, we keep many traditions
that are leading to good order [1 Corin-
thians 14:40] in the Church, such as the
order of Scripture lessons in the Mass and
41 the chief holy days. At the same time, we
warn people that such observances do not
justify us before God, and that it is not sin-
ful if we omit such things, without causing
42 offense. The Fathers knew of such freedom
43 in human ceremonies. In the East they
kept Easter at another time than at Rome.
When the Romans accused the Eastern
Church of schism, they were told by others
that such practices do not need to be the
44 same everywhere. Irenaeus says, "Diversity
concerning fasting does not destroy the har-
mony of faith." Pope Gregory says, in Dist.
XII, that such diversity does not violate the
45 unity of the Church. In the *Tripartite His-
tory*, Book 9, many examples of different
rites are gathered, and the following state-
ment is made:

> It was not the mind of the apostles to enact rules concerning holy days, but to preach godliness and a holy life.

ARTICLE XXVII
Monastic Vows

Note: This article has in view Martin Luther's experience in the monastery, along with what other former monks had to say about life in the cloister. The idea that a person should hide himself behind the walls of a monastery, and perform spiritual works to make himself more worthy of God's favor, has no biblical justification at all. During the Middle Ages, many common people believed that only priests, monks, or nuns were truly performing spiritual work. But such a view contradicts God's Word, which teaches how all of life is an opportunity to serve God—giving Him glory by serving our neighbor. Even today, it is assumed that activities at church are somehow of greater value than the common, everyday duties life requires of us. This article extols such biblical duties as being a faithful husband, wife, son, or daughter, and takes great care to reject monasticism and explain how harmful and dangerous it is for those who are entrapped in it. Forcing chastity on those who have not been given this gift is particularly harmful, since many are led to believe they merit God's grace by means of their sacrifice, not the sacrifice of Christ. (See also Ap XXVII; SA III XIV.)

It will be easier to understand what we 1
teach about monastic vows by considering
the state of the monasteries and how many
things were done every day contrary to
canon law. In Augustine's time they were 2
free associations. Later, when discipline was
corrupted, vows were added for the purpose
of restoring discipline, as in a carefully
planned prison. Gradually, many other regu- 3
lations were added besides vows. These 4
binding rules were laid upon many before
the lawful age, contrary to canon law.

5 Many entered monastic life through ig-
norance. They were not able to judge their
own strength, though they were old enough.
6 They were trapped and compelled to remain,
even though some could have been freed by
7 the kind provision of canon law. This was
more the case in convents of women than of
monks, although more consideration should
have been shown the weaker sex [1 Peter 3:7].
8 This rigor displeased many good people be-
fore this time, who saw that young men and
women were thrown into convents for a liv-
ing. They saw what unfortunate results came
of this procedure, how it created scandals,
and what snares were cast upon consciences!
9 They were sad that the authority of canon
law in so great a matter was utterly set aside
10 and despised. In addition to all these evil
things, a view of vows was added that dis-
pleased even the more considerate monks.
They taught that monastic vows were equal
11 to Baptism. They taught that a monastic life
merited forgiveness of sins and justification
12 before God. Yes, they even added that the
monastic life not only merited righteousness
before God, but even greater merit, since it
was said that the monastic life not only kept
God's basic law, but also the so-called "evan-
gelical counsels."

13 So they made people believe that the pro-
fession of monasticism was far better than
Baptism, and that the monastic life was
more meritorious than that of rulers, pastors,
and others, who serve in their calling accord-
ing to God's commands, without any man-
14 made services. None of these things can be
denied. This is all found in their own books
about monasticism.

15 How did all this come about in monas-
teries? At one time they were schools of the-
ology and other branches of learning, pro-
ducing pastors and bishops for the benefit of
the Church. Now it is another thing. It is
needless to go over what everyone knows.
Before, they came together for the sake of 16
learning, now they claim that monasticism is
a lifestyle instituted to merit grace and righ-
teousness. They even preach that it is a state
of perfection! They put monasticism far
above all other kinds of life ordained by God.
We have mentioned all these things without 17
hateful exaggeration so that our teachers'
doctrine on monasticism may be better un-
derstood.

First, concerning monks who marry, our 18
teachers say that it is lawful for anyone who is
not suited for the single life to enter into
marriage. Monastic vows cannot destroy
what God has commanded and ordained.
God's commandment is this, "Because of the 19
temptation to sexual immorality, each man
should have his own wife" (1 Corinthians
7:2). It is not just a command given by God. 20
God has created and ordained marriage for
those who are not given an exception to nat-
ural order by God's special work. This is what
is taught according to the text in Genesis
2:18, "It is not good that the man should be
alone." Therefore, those who obey this com- 21
mand and ordinance of God do not sin.

What objection can be raised to this? Let 22
people praise the obligation of a monastic
vow as much as they want, but they will
never be able to destroy God's command-
ment by means of a monastic vow. Canon 23
law teaches that superiors can make excep-
tions to monastic vows; how much less are
such monastic vows in force that are contrary
to God's commandments!

If, in fact, an obligation to a monastic 24
vow could never be changed for any reason,
the Roman popes could never have granted
exceptions to the vows. For it is not lawful for
someone to make an exception to what is
truly from God. The Roman pontiffs have 25
wisely judged that mercy is to be observed in

George, Margrave of Brandenburg (1484–1543)

A courageous ally of John the Steadfast. Stood up to the emperor at the Diet of Augsburg, telling Charles he would sooner have his head cut off than deny Christ and His Word. Also called George the Pious.

these monastic obligations. That is why we
read that many times they have made special
arrangements and exceptions with monastic
26 vows. The case of the King of Aragon, who
was called back from the monastery, is well
known, and there are also examples in our
own times.

27 In the second place, why do our adver-
saries exaggerate the obligation or effect of a
vow when, at the same time, they do not
have anything to say about the nature of the
vow itself? A vow should be something that
is possible; it should be a decision that is
made freely and after careful deliberation.
28 We all know how possible perpetual chastity
29 actually is in reality, and just how few peo-
ple actually do take this vow freely and de-
liberately! Young women and men, before
they are able to make their own decision
about this, are persuaded, and sometimes
even forced, to take the vow of chastity.
30 Therefore, it is not fair to insist so rigorously
on the obligation. Everyone knows that tak-
ing a vow that is not made freely and deliber-
ately is against the very nature of a true vow.

31 Most canonical laws overturn vows made
before the age of fifteen. Before that age a per-
son does not seem able to make a wise judg-
ment and to decide to make a lifelong com-
32 mitment like this. There is another canon law
that adds even more years to this limit, show-
ing that the vow of chastity should not be
made before the age of eighteen. So which of
33 these two canon laws should we follow? Most
people leaving the monastery have a valid ex-
cuse, since they took their vows before they
were fifteen or eighteen.

34 Finally, even though it might be possible
to condemn a person who breaks a vow, it
does not follow that it is right to dissolve
35 such a person's marriage. Augustine denies
that they ought to be dissolved (XXVII.
Quaest. I, Cap. *Nuptiarum*). Augustine's au-
thority should not be taken lightly, even
though some wish to do so today.

Although it appears that God's com- 36
mand about marriage delivers many from
their vows, our teachers introduce another
argument about vows to show that they are
void. Every service of God, established and
chosen by people to merit justification and
grace, without God's commandment, is
wicked. For Christ says in Matthew 15:9, "In
vain do they worship Me, teaching as doc-
trines the commandments of men." Paul 37
teaches everywhere that righteousness is not
to be sought in self-chosen practices and
acts of worship, devised by people. Righ-
teousness comes by faith to those who be-
lieve that they are received by God into grace
for Christ's sake.

It is clear for all to see that the monks 38
have taught that services made up by people
make satisfaction for sins and merit grace
and justification. What else is this than de-
tracting from Christ's glory and hiding and
denying the righteousness that comes
through faith? Therefore, it follows that 39
monastic vows, which have been widely
taken, are wicked services of God and, conse-
quently, are void. For a wicked vow, taken 40
against God's commandment, is not valid;
for (as the Canon says) no vow ought to bind
people to wickedness.

Paul says, "You are severed from Christ, 41
you who would be justified by the law; you
have fallen away from grace" (Galatians 5:4).
Therefore, anyone wanting to be justified by 42
his vows makes Christ useless and falls from
grace. Anyone who tries to connect justifica- 43
tion to monastic vows bases his justification
on his own works, which properly belongs to
Christ's glory.

It cannot be denied that the monks have 44
taught that they were justified and merited
forgiveness of sins by means of their vows

and observances. Indeed, they even invented
greater absurdities, saying that they could
45 give others a share in their works. If anyone
wanted to make more of this point, to make
our opponents look even worse, even more
things could be mentioned, things that even
46 the monks are ashamed of now. And on top
of all this, the monks persuaded people that
the services that they invented were a state of
47 Christian perfection. What else is this other
48 than assigning our justification to works? It
is no light offense in the Church to set be-
fore the people a service invented by people,
without God's commandment, and then to
teach them that such service justifies. For
the righteousness of faith, which ought to
be the highest teaching in the Church, is
hidden when these "wonderful" and "angel-
ic" forms of worship, with their show of
poverty, humility, and celibacy, are put in
front of people.

49 God's precepts, and God's true service,
are hidden when people hear that only
monks are in a state of perfection. True
Christian perfection is to fear God from the
heart, to have great faith, and to trust that for
Christ's sake we have a God who has been
reconciled [2 Corinthians 5:18–19]. It means
to ask for and expect from God His help in
all things with confident assurance that we
are to live according to our calling in life,
being diligent in outward good works, serv-
50 ing in our calling. This is where true perfec-
tion and true service of God is to be found. It
does not consist in celibacy or in begging or
51 in degrading clothes. The people come up
with all sorts of harmful opinions based on
52 the false praise of monastic life. They hear
celibacy praised without measure and feel
53 guilty about living in marriage. They hear
that only beggars are perfect, and so they
keep their possessions and do business with
guilty consciences. They hear that it is an 54
even higher work, a Gospel-counsel, not to
seek revenge. So some in private life are not
afraid to take revenge, for they hear that it is
but a counsel and not a commandment.
Others come to the conclusion that a Chris- 55
tian cannot rightly hold a civil office or be a
ruler.

There are on record examples of men 56
who hid themselves in monasteries because
they wanted to forsake marriage and partici-
pation in society. They called this fleeing 57
from the world, and said they were seeking a
kind of life that would be more pleasing to
God. They did not realize that God ought to
be served according to the commandments
that He Himself has given, not in command-
ments made up by people. Only a life that 58
has God's commandment is good and per-
fect. It is necessary to teach the people about 59
these things.

Before our times, Gerson rebukes the 60
monks' error about perfection. He testifies
that in his day it was a new saying that the
monastic life is a state of perfection. So 61
many wicked opinions are inherent in
monastic vows—that they justify, that they
cause Christian perfection, that they make it
possible to keep the counsels and command-
ments, that they are works over and above
God's commandments. All these things are 62
false and empty. They make monastic vows
null and void.

ARTICLE XXVIII

Church Authority

Note: Article XXVIII expands on Articles V and XIV. What authority, or power, do bishops have in the Church? Over the course of centuries, bishops had become not merely Church leaders, but political figures as well, claiming the right to govern both Church and State and to make and enforce laws in both realms. By returning to a biblical understanding of church, the Augsburg Confession clarifies that the true authority, or power, of bishops is the preaching of the Gospel, the forgiving and withholding of forgiveness of sins, and the administering of the Sacraments. The Church is not to interfere in the government, but is to keep its focus on the Gospel. This article is the foundation for the Lutheran understanding of the two kingdoms: God's work and rule in the world by means of the Church (the kingdom or regiment of the right hand) and the State (the kingdom or regiment of the left hand). Bishops, or pastors, have authority in the Church only to forgive sins in the name of Christ, to reject false doctrine and reprove those who uphold it, and to exclude persons who refuse to repent of open and manifest sin. This article, like the others, places the focus on the chief teaching of the Gospel: we are justified by God's grace through faith in Christ alone. (See also Ap XXVIII; SC Table of Duties.)

---

1 There has been great controversy about
the power of the bishops, in which some have
terribly confused the power of the Church
2 with the power of the State. This confusion
has produced great war and riot. All the
while the popes, claiming the Power of the
Keys, have instituted new services and bur-
dened consciences with Church discipline
and excommunication. But they have also
tried to transfer the kingdoms of this world
to the Church by taking the Empire away
3 from the emperor. Learned and godly peo-
ple have condemned these errors in the
4 Church for a long time. Therefore, our
teachers, in order to comfort people's con-
sciences, were constrained to show the differ-
ence between the authority of the Church
and the authority of the State. They taught
that both of them are to be held in reverence
and honor, as God's chief blessings on earth,
because they have God's command.

Our teachers' position is this: the author- 5
ity of the Keys [Matthew 16:19], or the au-
thority of the bishops—according to the
Gospel—is a power or commandment of
God, to preach the Gospel, to forgive and re-
tain sins, and to administer Sacraments.
Christ sends out His apostles with this com- 6
mand, "As the Father has sent Me, even so I
am sending you . . . Receive the Holy Spirit. If
you forgive the sins of anyone, they are for-
given; if you withhold forgiveness from any-
one, it is withheld" (John 20:21–22). And in 7
Mark 16:15, Christ says, "Go . . . proclaim the
Gospel to the whole creation."

This authority is exercised only by teach- 8
ing or preaching the Gospel and administer-
ing the Sacraments, either to many or to in-
dividuals, according to their calling. In this
way are given not only bodily, but also eter-
nal things: eternal righteousness, the Holy
Spirit, and eternal life. These things cannot 9
reach us except by the ministry of the Word
and the Sacraments, as Paul says, "The
Gospel . . . is the power of God for salvation
to everyone that believes" (Romans 1:16).
Therefore, the Church has the authority to 10
grant eternal things and exercises this au-
thority only by the ministry of the Word. So
it does not interfere with civil government
anymore than the art of singing interferes
with civil government. For civil government 11
deals with other things than the Gospel does.
Civil rulers do not defend minds, but bodies
and bodily things against obvious injuries.
They restrain people with the sword and
physical punishment in order to preserve
civil justice and peace [Romans 13:1–7].

Therefore, the Church's authority and the 12
State's authority must not be confused. The
Church's authority has its own commission

to teach the Gospel and to administer the
13 Sacraments [Matthew 28:19–20]. Let it not
break into the office of another. Let it not
transfer the kingdoms of this world to itself.
Let it not abolish the laws of civil rulers. Let it
not abolish lawful obedience. Let it not inter-
fere with judgments about civil ordinances
or contracts. Let it not dictate laws to civil
14 authorities about the form of society. As
Christ says, "My kingdom is not of this
15 world" (John 18:36). Also, "Who made Me a
judge or arbitrator over you?" (Luke 12:14).
16 Paul also says, "Our citizenship is in heaven"
17 (Philippians 3:20). And, "The weapons of
our warfare are not of the flesh but have di-
vine power to destroy strongholds" (2 Corin-
thians 10:4).

18 This is how our teachers distinguish be-
tween the duties of these two authorities.
They command that both be honored and
acknowledged as God's gifts and blessings.

19 If bishops have any authority of the State,
this is not because they are bishops. In other
words, it is not by the Gospel's commission.
It is an authority they have received from
kings and emperors for the purpose of ad-
ministering the civil affairs of what belongs
to them in society. This is another office, not
the ministry of the Gospel.

20 Therefore, when a question arises about
the bishops' jurisdiction, civil authority must
be distinguished from the Church's jurisdic-
21 tion. Again, the only authority that belongs
to the bishops is what they have according to
the Gospel, or by divine right, as they say. For
they have been given the ministry of the
Word and Sacraments. They have no other
authority according to the Gospel than the
authority to forgive sins, to judge doctrine, to
reject doctrines contrary to the Gospel, and
to exclude from the communion of the
Church wicked people, whose wickedness is
known. They cannot exclude people with
human force, but simply by the Word. Ac- 22
cording to this Gospel authority, as a matter
of necessity, by divine right, congregations
must obey them, for Luke 10:16 says, "The
one who hears you hears Me." But when 23
they teach or establish anything against the
Gospel, then the congregations are forbidden
by God's command to obey them.

> Beware of false prophets. (Matthew 7:15)

> But even if we or an angel from heaven 24
> should preach to you a Gospel con-
> trary to the one we preached to you,
> let him be accursed. (Galatians 1:8)

> For we cannot do anything against 25
> the truth, but only for the truth . . .
> the authority that the Lord has given 26
> me for building up, and not for tear-
> ing down. (2 Corinthians 13:8–10)

The Canonical Laws also command this 27
(II. Q. VII. Cap., *Sacerdotes*, and Cap. *Oves*)
And Augustine writes: 28

> Neither must we submit to catholic bishops if they chance to err, or hold anything contrary to the canonical Scriptures of God. (*Contra Petiliani Epistolam*)

If the bishops have any other authority or 29
jurisdiction, in hearing and judging certain cases, as of matrimony or of tithes, they have this authority only by human right. If the bishops do not carry out their duties in these areas, the princes are bound, even if they do not want to, to dispense justice to their subjects in order to maintain peace.

There is also a dispute about whether or 30
not bishops, or pastors, have the right to in-
troduce ceremonies in the Church, and to
make laws about meats, holy days, and
grades, that is, orders of ministers, and so on.
Those who say that the bishops do have this 31
right refer to this testimony of Christ in John

16:12–13, "I still have many things to say to
you, but you cannot bear them now. When
the Spirit of truth comes, He will guide you
32 into all the truth." They also refer to the ex-
ample of the apostles, who commanded that
Christians abstain from blood and from
33 things strangled (Acts 15:[20,] 29). They refer
to the Sabbath day as having been changed
into the Lord's Day, contrary to the Decalog,
as they understand it. In fact, they make
more of the supposed change of the Sabbath
day than any other example they can think
of. They say that the Church's authority is so
great, it has even done away with one of the
Ten Commandments.

34 But on this question, for our part (as we
have shown earlier) we teach that bishops
have no authority to decree anything
against the Gospel. The Canonical Laws
35 teach the same thing (Dist. IX). It is against
Scripture to establish or require the obser-
vance of any traditions for the purpose of
making satisfaction for sins, or to merit
36 grace and righteousness. When we try to
merit justification by observing such things,
we cause great harm to the glory of Christ's
37 merit. It is quite clear that by such beliefs,
traditions have almost multiplied to an infi-
nite degree in the Church, while at the same
time, the doctrine about faith and the righ-
teousness through faith has been sup-
pressed. Gradually more holy days were
made, fasts appointed, new ceremonies and
services in honor of saints instituted. Those
responsible for such things thought that by
38 these works they were meriting grace. So
the Penitential Canons increased. We still
see some traces of this in the satisfactions.

39 Those who establish such traditions are
acting contrary to God's command when
they locate sin in foods, days, and similar
things. They burden the Church with
bondage to the Law, as if there needs to be
something similar to the services command-
ed in Leviticus [chapters 1–7] in order to
merit justification. They say that Christ has
committed the arrangement of such services
to the apostles and bishops. They have writ- 40
ten about the Law of Moses in such a way
that the popes have been misled to some
degree. This is how they have burdened the 41
Church, by making it a mortal sin—even if
nobody else is offended—to do manual
labor on holy days, or to skip the canonical
hours, or that certain foods dirty the con-
science, or that fasting is a work that appeas-
es God. Or they say that, in a reserved case,
sin can only be forgiven by the person who
reserved the case, even though canon law
speaks only of reserving the ecclesiastical
penalty, not the guilt.

Who has given the bishops the right to 42
lay these traditions on the Church, by which
they snare consciences? In Acts 15:10,
Peter forbids us from putting a yoke on
the neck of the disciples, and Paul says in
2 Corinthians 13:10 that the authority given
to him was for edification, not for destruc-
tion. Why do the adversaries increase sins
with their traditions?

There are clear testimonies that forbid 43
creating traditions in such a way as to suggest
that they merit grace or are necessary to sal-
vation. Paul says in Colossians 2:16, "There- 44
fore let no one pass judgment on you in
questions of food and drink, or with regard
to a festival or a new moon or a Sabbath."
And later: 45

> If with Christ you died to the elemental spirits of the world, why, as if you were still alive in the world, do you submit to regulations—'Do not handle, Do not taste, Do not touch' (referring to things that all perish as they are used)—according to human precepts and teachings? These have

> indeed an appearance of wisdom.
> (Colossians 2:20–23)

46 Also in Titus 1:14 he openly forbids tradi-
tions with these words: "not devoting them-
selves to Jewish myths and the commands of
people who turn away from the truth."

47 In Matthew 15:14, Christ says of those
who require traditions, "Let them alone; they
48 are blind guides." In verse 13 He rejects such
services: "Every plant that My heavenly Fa-
ther has not planted will be rooted up."

49 If bishops have the right to burden
churches with infinite traditions, and to
snare consciences, why does Scripture so
often forbid making and listening to tradi-
tions? Why does it call them "teachings of
demons" (1 Timothy 4:1)? Did the Holy Spir-
it warn of these things in vain?

50 Therefore, ordinances instituted as
though they are necessary, or with the view
that they merit grace, are contrary to the
Gospel. Therefore, it follows that it is not
lawful for any bishop to institute and require
51 such services. It is necessary that the doc-
trine of Christian freedom be preserved in
the churches. In other words, the bondage
of the Law is not necessary in order to be
justified, as it is written in the Epistle to the
Galatians, "do not submit again to a yoke of
52 slavery" (5:1). It is necessary for the chief
article of the Gospel to be preserved, namely
that we obtain grace freely by faith in Christ,
and not by certain observances or acts of
worship devised by people.

53 What, then, are we to think of the Sunday
rites, and similar things, in God's house? We
answer that it is lawful for bishops, or pas-
tors, to make ordinances so that things will
be done orderly in the Church, but not to
teach that we merit grace or make satisfaction
for sins. Consciences are not bound to regard
them as necessary services and to think that it
is a sin to break them without offense to oth-
ers. So in 1 Corinthians 11:5, Paul concludes 54
that women should cover their heads in the
congregation and in 1 Corinthians 14:30, that
interpreters be heard in order in the church,
and so on.

It is proper that the churches keep such 55
ordinances for the sake of love and tran-
quility, to avoid giving offense to another, so
that all things be done in the churches in
order, and without confusion (1 Corin-
thians 14:40; comp. Philippians 2:14). It is 56
proper to keep such ordinances just so long
as consciences are not burdened to think
that they are necessary to salvation, or to re-
gard it as sin if they are changed without of-
fending others. For instance, no one will say
that a woman sins who goes out in public
with her head uncovered, as long as no of-
fense is given.

This kind of ordinance in the Church is 57
observing the Lord's Day, Easter, Pentecost,
and similar holy days and rites. It is a great 58
error for anyone to think that it is by the au-
thority of the Church that we observe the
Lord's Day as something necessary, instead of
the Sabbath Day. Scripture itself has abol- 59
ished the Sabbath Day [Colossians 2:16–17].
It teaches that since the Gospel has been re-
vealed, all the ceremonies of Moses can be
omitted. Yet, because it was necessary to 60
appoint a certain day for the people to know
when they ought to come together, it ap-
pears that the Church designated the Lord's
Day [Revelation 1:10] for this purpose. This
day seems to have been chosen all the more
for this additional reason: so people might
have an example of Christian freedom and
might know that keeping neither the Sabbath
nor any other day is necessary.

There are monstrous debates about 61
changing the law, ceremonies of the new
law, and changing the Sabbath Day. They

have all sprung from the false belief that in the Church there must be something similar to the services set forth in Leviticus [1–7], and that Christ had commissioned the apostles and bishops to come up with new
62 ceremonies necessary to salvation. These errors crept into the Church when the righteousness that comes through faith was
63 not taught clearly enough. Some debate whether or not keeping the Lord's Day is not a divine right, but similar to it. They prescribe the extent to which it is lawful to
64 work on holy days. What else are such disputes except traps for the conscience? Even when they try to modify the traditions, nobody will understand the modifications as long as the opinion remains that these traditions are necessary and must remain. There the righteousness of faith and Christian freedom is not known.

65 In Acts 15:20, the apostles commanded to abstain from blood. Who observes this now? Those who choose to eat blood do not sin, for not even the apostles themselves wanted to burden consciences with bondage to traditions. They forbid the eating of the blood for
66 a time to avoid giving offense. For in this decree we must always keep in mind what the aim of the Gospel is.

67 Scarcely any canon laws are kept with exactness. From day to day many go out of use, even among those who are the most zealous
68 advocates of traditions. In order to treat the conscience properly, we must realize that canon laws are to be kept without regarding them as necessary. No harm is done to the conscience even though traditions may go out of use.

69 The bishops might easily retain the legitimate obedience of the people if they would not insist upon the observance of traditions that cannot be kept with a good conscience.
70 Instead, they command celibacy and accept no preachers—unless they swear that they will not teach the Gospel's pure doctrine.
The churches are not asking the bishops to 71
restore concord at the expense of their honor, even though it would be proper for
good pastors to do this. They ask only that 72
the bishops release unjust burdens that are new and have been received contrary to the
custom of the universal Church. It may be 73
that in the beginning there were plausible reasons for some of these ordinances, but
they are not adapted to later times. It is also 74
clear that some were adopted through erroneous ideas. Therefore, it would be in keeping with the popes' mercy to change them now. Such a modification does not shake the Church's unity. Many human traditions have been changed over time, as the canons them-
selves show. But if it is impossible for the 75
adversaries to change those traditions, which they say is sinful to change, we must follow the apostolic rule, which commands us to "obey God rather than men" (Acts 5:29).

In 1 Peter 5:3, Peter forbids bishops to be 76
lords and rule over the churches. It is not 77
our intention to take oversight away from the bishops. We ask only this one thing, that they allow the Gospel to be taught purely, and that they relax a few observances that they claim
it is sinful to change. If they will not give 78
anything up, it is for them to decide how they will give an account to God for causing schism by their stubbornness.

Conclusion

These are the chief articles that seem to 1
be in controversy. We could have mentioned more abuses. But here we have set forth only the chief points in order to avoid making this Confession too long. From these chief points
the rest may be easily judged. There have 2
been, for example, great complaints about indulgences, pilgrimages, and the abuse of

excommunication. Our parishes have been
troubled in many ways by dealers in indul-
gences. There were endless arguments be-
tween the pastors and the monks about who
has the right in parishes to hear confessions,
do funerals, give sermons on extraordinary
3 occasions, and innumerable other things. We
have passed over such issues so that the chief
points in this matter, briefly set forth, might
4 be more easily understood. Nothing has
been said or brought up for the rebuke of
5 anyone. We have mentioned only those
things we thought it was necessary to talk
about so that it would be understood that in
doctrine and ceremonies we have received
nothing contrary to Scripture or the Church
universal. It is clear that we have been very
careful to make sure no new ungodly doc-
trine creeps into our churches.

We present these articles in accordance 6
with Your Imperial Majesty's edict, in order
to show our Confession and let people see a
summary of our teachers' doctrine. If there 7
is anything that anyone might desire in this
Confession, we are ready, God willing, to
present more thorough information accord-
ing to the Scriptures.

Your Imperial Majesty's faithful subjects: 8
John, Duke of Saxony, Elector. 9
George, Margrave of Brandenburg. 10
Ernest, Duke of Lüneberg. 11
Philip, Landgrave of Hesse. 12
John Frederick, Duke of Saxony. 13
Francis, Duke of Lüneberg. 14
Wolfgang, Prince of Anhalt. 15
Senate and Magistracy of Nürnberg. 16
Senate of Reutlingen. 17

Understanding Indulgences

Note: The following is a translation of an actual indulgence administered in 1515 by Albert, the Archbishop of Mainz and Magdeburg. It was designed to raise money for the completion of St. Peter's Cathedral in Rome. It guarantees forgiveness and provides for the reception of Communion, even when a person's territory was under a Communion ban (interdict) by the pope. For example,

> Simply visit the church or churches of your choice on a day in Lent or another holiday . . . you will obtain as many indulgences and forgiveness of sins as if you had visited the church or churches in Rome on that same day.

During an interdict, a bishop or pope would not permit Masses to be said or any other Sacraments to be administered in any churches of a given territory. Often interdicts were issued whenever the monarch of a country defied Church authority. It was an effective weapon used by the Medieval Church to keep monarchs in line. The common people, in fear of dying outside of a state of grace, would frequently pressure their king to yield to the Church's demands.

This sample indulgence is not part of the Book of Concord.

We Grant Indulgence

Albert, by the grace of God and of the Apostolic See: Archbishop of Mainz and Magdeburg, Administrator of the churches of Halberstadt, Primate of Germany, Arch-Chancellor and Elector-Prince of the Holy Roman Empire, Duke of Mark Brandenburg, Stettin, Pomerania, the Cashubians, and Slavs, Burggrave of Nürnberg, Prince of Rugia. Greetings in the Lord to those dear to us in Christ.

You have agreed to undertake an act of sincere and fervent devotion for the Church of Rome. You have given to the building of the Basilica of St. Peter, an immense undertaking requiring skillful production. Your contribution will not only benefit that city, but it also shows that you are obedient to our commands.

Since you have given generously to our cause, you encourage and persuade us to agree to [fulfill] your requests. You have long and fervently asked us that you might have an altar stone on which Mass can be said. You have been looking for an altar where Mass can be said without the meddling of foreign laws; we hereby grant your request.

If you should happen to enter into regions placed under ecclesiastical interdict by the authority of an ordinary bishop, nonetheless, you will not find yourself standing outside the doors of the church, excommunicated as it were. Instead, as long as you live, you will be able to celebrate Mass by yourself, if you are a priest. If you are a layperson, you may have Mass celebrated for you. You may use your own priest or any other priest. It does not matter whether the priest is a diocesan priest or a member of a religious order. This permission extends especially to the Easter Mass, even the Mass at sunrise. Of course, you may do this only if you yourself have not committed the sin that caused the land to be placed under the interdict.

You also may get as many indulgences and pardons for sin by visiting a church of your choice as if you had made a pilgrimage to Rome. Simply visit the church or churches of your choice on a day in Lent or another holiday when pilgrims visit the various churches around Rome. By taking a trip to a local church or churches, you will obtain as many indulgences and forgiveness of sins as if you had visited the church or churches in Rome on that same day.

You can also be given full Christian burial, even if you happen to die when your country is under an interdict. Of course, to receive this benefit you must not have committed the sin for which the land has been put under the interdict.

We issue this decree by the apostolic authority given to us by the letter "We Grant Indulgence," written by our Most Holy Lord Leo X, Pope by the grace of God. Nonetheless, please do not use a dispensation of this kind until the day you celebrate Mass or have it celebrated on your behalf. For when our Lord Jesus Christ (who is the radiance of eternal light) is being sacrificed in the liturgy of the altar, it is fitting that it not be done in the darkness of night but in the light. We order that the individual be communed into whose trust the present letter has been given and the seal has been affixed.

Date: In the year of our Lord 1515, on the ______________ day of the month of ____________________, during the pontificate of our aforementioned lord, the Pope.

THE APOLOGY OF THE AUGSBURG CONFESSION

Sacrifice of Isaac
From Luther's translation of the Pentateuch, 1523

Article IV of the Apology is the longest and most extensive explanation of the Christian faith's chief article: the doctrine of justification by grace through faith in Christ alone. This doctrine is the heartbeat of the entire Book of Concord. The offering of Isaac, and the ram sacrificed in his place, powerfully foreshadow the sacrifice of Jesus Christ.

Editor's Introduction to the Apology of the Augsburg Confession

Emperor Charles is an excellent man; he hopes to restore unity and peace. I don't know whether he will be able to do this, besieged as he is by so many demonic monsters.

—Martin Luther to Nicholaus Hausmann
September 23, 1530 (LW 49:422)

After the public reading and presentation of the Augsburg Confession on June 25, 1530, the Lutherans waited to receive the emperor's reply, which came on August 3. It was read to the Lutherans and soon became known as the *Pontifical Confutation of the Augsburg Confession*. They heard the reply, but were not given a copy of it. Couched in careful diplomatic language, the emperor's message was clear: Back down or else. Further meetings were called for between the Lutherans and the emperor's theologians.

Two series of meeting were held, the first, August 13–21, and the second, August 24. During these meetings, Philip Melanchthon was willing to compromise the Lutheran Confession. However, the Lutheran laymen prevailed and remained firm. In private, Emperor Charles tried everything he could think of to pressure the Lutheran princes to back down. He threatened to exile them from their territories and to seize by force all their property and possessions. Martin Luther, writing from the Coburg castle, encouraged them to stand strong. On September 22, Charles officially declared the Imperial Meeting to be in recess. He stated that the Pontifical Confutation had sufficiently answered the Lutheran Confession and gave the Lutherans until April 15, 1531, to concede to his demands. They refused.

The Lutherans were never given a copy of the Pontifical Confutation, but were ordered to do the following: accept all the conditions it imposed, accept the Confutation's conclusions, make no reply to it, and not allow it to be published. Such outrageous demands were wholly unacceptable to the Lutherans. Fortunately, while the Confutation was being read, professional stenographers were writing the Confutation down, word for word, so they had an accurate transcript of its contents. The Lutheran princes asked Chancellor Brück and Philip Melanchthon to work on a reply. By September 22, a first draft was ready. They tried to give Charles a copy, but he refused to accept it. Then the Lutheran party left Augsburg. Melanchthon began working on a thorough revision of what was called the "Apology of the Augsburg Confession." (The word *apology* in the Greek language, which Melanchthon taught at the university in Wittenberg, means "defense.") Not until 1573 did the Roman Church officially publish the *Confutation of the Augsburg Confession*. This was long after the Council of Trent (1546–63) had formally adopted the Confutation's conclusions.

Melanchthon worked on a thorough revision of the Apology of the Augsburg Confession from the end of September 1530 until April 15, 1531. Melanchthon was firm and confident as he replied to the Roman Church. He had taken courage from the example of the Lutheran laymen at Augsburg and was bolstered by Martin Luther personally, who continued to encourage him to remain strong.

The Apology of the Augsburg Confession is the longest and most detailed confession in the Book of Concord. It carefully works through the Roman response to the Augsburg Confession, refuting errors and setting forth the truth. The driving force in the Apology is the repeated insistence that the Bible's most important and comforting teaching is justification by grace alone, through faith alone, on account of Christ alone. Again and again, Melanchthon returns to this teaching.

The Apology of the Augsburg Confession was first released as Melanchthon's personal opinion, since it was not formally adopted by the Lutheran princes in Augsburg. It soon became popular throughout Lutheran Germany. Justas Jonas, colleague and friend of both Luther and Melanchthon, prepared the German translation of the Apology. In 1531, the Smalcaldic League, an organization of German territories and cities, was formed. A requirement of membership was acceptance of both the Augsburg Confession and the Apology of the Augsburg Confession. In 1533, in a letter to Christians in Leipzig, Luther urged them to "adhere to our [Augsburg] Confession *and apology*." In 1577, the Apology was included in the Formula of Concord's list of doctrinal statements.

The translation is from the 1584 Latin edition of the Book of Concord, which was the base text for the Apology in the Concordia Triglotta. See the User's Guide on page xxvii for details about the use of brackets and symbols. Please note that in the longer articles of the Apology some subheads are added for the convenience of the reader.

Justas Jonas (1493–1555)

Justas Jonas was a close friend and ally of Martin Luther. He came to Wittenberg in 1521 to lead the Foundation of All Saints at the Castle Church and helped Luther end this last bastion of Romanism in Wittenberg. With Luther, Bugenhagen, and Melanchthon, Jonas produced the Torgau Articles, a predecessor of the Augsburg Confession. He was at Luther's side when he died in 1546. Jonas translated the Apology into German. (Melanchthon affirmed his work.) He translated many of Luther's Latin writings into German.

TIMELINE

1530 *Torgau Articles* drafted, March

Augsburg Confession presented to Charles V at Diet of Augsburg, June 25

Meetings concerning *Augsburg Confession*, August

Augsburg Diet ends, September; Lutherans asked to concede by April 15, 1531

1531 *Augsburg Confession* and *Apology* published, April–May; *Apology*'s second edition published, September

Smalcaldic League formed, requires acceptance of *Augsburg Confession* and *Apology*

Ulrich Zwingli dies on Swiss battlefield at Kappel am Albis

1532 In exchange for religious tolerance, Protestant princes agree to assist Charles V in war against the Turks until religious issues can be resolved by church council and imperial court

Luther publishes *An Admonition to Prayer against the Turks*, September

1533 English King Henry VIII excommunicated

Luther urges Christians in Leipzig to adhere to *Augsburg Confession* and *Apology*

1534 Luther publishes complete German Bible

Ignatius of Loyola founds Society of Jesus (Jesuits)

1536 Luther, Melanchthon, and Englishmen Edward Fox and Robert Barnes agree to *Wittenberg Articles*; rejected by Zwinglians

John Calvin publishes *Institutes of the Christian Religion*

1538 Luther's *Smalcald Articles* published

OUTLINE

The outline for the Apology, or "defense," of the Augsburg Confession has two sets of numbers. Neither set is fully in order because of the way Melanchthon responded to the issues presented by the Pontifical Confutation (see introduction above).

The numbers on the left generally correspond with the articles of the Augsburg Confession. However, note that there is no Article VI, XXV, or XXVI in the Apology, since similar articles were treated together. (The article on "New Obedience" was treated with the article on "Justification"; the article on "Confession" was treated with the article on "Repentance"; and the article on "The Distinction of Meats" was treated with the article on the "The Mass.")

The numbers on the right, in parentheses, show which articles were disputed by the Pontifical Confutation. The section on "Confession and Satisfaction" is marked in some editions as Article VI.

Greeting

I. God

II. Original Sin (I)

III. Christ

IV. Justification (II)

- What Is Justifying Faith?
- Faith in Christ Justifies
- We Obtain Forgiveness of Sins through Faith Alone in Christ
- [Scripture Affirms This Teaching]
- [The Church Fathers Affirm This Teaching]
- [The Adversaries Reject This Teaching]

V. Love and Fulfilling the Law (III)

- [No One Can Keep the Law Perfectly]

The Apology of the Augsburg Confession

Philip Melanchthon Presents His Greeting to the Reader

1 After our princes' Confession was read publicly, certain theologians and monks prepared a "Confutation." His Imperial Majesty had it read in the assembly of the princes. Then he demanded that the princes agree with it.

2 Our princes heard that many articles were not approved, which they could not abandon without offense to conscience. Therefore, they asked for a copy of the Confutation so they could see what the adversaries condemned and refute their arguments.

In such an important matter of religion and the instruction of consciences, they thought that the adversaries would share their writing without any hesitation.

But our princes could only get a copy under the most dangerous conditions, which were impossible for them to accept.

3 Negotiations for peace were begun. It was
clear that our princes avoided no burden,
however grievous, that could be borne with-
4 out offense to conscience. But the adversaries
stubbornly demanded that we approve certain clear abuses and errors. Since we could not do this, His Imperial Majesty again demanded that our princes agree with the Confutation. Our princes refused to do so.

For in a matter of religion, how could our princes agree with a writing they had not seen, especially since they had heard some articles condemned? It was impossible for them, without grievous sin, to approve the adversaries' opinions.

5 They commanded me and some others
to prepare an *Apology of the Confession.* This
would be set forth for His Imperial Majesty
the reasons why we could not receive the
Confutation. The adversaries' objections
would also be refuted. During the reading 6
[of the Confutation] some of us had taken
down the chief points of the topics and ar-
guments. The princes offered this Defense 7
to His Imperial Majesty ‹when they left Augsburg›, so that he would know that we were hindered from approving the Confutation by the greatest and most important reasons. But His Imperial Majesty did not receive the offered writing.

Afterward, a decree was published in 8
which the adversaries boast that they have refuted our Confession from the Scriptures.

Reader, you now have our Apology. 9
From it you will understand not only what the adversaries said about our Confession (for we have reported in good faith), but also that—contrary to the clear Scripture of the Holy Spirit—they condemned several articles. That is how far they are from overthrowing our statements by means of the Scriptures.

Originally we drew up the Apology after 10
consulting with others. Yet, as it passed through the press, I made some additions. That is why I give my name, so that no one can complain that the book has been published anonymously.

In these controversies, as far as I was able 11
at all, it has always been my custom to keep the traditional form of doctrine. I did this so that at some time unity could be reached more readily. I am not departing far from this custom now, even though I could justly

lead people today even farther away from the opinions of the adversaries.

12 The adversaries are dealing with these issues in a way that shows they are seeking neither truth nor concord, but to drain our blood.

13 I have written with the greatest moderation possible. If any expression appears too severe, I must say that I am arguing with the theologians and monks who wrote the Confutation, not with the emperor or the
14 princes, whom I hold in due esteem. I recently saw the Confutation and noticed how cunningly and slanderously it was written, so that on some points it could deceive even the cautious.

15 Yet I did not discuss all their sophistries, for it would be an endless task. Instead I deal with the chief arguments, so that all nations will have a clear testimony from us that we hold the Gospel of Christ correctly and pi-
16 ously. Disagreement does not delight us, neither are we indifferent to our danger. We readily understand the extent of it when we see how inflamed our adversaries are by bitterness and hatred. Yet we cannot abandon truth that is clear and necessary for the Church.

That is why we believe that troubles and dangers for Christ's glory and the Church's good should be endured. We are confident that God approves our faithfulness to duty. We hope that the judgment of future generations about us will be more just.

17 It is undeniable that many topics of Christian doctrine, whose place in the Church is most important, have been brought to view and explained by our theologians. We are not inclined to repeat here under what sort of opinions, and how dangerously, these topics used to lay buried in the writings of the monks, canonists, and sophistic theologians.

We have the public testimony of many good men, who give thanks to God for this great blessing: our Confession teaches many necessary things better than any of our adversaries' books. 18

We will commend our cause to Christ, who will someday judge these controversies. We beg Him to look upon the afflicted and scattered churches and to bring them back to godly and continuous harmony. 19

Apology of the Augsburg Confession

ARTICLE I
God

Note: Lutherans clearly identify themselves with the historic Church of all times and places by confessing the biblical doctrine of the Holy Trinity and by rejecting the teachings of all those who deny the one, true God: Father, Son, and Holy Spirit. (See the Apostles', Nicene, and Athanasian Creeds; AC I; SA I; SC II; LC II.)

Our adversaries approve Article I of our Confession, in which we declare that we believe and teach that there is one divine, undivided essence. Yet, there are three distinct persons, of the same divine essence, and co- 1
eternal: Father, Son, and Holy Spirit. We have 2
always taught and defended this article. We believe that it has sure and firm testimonies in Holy Scripture that cannot be overthrown. We constantly affirm that those thinking otherwise are outside of Christ's Church, are idolaters, and insult God.

God Creates the World

The Fall

ARTICLE II (I)

Original Sin

Note: By the sixteenth century, Roman theologians had come to view original sin merely as a weakness in human nature. The Scriptures, however, teach that original sin is the absence of original righteousness and the root cause of all sinful thoughts, words, and deeds. Original sin damns a person to hell, the Bible asserts, so clear definitions were needed. Rome sought some way to preserve mankind's ability to choose God's grace and cooperate with it. So it regarded *concupiscence,* the powerfully strong tendency in us to sin, not as sin, but as mere tinder (Latin: *fomes*), which could ignite into sinful behavior. The Bible, as the Lutherans were concerned to prove, also names as sin our inborn tendency to sin.

Article II of the Apology is essential for understanding what follows in Articles III and IV. Melanchthon points out the key comforting truth of God's Word: In Christ, God removes the condemnation of all sin, including concupiscence. He does so by forgiving us our sins through Christ's blood and by applying to us Christ's righteousness, holiness, and innocence. So, while in this life sin remains, the Holy Spirit continually brings it under check, beats it down and kills it, and works within us to increase and strengthen our faith in God and love for our neighbor. (See AC II; SA III I; FC Ep I and SD I.)

1 The adversaries approve Article II, "Original Sin," but in such a way that they actually condemn our definition of original sin, which we gave in passing. Here, right at the outset, Your Majesty will discover that the Confutation's writers were lacking not only judgment, but also honesty. We simply wanted to mention the things that original sin includes. But these men, by creating a misleading interpretation, cleverly twist a statement that in itself contains nothing wrong. So they say, "To lack fear of God and to lack faith is actual guilt." Therefore, they deny it is original sin.

Clearly, these sorts of subtleties start in 2
the schools, not in the emperor's council. Even though such sophistry can be easily refuted, we ask that the Augsburg Confession in German be examined, so that all good people will understand that we do not teach anything absurd in this matter. This will free us from the suspicion of teaching something new. For there it is written:

> It is further taught that since Adam's fall all human beings, who are naturally conceived, are born in sin. From their mother's womb they are all filled with evil desire and the inclination toward evil. By nature, they have no true fear of God and no true faith in God.

As this passage demonstrates, we teach 3
that those who are born according to the fleshly nature have concupiscence. This means people not only lack fear and trust in God, but also do not even have the power or gifts to produce fear and trust in God. What fault can be found with this point? Indeed, we think that we have explained and defended ourselves well enough to good men. For in this sense the Latin description denies to nature the ability, gifts, and energy to produce fear and trust in God. In adults, we deny the ability actually to do anything truly good. So, when we mention concupiscence, we understand not only the acts or fruit, but also the constant inclination of the nature.

Now we will show more fully that our de- 4
scription agrees with the usual and ancient definition. First, we must show why we prefer to use these words in this place. In their schools, the adversaries confess that "the material" (as they call it) "of original sin is con-

cupiscence." We should not have passed by
this fact in framing our definition, precisely
because some are offering philosophical
speculations in a way that is not appropriate
for teachers of religion.

5 Some of them claim that original sin is
not a depravity or corruption in human na-
ture, but only servitude, or a condition of
mortality. ‹They say that it is not inherent in
our nature, but is rather a burden› put on us
‹as a result of Adam's sin›, not that we have
any such depravity of our own. Besides, they
add that no one is condemned to eternal
death on account of original sin, just as a
child born of a slave woman becomes a slave
not as a result of any personal fault, but as a
6 result of his mother's condition. To show that
this impious opinion is displeasing to us, we
used the word *concupiscence*. With the best
intention, we have explained this term as
"diseases" and said that "the nature of human
beings is born corrupt and full of faults."

7 We have not only used the word *concupis-
cence*, but we have also said that "the fear of
God and faith are lacking." We added this
comment because the scholastic teachers do
not understand the definition of original sin
well enough. They take what they received
from the Fathers and extend the definition of
original sin. They argue that the evil inclina-
tion (*fomes*) is a quality (like a blemish) on
the body. With their usual folly, they ask
whether this quality is caused from the con-
tagiousness of the apple or from the breath of
the serpent, and whether medicines can cure
the condition. They suppress the main point
8 with such questions. So, when they talk
about original sin, they do not mention the
more serious faults of human nature, such as
ignorance of God, contempt for God, total
lack of fear of God and confidence in God,
hatred of God's judgment, fleeing from God
when He judges us, anger toward God, de-
spairing of God's grace, putting trust in
things of this world, and so forth. The
Scholastics do not notice all these diseases
that are totally contrary to God's Law. They
even say that human nature is entirely capa-
ble of loving God above all things and fulfill-
ing God's commandments "according to the
substance of the act." These diseases are to-
tally contrary to God's Law, but the Scholas-
tics do not notice them. They do not even re-
alize that they are contradicting themselves.
For what else is being able, by one's own 9
strength, to love God above all things and
fulfill His commandments except original
righteousness? If human nature is so strong 10
that it is able, on its own, to love God above
all things, as the Scholastics confidently af-
firm, what then is original sin? Why do we
need Christ's grace if we can be justified as a
result of our own righteousness? Why do we
need the Holy Spirit if we are strong enough
on our own to love God above all things and
fulfill God's commandments? Is there anyone 11
who does not realize that our adversaries'
ideas are absurd? They recognize the less se-
rious diseases in human nature, but the more
serious they do not even acknowledge. Scrip-
ture everywhere warns us, as the Prophets
constantly complain, about putting our con-
fidence in our human abilities, contempt for
God, hating God, and similar faults with
which we are born. [See Psalm 13 and other
passages, such as Psalm 14:1–3; 140:3; 36:1.]
After the Scholastics mixed philosophical 12
speculations about the perfection of nature
[the light of reason] with Christian doctrine,
they credited more than was possible to the
ability of free will. They taught that people
are justified before God by philosophical or
civic righteousness. We, too, confess that
such things are subject to reason, and so to
some degree are within our power. However,
as a result of their speculations they could

not see the inner uncleanness of human na-
13 ture. This can only be evaluated and under-
stood on the basis of God's Word, which the
Scholastics do not use very often in their
discussions.

14 These were the reasons why we also men-
tioned concupiscence in our description of
original sin, and why we deny to human na-
ture the ability to fear and trust in God. We
wanted to show that original sin contains
these diseases: ignorance of God, contempt
for God, not having fear and trust in God,
the inability to love God. These are the chief
faults of human nature because they conflict
with the First Table of the Ten Command-
ments [Exodus 20:3–11].

15 We have not said anything new. The an-
cient definition of original sin, understood
correctly, says precisely the same thing.
"Original sin is the absence of original righ-
teousness." But what is righteousness? Here
the Scholastics wrangle over philosophical
questions. They do not explain what original
16 righteousness is. In the Scriptures, righ-
teousness consists not only in obeying the
Second Table of the Ten Commandments
‹which are about good works in serving our
fellowman›, but also the First Table, which
teaches about fearing God, faith, and loving
17 God. Therefore, original righteousness in-
cludes not only physical health in all ways, as
they contend, but also these gifts: a sure and
certain knowledge of God, fear of God, con-
fidence in God, and the desire and ability to
18 give God these things. Scripture testifies to
this when it says in Genesis 1:27 that man
was made in the image and likeness of God.
What else was this image and likeness other
than that man was created with wisdom and
righteousness so that he could apprehend
God and reflect God? Mankind was given the
gift of knowing God, fearing God, and being
19 confident in God. This is how Irenaeus and
Ambrose interpret the likeness to God. Am-
brose not only says many things to this effect,
but especially declares, "That soul is not,
therefore, in the image of God, in which God
is not [dwelling] at all times." Paul shows in 20
Ephesians 5:9 and Colossians 3:10 that the
image of God is the knowledge of God, righ-
teousness, and truth. Lombard is not afraid 21
to say that original righteousness "is the very
likeness to God which God implanted in
man." We recount the opinions of the an- 22
cients, which in no way interfere with Augus-
tine's interpretation of the image.

The ancient definition of original sin is 23
that it is a lack of righteousness. This defini-
tion not only denies that mankind is capable
of obedience in his body, but also denies that
mankind is capable of knowing God, placing
confidence in God, fearing and loving God,
and certainly also the ability to produce such
things. For even the theologians themselves
teach in their schools that these are not pro-
duced without certain gifts and the aid of
grace. In order that the matter may be un-
derstood, we say that these gifts are precisely
the knowledge of God and fear and confi-
dence in God. From these facts it appears
that the ancient definition says precisely the
same thing that we say, denying fear and con-
fidence toward God. It denies not only the
actions, but also the gifts and ability to pro-
duce these acts.

Of equal importance is the definition of 24
original sin found in the writings of
Augustine. He is used to defining original sin
as concupiscence (wicked desire). He means
that when righteousness had been lost, con-
cupiscence came in its place. Since diseased
nature cannot fear and love God and believe
God, it seeks and loves carnal things. By na-
ture, when we are secure, we hold God's
judgment in contempt. When we are terri-
fied, we hate God's judgment. This is why

Augustine includes both the defect and the vicious habit that has come in its place in his
25 definition of original sin. Concupiscence is not only a corruption of physical qualities, but also, in the higher powers, a vicious turning to fleshly things. These people do not realize the contradiction in what they are saying. At the same time, they attribute to mankind a concupiscence that is not entirely destroyed by the Holy Spirit and also the ability to love God above all things.

26 We are right in our description of original sin when we say that it is not being able to believe God and not being able to fear and love God. We are right when we say that it includes concupiscence, which seeks fleshly things contrary to God's Word. This means when it seeks not only the pleasure of the body, but also fleshly wisdom and righteousness. Therefore, it holds God in contempt when it trusts in these as good things.
27 It is not only the ancient teachers, but even the more recent teachers (at least the wiser ones among them), who teach that original sin is both the defects I have mentioned and concupiscence. Thomas Aquinas says:

> Original sin includes the loss of original righteousness, and with this a disorderly arrangement of the parts of the soul; therefore, it is not pure loss, but a corrupt habit.

28 Bonaventure says:

> When the question is asked, "What is original sin?" the correct answer is that it is immoderate concupiscence. The correct answer is, also, that it is a lack of the righteousness that is due. And in one of these replies the other is included.

29 This is also Hugo's opinion when he says that "original sin is ignorance in the mind and concupiscence in the flesh." He is saying that when we are born, we bring with us ignorance of God, unbelief, distrust, con-
tempt, and hatred of God. When he men- 30
tions ignorance, he includes these other things. These opinions also agree with Scripture. Paul sometimes clearly calls it a defect, as in 1 Corinthians 2:14, "The natural person does not accept the things of the Spirit of God." In another place, he calls it concupiscence, "at work in our members to bear
fruit for death" (Romans 7:5). We could cite 31
more passages relating to both parts, but when a fact is so clear there is no need of further testimonies. The intelligent reader realizes easily that to be without the fear of God and without faith are more than actual guilt. They are abiding defects in our unregenerate nature.

When it comes to original sin, we hold 32
nothing different from either Scripture or the Church catholic. Rather, we cleanse from corruptions and restore to light the most important declarations of Scripture and the Fathers, which have been covered over by the sophistry and controversies of the theologians of our day. It is more than clear that modern theologians do not notice what the Fathers mean when they speak about a "de-
fect." The knowledge of original sin is ab- 33
solutely necessary. The magnitude of Christ's grace cannot be understood unless our diseases are recognized. ‹Christ says in Matthew 9:12 and Mark 2:17, "Those who are well have no need of a physician."› The entire notion that a person is righteous is mere hypocrisy before God. We must acknowledge that our heart is, by nature, destitute of fear,
love, and confidence in God. For this reason 34
the prophet Jeremiah says, "After I was instructed, I slapped my thigh; I was ashamed, and I was confounded" (31:19). Likewise, "I said in my alarm, 'All mankind are liars' "

(Psalm 116:11). That is, they do not think correctly about God.

35 Here our adversaries attack Martin
Luther because he wrote that "original sin remains after Baptism." They add that this point was justly condemned by Leo X. But His Imperial Majesty will discover a clear slander on this point. Our adversaries know in what sense Luther intended this remark that original sin remains after Baptism. Luther always writes that Baptism removes the guilt of original sin. However, the *material*, as they call it, of the sin (concupiscence) remains. He also adds that the Holy Spirit, given through Baptism, begins to put to death the concupiscence and begins to create
36 new movements within a person. Augustine
speaks in the same way when he says, "Sin is forgiven in Baptism, not in such a way that it no longer exists, but so that it is not charged." Here he confesses openly that sin exists. It remains, although it is not counted against us any longer. Augustine's judgment on this point was so agreeable to those who came after him that it is often quoted in the decrees of Church councils. In *Against Julian*, Augustine says:

> The Law, which is in the members, has been overturned by spiritual regeneration and remains in the mortal flesh. It has been overturned because the guilt has been forgiven in the Sacrament, by which believers are born again; but it remains, because it produces desires, against which believers struggle.

37 Our adversaries know that Luther believes
and teaches this, and since they cannot deny this, they instead try to pervert his words in an effort to crush an innocent man.

38 They argue that concupiscence is a penal-
ty, but not a sin. Luther maintains that it is a sin. It has been said above that Augustine defines original sin as concupiscence. If they don't like this, then let them argue with Au-
gustine. Besides, Paul says in Romans 7:7, "I 39
would not have known what it is to covet [concupiscence] if the law had not said, 'You shall not covet.'" Likewise, "I see in my members another law waging war against the law of my mind and making me captive to the law of sin that dwells in my members" (Ro-
mans 7:23). No amount of sophistry can 40
overthrow these points. They clearly call concupiscence sin, which is not charged against those who are in Christ [Romans 8:1], although by nature it is deserving of death
[Romans 6:23] where it is not forgiven. All 41
controversies aside, this is what the Fathers believe. Augustine, in a long discussion, refutes the opinion of those who think that concupiscence in a person is not a fault, but merely an incidental and inconsequential matter just as color of the body or ill health is said to be an adiaphoron.

But when our adversaries argue that the 42
evil inclination (*fomes*) is an adiaphoron, not only many passages of Scripture, but simply the entire Church, contradict them. Who has ever dared to say that the following things, even if perfect agreement could not be reached, are indifferent matters: doubt about God's wrath, His grace, God's Word, anger at the judgments of God, being provoked because God does not at once deliver one from afflictions, murmuring because the wicked enjoy a better fortune than the good, to be urged on by wrath, lust, the desire for
glory, wealth, and so on? Godly people ac- 43
knowledge these things in themselves, as appears in the Psalms and the Prophets. But in the scholastic academies they took from philosophy entirely different ideas: desires and inclinations are neither good nor evil, neither praiseworthy nor worthy of blame. Likewise,

that sin is only sin if it is a voluntary action. Philosophers were expressing such ideas about civil righteousness, not about God's judgment. They unwisely add other ideas as well, saying that nature is not evil. Properly understood, we do not reject this idea, but it is not right to take this understanding of what God creates as good and apply it to original sin. This is precisely what we read in the works of the Scholastics, who wrongly mingle philosophy or civil teachings about
44 ethics with the Gospel. These matters were not only disputed in the schools, but as is usually the case, were carried from the schools to the people. These teachings prevailed and nourished confidence in human strength and suppressed the knowledge of
45 Christ's grace. Therefore, Luther wanted to declare how great the consequences of original sin are and how weak human beings are as a result. So he taught that these remnants of original sin [after Baptism] are not, by nature, adiaphora in people, but that we need Christ's grace so that they are not counted against us as sin. And, to put them to death [mortify them], we need the Holy Spirit [Romans 8:13].

46 The Scholastics minimize sin and punishment when they teach that people can fulfill God's commandments under their own power. But in Genesis, the punishment imposed because of original sin is described differently. For there human nature is subjected not only to death and other bodily evils, but also to the devil's kingdom. In Genesis 3:15, there is this fearful sentence that proclaims, "I will put enmity between you and the woman, and between your off-
47 spring and her offspring." Defects and concupiscence are both sin and punishment. Death and other bodily evils, and the dominion of the devil, are properly understood to be punishments. Human nature has been delivered into slavery and is held captive by the devil [Colossians 1:13]. He fills human nature with a passionate desire for wicked opinions and errors and pushes it to sins of every kind. Just as the devil cannot be con- 48
quered except by Christ's help, so we cannot free ourselves from this slavery by our own strength. World history shows how great 49
and powerful the devil's kingdom is. The world is full of blasphemies against God and wicked opinions. The devil keeps all tied up many hypocrites who appear holy and who are wise and righteous in the world's eyes. Even greater vices are seen in other people. 50
Since Christ was given to us to remove both these sins and these punishments and to destroy the devil's kingdom, sin, and death [1 John 3:8], we will never be able to recognize Christ's benefits unless we understand our evils. For this reason our preachers have diligently taught all about these things. They have not delivered anything that is new, but have set forth Holy Scripture and the judgment of the Holy Fathers.

We think this will satisfy His Imperial 51
Majesty about the childish and trivial sophistry the adversaries use to pervert our article on original sin. We know that we believe correctly, in harmony with the Church catholic of Christ. If the adversaries renew this controversy, there will be more than enough of us to reply and to defend the truth. In this case our adversaries, to a great extent, do not understand what they are saying. They often speak in a contradictory way and do not explain, either correctly or logically, what is the essence of original sin and what they call a "defect." We are unwilling here to examine their arguments in any further subtle detail. We think it is worthwhile just to recite, in customary and well-known words, the belief of the Holy Fathers, which we also follow.

ARTICLE III

Christ

Note: It was very important for the Lutherans to affirm the historic biblical confession of the Church: Christ is fully God and fully man. In his *Confession concerning Christ's Supper* of 1528, Luther wrote,

> Here you must take your stand and say that wherever Christ is according to His divinity, He is there as a natural divine person and He is also naturally and personally there, as His conception in His mother's womb proves conclusively. For if He was the Son of God, He had to be in His mother's womb naturally and personally, and become Man. . . . He is not two separate persons but a single person. Wherever this person is, it is the single, indivisible person, and if you can say, "Here is God," then you must also say, "Christ the Man is present too."

The article on justification is rooted in this article on Christ. (See the Apostles', Nicene, and Athanasian Creeds; AC III; SA II I; SC II; LC II; FC Ep VIII and SD VIII.)

52 The adversaries approve Article III, in which we confess that there are two natures in Christ. The human nature was assumed by the Word into the unity of His person [John 1:14]. Christ suffered and died to reconcile the Father to us and was raised again to reign, to justify, and to sanctify believers according to the Apostles' Creed and the Nicene Creed.

ARTICLE IV (II)

Justification

Note: Article IV of the Apology is the most complex article in the entire Book of Concord. Because it deals with our salvation, that is, how God has forgiven our sins and has reconciled us to Himself in Christ, it is also the most important. This article is the very heart of the Gospel and the most important teaching in the Holy Scriptures; therefore, the Apology goes into great detail about the doctrine of justification. All Scripture leads us to, from, and back to the truth of Christ's work of atonement. God applies Christ's work to individuals freely by grace, through faith, without works. The article on Christ (AC III) proclaims how God atones for sins. The article on the Church's ministry of the means of grace (AC V) confesses how God applies to individuals the merits won by Christ. What brings these two articles together is the article on justification (AC IV), which describes how we are justified, that is, declared righteous by God. (See AC IV; SA III XIII; FC Ep III and SD III.)

In Articles IV, V, VI, and XX, they con- 1
demn us for teaching that "people obtain forgiveness of sins not because of their own merits, but freely for Christ's sake, through faith in Christ." They condemn us both for denying that people obtain forgiveness of sins because of their own merits and for affirming that—through faith—people obtain forgiveness of sins and are justified through
faith in Christ. But in this controversy, the 2
chief topic of Christian doctrine is treated. When it is understood correctly, it illumines and amplifies Christ's honor ‹which is especially useful for the clear, correct understanding of the entire Holy Scriptures, and alone shows the way to the unspeakable treasure and right knowledge of Christ, and alone

opens the door to the entire Bible›. It brings
necessary and most abundant consolation to
devout consciences. Therefore, we ask His
Imperial Majesty to hear us with patience in
3 matters of such importance. For the adver-
saries do not understand what the forgive-
ness of sins or faith or grace or righteousness
is. Therefore, they sadly corrupt this topic,
hide Christ's glory and benefits, and rob de-
vout consciences of the consolation offered
4 in Christ. In order that we may strengthen
the position of our Confession, and also re-
move the charges that the adversaries ad-
vance against us, certain points are to be set
forth in the beginning. Then the sources of
both kinds of doctrine (that of our adver-
saries and our own) may be known.

5 All Scripture ought to be distributed into
these two principal topics: the Law and the
promises. For in some places Scripture pre-
sents the Law, and in others the promises
about Christ. In other words, in the Old Tes-
tament, Scripture promises that Christ will
come, and it offers, for His sake, the forgive-
ness of sins, justification, and life eternal. Or
in the Gospel, in the New Testament, Christ
Himself (since He has appeared) promises
the forgiveness of sins, justification, and life
6 eternal. Furthermore, in this discussion, by
Law we mean the Ten Commandments,
wherever they are read in the Scriptures. We
say nothing at present about the ceremonies
and judicial laws of Moses.

7 Of these two parts of Scripture the adver-
saries choose the Law, because in some way
human reason naturally understands the
Law (for it has the same judgment divinely
written in the mind). By the Law they seek
8 the forgiveness of sins and justification. The
Ten Commandments require outward civil
works, which reason can in some way pro-
duce. But they also require other things
placed far above reason: truly to fear God,
truly to love God, truly to call upon God,
truly to be convinced that God hears us, and
to expect God's aid in death and in all afflic-
tions. Finally, the Law requires obedience to
God, in death and all afflictions, so that we
may not run from these commandments or
refuse them when God lays them upon us.

Here the Scholastics have followed the 9
philosophers. They teach only a righteousness
of reason. That is, they teach civil works. Be-
sides that, they imagine reason can love God
above all things without the Holy Spirit. For,
as long as the human mind is at ease, and
does not feel God's wrath or judgment, it can
imagine that it wants to love God, that it
wants to do good for God's sake. In this way,
they teach that people merit forgiveness of
sins by doing what is in them, namely, when
reason produces an act of love toward God by
grieving over sin or when reason is active in
doing what is good for God's sake. Because 10
this notion naturally flatters people, it has
brought forth and multiplied in the Church
many services, monastic vows, and abuses of
the Mass. In the course of time with this
opinion, someone has come up with one act
of worship and observances, and someone
else, others. To nourish and increase confi- 11
dence in such works, the Scholastics have as-
serted that God must give grace to a person
who does such works, not that He is forced
to, but that God will not change ‹what He
ordered›.

In this opinion there are many great and 12
deadly errors, which would be too boring to
list. Let the careful reader think only about
this: If this is Christian righteousness, what
difference is there between philosophy and
Christ's teaching? If we merit forgiveness of
sins by these acts, of what benefit is Christ? If
we can be justified by reason and the works
of reason, what need is there of Christ or re-
generation [1 Peter 1:18–21]? From these 13
opinions the matter has now reached the
point that many ridicule us because we teach
that a righteousness different from philo-
sophic righteousness must be sought. We 14

have heard that some preachers, after setting
aside the Gospel, have explained Aristotle's
ethics instead of a sermon. Not that such
men err if those things the adversaries de-
fend are true. For Aristotle wrote about civil
morals in such a learned way that nothing
further about the topic needs to be de-
15 manded. We see books published in which
certain sayings of Christ are compared with
the sayings of Socrates, Zeno, and others. It's
as though Christ had come to deliver certain
laws through which we might merit forgive-
ness of sins, as though we did not receive this
16 freely because of His merits. Therefore, if we
here accept the teaching of the adversaries—
that by the works of reason we merit forgive-
ness of sins and justification—there will be
no difference between righteousness of
philosophers (or certainly of Pharisees) and
of Christians.

17 Yet the adversaries do not pass by Christ
completely. They require a knowledge of the
history about Christ. They credit Him by
writing that from His merit a way of life is
given to us or, as they say, "first grace" (*prima
gratia*). They understand this as a *habit*, in-
clining us to love God more readily. Yet,
what they credit to this habit is of little im-
portance. For they imagine that the human
will's acts are the same before and after this
habit. They imagine that the will can love
God; but, nevertheless, this habit stimulates
it to love more cheerfully. They tell us, "First,
merit this habit by your earlier merits." Then
they tell us we should merit an increase of
this habit and life eternal by the works of the
18 Law. In this way they bury Christ, so that
people may not benefit from Him as a Medi-
ator and believe that they freely receive for-
giveness of sins and reconciliation for His
sake. They let people dream that by their
own fulfillment of the Law, they merit for-
giveness of sins, that by their own fulfillment
of the Law, they are counted righteous be-
fore God. However, the Law is never satisfied
since reason does nothing except certain
civil works. In the meantime, a person nei-
ther fears God nor truly believes that God
cares. Although they speak about this habit,
God's love cannot exist in a person without
the righteousness of faith, nor can His love
be understood.

They make up a distinction between due 19
merit and true, complete merit (*meritum
congrui* and *meritum condigni*). This is only a
tactic, so that they do not appear to agree
openly with the Pelagians. If God must give
grace for the due merit, it is no longer due
merit, but a true duty and complete merit.
They do not know what they are saying. After
this habit of love is in a person, they imagine
that such a person can gain merit in a whol-
ly deserving way (*de condigno*). Yet they tell
us to doubt whether there is a habit present.
Therefore, how do they know whether they
gain merit in a merely agreeable way or a
wholly deserving way (*de congruo* or *de
condigno*)? This whole matter was made up 20
by idle men. They did not know how forgive-
ness of sins happens and how, by God's judg-
ment and the terrors of conscience, trust in
works is driven out of us. Secure hypocrites
always judge that they gain merit in a wholly
deserving way, whether the habit is present
or is not present, because people naturally
trust in their own righteousness. But terrified
consciences waver and hesitate. Then they
seek and heap up other works in order to
find peace. Such consciences never think that
they gain merit in a wholly deserving way,
and they rush into despair unless they hear—
in addition to the teaching of the Law—the
Gospel about free forgiveness of sins and
righteousness of faith.

So the adversaries teach nothing but righ- 21
teousness of reason, or certainly about the Law.

The Bronze Snake in the Wilderness

The Sacrifice of Isaac

They see the Law just like the Jewish people see Moses' veiled face. In self-secure hypocrites, who think that they fulfill the Law, they stir up assumptions and empty confidence in works and cause them to have contempt for the grace of Christ. On the other hand, they also drive timid consciences to despair. The timid labor with doubt. They can never experience what faith is and how effective it is. So at last they completely despair.

22 We think about the righteousness of reason like this: God requires it. Because of God's commandment, the honorable works commanded by the Ten Commandments must be done, according to Galatians 3:24, "The law was our guardian." Likewise, 1 Timothy 1:9 says, "The law is not laid down for the just but for the lawless." For God wants wild sinners to be restrained by civil discipline. To maintain discipline, He has given laws, letters, doctrine, rulers, and penalties.
23 To a certain extent reason can, by its own strength, perform this civil righteousness. Yet it is often overcome by natural weakness and by the devil pushing it to do obvious crimes.
24 We cheerfully credit this righteousness of reason with the praises that are due it. (This corrupt nature has no greater good.) Aristotle rightly says, "Neither the evening star nor the morning star is more beautiful than righteousness," and God also honors it with bodily rewards. However, it ought not to be praised by dishonoring Christ.

25 So it is false that we merit forgiveness of sins by our works.

26 It is false that people are counted righteous before God because of the righteousness of reason.

27 It is false that reason, by its own strength, is able to love God above all things and to fulfill God's Law. In other words, reason cannot truly fear God, be truly confident that God hears prayer, be willing to obey God in death and other divine matters, not covet what belongs to others, and so on. Yet reason can do civil works.

The following is also false and dishonor- 28
ing to Christ: people do not sin who, without grace, do God's commandments.

We have testimonies in favor of our belief 29
not only from the Scriptures, but also from the Fathers. For in opposition to the Pelagians, Augustine argues at great length that grace is not given because of our merits. In *On Nature and Grace,* he says:

> If natural ability, through the free will, is enough for learning how one ought to live and for living aright, then Christ has died in vain. Then the offense of the cross is made void. Why may I not also cry out about
> this? Yes, I will cry out! And, with 30
> Christian grief, I will rebuke them: "You are severed from Christ, you who would be justified by the law; you have fallen away from grace" (Galatians 5:4; cf. 2:21). For they, being ignorant of God's righteousness, and going about to establish their own righteousness, have not submitted themselves unto God's righteousness. "For Christ is the end of the law for righteousness to everyone who believes" (Romans 10:4).

John 8:36 says, "If the Son sets you free, you 31
will be free indeed." Therefore, by reason we cannot be freed from sins and merit forgiveness of sins. In John 3:5, it is written, "Unless one is born of water and the Spirit, he cannot enter the kingdom of God." But if it is necessary to be born again of the Holy Spirit, the righteousness of reason does not justify us
before God and does not fulfill the Law. Ro- 32
mans 3:23 says, "All have sinned and fall short of the glory of God." They totally lack the wisdom and righteousness of God, which

acknowledges and glorifies God. Likewise, Romans 8:7–8 says, "For the mind that is set on the flesh is hostile to God, for it does not submit to God's law; indeed, it cannot. Those who are in the flesh cannot please God."
33 These testimonies are so clear that, to use Augustine's words in this case, they do not need a keen understanding, but only an attentive hearer. If the carnal mind is hostile against God, the flesh certainly does not love God. If it cannot be subject to God's Law, it cannot love God. If the carnal mind is hostile against God, the flesh sins, even when we do outward civil works. If it cannot be subject to God's Law, it certainly sins even when it has deeds that are excellent and praiseworthy according
34 to human judgment. The adversaries consider only the teachings of the Second Table, which contain civil righteousness that reason understands. Content with this, they think that they fulfill God's Law. In the meantime, they do not see the First Table, which commands that we love God, that we declare God is certainly angry with sin, that we truly fear God, that we declare God certainly hears prayer. But the human heart without the Holy Spirit either feels secure and despises God's judgment, or in punishment flees from
35 God and hates Him when He judges. Therefore, it does not obey the First Table. So, contempt for God, doubt about God's Word, and doubt about the threats and promises dwell in human nature. People truly sin, even when—without the Holy Spirit—they do virtuous works. This is because they act with a wicked heart according to Romans 14:23: "Whatever does not proceed from faith is sin." For such people do their works with contempt for God, just as Epicurus does not believe that God cares for him or that he is regarded or heard by God. This contempt ruins works that seem virtuous because God judges the heart.

Lastly, it was very foolish for the adver- 36
saries to write that people who are under eternal wrath merit forgiveness of sins by an act of love, which springs from their mind. For it is impossible to love God unless forgiveness of sins is received first by faith. The heart, truly feeling that God is angry, cannot love God unless He is shown to have been reconciled. As long as He terrifies us and seems to cast us into eternal death, human nature is not able to take courage. It cannot love a wrathful, judging, and punishing God.
It is easy for idle men to invent such dreams 37
about love, such as a person guilty of mortal sin can love God above all things, because they do not feel what God's wrath or judgment is. But in agony of conscience and in conflicts ‹with Satan›, conscience experiences the emptiness of these philosophical specula-
tions. Paul says in Romans 4:15, "The law 38
brings wrath." He does not say that by the Law people merit forgiveness of sins. For the Law always accuses and terrifies consciences. Therefore, it does not justify, because a conscience terrified by the Law runs from God's judgment. They err who assume that by the Law—by their own works—they merit for-
giveness of sins. It is enough for us to have 39
said these things about the righteousness of reason or of the Law, which the adversaries teach. Later, when we will declare our belief about the righteousness of faith, the subject itself will drive us to present more testimonies. These also will be of service in overthrowing the adversaries' errors that we have reviewed so far.

By their own strength, people cannot ful- 40
fill God's Law. They are all under sin, subject to eternal wrath and death. Because of this, we cannot be freed by the Law from sin and be justified. But the promise of forgiveness of sins and of justification has been given us for Christ's sake, who was given for us in order

that He might make satisfaction for the sins
of the world. He has been appointed as the
41 Mediator and Atoning Sacrifice. This prom-
ise does not depend on our merits, but freely
offers forgiveness of sins and justification, as
Paul says in Romans 11:6, "But if it is by
grace, it is no longer on the basis of works;
otherwise grace would no longer be grace."
And in another place, Romans 3:21, "The
righteousness of God has been manifested
apart from the law." In other words, forgive-
ness of sins is freely offered. Nor does recon-
42 ciliation depend on our merits. Because if
forgiveness of sins were to depend on our
merits, and reconciliation were from the Law,
it would be useless. Since we do not fulfill the
Law, it would also follow that we would never
gain the promise of reconciliation. Paul rea-
sons this way in Romans 4:14, "For if it is the
adherents of the law who are to be the heirs,
faith is null and the promise is void." If the
promise would depend on our merits and
the Law, which we never fulfill, it would fol-
low that the promise would be useless.

43 Since justification is gained through the
free promise, it follows that we cannot justi-
fy ourselves. Otherwise, why would there be a
need to promise? Since the promise can only
be received by faith, the Gospel (which is
properly the promise of forgiveness of sins
and of justification for Christ's sake) pro-
claims the righteousness of faith in Christ.
The Law does not teach this, nor is this the
44 righteousness of the Law. For the Law de-
mands our works and our perfection. But,
for Christ's sake, the Gospel freely offers rec-
onciliation to us, who have been vanquished
by sin and death. This is received not by
works, but by faith alone. This faith does not
bring to God confidence in one's own merits,
but only confidence in the promise, or the
45 mercy promised in Christ. This special faith
(by which an individual believes that for
Christ's sake his sins are forgiven him, and
that for Christ's sake God is reconciled and
sees us favorably) gains forgiveness of sins
and justifies us. In repentance, namely, in ter-
rors, this faith comforts and encourages
hearts. It regenerates us and brings the Holy
Spirit so that we may be able to fulfill God's
Law: to love God, truly fear God, truly be
confident that God hears prayer, and obey
God in all afflictions. This faith puts to death
concupiscence and the like. So faith freely re- 46
ceives forgiveness of sins. It sets Christ, the
Mediator and Atoning Sacrifice, against
God's wrath. It does not present our merits
or our love. This faith is the true knowledge
of Christ and helps itself to the benefits of
Christ. This faith regenerates hearts and
comes before the fulfilling of the Law. Not a 47
syllable exists about this faith in the teaching
of our adversaries. Therefore, we find equal
fault with the adversaries because (a) they
teach only the righteousness of the Law, and
(b) they do not teach the righteousness of the
Gospel, which proclaims the righteousness of
faith in Christ.

What Is Justifying Faith?

Note: No other article in the Book of Concord so thoroughly presents how the Roman Church errs when it comes to the central teaching of Scripture. The Pontifical Confutation stated adamantly that justification is "not by faith alone, which some incorrectly teach, but faith which works through love." This view was affirmed by the Council of Trent and remains the doctrine of the Roman Catholic Church to this day. The Council of Trent condemns the Bible's teaching that man is saved apart from any works, by grace alone, through faith alone. This condemnation is still clearly evident in the most recent edition of the Catholic Catechism.

48 The adversaries imagine that faith is only a knowledge of the history of Christ. Therefore, they teach that it can coexist with mortal sin. They say nothing about faith, by which Paul so frequently says that people are justified. For those who are counted as righteous before God do not live in mortal sin. But the faith that justifies is not merely a knowledge of history. It is to believe in God's promise. In the promise, for Christ's sake, forgiveness of sins and justification are freely offered. And so that no one may suppose that this is mere knowledge, we will add further: it is to want and to receive the offered promise of forgiveness of sins and of justification.

49 The difference between this faith and the righteousness of the Law can be easily discerned. Faith is the divine service (*latreia*) that receives the benefits offered by God. The righteousness of the Law is the divine service (*latreia*) that offers to God our merits. God wants to be worshiped through faith so that we receive from Him those things He promises and offers.

50 Faith means not only a knowledge of the history, but the kind of faith that believes in the promise. Paul plainly testifies about this when he says in Romans 4:16, "That is why it depends on faith, in order that the promise may rest on grace and be guaranteed." He judges that the promise cannot be received unless it comes through faith. Therefore, he puts them together as things that belong to one another. He connects the promise and
51 faith. It will be easy to decide what faith is if we consider the Creed, where this article certainly stands: the forgiveness of sins. It is not enough to believe that Christ was born, suffered, was raised again, unless we add also this article, which is the purpose of the history: the forgiveness of sins. To this article the rest must be referred, namely, that for Christ's sake, and not because of our merits, forgive-
ness of sins is given to us. For what need was 52
there that Christ was given for our sins if our merits can make satisfaction for our sins?

Whenever we speak of justifying faith, we 53
must keep in mind that these three objects belong together: the promise, grace, and Christ's merits as the price and atonement. The promise is received through faith. Grace excludes our merits and means that the benefit is offered only through mercy. Christ's merits are the price, because there must be a
certain atonement for our sins. Scripture fre- 54
quently cries out for mercy; the Holy Fathers
often say that we are saved by mercy. There- 55
fore, whenever mercy is mentioned, we must keep in mind that faith, which receives the promise of mercy, is required there. Again, whenever we speak about faith, we want an object of faith to be understood, namely, the
promised mercy. For faith justifies and saves, 56
not because it is a worthy work in itself, but only because it receives the promised mercy.

Throughout the Prophets and the Psalms 57
this worship (this *latreia*) is highly praised, even though the Law does not teach the free forgiveness of sins. The Old Testament Fathers knew the promise about Christ, that God for Christ's sake wanted to forgive sins. They understood that Christ would be the price for our sins. They knew that our works are not a price for so great a matter. So they received free mercy and forgiveness of sins by faith, just as the saints in the New Testament.
To this point belong those frequent repeti- 58
tions about mercy and faith that appear in the Psalms and the Prophets. For example, Psalm 130:3 says, "If You, O LORD, should mark iniquities, O Lord, who could stand?" Here David confesses his sins and does not list his merits. He adds, "But with You there is forgiveness" (v. 4). Here he comforts himself by his trust in God's mercy, and he refers to the promise, "I wait for the LORD, my soul

waits, and in His word I hope" (v. 5). This
means, "Because You have promised the for-
giveness of sins, I am sustained by Your
59 promise." Therefore, the Fathers also were
justified, not by the Law, but by the promise
and faith. It is amazing that the adversaries
diminish faith to such a degree, even though
they see that it is everywhere praised as a
great service. For example, Psalm 50:15
says, "Call upon Me in the day of trouble; I
60 will deliver you." God wants Himself to be
known, He wants Himself to be worshiped,
so that we receive benefits from Him and re-
ceive them because of His mercy, not be-
cause of our merits. This is the richest con-
solation in all afflictions. The adversaries
ban such consolation when they diminish
and disparage faith and teach only that by
means of works and merits people interact
with God.

Faith in Christ Justifies

Note: While the Roman Church does not bypass Christ or God's grace, it does base its doctrine of justification on our cooperation with God's grace rather than on Christ's work alone. Inclination toward goodness is increased by participation in the Church's sacramental system, whereby we receive grace from the merits of Christ and the saints. Through our cooperation with this grace, we earn eternal life. This teaching is subtly and deceptively nuanced, and must be exposed as false and potentially damning (Galatians 3:10–14). It diverts our eyes from Christ and His full, complete, and perfect satisfaction for sins. Through careful analysis of religious terms and their use, Melanchthon shows that the Roman Catholic teaching on justification is contrary to the Holy Scriptures, that it confuses grace and works, and that it obscures the merit and glory of Jesus Christ.

In the first place, lest anyone think that we 61
speak about an idle knowledge of history, we
must state how faith is obtained. Afterward,
we will show both that faith justifies and how
this ought to be understood. We will also ex-
plain the objections of the adversaries.
Christ, in the last chapter of Luke, com- 62
mands "that repentance and forgiveness of
sins should be proclaimed in His name"
(24:47). The Gospel convicts all people that
they are under sin, that they are subject to
eternal wrath and death. It offers, for Christ's
sake, forgiveness of sin and justification,
which is received through faith. The preach-
ing of repentance (which accuses us) terrifies
consciences with true and grave terrors. In
these matters, hearts ought to receive conso-
lation again. This happens if they believe
Christ's promise, that for His sake we have
forgiveness of sins. This faith, encouraging
and consoling in these fears, receives forgive-
ness of sins, justifies, and gives life. For this
consolation is a new ‹birth› and spiritual life.
These things are plain and clear and can be 63
understood by the pious. They also have tes-
timonies of the Church. The adversaries can-
not say how the Holy Spirit is given. They
imagine that the Sacraments give the Holy
Spirit by the outward act (*ex opere operato*),
without a good emotion in the one receiving
them, as though, indeed, the gift of the Holy
Spirit were a useless matter.

We speak of the kind of faith that is not 64
an idle thought, but that liberates from
death and produces a new life in hearts. This
is the work of the Holy Spirit. This does not
coexist with mortal sin. As long as faith is
present, it produces good fruits, as we will
explain later. About the conversion of the 65
wicked, or about the way of regeneration,
what can be said that is simpler and clearer?
Let the Scholastics, from so great a host of
writers, produce a single commentary upon
the *Sentences* that speaks about the way of
regeneration. When they speak of the habit 66

of love, they imagine that people merit it through works. They do not teach that it is received through the Word. They teach just
67 like the Anabaptists teach at this time. But God cannot be interacted with, God cannot be grasped, except through the Word. So justification happens through the Word, just as Paul says in Romans 1:16, "[The Gospel] is the power of God for salvation to everyone who believes." Likewise, he says in 10:17, "Faith comes from hearing." Proof can be derived even from this: faith justifies because, if justification happens only through the Word, and the Word is understood only by faith, it follows that faith jus-
68 tifies. There are other and more important reasons. We have said these things so far in order that we might show the way of regeneration and that the nature of faith ‹what faith is or is not›, about which we speak, might be understood.

69 Now we will show that faith justifies ‹and nothing else›. Here, in the first place, readers must be taught about this point: Just as it is necessary to keep this statement—Christ is Mediator—so is it necessary to defend that faith justifies. For how will Christ be Mediator if we do not use Him as Mediator in justification, if we do not hold that we are counted righteous for His sake? To believe is to trust in Christ's merits, that for His sake God certainly wishes to be reconciled with
70 us. Here is a similar point: Just as we should defend that the promise of Christ is necessary apart from the Law, so also we should defend that faith justifies. For the Law cannot be performed unless the Holy Spirit is received first. It is, therefore, necessary to defend that the promise of Christ is necessary. But this cannot be received except through faith. Therefore, those who deny that faith justifies teach nothing but the Law, both Christ and the Gospel being set aside.

When it is said that faith justifies, some 71
perhaps understand it to mean that faith is the beginning of justification or the preparation for justification. Then it is not faith through which we are accepted by God, but the works that follow. So they dream that faith is highly praised because it is the beginning. For great is the importance of the beginning, as they commonly say, "The beginning is half of everything." They speak as if one would say that grammar makes the teachers of all arts, because it prepares for other arts. (In fact, it is one's own art that makes everyone an artist.) We do not believe like this about faith, but we hold—properly and truly—we are for Christ's sake counted righteous, or are acceptable to God through
faith itself. "To be justified" means that just 72
people are made out of unjust people, or born again. It also means that they are pronounced, or counted, as just. For Scripture speaks in both ways. So we wish to show this first: Faith alone makes a just person out of an unjust person; in other words, that person receives forgiveness of sins.

The term *alone* [*sola*] offends some peo- 73
ple, even though Paul says in Romans 3:28, "For we hold that one is justified by faith apart from works of the law." He says in Ephesians 2:8–9, "It is the gift of God, not a result of works, so that no one may boast." He says in Romans 3:24, "justified by His grace as a gift." If the exclusive term *alone* displeases, let them remove from Paul also the exclusives *freely, not of works, it is the gift*, and so on. For these also are exclusives. It is, however, the notion of merit that we exclude. We do not exclude the Word or Sacraments, as the adversaries falsely charge against us. We have said earlier that faith is conceived from the Word. We honor the ministry of the Word ‹Preaching Office and Word› in the highest degree.
Love and works must also follow faith. 74

Therefore, they are not excluded so that they do not follow faith, but confidence in the merit of love or of works is excluded in justification. We will clearly show this.

We Obtain Forgiveness of Sins through Faith Alone in Christ

Note: The Bible teaches that mankind stands entirely damned before God. He demands that we be righteous and holy in His sight, without exception. Certainly we are able to perform works that are considered worthy in the eyes of the world (Ap IV 23), but these are insufficient for God's requirements and cannot atone for our sins. There is nothing within us that merits His grace and mercy. As sinners, how can we stand before a holy, righteous, and just God? We can, but only by His grace. God restores us to a right relationship with Himself through Christ Jesus. By grace, God justifies us through faith in His Son.

The biblical definition of grace is God's unmerited favor in Christ, His love active in the salvation brought about by Christ (Titus 2:11). Saving, or justifying, grace is the undeserved kindness that God gives sinful people because of what Christ has done (John 3:16; Titus 3:4–5). Grace stands in stark contrast to the works that human beings do. The Bible clearly teaches that since our salvation is purely by grace, all human works are entirely excluded from justification (Romans 11:6; Ephesians 2:8–9). This biblical definition of grace is important. If we relied on ourselves for justification before God, one of three things would happen: we could despair of our efforts to earn God's favor, we could become self-righteous hypocrites, or we could completely reject our Savior.

In the Roman Church, both then and now, "grace" is more of a quality or power that God infuses into man's natural goodness, allowing him to reach a point where he pleases God. The Catechism of the Catholic Church carefully states that man is involved in the process of his own justification. Through grace, God begins the process, but it is up to man to complete his justification before God. Man's good works, begun by God's grace, merit for him a right relationship with God. True, it is claimed that these merits are ultimately derived from the operation of the Holy Spirit. But in the end, man contributes to his own justification. This is a dangerous mixture of grace and works. In this system, how can we be sure of a right standing with God? How can we know if we are justified?

We think even the adversaries acknowledge that the forgiveness of sins is necessary first in justification. We are all under sin. Therefore, we reason as follows: 75

To receive the forgiveness of sins is to be justified, according to Psalm 32:1, "Blessed is the one whose transgression is forgiven." 76
By faith alone in Christ—not through love, not because of love or works—we receive the forgiveness of sins, although love follows faith. 77
Therefore, by faith alone we are justified. We understand justification as the making of a righteous person out of an unrighteous one, or that a person is regenerated. 78

It will become easy to state the minor premise ‹that we receive forgiveness of sin by faith, not by love› if we know how forgiveness of sins happens. With great indifference the adversaries dispute whether forgiveness of sins and infusion of grace are the same change. Being useless men, they did not know how to answer this question. In the forgiveness of sins, the terrors of sin and of eternal death must be overcome in the heart. Paul testifies about this in 1 Corinthians 15:56–57, "The sting of death is sin, and the power of sin is the law. But thanks be to God, who gives us the victory through our Lord Jesus Christ." In other words, sin terrifies consciences. This happens through the Law, which shows God's wrath against sin. But we 79

The Crucifixion

gain the victory through Christ. How?
Through faith, when we comfort ourselves
by confidence in the mercy promised for
80 Christ's sake. Therefore, we prove the minor
premise. God's wrath cannot be appeased if
we set our own works against it. For Christ
has been set forth as an Atoning Sacrifice so,
that for His sake, the Father may be recon-
ciled to us. But Christ is not received as a Me-
diator except by faith. Therefore, by faith
alone we receive forgiveness of sins when we
comfort our hearts with confidence in the
81 mercy promised for Christ's sake. Likewise,
Paul says in Romans 5:2, "Through Him we
have also obtained access" and adds, "by
faith." Therefore, we are reconciled to the Fa-
ther and receive forgiveness of sins when we
are comforted with confidence in the mercy
promised for Christ's sake. The adversaries
regard Christ as Mediator and Atoning Sacri-
fice for this reason: He has merited the habit
of love. They do not encourage us to use Him
now as Mediator. They act as though Christ
were certainly in the grave. They imagine
that we have access to God through our own
works. They think they merit this habit
through these, and afterward, by this love,
come to God. Is this not to bury Christ alto-
gether and to take away the entire teaching of
faith? Paul, on the contrary, teaches that we
have access to God (that is, reconciliation)
through Christ. To show how this happens,
he adds that we have access by faith. By faith,
for Christ's sake, we receive forgiveness of
sins. We cannot set up our own love and our
own works against God's wrath.

82 *Second.* It is certain that sins are forgiven for the sake of Christ as our Atoning Sacrifice, "whom God put forward as a propitiation" (Romans 3:25). Furthermore, Paul adds, "by faith." Therefore, this atonement benefits us in this way: We receive the mercy promised in Him by faith and set it against God's wrath and judgment. To the same effect, it is written in Hebrews 4:14, 16, "Since then we have a great high priest . . . let us then with confidence draw near." The apostle tells us to come to God, not with confidence in our own merits, but with confidence in Christ as the High Priest. The apostle requires faith.

Third. Peter says in Acts 10:43, "To Him all 83
the prophets bear witness that everyone who believes in Him receives forgiveness of sins through His name." How could this be said more clearly? Peter says we receive forgiveness of sins through Christ's name, that is, for His sake. It is not for the sake of our merits, not for the sake of our contrition, attrition, love, worship, or works. He adds: *When we believe in Him.* Peter requires faith. For we cannot receive Christ's name except by faith. Besides, he refers to the agreement of all the prophets. This is truly to cite the authority of the Church. We will speak again later on this topic, when describing "repentance."

Fourth. Forgiveness of sins is something 84
promised for Christ's sake. It cannot be received except through faith alone. For a promise cannot be received except by faith alone. Romans 4:16 says, "That is why it depends on faith, in order that the promise may rest on grace and be guaranteed." It is as though he says, "If the matter were to depend on our merits, the promise would be uncertain and useless. For we never could determine when we would have enough merit." Experienced consciences can easily understand this. So Paul says in Galatians 3:22, "But the Scripture imprisoned everything under sin, so that the promise by faith in Jesus Christ might be given to those who believe." He takes merit away from us because he says that all are guilty and included under sin. Then he adds that the promise (namely, forgiveness of sins and justification) is given,

and he shows how the promise can be received—by faith. This reasoning, derived from the nature of a promise, is the chief reasoning in Paul and is often repeated. Nor can anything be devised or imagined by which
85 Paul's argument can be overthrown. Therefore, let not good minds allow themselves to be forced from the conviction that we receive forgiveness of sins for Christ's sake, through faith alone. In this they have sure and firm consolation against the terrors of sin, against eternal death, and against all the gates of hell.

[Scripture Affirms This Teaching]

Note: The Bible teaches that "to justify" is to declare righteous. In the Gospel of Christ, God declares that we are forgiven, righteous, and holy in His sight. Melanchthon elaborates on this point in Article IV. St. Paul teaches that justification is only by grace, through faith, apart from any works of righteousness on man's part (Romans 3:28). Lutherans insist that justification is not a process through which God brings us up to a certain level of holiness, which then qualifies us to receive more grace. Rather, it is God's declaration that the dead are alive, the condemned are not guilty, and the sinful are forgiven because of Jesus.

In contrast to biblical justification, the Roman Church teaches that God's grace is a power infused to begin good works, and that justification is the entire process by which this occurs. This confuses justification (whereby God declares us righteous because of Christ) and sanctification (whereby He begins to conform us to Christ). Such a teaching causes grave doubts in the heart of the believer, who may never be sure whether he is truly justified. The Scriptures provide hope, comfort, peace, and joy in knowing that Christ has accomplished all for us through His life, death, and resurrection. The Roman Church's teaching leads to doubt and despair.

We are justified through faith. Melanchthon explains at length what the Bible teaches about faith. Christ's perfect obedience to His Father's will (Galatians 4:4–5) and His sacrificial death on the cross (Colossians 1:22) won forgiveness of sins for the whole world (1 John 2:2). How do we personally receive Christ's universal righteousness and atonement? We receive these gifts through faith and faith alone. God gives us faith as a gift, through which Christ's righteousness is credited to us (Ephesians 2:8–9) and our sins are forgiven (Romans 3:22–24). Melanchthon carefully states that by no means do the Lutherans consider faith to be mere intellectual assent to historic truths; the devil and ungodly people have this sort of "faith." Justifying faith is God-instilled trust that believes the life, death, and resurrection of Christ is "for me." It is firm acceptance of God's offer promising forgiveness of sins and justification. Faith is always personal and individual. No one can have faith for another.

Since we receive forgiveness of sins and 86
the Holy Spirit through faith alone, faith alone justifies. For those reconciled are counted as righteous and as God's children. This is not because of their own purity, but through mercy for Christ's sake, provided only that they receive this mercy through faith. So Scripture testifies that *by faith we are accounted righteous* (Romans 3:26). We will add testimonies that clearly declare that faith is that very righteousness through which we are accounted righteous before God. This is not because faith is a work that is worthy in itself. It is because faith receives the promise by which God has declared that, for Christ's sake, He wishes to show favor to those believing in Him, or because God knows that Christ Jesus was "made our wisdom and our righteousness and sanctification and redemption" (1 Corinthians 1:30).

In the Epistle to the Romans, Paul dis- 87
cusses this topic specifically. He declares that when we believe God (for Christ's sake) is

reconciled to us, we are justified freely through faith. This point, which contains the statement of the entire discussion, Paul sets forth in the third chapter: "For we hold that one is justified by faith apart from works of the law" (Romans 3:28). The adversaries conclude that this passage refers to Levitical ceremonies. But Paul speaks not only of the ceremonies, but of the whole Law. For he quotes afterward (7:7) from the Ten Commandments: "You shall not covet." If moral works would merit the forgiveness of sins and justification, there would also be no need for Christ and the promise. All that Paul says about the promise would be overthrown. He would also have been wrong in writing to the Ephesians, "For by grace you have been saved through faith. And this is not your own doing; it is the gift of God, not a result of works" (2:8–9). Paul, likewise, refers to Abraham and David in Romans 4:1, 6. But they had God's command for circumcision. Therefore, if any works justified, these works must also have justified at the time that they had a command. But Augustine teaches correctly that Paul speaks of the entire Law, as he discusses at length in his book *On the Spirit and the Letter*, where he finally says:

> These matters, having been considered and treated, according to the ability that the Lord has thought worthy to give us, we conclude that a person is not justified by the precepts of a good life, but by faith in Jesus Christ.

88 Lest we may decide that "faith justifies"
came from Paul without consideration, he
fortifies and confirms this teaching by a long
discussion in Romans 4. Afterward, he re-
89 peats it in all his letters. So he says in Romans
4:4–5:

> Now to the one who works, his wages are not counted as a gift but as his due. And to the one who does not work but trusts Him who justifies the ungodly, his faith is counted as righteousness.

Here he clearly says that faith itself is credit-
ed for righteousness. Faith is that thing God
declares to be righteousness. Paul adds that
righteousness is credited freely. He says that
it could not be credited freely if it were due
because of works. Therefore, he excludes also
the merit of moral works. For if justification
before God were due to these moral works,
faith would not be credited for righteousness
without works. Afterward, in Romans 4:9, 90
"We say that faith was counted to Abraham
as righteousness." Romans 5:1 says, "Since we 91
have been justified by faith, we have peace
with God." This means we have consciences
that are peaceful and joyful before God.
Romans 10:10 says, "With the heart one be- 92
lieves and is justified." Here he declares that
faith is the righteousness of the heart.

> We also have believed in Christ Jesus, in order to be justified by faith in Christ and not by works of the law. (Galatians 2:16) 93

> For by grace you have been saved through faith. And this is not your own doing; it is the gift of God, not a result of works, so that no one may boast. (Ephesians 2:8–9)

> But to all who did receive Him, who believed in His name, He gave the right to become children of God, who were born, not of blood nor of the will of the flesh nor of the will of man, but of God. (John 1:12–13) 94

> And as Moses lifted up the serpent in the wilderness, so must the Son of Man be lifted up, that whoever believes in Him may have eternal life. (John 3:14–15) 95

Preaching Justification

> 96 For God did not send His Son into the world to condemn the world, but in order that the world might be saved through Him. Whoever believes in Him is not condemned. (John 3:17–18)

> 97 Let it be known to you therefore, brothers, that through this man forgiveness of sins is proclaimed to you, and by Him everyone who believes is freed from everything from which you could not be freed by the law of Moses. (Acts 13:38–39)

How could the office of Christ and justification be declared more clearly? Paul says that the Law does not justify. Therefore, Christ was given, that we may believe that for His sake we are justified. He plainly denies justification by the Law. So for Christ's sake we are accounted righteous when we believe that God, for His sake, has been reconciled to us.

> 98 This Jesus is the stone that was rejected by you, the builders, which has become the cornerstone. And there is salvation in no one else, for there is no other name under heaven given among men by which we must be saved. (Acts 4:11–12)

Christ's name is received only by faith.
Therefore, we are saved by confidence in
Christ's name, and not by confidence in our
works. For "the name" here means the cause
that is mentioned, because of which salva-
tion is gained. To call upon Christ's name is
to trust in His name as the cause, or price,
99 because of which we are saved. Acts 15:9 says,
"cleansed their hearts by faith." Therefore,
the faith that the apostles speak about is not
useless knowledge, but a reality. It receives
the Holy Spirit and justifies us.

100 Habakkuk 2:4 says, "The righteous shall
live by his faith." Here he says, first, that people
are just by faith. By faith they believe that God
is favorable, and he adds that the same faith
gives life because this faith produces peace and
joy in the heart and eternal life.

Isaiah 53:11 says, "By His knowledge shall 101
the righteous one, My servant, make many to be accounted righteous." What is Christ's knowledge unless it means to know Christ's benefits, the promises He has scattered throughout the world by the Gospel? To know these benefits is properly and truly to believe in Christ, to believe that He will certainly fulfill what God has promised for Christ's sake.

Scripture is full of such testimonies. For 102
in some places it presents the Law, and in others it presents the promises about Christ, forgiveness of sins, and free acceptance of the sinner for Christ's sake.

[The Church Fathers Affirm This Teaching]

Note: In the Apology, Melanchthon strongly refutes the Roman Church's understanding of faith, drawing on examples from Scripture and the church fathers. The Roman Church teaches that grace is infused into the human soul. Man cooperates with this infused grace to produce certain virtues, faith being among them. By freely assenting to the doctrines of the Roman Church, one demonstrates "faith." This view of faith reduces God's gracious, supernatural gift to a mere initiating power. It also diminishes personal faith in Christ to simple agreement with the teachings of the Church. Instead of heartfelt trust in our gracious God and Savior, faith becomes mere intellectual assent to the history of Jesus.

In the Roman Church's theology, justification is given only partially in this life. The Scriptures and Article IV of the Apology, however, clearly teach and confess that justification is complete and total because of the sufficient, atoning, once for all sacrifice of Christ on the cross.

---

103 Here and there among the Fathers similar testimonies exist. For Ambrose says in his letter to a certain Irenaeus:

> Furthermore, the world was subject to God by the Law because, according to the command of the Law, all are indicted. And yet, by the works of the Law, no one is justified. For, by the Law, sin is perceived, but guilt is not taken away. The Law, which declared all people sinners, seemed to have done harm. But when the Lord Jesus Christ came, He forgave to all people the sin, which no one could avoid. And, by the shedding of His own blood, He blotted out the handwriting that was against us. This is what he says in Romans 5:20, "The law came in to increase the trespass, but where sin increased, grace abounded all the more." Because after the whole world became subject, Christ took away the sin of the whole world, as John testified, saying in John 1:29, "Behold, the Lamb of God, who takes away the sin of the world!" And for this reason let no one boast about works, because no one is justified by his deeds. But he who is righteous has righteousness given to him because he was justified from the washing of Baptism. Faith, therefore, is that which frees through the blood of Christ, because he is blessed "whose transgression is forgiven, whose sin is covered" (Psalm 32:1).

104 These are the words of Ambrose, which clearly favor our doctrine. He denies justification to works and teaches that faith sets us
105 free through the blood of Christ. Let all the commentators on the *Sentences*, who are adorned with magnificent titles, be collected into one heap. For some are called "angelic," others "subtle," and others "unanswerable" ‹that is, doctors who cannot err›. When all these have been read and reread, they will not be worth half as much for understanding Paul as is this one passage of Ambrose.

In the same way, Augustine writes many 106
things against the Pelagians. In *On the Spirit and the Letter,* he says:

> The righteousness of the Law—that he who has fulfilled the Law shall live in it—is set forth for this reason: when anyone has recognized his weakness he may attain and do the Law and live in it, reconciling the Justifier not by his own strength nor by the letter of the Law itself (which cannot be done), but by faith. In a justified person, there is no right work by which he who does that work may live. But justification is received by faith.

Here Augustine clearly says that the Justifier is reconciled by faith and that justification is received by faith. A little after:

> By the Law we fear God; by faith we hope in God. But to those fearing punishment grace is hidden. And the soul laboring under this fear resorts by faith to God's mercy, in order that He may give what He commands.

Here he teaches that hearts are terrified by the Law, but they receive consolation by faith. He also teaches us to receive mercy by faith, before we try to fulfill the Law. We will quote certain other passages shortly.

[The Adversaries Reject This Teaching]

Truly, it is amazing that the adversaries 107
are in no way moved by so many passages of Scripture, which clearly credit justification to

faith. Indeed, Scripture denies this ability to
108 works. Do they think that the same point is
repeated so often for no purpose? Do they
think that these words fell thoughtlessly from
109 the Holy Spirit? But they have also come up
with sophisticated tricks by which they es-
cape these passages. They say that these pas-
sages of Scripture (that speak of faith) ought
to be received as referring to faith that has
been formed (*fides formata*). This means they
do not credit justification to faith except on
account of love. Yes, they do not credit justi-
fication to faith in any way, but only to love,
because they dream that faith can coexist
110 with mortal sin. Where does this go? They
again abolish the promise and return to the
Law. If faith receives forgiveness of sins be-
cause of love, forgiveness of sins will always
be uncertain, because we never love as much
as we ought to. Indeed, we do not love unless
our hearts are firmly convinced that forgive-
ness of sins has been granted to us. So the ad-
versaries, in forgiveness of sins and justifica-
tion, require confidence in one's own love. In
this way, they completely abolish the Gospel
about the free forgiveness of sins; although,
at the same time, they do not offer this love
or understand it, unless they believe that for-
giveness of sins is freely received.

111 We also say that love ought to follow
faith, as Paul also says in Galatians 5:6: "For
in Christ Jesus neither circumcision nor un-
circumcision counts for anything, but only
faith working through love."

112 Yet, we must not think that by confidence
in this love, or because of this love, we receive
forgiveness of sins and reconciliation, just as
we do not receive forgiveness of sins because
of other works that follow. But forgiveness of
sins is received by faith alone. Indeed, this is
properly called faith because the promise
113 cannot be received except by faith. Faith,
properly called, is what believes this promise.
Scripture speaks of this faith. Because faith 114
receives forgiveness of sins and reconciles us
to God, we are ‹like Abraham› counted as
righteous for Christ's sake before we love and
before we do the works of the Law, although
love necessarily follows.

Nor, indeed, is this faith an idle knowl- 115
edge, neither can it coexist with mortal sin. It
is a work of the Holy Spirit, by which we are
freed from death and terrified minds are en-
couraged and brought to life. Because this 116
faith alone receives forgiveness of sins, makes
us acceptable to God, and brings the Holy
Spirit, it could be more correctly called
"grace making one pleasing to God" (*gratia
gratum faciens*). It could not be called an ef-
fect following faith (i.e., love).

In order that the subject might be made 117
quite clear, we have shown well enough so
far, both from testimonies of Scripture and
arguments derived from Scripture, that we
receive forgiveness of sins for Christ's sake
through faith alone. We have shown that
through faith alone we are justified, that is,
unrighteous people are made righteous, or
regenerated. How necessary the knowledge 118
of this faith is can be easily judged. Because
Christ's office is recognized in this alone, we
receive Christ's benefits by this alone. Only
this teaching brings sure and firm consola-
tion to pious minds. In the Church there 119
must be the teaching by which the pious may
receive the sure hope of salvation. For the ad-
versaries give people bad advice when they
tell them to doubt whether they receive for-
giveness of sins. How will such persons sus-
tain themselves in death who have heard
nothing of this faith and think that they
ought to doubt whether they receive forgive-
ness of sins? Besides, it is necessary that the 120
Gospel be kept in Christ's Church, namely,
the promise that sins are freely forgiven for
Christ's sake. Those who teach nothing of

The Risen Christ

this faith we speak about, completely abolish
121 the Gospel. But the Scholastics mention not even a word about this faith. Our adversaries follow them and reject this faith. Nor do they see that by rejecting this faith they abolish the entire promise about the free forgiveness of sins and the righteousness of Christ.

ARTICLE V (III)

Love and Fulfilling the Law

Note: Good works do not cause justification; rather, they are the result of justification. Melanchthon carefully distinguishes between the effect of the Law before a person is justified and the effect of the Law after a person is justified. Rome had garbled these critical biblical distinctions with disastrous consequences. Melanchthon returns to them constantly, writing the longest article in the Apology. Lutherans believe that Christians improve at keeping the Law, and they require good works. However, good works are not necessary for salvation, but are the necessary fruit of salvation.

Justification is not merely an initial grace, but the entire reconciliation we receive from God for Christ's sake. While the Law always accuses us, any beginnings we make at keeping God's Law pleases Him only because of faith, which holds on to Christ. This important discussion of faith and works proceeds with absolute clarity. Melanchthon goes right to the heart of the matter by stating that we can never pit our works against the wrath and judgment of God. Only Christ, our Mediator, can stand for us in our place, take God's wrath and punishment (which we deserve), and win for us eternal life, joy, and peace. (See AC VI; SA III XIII; FC Ep IV, V, and VI; FC SD IV, V, and VI.)

1 On this topic the adversaries quote
*[122] against us, "If you would enter life, keep the commandments" (Matthew 19:17); likewise, "It is the doers of the law who will be justified" (Romans 2:13), and many other things about the Law and works. Before we reply to this, we must first declare *what we believe about love and the fulfilling of the Law.*

> I will put My law within them, and I 2
> will write it on their hearts. (Jeremiah 31:33) [123]
>
> Do we then overthrow the law by this faith? By no means! On the contrary, we uphold the law. (Romans 3:31)
>
> If you would enter life, keep the commandments. (Matthew 19:17)
>
> But [if I] have not love, I gain nothing. (1 Corinthians 13:3)

These and similar sentences testify that we 3
are to keep the Law when we have been justi- [124]
fied by faith, and so grow in fulfilling the Law more and more ‹by the Spirit›. Furthermore, we are not talking about ceremonies, but about the Law that addresses the movements of the heart, namely, the Ten Command-
ments. Faith brings the Holy Spirit and pro- 4
duces a new life in hearts. It must also pro- [125]
duce spiritual movements in hearts. The prophet Jeremiah shows what these movements are when he says, "I will put My law within them, and I will write it on their hearts" (31:33). Therefore, when we have been justified by faith and regenerated, we begin to fear and love God, to pray to Him, to expect aid from Him, to give thanks and praise Him, and to obey Him in times of suffering. We also begin to love our neighbors, because our hearts have spiritual and holy movements.

These things cannot happen until we 5
have been justified through faith and regen- [126]
erated (we receive the Holy Spirit). First, because the Law cannot be kept without Christ;

* A different numbering system appears in some editions of the Apology.

likewise, the Law cannot be kept without the
6 Holy Spirit. But the Holy Spirit is received
[127] through faith, as Paul declares in Galatians
3:14, "that we might receive the promised
7 Spirit through faith." Also remember, how
[128] can the human heart love God while it knows
that He is terribly angry and is oppressing us
with earthly and endless distress? The Law always accuses us. It always shows that God is
8 angry. God is not loved until we receive
[129] mercy through faith. Not until then does He
become someone we can love.

9 Civil works (i.e., the outward works of
[130] the Law) can be done in some measure, without Christ and without the Holy Spirit. Nevertheless, from what we have said, it seems that what belongs only to the divine Law (i.e., the heart's affections toward God), which are commanded in the First Table,
10 cannot be done without the Holy Spirit. But
[131] our adversaries are fine theologians. They
focus on the Second Table and political works. They don't care about the First Table. They act as though the First Table were of no matter. They certainly require only outward fulfillment of the Law. They in no way consider the Law that is eternal and placed far above the sense and intellect of all creatures. Deuteronomy 6:5 says, "You shall love the LORD your God with all your heart."

11 Christ was given for this purpose, that
[132] forgiveness of sins might be bestowed on us
for His sake. He was also given so that the Holy Spirit might bring forth in us new and eternal life and eternal righteousness. Therefore, the Law cannot truly be kept unless the Holy Spirit is received through faith. So Paul says that *the Law is established through faith, and not made useless,* because the Law can only be kept when the Holy Spirit is given.
12 Paul teaches, *The veil that covered the face of*
[133] *Moses cannot be removed except by faith in*
Christ, by which the Holy Spirit is received. (See 2 Corinthians 3:14–18.) For he says, "Yes, to this day whenever Moses is read a veil lies over their hearts. But when one turns to the Lord, the veil is removed. Now the Lord is the Spirit, and where the Spirit of the Lord is, there is freedom" [2 Corinthians 3:15–17].
Paul understands by the "veil" the human 13
opinion about the entire Law, the Ten Com- [134]
mandments and the ceremonies. In other words, hypocrites think that outward and civil works satisfy God's Law, and that sacrifices and observances justify a person before God by the outward act (*ex opere operato*).
But then this veil is removed from us (i.e., we 14
are freed from this error) when God shows to [135]
our hearts our uncleanness and the hatefulness of sin. Then, for the first time, we see that we are far from fulfilling the Law. We learn to know how flesh is self-secure and doesn't care. It does not fear God and is not completely certain that we are cared for by God. It imagines that people are born and die by chance. Then we experience that we do not believe that God forgives and hears us. But when we hear about the Gospel and the forgiveness of sins, we are consoled through faith, we receive the Holy Spirit so that now we are able to think correctly about God, to fear and believe God, and so on. From these facts it is clear that the Law cannot be kept without Christ and the Holy Spirit.

We profess that the work of the Law must 15
be begun in us, and that it must be kept con- [136]
tinually more and more. At the same time we also speak about both spiritual movements and outward good works. Therefore, the adversaries falsely charge that our theologians do not teach good works. They not only require good works, but they also show
how they can be done. The result convicts 16
the hypocrites, who by their own powers try [137]
to fulfill the Law. For they cannot do the
things they attempt. Human nature is far too 17

John Agricola (1494?–1566)

John Agricola taught that God's Law plays no part in the life of a person who has been converted by the Gospel. Luther opposed Agricola's antinomian (anti-law) views. Years later a similar controversy over good works surfaced and was resolved by Article VI of the Formula of Concord.

[138] weak to resist the devil by its own powers.
He holds as captive everyone who has not
18 been freed through faith. There is need for
[139] Christ's power against the devil. For we
know that for Christ's sake we are heard and
have the promise. We may pray for the gov-
ernance and defense of the Holy Spirit, that
we may neither be deceived and err, nor be
pushed to do anything against God's will.
Psalm 68:18 teaches this very thing: "You as-
cended on high, leading a host of captives in
Your train and receiving gifts among men."
Christ has overcome the devil, and has given
to us the promise and the Holy Spirit, in
order that—by divine aid—we ourselves
may also overcome. So 1 John 3:8 says, "The
reason the Son of God appeared was to de-
19 stroy the works of the devil." Again, we teach
[140] not only how the Law can be kept, but also
how God is pleased if anything is done. This
is not because we satisfy the Law, but be-
cause we are in Christ, as we shall explain
shortly. Therefore, it is clear that we require
20 good works. In fact, we also say this: Our
[141] love for God, even though it is small, cannot
possibly be separated from faith. For we
come to the Father through Christ. When
forgiveness of sins has been received, then
we are truly certain that we have a God [Ex-
odus 20:3], that is, that God cares for us. We
call upon Him, we give Him thanks, we fear
Him, we love Him as 1 John 4:19 teaches,
"We love because He first loved us." In other
words, we love Him because He gave His
Son for us and forgave us our sins. In this
way John shows that faith comes first and
21 love follows. Likewise, the faith of which we
[142] speak exists in repentance. I mean that faith
is conceived in the terrors of conscience,
which feels God's wrath against our sins and
seeks forgiveness of sins, seeks to be freed
from sin. In such terrors and other troubles,
this faith ought to grow and be strength-
ened. Therefore, it cannot exist in people 22
who live by the flesh, who are delighted by [143]
their own lusts and obey them. So, Paul says
in Romans 8:1, "There is therefore now no
condemnation for those who are in Christ
Jesus." So, too, "We are debtors, not to the
flesh, to live according to the flesh. For if you
live according to the flesh you will die, but if
by the Spirit you put to death the deeds of
the body, you will live" (8:12–13). Paul is 23
writing about faith that receives forgiveness [144]
of sins in a terrified heart and flees from sin.
Such faith does not remain in those who
obey their desires, neither does it dwell with
mortal sin.

From these effects of faith the adversaries 24
select one, namely, love, and teach that love [145]
justifies. It is clear that they only teach the
Law. They do not teach that forgiveness of
sins is first received through faith. They do
not teach about Christ as Mediator, that we
have a gracious God for Christ's sake, but for
the sake of our love. Yet, they do not say
what the nature of this love is, neither can
they say. They proclaim that they fulfill the 25
Law, although this glory belongs to Christ [146]
alone. They set up confidence in their own
works against God's judgment. For they say
that they merit according to righteousness
(*de condigno*) grace and eternal life. This
confidence is absolutely ungodly and useless.
For in this life we cannot satisfy the Law, be-
cause the sinful nature does not stop bring-
ing forth ‹evil inclination and desire›, even
though the Spirit in us resists them.

But someone may say, "Since we also con- 26
fess that love is a work of the Holy Spirit, and [147]
since it is righteousness, because it is the ful-
filling of the Law, why do we not teach that
love justifies?" To this we must reply: In the
first place, it is certain that we do not receive
forgiveness of sins through our love or for
the sake of our love, but for Christ's sake, by

27 faith alone. Faith alone looks upon the
[148] promise. It knows that because of the prom-
ise, it is absolutely certain that God forgives,
because Christ has not died in vain. Such
faith overcomes the terrors of sin and death.
28 If anyone doubts whether sins are forgiven
[149] him, he dishonors Christ. For he judges that
his sin is greater or more effective than
Christ's death and promise, even though Paul
says, "Where sin increased, grace abounded
all the more" (Romans 5:20). This means that
29 mercy is more comprehensive than sin. If
[150] anyone thinks that he receives forgiveness of
sins because he loves, he dishonors Christ
and will discover in God's judgment that this
confidence in his own righteousness is
wicked and useless. Likewise, it is necessary
30 that faith alone reconciles and justifies. We
[151] do not receive forgiveness of sins through
other powers of the Law, or because of these:
patience, chastity, obedience toward magis-
trates, and so on. (Nevertheless, these virtues
ought to follow faith.) Likewise, we do not
receive forgiveness of sins because of love for
31 God, even though this must follow. Besides,
[152] this way of speaking is well known. At times
we use a word for something and we use the
same word for the cause and effects of that
thing *(synecdoche)*. For example, in Luke
7:47, Christ says, "Her sins, which are many,
are forgiven—for she loved much." Christ
Himself interprets this when He adds, "Your
faith has saved you" [7:50]. Christ did not
mean that the woman had merited forgive-
32 ness of sins by that work of love. That is why
[153] He adds, "Your faith has saved you." But faith
is that which freely obtains God's mercy be-
cause of God's Word. If anyone denies that
this is faith, he does not understand at all
33 what faith is. The story in this passage shows
[154] what Christ calls "love." The woman came
with the opinion that forgiveness of sins
should be sought in Christ. This worship is
the highest worship of Christ. She could
think nothing greater about Christ. To seek
forgiveness of sins from Him was truly to ac-
knowledge the Messiah. To think of Christ
this way, to worship Him this way, to em-
brace Him this way, is truly to believe. Fur-
thermore, Christ used the word *love* not to-
ward the woman, but against the Pharisee.
He contrasted the entire worship of the
Pharisee with the entire worship offered by
the woman. He rebuked the Pharisee be-
cause he did not acknowledge that He was
the Messiah, even though he performed the
outward duties that a guest and a great and
holy man deserved. Christ points to the
woman and praises her worship, ointment,
tears, and so forth. These were all signs of
faith and a confession—with Christ she
sought forgiveness of sins. It is indeed a
great example. Not without reason, this
moved Christ to rebuke the Pharisee, who
was a wise and honorable man, but not a
believer. He charges him with lack of holi-
ness and admonishes him by the example of
the woman. In this way, Christ shows that it
is disgraceful for the Pharisee. While an un-
learned woman believes God, he, a doctor of
the Law, does not believe. He does not ac-
knowledge the Messiah and does not seek
from Him forgiveness of sins and salvation.
So Christ praises her entire worship. This 34
often happens in the Scriptures, that by one [155]
word we embrace many things. Below we
shall speak at greater length about similar
passages such as Luke 11:41, "But give as
alms those things that are within, and be-
hold, everything is clean for you." He re-
quires not only alms, but also the righ-
teousness of faith. He says here, "Her sins,
which are many, are forgiven—for she loved
much" [Luke 7:47]. This means she has
truly worshiped Me with faith and faith's
exercises and signs. He means the entire

worship. Meanwhile, He teaches this: Forgiveness of sins is properly received by faith, even though love, confession, and other good fruit ought to follow. He does not mean that these fruit are the price, or are the atonement that reconciles us to God, because of which the
35 forgiveness of sins is given. We are disputing
[156] about a great subject, about Christ's honor, and where good minds may seek for sure and firm consolation. We are disputing whether confidence is to be placed in Christ or in our
36 works. If it is to be placed in our works, the
[157] honor of Mediator and Atoning Sacrifice will be withdrawn from Christ. Yet we shall find, in God's judgment, that this confidence is useless. From this confidence, consciences rush directly into despair. If forgiveness of sins and reconciliation do not happen freely for Christ's sake, but for the sake of our love, no one will have forgiveness of sins. He would only have it when he had fulfilled the entire Law, because the Law does not justify as long
37 as it can accuse us. Therefore, it is clear that
[158] we are justified through faith, since justification is reconciliation for Christ's sake. For it is very certain that forgiveness of sins is received through faith alone.

[No One Can Keep the Law Perfectly]

38 Now let us reply to the objection stated
[159] above: The adversaries are right in thinking that love is the fulfilling of the Law and that obedience to the Law is certainly righteousness. But they make a mistake in this matter. They think that we are justified by the Law. Since we are not justified by the Law, we receive forgiveness of sins and reconciliation through faith for Christ's sake. This is not because of love or the fulfilling of the Law; it follows necessarily that we are justified through faith in Christ.

39 In the second place, this fulfilling of the
[160] Law, or obedience toward the Law, is indeed righteousness, when it is complete. But it is small and impure in us. So our righteousness is not pleasing for its own sake and
is not accepted for its own sake. From what 40
has been said above, it is clear that *justifica- [161]
tion* means not the beginning of the renewal, but the reconciliation by which we are accepted afterward. It can now be seen much more clearly that starting to fulfill the Law does not justify, because such fulfillment is only accepted on account of faith. Nor must we trust that we are accounted righteous before God by our own perfection and fulfilling of the Law, but rather for Christ's sake.

‹In the third place,› Christ does not stop 41
being our Mediator after we have been re- [162]
newed. They err who imagine that He has merited only a first grace, and that, afterward, we please God and merit eternal life
by our fulfilling of the Law. Christ remains 42
Mediator, and we should always be confi- [163]
dent that for His sake we have a reconciled God, even though we are unworthy. Paul clearly teaches this when he says, "I am not aware of anything against myself, but I am not thereby acquitted" (1 Corinthians 4:4). Paul knows that through faith he is counted righteous for Christ's sake, according to the passage "Blessed is the one whose transgression is forgiven" (Psalm 32:1; see also Romans 4:7). But this forgiveness is always received through faith. Likewise, the credit for the righteousness of the Gospel comes from the promise. Therefore, it is always received through faith. It must always be regarded as certain that we are counted righteous
through faith for Christ's sake. If the regener- 43
ate afterward think that they will be accepted [164]
because of the fulfilling of the Law, when would a conscience be certain that it pleased
God? We never satisfy the Law! So we must al- 44
ways run back to the promise. Our infirmity [165]

must be recognized in this matter. We must regard it as certain that we are counted righteous for the sake of Christ, "who is at the right hand of God, who indeed is interceding for us" (Romans 8:34). If anyone thinks that he is righteous and accepted because of his own fulfillment of the Law, and not because of Christ's promise, he dishonors this High Priest. This cannot be understood. How could someone imagine that a person is righteous before God when Christ is excluded as the Atoning Sacrifice and Mediator?

45 ‹In the fourth place,› what need is there of
[166] a long discussion? All Scripture, all the
Church cries out that the Law cannot be satisfied. Therefore, starting to fulfill the Law
does not please on its own account, but on
46 account of faith in Christ. Otherwise, the
[167] Law always accuses us. For who loves or fears
God enough? Who has enough patience to bear the troubles brought by God? Who does not frequently doubt whether human affairs are ruled by God's counsel or by chance? Who does not frequently doubt whether he is heard by God? Who is not frequently enraged because the wicked enjoy a better life than the righteous, because the righteous are oppressed by the wicked? Who fulfills his
own calling? Who loves his neighbor as him-
47 self? Who is not tempted by lust? Paul says,
[168] "For I do not do the good I want, but the evil
I do not want is what I keep on doing" (Romans 7:19). Likewise, "I myself serve the law of God with my mind, but with my flesh I serve the law of sin" (7:25). Here he openly declares that he serves the law of sin. David says in Psalm 143:2, "Enter not into judgment with Your servant, for no one living is righteous before You." Here even God's servant prays for the removal of judgment. Likewise, "Blessed is the man against whom the LORD counts no iniquity" (Psalm 32:2). Therefore, in our weakness sin is always present, which could be charged against us. A little while after he says, "Therefore let everyone who is godly offer prayer to You" (32:6).
Here he shows that even saints ought to seek
forgiveness of sins. They are more than blind 48
who do not realize that wicked desires in the [169]
flesh are sins, of which Paul says, "For the desires of the flesh are against the Spirit, and
the desires of the Spirit are against the flesh"
(Galatians 5:17). The flesh distrusts God, 49
trusts in present things, seeks human aid in [170]
trouble, even contrary to God's will. It flees from suffering, which it ought to bear because of God's commands. It doubts God's mercy and so on. The Holy Spirit in our hearts fights against such tendencies in order to suppress and kill them and to produce
new spiritual motives. We will collect more 50
testimonies below about this topic, although [171]
they are clearly everywhere not only in the Scriptures, but also in the Holy Fathers.

[Church Fathers and St. Paul Affirm Justification through Faith]

Augustine well says, "All God's com- 51
mandments are fulfilled when whatever is [172]
not done, is forgiven." Therefore, he requires faith even in good works. He says this to show that we may believe we please God for Christ's sake, and even our works are not
worthy and pleasing of themselves. Jerome, 52
against the Pelagians, says: [173]

> Then we are righteous when we confess that we are sinners, and that our righteousness stands not in our own merit, but in God's mercy.

Therefore, when starting to fulfill the Law, 53
faith ought to be present, which certainly [174]
believes that we have a reconciled God for Christ's sake. For mercy cannot be received

except through faith, as has been repeatedly
54 said above. Paul says in Romans 3:31, "Do we
[175] then overthrow the law by this faith? By no
means! On the contrary, we uphold the law."
Here's what we ought to understand: People
regenerated through faith not only receive the
Holy Spirit, and have motives that agree with
God's Law, but we ought also to realize that
they are far distant from the Law's perfection.
This point has the greatest importance by far,
55 and we must add it to the argument also. We
[176] cannot conclude that we are counted righ-
teous before God because of our fulfilling of
the Law. Justification must be sought else-
where in order that the conscience may be-
come peaceful. For we are not righteous
before God as long as we flee from God's
56 judgment and are angry with God. There-
[177] fore, we must conclude that we are counted
righteous for Christ's sake being reconciled
through faith. This is not because of the Law
or our works. Because of faith, beginning to
fulfill the Law pleases God. Because of faith,
there is no charge that we fulfill the Law im-
perfectly, even though the sight of our impu-
rity terrifies us. If justification is to be sought
elsewhere, our love and works do not justify.
57 Christ's death and satisfaction ought to be
[178] placed far above our purity, far above the Law
itself. This truth ought to be set before us so
that we can be sure of this: We have a gracious
God because of Christ's satisfaction and not
because of our fulfilling the Law.

58 Paul teaches this in Galatians 3:13, when
[179] he says, "Christ redeemed us from the curse
of the law by becoming a curse for us." This
means that the Law condemns all people.
But Christ—without sin—has borne the
punishment of sin. He has been made a vic-
tim for us and has removed that right of the
Law to accuse and condemn those who be-
lieve in Him. He Himself is the Atonement
for them. For His sake they are now counted
righteous. Since they are counted righteous,
the Law cannot accuse or condemn them,
even though they have not actually satisfied
the Law. Paul writes the same way to the
Colossians, "You have been filled in Him"
(2:10). This is like saying, "Although you are
still far from the perfection of the Law, the
remnants of sin do not condemn you. For
Christ's sake we have a sure and firm recon-
ciliation, if you believe, even though sin
dwells in your flesh."

The promise should always be in sight. Be- 59
cause of His promise, God wishes to be gra- [180]
cious and to justify for Christ's sake, not be-
cause of the Law or our works. In this promise
timid consciences should seek reconciliation
and justification. By this promise they should
sustain themselves and be confident that they
have a gracious God for Christ's sake, because
of His promise. So works can never make a
conscience peaceful. Only the promise can. If 60
justification and peace of conscience must be [181]
sought in something other than love and
works, then love and works do not justify. This
is true even though they are virtues and be-
long to the righteousness of the Law, insofar as
they are a fulfilling of the Law. Obedience to
the Law justifies by the righteousness of the
Law—if a person fulfills it. But imperfect righ-
teousness of the Law is not accepted by God
unless it is accepted because of faith. So legal
righteousness does not justify, that is, it nei-
ther reconciles nor regenerates nor by itself
makes us acceptable before God.

From this it is clear that we are justified 61
before God through faith alone. Through [182]
faith alone we receive forgiveness of sins and
reconciliation, because reconciliation or jus-
tification is a matter promised for Christ's
sake, not for the Law's sake. Therefore, it is
received through faith alone, although, when
the Holy Spirit is given, the fulfilling of the
Law follows.

Reply to the Adversaries' Arguments

62 Now, when the grounds of this case have
[183] been understood (the distinction between
the Law and the promises, or the Gospel), it
will be easy to resolve the adversaries' objec-
tions. For they quote passages about the Law
and works and leave out passages about the
63 promises. But a final reply can be made to all
[184] opinions about the Law, namely, that the Law
cannot be kept without Christ, and that if
civil works are done without Christ, they do
not please God. Therefore, when works are
commended, it is necessary to add that faith
is required. They are commended because of
faith. They are the fruit and testimonies of
64 faith. Ambiguous and dangerous cases pro-
[185] duce many and various solutions. For the
judgment of the ancient poet is true:

> An unjust cause, being in itself sick,
> requires skillfully applied remedies.

In just and sure cases, one or two explana-
tions derived from the sources correct all
things that seem to offend. This happens also
in our case here. For the rule I have just quot-
ed explains all the passages that are quoted
65 about the Law and works. We acknowledge
[186] that Scripture teaches the Law in some places
and the Gospel in other places (i.e., the free
promise of forgiveness of sins for Christ's
sake). But our adversaries absolutely abolish
the free promise when they deny that faith
justifies and when they teach that we receive
forgiveness of sins and reconciliation be-
66 cause of love and our works. If forgiveness of
[187] sins depends on our works, it is completely
uncertain. The promise will be abolished.
67 Therefore, we tell godly minds to consider
[188] the promises, and we teach about free for-
giveness of sins and about reconciliation,
which happens through faith in Christ. Af-
terward, we add also the teaching of the Law.
It is necessary to distinguish these things
aright, as Paul says in 2 Timothy 2:15. We
must see what Scripture says about the Law
and what it says about the promises. For it
praises works in such a way that it does not
remove the free promise.

Good works are to be done because of 68
God's command and for the exercise of [189]
faith—confessing the faith and giving
thanks. Good works must be done for these
reasons. They are done in the flesh, which is
not as yet entirely renewed. The flesh hinders
the Holy Spirit's motives and adds some of
its uncleanness to the works. Yet, because of
Christ, they are holy, divine works, sacrifices,
and acts belonging to the rule of Christ, who
in this way displays His kingdom before this
world. For in these works He sanctifies hearts
and represses the devil. In order to retain the
Gospel among people, He openly sets the
confession of saints against the kingdom of
the devil and, in our weakness, declares His
power. Consider the dangers, labors, and ser- 69
mons of the apostle Paul, of Athanasius, Au- [190]
gustine, and the rest who taught the church-
es. These deeds are holy works and true
sacrifices acceptable to God. They are
Christ's battles [Colossians 2:15] through
which He repressed the devil and drove him
away from those who believed. David's 70
labors, in waging wars and in his home gov- [191]
ernment, are holy works, true sacrifices, and
battles fought by God. They defend the peo-
ple who had God's Word against the devil, in
order that the knowledge of God might not
be entirely extinguished on earth. We think 71
this way also about every good work in the [192]
humblest callings and in private affairs.
Through these works Christ celebrates His
victory over the devil, just as the distribution
of alms by the Corinthians (1 Corinthians
16:1) was a holy work, a sacrifice and battle
of Christ against the devil, who labors so that
nothing may be done to praise God. To 72

Christ Confronts Saul on the Road to Damascus

[193] demean such works (the confession of doc-
trine, sufferings, works of love, suppression
of the flesh) would be to demean the out-
ward rule of Christ's kingdom among people.
73 Here also we add something about rewards
[194] and merits. We teach that rewards have been
offered and promised for the works of be-
lievers. We teach that good works have merit,
not for forgiveness of sins, for grace, or for
justification (for these we receive only
through faith), but for other rewards, bodily
and spiritual, in this life and after this life. For
Paul says in 1 Corinthians 3:8, "Each will
receive his wages according to his labor."
74 There will be different rewards according to
[195] different labors. But forgiveness of sins is
given alike and equal to all people, just as
Christ is one, and is offered freely to all who
believe that for His sake their sins are forgiv-
en. Therefore, forgiveness of sins and justifi-
cation are received only through faith, not
because of any works. This is clear because of
the terrors of conscience, because none of
our works can turn away God's wrath, as
Paul clearly says in Romans 5:1, "Therefore,
since we have been justified by faith, we have
peace with God through our Lord Jesus
Christ. Through Him we have also obtained
access by faith." Because faith makes sons of
75 God, it also makes coheirs with Christ. Be-
[196] cause by our works we do not merit justifi-
cation, through which we are made sons of
God, and coheirs with Christ. We do not
merit eternal life by our works. Faith receives
it because faith justifies us and has a recon-
ciled God. But eternal life is due to the justi-
fied, according to the passage in Romans
8:30, "Those whom He justified He also glo-
76 rified." Paul (Ephesians 6:2) tells us the com-
[197] mandment about honoring parents, by
mentioning the reward added to that com-
mandment. He does not mean that obedi-
ence to parents justifies us before God. But
when obedience happens in those who have
been justified, it merits other great rewards.
God puts His saints to work in various ways 77
and often holds back the rewards of works- [198]
righteousness. He does this so that they may
learn not to trust in their own righteousness
and may learn to seek God's will rather than
the rewards. This can be seen with Job,
Christ, and other saints. And many psalms
teach us about this. They console us against
the happiness of the wicked, as Psalm 37:1
says, "Be not envious." Christ says in
Matthew 5:10, "Blessed are those who are
persecuted for righteousness' sake, for theirs
is the kingdom of heaven." By these praises of 78
good works, believers are undoubtedly [199]
moved to do good works. Meanwhile, the 79
teaching of repentance is also proclaimed [200]
against the godless, whose works are wicked.
God's wrath, which He has threatened
against all who do not repent, is displayed.
Therefore, we praise and require good 80
works and show many reasons why they [201]
ought to be done.

Paul also teaches this about works when
he says in Romans 4:9–25 that Abraham re-
ceived circumcision. He did not seek to be
justified by this work, for he had already at-
tained justification through faith. He was
counted righteous. But circumcision was
added so that (a) Abraham might have a
written sign in his body, (b) admonished by
this, he might exercise faith, and (c) by this
work he might also confess his faith before
others and, by his testimony, invite others to
believe. "By faith Abel offered to God a 81
more acceptable sacrifice" (Hebrews 11:4). [202]
Because he was just by faith, the sacrifice
that he made was pleasing to God. It is not
that he merited forgiveness of sins and grace
by this work, but he exercised his faith and
showed it to others, in order to invite them
to believe.

82 In this way good works ought to follow
[203] faith. Yet people who cannot believe and be
sure that they are freely forgiven for Christ's
sake, and that freely they have a reconciled
God for Christ's sake, use works in a far dif-
ferent way. When they see the works of
saints, they judge in a human way that
saints have merited forgiveness of sins and
grace through these works. So they imitate
them, thinking that through similar works
they merit forgiveness of sins and grace.
They think that through these works they
appease God's wrath and are counted righ-
83 teous for the sake of these works. We con-
[204] demn this godless opinion about works. In
the first place, it hides Christ's glory when
people offer to God these works as a price
and atonement. This honor, due to Christ
alone, is credited to our works. Second, they
do not find peace of conscience in these
works. In true terrors, heaping up works
upon works, they eventually despair be-
cause they find no work pure ‹important
and precious› enough. The Law always ac-
cuses and produces wrath. Third, such per-
sons never attain the knowledge of God. For
in anger they run from God, who judges
and afflicts them. They never believe that
84 they are heard. But faith shows God's pres-
[205] ence, since it is certain that God freely for-
gives and hears us.

85 Furthermore, this godless opinion about
[206] works always has existed in the world. The
heathen had sacrifices, derived from the fa-
thers. They imitated their works. They did
not maintain their faith, but thought that
the works were an atonement and price by
which God would be reconciled to them.
86 The people in the Law ‹the Israelites› imitat-
[207] ed sacrifices with the opinion that they
would appease God by means of these
works, so to say, *ex opere operato*. We see
here how seriously the prophets rebuke the
people: Psalm 50:8, "Not for your sacrifices
do I rebuke you," and Jeremiah 7:22, "I did
not speak to your fathers or command them
concerning burnt offerings and sacrifices."
Such passages do not condemn works, which
God certainly had commanded as outward
exercises in this government. They condemn
the godless opinion that people thought, that
by their works they appeased God's wrath,
and so cast away faith. Because no works ease 87
the conscience, new works, in addition to [208]
God's commands, were made up from time
to time. The people of Israel had seen the
prophets sacrificing on high places [e.g.,
1 Samuel 9:10–14, 19]. Besides, the examples
of the saints very greatly move the minds of
people who hope to obtain grace by similar
works just as these saints received it. There-
fore, the people began, with remarkable zeal,
to imitate their work, in order that by such a
work they might merit forgiveness of sins,
grace, and righteousness. But the prophets
had been sacrificing on high places, not so
that they might merit forgiveness of sins and
grace by these works, but because they taught
on these places. So they presented a testimo-
ny of their faith there. The people had heard 88
that Abraham had sacrificed his son [Genesis [209]
22]. Therefore, they also, in order to appease
God by a most cruel and difficult work, put
their sons to death [e.g., 2 Kings 16:3]. But
Abraham did not sacrifice his son with the
opinion that this work was a price and aton-
ing work by which he was counted righteous.
In a similar way, the Lord's Supper was insti- 89
tuted in the Church. So by remembering [210]
Christ's promises (about which we are taught
in this Sacrament), faith would be strength-
ened in us, and we would publicly confess
our faith and proclaim Christ's benefits, as
Paul says in 1 Corinthians 11:26, "For as
often as you eat this bread and drink the cup,
you proclaim the Lord's death until He

comes." But our adversaries contend that the
Mass is a work that justifies us by the out-
ward work (*ex opere operato*) and removes
the guilt and liability to punishment in those
for whom it is celebrated. That's what
Gabriel Biel writes.
90 Anthony, Bernard, Dominic, Francis,
[211] and other Holy Fathers selected a certain
kind of life either for the sake of study or
other useful exercises. In the meantime, they
believed that by faith they were counted
righteous for Christ's sake and that God was
gracious to them, not because of their own
exercises. But the multitude since then has
imitated not the faith of the Fathers, but
their example without faith. By such works
the multitude thought they might merit for-
giveness of sins, grace, and righteousness.
They did not believe that they received these
freely on account of Christ as the Atoning
91 Sacrifice. The world judges that all works are
[212] an atonement by which God is appeased.
They are a price by which we are counted
righteous. It does not believe that Christ is
the Atonement. It does not believe that
through faith we are freely counted righ-
teous for Christ's sake. Since works cannot
ease the conscience, other works are contin-
ually chosen, new rites are performed, new
vows are made, and new orders of monks
are formed beyond God's command, in
order that some great work may be sought
that may be set against God's wrath and
92 judgment. Contrary to Scripture, the adver-
[213] saries uphold these godless opinions about
works. They say these things about our
works: they are an atonement, they merit
forgiveness of sins and grace, and we are
counted righteous before God by them (and
not through faith, for Christ's sake as the
Atonement). What is this other than to deny
Christ the honor of Mediator and Atoning
93 Sacrifice? We believe and teach that good
works must be done (*fulfilling of the Law* [214]
ought to follow faith). Nevertheless, we give
Christ His own honor. We believe and teach
that through faith, for Christ's sake, we are
counted righteous before God. We are not
counted righteous because of works without
Christ as Mediator. We do not merit forgive-
ness of sins, grace, and righteousness by
works. We cannot set our works against
God's wrath and justice. Works cannot over-
come the terrors of sin. But the terrors of sin
are overcome through faith alone. Only
Christ the Mediator is to be presented by
faith against God's wrath and judgment. If 94
anyone thinks differently, he does not give [215]
Christ due honor. Christ has been set forth
so that He might be an Atonement, that
through Him we might have access to the
Father. We are speaking now about the righ- 95
teousness through which we approach God [216]
(not humans) but by which we receive grace
and peace of conscience. Conscience, how- 96
ever, cannot be eased before God, unless [217]
through faith alone. Faith is certain that
God for Christ's sake is reconciled to us, ac-
cording to Romans 5:1, "Therefore, since we
have been justified by faith, we have peace."
This is because justification is only a matter
freely promised for Christ's sake. Therefore,
it is always received before God through
faith alone.

[Passages the Adversaries Misuse]

Now we will reply to those passages that 97
the adversaries quote in order to prove that [218]
we are justified by love and works. From
1 Corinthians 13:2, they quote, "If I have all
faith . . . but have not love, I am nothing."
Here they triumph greatly. Paul testifies to
the entire Church (they say) that faith alone
does not justify. But a reply is easy after we 98
have shown above what we teach about love [219]
and works. This passage of Paul requires

love. We also require this. For we have said
above that renewal and beginning to fulfill
the Law must exist in us, according to Jere-
miah 31:33, "I will put My law within them,
and I will write it on their hearts." If anyone
should cast away love, even though he has
great faith, he does not keep his faith. For he
99 does not keep the Holy Spirit. Nor indeed
[220] does Paul in this passage talk about the way
of justification. Instead, he writes to those
who, after they had been justified, should be
urged to bring forth good fruit lest they lose
100 the Holy Spirit. Furthermore, the adversaries
[221] treat the matter in a ridiculous way. They
quote this one passage, in which Paul teaches
about fruit. Yet they leave out many other
passages in which he discusses the way of jus-
tification in a regular order. Besides, they al-
ways add a correction to the other passages
that speak of faith, namely, that the passages
ought to be understood as applying to "faith
formed by love." They add no correction that
there is also need for faith, which believes we
are counted righteous for Christ's sake as the
Atonement. So the adversaries exclude Christ
from justification and teach only a righ-
101 teousness of the Law. But let us return to
[222] Paul. No one can conclude anything more
from this text than this: love is necessary. We
confess this. It is also necessary not to steal.
But the reasoning will not be correct if some-
one would put the argument like this: "Not
to commit theft is necessary. Therefore, not
to commit theft justifies." Justification is not
the approval of a particular work, but of the
entire person. Therefore, this passage from
Paul does not harm us. Only, the adversaries
must not add to it whatever they please by
imagination. Paul does not say that love jus-
tifies. He says, "I am nothing" [1 Corinthians
13:2]. In other words, faith—however great it
may have been—is extinguished. He does not
say that love overcomes the terrors of sin and
of death, that we can set our love against
God's wrath and judgment, or that our love
satisfies God's Law. He does not say that we
have access to God by our love without
Christ as the Atoning Sacrifice, that we re-
ceive the promised forgiveness of sins by our
love. Paul says nothing about this. He does
not, therefore, think that love justifies, be-
cause we are justified only when we receive
Christ as the Atoning Sacrifice and believe
that for Christ's sake God is reconciled to us.
Neither is justification even to be dreamed of
without Christ as the Atonement. If there is 102
no need of Christ, if we can overcome death [223]
by our love, if we have access to God by our
love without Christ as the Atonement, then
let our adversaries remove the promise about
Christ. Let them abolish the Gospel. The ad- 103
versaries corrupt very many passages, be- [224]
cause they bring to them their own opinions
and do not derive the meaning from the pas-
sages themselves. For what difficulty is there
in this passage if we remove the interpreta-
tion that the adversaries attach to it out of
their own mind? They do not understand
what justification is or how it occurs. The
Corinthians, being justified before, had re-
ceived many excellent gifts. In the beginning,
they glowed with zeal, just as is generally the
case. Then dissensions began to arise among
them, as Paul points out. They began to dis-
like good teachers. So Paul rebuked them,
calling them back to offices of love. These are
necessary. Yet it would be foolish to imagine
that works of the Second Table (through
which we interact with humans and not
properly with God) justify us. But in justifi-
cation we interact with God. His wrath must
be appeased and conscience must be eased
about God. None of these happen through
the works of the Second Table.

But they object that love is preferred to 104
faith and hope. For Paul says in 1 Corinthians [225]

13:13, "The greatest of these is love." Now, it is reasonable that the greatest and chief virtue
105 should justify. Yet Paul, in this passage, prop-
[226] erly speaks about love toward one's neighbor
and indicates that love is the greatest, because it has the most fruit. Faith and hope have to do only with God. But love has infinite offices outwardly toward humanity. Indeed, let us grant to the adversaries that love toward God and our neighbor is the greatest virtue, because the chief commandment is this: "You shall love the Lord your God" (Matthew 22:37). But how will they conclude from this
106 that love justifies? They say, "The greatest
[227] virtue justifies." By no means! For just as the
greatest, or first, Law does not justify, so also the Law's greatest virtue does not justify. But the virtue that justifies receives Christ, which brings to us Christ's merits, by which we receive grace and peace from God. This virtue is faith. As it has often been said, faith is not just knowledge. But it is willing to receive or take hold of those things that are offered in the
107 promise about Christ. Furthermore, this obe-
[228] dience toward God (i.e., to want to receive the
offered promise) is no less a divine service (*latreia*) than is love. God wants us to believe Him and to receive from Him blessings. He declares this to be true divine service.

108 The adversaries base justification on love
[229] because they everywhere teach and require
the righteousness of the Law. We cannot deny that love is the Law's highest work. Human wisdom gazes at the Law and seeks justification in it. So the scholastic doctors, great and talented men, proclaim love as the Law's highest work and base justification on this work. Deceived by human wisdom, they did not look upon the uncovered, but upon the veiled face of Moses, just like the Pharisees, philosophers, and followers of Muham-
109 mad. But we preach the foolishness of the
[230] Gospel, in which another righteousness is re-
vealed: for Christ's sake as the Atonement, we are counted righteous when we believe that God has been reconciled to us for Christ's sake. Neither are we ignorant about how far distant this teaching is from the judgment of reason and the Law. Nor are we ignorant that the Law's teaching about love makes a much greater show. For it is wisdom. But we are not ashamed of the Gospel's foolishness. We defend this truth for the sake of Christ's glory and ask Christ, by His Holy Spirit, to help us so that we may be able to make this clear and obvious.

The adversaries, in the Confutation, have 110
also quoted Colossians 3:14 against us, "love, [231]
which binds everything together in perfect harmony." From this they conclude that love justifies because it makes people perfect. Although a reply about perfection could be made here in many ways, we will simply recite Paul's meaning. It is certain that Paul spoke about love toward one's neighbor. We must not think that Paul would credit either justification or perfection to the works of the Second Table, rather than to the works of the First. If love makes people perfect, there will then be no need of Christ as the Atonement (for faith receives Christ as the only Atonement). This is far distant from Paul's meaning, who never allows Christ to be excluded
as the Atonement. Therefore, he speaks not 111
about personal perfection, but about the in- [232]
tegrity common to the Church. For this reason, he says that love is a bond or connection to show that he speaks about the binding and joining together of the many members of the Church. In all families and in all states unity should be nourished by mutual offices, and peace cannot be maintained unless people overlook and forgive certain mistakes among themselves. In a similar way, Paul commands that there should be love in the Church in order that it may preserve unity, bear with

the harsher manners of brethren as there is need, and overlook certain less serious mistakes. This must happen or else the Church will fly apart into various schisms, and hostilities and factions and heresies will arise from the schisms.

112 Unity cannot last (is necessarily dis-
[233] solved) whenever the bishops impose heavier burdens upon the people, or when they have no respect for weakness in the people. Dissensions arise when the people judge too severely the conduct of teachers or despise the teachers because of certain less serious faults. For then, another kind of teaching and other
113 teachers are sought after. On the other hand,
[234] perfection (i.e., the Church's integrity) is preserved when the strong bear with the weak, when the people put up with some faults in the conduct of their teachers, and when the bishops make some allowances for the peo-
114 ple's weakness. The books of all the wise are
[235] full of these teachings about fairness, namely, that in everyday life we should make many allowances mutually for the sake of common peace. Paul teaches about this frequently both here and elsewhere. Therefore, the adversaries do not argue carefully from the term *perfection* that love justifies. For Paul speaks of common integrity and peace. Ambrose interprets this passage in this way, "Just as a building is said to be perfect or entire when all its parts are fitly joined together
115 with one another." Furthermore, it is dis-
[236] graceful for the adversaries to preach so much about love while they don't show it anywhere. What are they doing now? They are tearing apart churches. They are writing laws in blood and asking the most merciful prince, the emperor, to enforce them. They are killing priests and other good men if any one of them has slightly indicated that he does not entirely approve of their clear abuses. What they are doing is not consistent with their claims of love, which if the adversaries would follow, the churches would be peaceful and the state would have peace. This turmoil would be lessened if the adversaries would stop being so bitter about certain traditions. These traditions are useless for godliness and are hardly observed by those very persons who most earnestly defend them. The adversaries easily forgive themselves, but do not likewise forgive others according to the passage in the poet, " 'I forgive myself,' Maevius said." But what they do is very far 116
from those praises of love that they recite [237]
here from Paul. They do not understand the word any more than the walls of a building that echo it back. They cite also this sentence 117
from Peter, "Love covers a multitude of sins" [238]
(1 Peter 4:8). Peter also speaks of love toward one's neighbor because he joins this passage to the rule that commands love for one another. No apostle would have imagined (a) our love overcomes sin and death, (b) love satisfies God's wrath and reconciles us to God, while excluding Christ as Mediator, and (c) love in and of itself is righteousness before God without Christ as Mediator. For this love, if such a thing could exist, would be a righteousness of the Law, not of the Gospel. The Gospel promises reconciliation and righteousness to us if we believe that, for the sake of Christ as Reconciler, the Father has been reconciled, and that Christ's merits are given to us. Peter urges us, a little before, to 118
come to Christ that we may be built upon [239]
Him. He adds in 1 Peter 2:6, "Whoever believes in Him will not be put to shame." When God judges and convicts us, our love does not free us from confusion. But faith in Christ frees us from these fears because we know that for Christ's sake we are forgiven.

Besides, this sentence about love is taken 119
from Proverbs 10:12, where the complete [240]
opposite clearly shows how love ought to be

understood, "Hatred stirs up strife, but love
120 covers all offenses." This verse teaches pre-
[241] cisely the same thing as Paul does in Colos-
sians: if any dissensions would occur, they
should be moderated and settled by our fair
and patient conduct. Dissensions, it says, in-
crease by means of hatred. We often see that
tragedies arise from the most trifling offens-
es. Certain petty offenses occurred between
Gaius Caesar and Pompey. If one had yield-
ed a very little to the other, civil war would
not have arisen. But while each gave in to his
own hatred, the greatest commotions arose
121 from a matter of no importance. Many here-
[242] sies have also arisen in the Church only from
the hatred of the teachers. Therefore, this
verse does not refer to a person's own faults,
but to the faults of others. When it says that
"love covers a multitude of sins," it means
those of others. Even though these offenses
occur, love overlooks, forgives, and yields to
them, not carrying all things to the extremi-
ty of justice. Peter, therefore, does not mean
that love merits the forgiveness of sins in
God's sight or that it is an atoning sacrifice
excluding Christ as Mediator. He also does
not mean that such love regenerates and jus-
tifies, but that it is not gloomy, harsh, and
uncooperative toward people. It overlooks
the mistakes of its friends, while it deplores
the harsher manners of others. A well-
known saying puts it this way: *Know, but do*
122 *not hate, the manners of a friend*. Nor did the
[243] apostle thoughtlessly teach so often about
this office what the philosophers call lenien-
cy (*epieikeia*). For this virtue is necessary for
keeping public harmony ‹in the Church and
the civil government›. Harmony in the
Church cannot last unless pastors and
churches mutually overlook and pardon
many things.

123 From James 2:24, they cite, "You see that a
[244] person is justified by works and not by faith
alone." No other passage is supposed to be
more contrary to our belief. But the reply is
easy and plain. If the adversaries do not at-
tach their own opinions about the merits of
works, the words of James have in them
nothing that is unhelpful to us. But wherever
there is mention of works, the adversaries
add their own false, godless opinions. They
say we merit the forgiveness of sins by means
of good works, that good works are a satis-
faction and price on account of which God is
reconciled to us, and that good works over-
come the terrors of sin and of death. They
also say that good works are accepted in
God's sight on account of their goodness,
and that they do not need mercy and Christ
as Reconciler. None of these things came into
James's mind. Yet, the adversaries defend
such teachings like this passage of James as
an excuse.

First, we must consider that the passage is 124
more against the adversaries than against us. [245]
For the adversaries teach that a person is jus-
tified by love and works. They say nothing
about faith, by which we receive Christ as
Reconciler. In fact, they condemn this faith,
not only in sentences and writings, but also
by the sword and capital punishment. They
endeavor to exterminate it in the Church.
James teaches much better. He does not leave
out faith, or present love in preference to
faith, but retains faith, so that in justification
Christ may not be excluded as Reconciler!
When Paul forms a summary of the Chris-
tian life, he also includes faith and love in
1 Timothy 1:5, "The aim of our charge is love
that issues from a pure heart and a good con-
science and a sincere faith."

Second, the subject matter itself shows 125
that the works spoken of here follow faith [246]
and that such faith is not dead, but living
and effective in the heart. James did not be-
lieve that we earn the forgiveness of sins and

grace by good works. After all, he is talking about the works of those who have been justified, who have already been reconciled and accepted, and who have received forgiveness of sins. Therefore, the adversaries err when they conclude that James teaches that we merit forgiveness of sins and grace by good works and that we have access to God by our works, apart from Christ as Reconciler.

126 Third, James said a little earlier that re-
[247] generation happens through the Gospel. For he says in James 1:18, "Of His own will He brought us forth by the word of truth, that we should be a kind of firstfruits of His creatures." When James says that we have been reborn by the Gospel, he teaches that we have been born again and justified through faith. For the promise about Christ is grasped only through faith when we set it against the terrors of sin and of death. James does not, therefore, think that we are born again through our works.

127 From these things it is clear that James
[248] does not contradict us. He criticized lazy and secure minds that imagine they have faith, although they do not have it. He made a dis-
128 tinction between dead and living faith. He
[249] says that faith that does not bring forth good works is dead. He also says that a living faith brings forth good works. Furthermore, we have shown already several times what we mean by faith. For we do not mean passive knowledge, such as devils have. Instead, we mean faith that resists the terrors of conscience and encourages and comforts terri-
129 fied hearts. Such faith is not an easy matter,
[250] as the adversaries dream. Neither is it a human power, but it is a divine power. Through faith we are reborn and overcome the devil and death. Paul says to the Colossians that faith is powerful through the power of God and overcomes death, "In which you were also raised with Him through faith in the powerful working of God" (2:12). Since this faith is a new life, it necessarily produces new movements and works. So James is right in denying that we are justified by such a faith that is without
works. But when he says that we are justified 130
by faith and works, he certainly does not say [251]
that we are born again by works. Neither does he say that Christ is our Reconciler only partly, and our works are our atoning sacrifice in part. Nor does he describe the way of justification, but only the nature of the just, after they have already been justified and re-
generated. Here "to be justified" does not 131
mean that a righteous person is made from a [252]
wicked person. It means to be pronounced righteous in a judicial sense, as in Romans 2:13, "For it is not the hearers of the law who are righteous before God, but the doers of the law who will be justified." These words "doers of the law who will be justified" contain nothing contrary to our doctrine. We, too, believe about James's words, "A person is justified by works and not by faith alone" (2:24) because people are certainly pronounced righteous having faith and good works. As we have said, the saints' good works are righteous and please God because of faith. For James praises only works produced by faith, as he testifies when he says of Abraham, "Faith was completed by his works" (2:22). "Doers of the law who will be justified," namely, those who believe God from the heart are pronounced righteous. Afterward, they have good fruit, which please Him because of faith. So they are the fulfill-
ment of the Law. These things, simply put, 132
contain nothing incorrect. However, they are [253]
distorted by the adversaries, who attach to them godless opinions made in their mind. For it does not follow that (a) works earn the forgiveness of sins, (b) works regenerate

hearts, (c) works are an atoning sacrifice, (d) works please without Christ as the Atoning Sacrifice, and (e) works do not need Christ as the Atoning Sacrifice. James says nothing about these things. Yet, the adversaries shamelessly conclude such things from James's words.

133 Certain other passages about works are
[254] also cited against us.

> Forgive, and you will be forgiven. (Luke 6:37)
>
> Is it not to share your bread with the hungry? . . . Then you shall call, and the LORD will answer. (Isaiah 58:7, 9)
>
> Break off your sins . . . by showing mercy to the oppressed. (Daniel 4:27)
>
> Blessed are the poor in spirit, for theirs is the kingdom of heaven. (Matthew 5:3)
>
> 134 Blessed are the merciful, for they shall
> [255] receive mercy. (Matthew 5:7)

Even these passages would contain nothing contrary to us if the adversaries would not falsely attach something to them. For they contain two things. One is a preaching either of the Law or of repentance. This preaching not only convicts those doing wrong, but also commands them to do what is right. The other is a promise that is added. But it is not said that sins are forgiven without faith, or that works themselves are an atoning sacri-
135 fice. Furthermore, these two things should
[256] always be understood in the preaching of the
Law. First, the Law cannot be obeyed unless we have been reborn through faith in Christ, just as Christ says in John 15:5, "Apart from Me you can do nothing." Second, some outward works can certainly be done. But this general judgment, which interprets the whole Law, must be retained. "Without faith it is impossible to please [God]" (Hebrews 11:6). The Gospel must also be retained, that through Christ we have access to the Father.
(See Hebrews 10:19; Romans 5:2.) For it is 136
clear that we are not justified by the Law. [257]
Otherwise, why would we need Christ or the Gospel, if the preaching of the Law alone would be enough? So, in the preaching of repentance, it is not enough to preach the Law, or the Word that convicts of sin. The Law works wrath and only accuses. The Law terrifies consciences, because consciences never are at rest unless they hear God's voice clearly promising the forgiveness of sins. So the Gospel must be added, that for Christ's sake sins are forgiven and that we obtain the forgiveness of sins by faith in Christ. If the adversaries exclude Christ's Gospel from the preaching of repentance, they are rightly judged blasphemers against Christ.

Isaiah preaches repentance as follows: 137

> Cease to do evil, learn to do good; [258]
> seek justice, correct oppression; bring justice to the fatherless, plead the widow's cause. "Come now, let us reason together, says the Lord: though your sins are like scarlet, they shall be as white as snow." (Isaiah 1:16–18)

So the prophet both urges repentance and adds the promise. But in such a sentence it would be foolish to consider only the words "correct oppression; bring justice to the fatherless." For he says in the beginning, "Cease to do evil," where he criticizes impiety of heart and requires faith. Also, the prophet does not say that through the works "correct oppression; bring justice to the fatherless," they can merit the forgiveness of sins by the outward act (*ex opere operato*), but he insists that such works are necessary in the new life. At the same time, he means that the forgiveness of sins is received through faith. So the
promise is added. We must understand all 138
similar passages in this way. Christ preaches [259]
repentance when He says, "Forgive," and He

adds the promise, "and you will be forgiven" (Luke 6:37). He does not say that when we forgive we merit the forgiveness of sins by our outward act (*ex opere operato*) as they term it. But He requires a new life, which certainly is necessary. At the same time, He means that forgiveness of sins is received through faith. So when Isaiah says, "Share your bread with the hungry" (58:7), he requires a new life. Nor does the prophet speak of this work alone, but, as the text shows, of the entire repentance. At the same time, he means that the forgiveness of sins is received
139 through faith. For the following is sure, and
[260] none of the gates of hell can overthrow it: the
preaching of the Law is not enough in the preaching of repentance. This is true because the Law works wrath and always accuses. But the preaching of the Gospel should be added so that forgiveness of sins is granted us. Our sins are forgiven if we believe that our sins are forgiven for Christ's sake. Otherwise, why would we need the Gospel? Why would we need Christ? This belief should always be in view so that it may oppose those who cast Christ and the Gospel aside and wickedly distort the Scriptures to human opinions, such as the idea that we purchase the forgiveness of sins by our works.

140 Faith is required also in the sermon of
[261] Daniel (4:24[–27]). For Daniel did not mean
that the king should only give alms. He includes repentance when he says, "Break off your . . . iniquities by showing mercy to the oppressed" [4:27]. This means, break off your sins by a change of heart and works. Here also, faith is required. Daniel proclaims to him many things about the worship of the only God, the God of Israel. He converts the king not only to give alms, but much more, to have faith. For we have the excellent confession of the king about the God of Israel, "There is no other god who is able to rescue in this way" (Daniel 3:29). Therefore, in Daniel's sermon there are two parts. One part gives a commandment about the new life and the works of the new life. In the other part, Daniel promises the forgiveness of sins to the king. This promise of the forgiveness of sins is not a preaching of the Law, but a truly prophetic and evangelical voice. Daniel certainly meant that the promise should be
received in faith. For Daniel knew that the 141
forgiveness of sins in Christ was promised [262]
not only to the Israelites, but also to all nations. Otherwise, he could not have promised to the king the forgiveness of sins. For without God's sure Word about His will, a person has no power to claim, especially when terrified by sin, that God ceases to be angry. In his own language, Daniel speaks clearly about repentance and even more clearly brings out the promise, "Break off your sins by practicing righteousness, and your iniquities by showing mercy to the oppressed" [4:27]. These words teach about all of repentance. They direct the king to become righteous, then to do good works, to defend the miserable against injustice, as was the king's duty.
Righteousness is faith in the heart. Further- 142
more, sins are redeemed by repentance. In [263]
other words, the obligation or guilt is removed because God forgives those who repent, as it is written in Ezekiel 18:21–22. Nor are we to conclude from this that He forgives on account of works that follow, on account of alms. Rather, He forgives only those who take hold of it on account of His promise. Only those who truly believe take hold of this promise, and through faith overcome sin and death. These, being reborn, should produce fruit worthy of repentance, just as John the Baptist says. (See Matthew 3:8.) The promise, therefore, was added, "There may perhaps be a lengthening of your prosperity" (Daniel
4:27). Jerome expresses some doubt here, 143

[264] which is beside the matter. In his commentaries he argues much more unwisely that the forgiveness of sins is uncertain. But let us remember that the Gospel gives a sure promise of the forgiveness of sins. To deny that there must be a sure promise of the forgiveness of sins would completely abolish the Gospel. Let us dismiss Jerome concerning this passage. The promise is displayed even in the words “Break off,” for it shows that the forgiveness of sins is possible, that sins can be redeemed, that is, that their obligation or guilt can be removed or God’s anger can be appeased. But our adversaries, overlooking the promises everywhere, consider only the laws. They falsely attach the human opinion that forgiveness happens on account of works. The text does not say this, but instead requires faith. For wherever a promise is, there faith is required. For a promise cannot be received unless through faith.

144 Works are recognizable among human
[265] beings. Human reason naturally admires
works. Reason sees only works and does not
understand or consider faith. Therefore, it
dreams that these works merit forgiveness of
sins and justify. This opinion of the Law naturally sticks in people’s minds. It cannot be
driven out, unless we are divinely taught.
145 The mind must be recalled from such earth-
[266] ly opinions to God’s Word. We see that the
Gospel and the promise about Christ have
been laid before us. When, therefore, the Law
is preached, when works are commanded, we
should not reject the promise about Christ.
But the promise must first be grasped, in
order that we may be able to produce good
works pleasing to God, as Christ says, “Apart
from Me you can do nothing” (John 15:5).
Therefore, if Daniel would have used words
like these, “Redeem your sins by repentance,”
the adversaries would not have noticed this
passage. Since Daniel has actually expressed
this thought in other words, the adversaries
distort his words to the harm of the doctrine
of grace and faith. However, Daniel meant
his words most especially to include faith.
Therefore, we respond to the words of Daniel 146
as follows: Since he is preaching repentance, [267]
he is teaching not only about works, but also
about faith, as the story itself testifies in the
context. Second, because Daniel clearly presents the promise, he necessarily requires
faith, which believes that sins are freely forgiven by God. In repentance he mentions
works. Yet he does not say that we merit the
forgiveness of sins by these works. Daniel
speaks not only about the forgiveness of the
punishment, for forgiveness of the punishment is sought in vain unless the heart first
receives the forgiveness of guilt. Besides, if 147
the adversaries understand Daniel as speak- [268]
ing only about the forgiveness of punishment, this passage will prove nothing against
us. It will then become necessary for them
also to confess that the forgiveness of sin and
free justification come before good works.
Afterward, even we concede that the punishments by which we are chastised are soothed.
This happens by our prayers, by our good
works, and finally by our entire repentance,
according to 1 Corinthians 11:31, “But if we
judged ourselves truly, we would not be
judged.”

> If you return, I will restore you. (Jeremiah 15:19)
>
> Return to Me, says the LORD of hosts, and I will return to you, says the LORD of hosts. (Zechariah 1:3)
>
> Call upon Me in the day of trouble. (Psalm 50:15)

Therefore, in all our praising of works and 148
in the preaching of the Law, let us keep this [269]
rule: the Law is not kept without Christ. As
He Himself has said, “Apart from Me you can

do nothing" [John 15:5]. Likewise, "Without faith it is impossible to please [God]" (Hebrews 11:6). For it is very certain that the doctrine of the Law is not intended to remove the Gospel and to remove Christ as the Atoning Sacrifice. Let the Pharisees, our adversaries, be cursed. They interpret the Law to assign Christ's glory to works. (In other words, they say works are an atoning sacrifice, that they merit the forgiveness of sins.) Works are always rightly praised in this way: they are pleasing because of faith. For works do not please without Christ as the Atoning Sacrifice. "Through Him we have also obtained access [to God]" (Romans 5:2), not by works with-
149 out Christ as Mediator. Therefore, when it is
[270] said in Matthew 19:17, "If you would enter
life, keep the commandments," we must believe that without Christ the commandments are not kept and cannot please. So in the Decalogue itself, in the First Commandment, the most liberal promise of the Law is added, "But showing steadfast love to thousands of those who love Me and keep My commandments" (Exodus 20:6). But this Law is not kept without Christ. For it always accuses the conscience that does not satisfy the Law. Therefore, the conscience flies in terror from the Law's judgment and punishment. For the Law works anger (Romans 4:15). A person keeps the Law when he hears that for Christ's sake God is reconciled to us, even though we cannot satisfy the Law. When Christ is apprehended as Mediator through this faith, the heart finds rest and begins to love God and to keep the Law. It knows that now, because of Christ as Mediator, it is pleasing to God, even though the incomplete fulfilling of the Law is
150 far from perfection and is very impure. We
[271] must conclude this about the preaching of re-
pentance. For although the Scholastics have said nothing at all about faith in the doctrine of repentance, yet we think that none of our adversaries is so mad as to deny that Absolution is a voice of the Gospel. And Absolution ought to be received through faith, in order that it may comfort the terrified conscience.

The doctrine of repentance—because it 151
not only commands new works, but also [272]
promises the forgiveness of sins—necessarily requires faith. The forgiveness of sins is not received unless through faith. Therefore, in those passages that refer to repentance, we should always understand that not only works, but also faith is required. For example, Matthew 6:14 says, "For if you forgive others their trespasses, your heavenly Father will also forgive you." Here a work is required, and the promise of the forgiveness of sins is added. This does not happen because of the work,
but through faith, because of Christ. Just as 152
Scripture testifies in many passages: [273]

> To Him all the prophets bear witness that everyone who believes in Him receives forgiveness of sins through His name. (Acts 10:43)
>
> Your sins are forgiven for His name's sake. (1 John 2:12)
>
> We have redemption through His blood, the forgiveness of our trespasses. (Ephesians 1:7)

What need is there to recite testimonies? 153
This is the very voice unique to the Gospel, [274]
namely, that for Christ's sake, and not for the sake of our works, we obtain the forgiveness of sins through faith. Our adversaries work to suppress this voice of the Gospel by means of distorted passages, which contain the doctrine of the Law or of works. It is true that in the doctrine of repentance works are required, because certainly a new life is required. But here the adversaries wrongly add that by such works we merit the forgiveness
of sins, or justification. Christ often connects 154
the promise of the forgiveness of sins to good [275]

works, yet not because He means that good works are an atoning sacrifice (for they follow reconciliation). Christ makes this connection for two reasons. One is because good fruit must necessarily follow. He reminds us that if good fruit do not follow, the repentance is hypocritical and fake. The other reason is that we have need of outward signs of so great a promise. A conscience full of fear
155 has need of much consolation. Baptism and
[276] the Lord's Supper are signs that continually remind, cheer, and encourage despairing minds to believe more firmly that their sins are forgiven. So the same promise is written and portrayed in good works, in order that these works may remind us to believe more firmly. Those who produce no good works do not encourage themselves to believe, but despise these promises. On the other hand, the godly embrace them and rejoice that they have the signs and testimonies of so great a promise. So they exercise themselves in these signs and testimonies. Therefore, just as the Lord's Supper does not justify us by the outward act (*ex opere operato*) without faith, so alms do not justify us by the outward act (*ex opere operato*) without faith.

156 The address of Tobit 4:11 ought to be re-
[277] ceived this way also, "Alms free from every sin and from death." We will not say that this is an exaggeration, although we should see it that way so that we do not detract from the praise of Christ, whose right it is to free from sin and death. But we must come back to the rule that without Christ, the doctrine of the
157 Law is of no profit. Therefore, those alms
[278] please God that follow reconciliation or justification, and not those that come before. They do not free from sin and death by the outward act (*ex opere operato*). As we have said above about repentance, we ought to embrace faith and its fruit. So here we must say about alms that this entire newness of life saves. Alms also are the exercises of faith, which receives the forgiveness of sins and overcomes death, while it exercises itself more and more, and in these exercises receives strength. We grant also this, that alms merit many favors from God, lessen punishments, and merit our defense in the dangers of sins and of death, as we have said a little before about the entire repentance. Tobit's 158
address, regarded as a whole, shows that faith [279]
is required before alms, "Be mindful of the Lord, your God, all your days" [4:5]. Afterward, "Bless the Lord, your God, always, and desire of Him that your ways be directed by Him" [4:19]. This, however, belongs properly to that faith, which believes that God is reconciled to it because of His mercy, and which wishes to be justified, sanctified, and governed by God. But our adversaries, 159
charming men, pick out mutilated sentences [280]
in order to deceive those who are unskilled. Afterward, they attach something from their own opinions. Therefore, entire passages are to be required. According to the common rule it is inappropriate, before the entire Law is thoroughly examined, to judge or reply when any single clause of it is presented. When produced in their entirety, passages very frequently bring the interpretation with them.

Luke 11:41 is also cited in a mutilated 160
form, namely, "But give as alms those things [281]
that are within, and behold, everything is clean for you." The adversaries are very stupid. Time and again we have said that the Gospel about Christ should be added to the preaching of the Law. Because of Christ, good works are pleasing. But our adversaries teach everywhere that, Christ being excluded, justification is merited by the works of the Law. When this passage is produced unmuti- 161
lated, it will show that faith is required. [282]
Christ rebukes the Pharisees, who think that they are cleansed before God (that is, that

The Golden Calf

Moses appears in this woodcut with horns on his head. (And also on pp. 85, 553, and 562.) Why? In Exodus 34:29–30, we read that after Moses received the Ten Commandments, his face "shone" or, literally, in the original Hebrew, it "sent forth beams of light." When the Latin translation was made in the fourth century, the word *beams* was incorrectly translated as *horns*, and thus it was that art from that point forward showed Moses with horns.

they are justified) by frequent bathings. This is just as some pope or other who says that holy water "sanctifies and cleanses the people," and the gloss says that it cleanses "from venial" sins. Such also were the opinions of the Pharisees that Christ rebuked. Against this phony cleansing He sets up a double cleanness: one inward, the other outward. He bids them be cleansed inwardly and adds concerning the outward cleanness: "But give as alms those things that are within, and
162 behold, everything is clean for you." The ad-
[283] versaries do not rightly apply the phrase "everything," for Christ adds this conclusion to both parts: "All things will be clean unto you, if you will be clean within, and will outwardly give alms." He shows that outward cleanness is to be connected to works commanded by God, and not to human traditions. These traditions were the bathings held at that time, like the daily sprinkling of water. (The clothing of monks, the distinctions of food, and similar pompous acts appear this way to us now.) But the adversaries distort the meaning by transferring the universal phrase to only one part like Sophists: "All things will be clean to those having given
163 alms." Yet Peter says in Acts 15:9, "having
[284] cleansed their hearts by faith." When this entire passage is examined, it presents a meaning harmonizing with the rest of Scripture. If the hearts are cleansed and then outwardly alms are added (i.e., all the works of love), they are entirely clean (i.e., not only within, but also without). Why is not Christ's entire speech added to it? There are many parts of the rebuke, some of which give commandments about faith and others about works. It is not the place of an honest reader to pick out the commands about works, while the passages about faith are skipped.

164 Last, readers are to be reminded of this:
[285] the adversaries give the worst advice to godly consciences when they teach that the forgiveness of sins is earned by works. Conscience, in seeking forgiveness through works, cannot be confident that the work will satisfy God. It is always tormented, and continually invents other works and other acts of worship, until it completely despairs. This course is described by Paul in Romans 4:5. There he proves that the promise of righteousness is not obtained because of our works. We could never affirm that we had a reconciled God, for the Law always accuses. So the promise would be in vain and uncertain. He concludes that this promise of the forgiveness of sins and of righteousness is received through faith, not because of works. This is Paul's true, simple, and genuine meaning. In it the greatest consolation is offered to godly consciences, and Christ's glory is shown forth. He certainly was given to us for this purpose, namely, that through Him we might have grace, righteousness, and peace.

So far we have reviewed the chief passages 165
that the adversaries cite against us. They [286]
point to these passages to try to show that faith does not justify, and that we merit the forgiveness of sins and grace by our works. But we hope that we have shown clearly enough to godly consciences that (a) these passages are not opposed to our doctrine; (b) the adversaries wickedly distort the Scripture to their opinions; (c) most of the passages that they cite have been garbled; (d) while leaving out the clearest passages about faith, they only select from the Scripture passages about works, and even these they distort; (e) everywhere they add certain human opinions to what the words of Scripture say; (f) they teach the Law in such a way as to sup-
press the Gospel about Christ. The entire 166
doctrine of the adversaries is, in part, derived [287]
from human reason. In part, it is a doctrine of the Law, not of the Gospel. For they teach

two ways of justification: one derived from reason, and the other derived from the Law, not from the Gospel, or the promise about Christ.

[The Adversaries' Teaching Based on Reason and the Law]

167
[288] The former way of justification they teach is that people merit grace by good works both in a merely agreeable way (*de congruo*) and in a wholly deserving way (*de condigno*). This way is a doctrine of reason. For reason, not seeing the uncleanness of the heart, thinks that it pleases God if it performs good works. Therefore, other works and other acts of worship are constantly invented by people in great peril, to defend against the terrors of conscience. The pagans and the Israelites slew human victims and undertook many other most painful works in order to appease God's anger. Afterward, orders of monks were invented, and these challenged each other in the severity of their observances against the terrors of conscience and God's anger. This way of justification (because it is according to reason and is completely occupied with outward works) can be understood and be done to a certain extent. To this end the canon lawyers have distorted the misunderstood Church ordinances, which were enacted by the Fathers for a far different purpose. The Fathers did not intend that we follow the ordinances in order to seek after righteousness, but they were given for the sake of mutual peace among people, so there might be a certain order in the Church. In this way, the canon lawyers also distorted the Sacraments, and most especially the Mass. Through them they seek righteousness, grace, and salvation by the outward act.

168
[289] Another way of justification is handed down by the scholastic theologians when they teach that we are righteous through a habit infused by God, which is love. They say that, aided by this habit, we keep God's Law outwardly and inwardly, and that this fulfilling of the Law is worthy of grace and of eternal life. This doctrine is plainly the doctrine of the Law. For what the Law says is true, "You shall love the LORD your God" (Deuteronomy 6:5). Also, "You shall love your neighbor" (Leviticus 19:18). Love is, therefore, the fulfilling of the Law.

But it is easy for a Christian to judge 169
about both of these ways [of justification] [290]
because both exclude Christ. They are, therefore, to be rejected. In the former, which teaches that our works are an atoning sacrifice for sin, the impiety is clear. The latter way contains much that is harmful. It does not teach that, when we are born again, we make use of Christ. It does not teach that justification is the forgiveness of sins. It does not teach that we attain the forgiveness of sins before we love, but falsely represents that we rouse in ourselves the act of love, through which we merit the forgiveness of sins. Nor does it teach that we overcome the terrors of sin and death through faith in Christ. It falsely claims that, by their own fulfilling of the Law, without Christ as the Atoning Sacrifice, people come to God. Finally, it claims that this very fulfilling of the Law, without Christ as the Atoning Sacrifice, is righteousness worthy of grace and eternal life. Nevertheless, scarcely a weak and feeble fulfilling of the Law happens even in saints.

Truly, if anyone will think about it, he will 170
most easily understand that the Gospel has [291]
not been given in vain to the world, and that Christ has not been promised and set forth, has not been born, has not suffered, has not risen again in vain. He will most easily understand that we are justified not by reason or by the Law. Therefore, in regard to justification, we are compelled to disagree with the

adversaries. For the Gospel shows another
way. The Gospel compels us to make use of
Christ in justification. The Gospel teaches
that through Christ we have access to God
through faith. It teaches that we ought to set
Him as Mediator and Atoning Sacrifice
against God's anger. The Gospel teaches that
through faith in Christ the forgiveness of sins
and reconciliation are received, and the ter-
171 rors of sin and of death are overcome. Paul
[292] also says that righteousness is not of the Law,
but of the promise. The Father has promised
that He wants to forgive, that for Christ's sake
He wants to be reconciled. This promise,
however, is received through faith alone, as
Paul testifies in Romans 4:13. This faith alone
receives the forgiveness of sins, justifies, and
regenerates. Then love and other good fruit
follow. Therefore, we teach that a person is
justified (as we have said above) when con-
science, terrified by the preaching of repen-
tance, is cheered and believes that for Christ's
sake it has a reconciled God. "Faith is count-
ed as righteousness [before God]" (Romans
172 4:3, 5). When the heart is cheered and quick-
[293] ened through faith in this way, it receives the
Holy Spirit. He renews us, so that we are able
to keep the Law, to love God and God's
Word, to be submissive to God in afflictions,
to be chaste, to love our neighbor, and so on.
Even though these works are far from the
perfection of the Law, on account of faith
they please God. Through faith we are ac-
counted righteous, because we believe that
for Christ's sake we have a reconciled God.
These things are plain and in harmony with
the Gospel and can be understood by per-
173 sons of sound mind. From this foundation it
[294] can easily be decided why we attribute justi-
fication to faith, and not to love. Love follows
faith, because love is the fulfilling of the Law
[Romans 13:10]. But Paul teaches that we are
justified not from the Law, but from the
promise, which is received only through
faith. We neither come to God without
Christ as Mediator, nor receive the forgive-
ness of sins for the sake of our love, but for
the sake of Christ. Likewise, we are not able 174
to love God while He is angry, and the Law [295]
always accuses us, always presents an angry
God to us. Therefore, we must first take the
promise through faith that for Christ's sake
the Father is reconciled and forgives. After- 175
ward, we begin to keep the Law. Our eyes are [296]
to be cast—far away from human reason, far
away from Moses—upon Christ. We are to
believe that Christ is given to us, in order that
for His sake we may be counted righteous. In
the flesh we never satisfy the Law. Therefore, 176
we are counted righteous, not because of the [297]
Law, but because of Christ. His merits are
granted us, if we believe on Him. We are not
justified by the Law, because human nature
cannot keep God's Law and cannot love God.
We are justified from the promise, in which,
for Christ's sake, reconciliation, righ-
teousness, and eternal life have been prom-
ised. If anyone, therefore, has considered
these foundations, he will easily understand
that justification must necessarily be attrib-
uted to faith. It is not in vain that Christ has
been promised and set forth, that He has
been born and has suffered and been raised
again. The promise of grace in Christ is not
in vain. It was made immediately from the
beginning of the world, apart from and be-
yond the Law. The promise should be re-
ceived through faith, as 1 John 5:10–12 says:

> Whoever does not believe God has made Him a liar, because he has not believed in the testimony that God has borne concerning His Son. And this is the testimony, that God gave us eternal life, and this life is in His Son. Whoever has the Son has life; whoever does not have the Son of God does not have life.

Christ says, "So if the Son sets you free,
you will be free indeed" (John 8:36). Paul
says in Romans 5:2, "Through Him we have
also obtained access by faith into this grace in
which we stand." By faith in Christ, therefore,
the promise of the forgiveness of sins and of
righteousness is received. Neither are we jus-
tified before God by reason or by the Law.
177 These things are so plain and so clear we
[298] wonder how the insanity of the adversaries is
so great that it calls them into doubt. The
proof is clear. Since we are justified before
God not from the Law, but from the promise,
it is necessary to attribute justification to
faith. What can be opposed to this proof, un-
less someone wishes to abolish the entire
178 Gospel and the entire Christ? Christ's glory
[299] becomes more brilliant when we teach that
we make the most of Him as our Mediator
and Atoning Sacrifice. Godly consciences see
that the most abundant consolation is of-
fered to them in this doctrine. They see that
they ought to believe and most firmly assert
that they have a reconciled Father for
Christ's sake, and not for the sake of our
righteousness. Yet, they also see that Christ
aids us, so that we are able to keep the Law as
179 well. The adversaries deprive the Church of
[300] such great blessings as these when they con-
demn, and work to wipe out, the doctrine
about the righteousness of faith. Therefore,
let all good minds beware of consenting to
the godless counsels of the adversaries. In the
adversaries' teaching about justification, no
mention is made of Christ and how we ought
to set Him against God's anger, as though we
were able to overcome His anger by love, or
to love an angry God. In regard to these
180 things, consciences are left in uncertainty.
[301] For if they think that they have a reconciled
God because they love and keep the Law, they
will always doubt whether they have a recon-
ciled God. This is so because they either do
not feel this love, as the adversaries acknowl-
edge, or they certainly feel that it is very
small. Much more often they feel that they
are angry at God's judgment. They feel He
oppresses human nature with many terrible
evils, with troubles of this life, the terrors of
eternal anger, and so on. When, therefore,
will conscience be at rest? When will it be
quieted? When, in this doubt and in these
terrors, will it love God? What else is the doc-
trine of the Law than a doctrine of despair?
Let any one of our adversaries come forward 181
to teach us about this love, how he himself [302]
loves God. They do not at all understand
what they say. They only echo, just like the
walls of a house, the little word *love* without
understanding it. Their teaching is confused
and shadowy. It not only transfers Christ's
glory to human works, but also leads con-
sciences either to arrogance or to despair. But 182
our teaching, we hope, is readily understood [303]
by pious minds and brings godly and whole-
some consolation to terrified consciences.
For as the adversaries mock that "also many
wicked people and devils believe" [cf. James
2:19], we have frequently said already that we
speak of faith in Christ, namely, of faith in
the forgiveness of sins, of faith that truly and
heartily assents to the promise of grace. This
is not brought about without a great struggle
in human hearts. People of sound mind can
easily judge the faith that believes we are
cared for by God, that we are forgiven and
heard by Him. It is something that surpasses
nature. For by itself the human mind makes
no such decision about God [1 Corinthians
2:14–16]. Therefore, this faith of which we
speak is neither in the wicked nor in devils.

Furthermore, if any learned person ob- 183
jects that righteousness is in the will and, [304]
therefore, it cannot be attributed to faith,
which is in the intellect, the reply is easy. In
the schools even such persons acknowledge

that the will commands the intellect to agree
with God's Word. We say also quite clearly,
"Just as the terrors of sin and death are not
only thoughts of the intellect, but also horri-
ble movements of the will fleeing God's judg-
ment, so faith is not only knowledge in the
intellect, but also confidence in the will. In
other words, it is to want and to receive that
which is offered in the promise, namely, rec-
onciliation and the forgiveness of sins."
184 Scripture uses the term *faith* this way, as the
[305] following sentence of Paul testifies in Ro-
mans 5:1, "Therefore, since we have been jus-
tified by faith, we have peace with God
through our Lord Jesus Christ." Further-
more, in this passage, to justify means (ac-
cording to court language) to acquit a guilty
person and declare him righteous. But this
happens because of the righteousness of an-
other, namely, of Christ. This righteousness
185 is communicated to us through faith. There-
[306] fore, since our righteousness in this passage
is the credit of the righteousness of another,
we must here speak about righteousness in a
way different than in philosophy or in a civil
court. (There we seek after the righteousness
of one's own work, which certainly is in the
will.) So Paul says in 1 Corinthians 1:30, "He
is the source of your life in Christ Jesus,
whom God made our wisdom and our righ-
teousness and sanctification and redemp-
tion." And in 2 Corinthians 5:21, "For our
sake He made Him to be sin who knew no
sin, so that in Him we might become the
186 righteousness of God." But because Christ's
[307] righteousness is given to us through faith,
faith is righteousness credited to us. In other
words, it is that by which we are made ac-
ceptable to God on account of the credit and
ordinance of God, as Paul says, "Faith is
counted as righteousness" (Romans 4:3, 5).
187 Although, because of certain hard-to-please
[308] people, we must say technically: Faith is truly
righteousness, because it is obedience to the
Gospel. For it is clear that obedience to the
command of a superior is truly a kind of dis-
tributive justice. This obedience to the
Gospel is credited for righteousness. So, only
because of this—because we grasp Christ as
the Atoning Sacrifice—are good works, or
obedience to the Law, pleasing. We do not
satisfy the Law, but for Christ's sake this is
forgiven us, as Paul says, "There is therefore
now no condemnation for those who are in
Christ Jesus" (Romans 8:1). This faith gives 188
God the honor, gives God that which is His [309]
own. By receiving the promises, it obeys
Him. Just as Paul also says, "No distrust made
him waver concerning the promise of God,
but he grew strong in his faith as he gave
glory to God" (Romans 4:20). So the worship 189
and divine service of the Gospel is to receive [310]
gifts from God. On the contrary, the worship
of the Law is to offer and present our gifts to
God. However, we can offer nothing to God
unless we have first been reconciled and born
again. This passage, too, brings the greatest
comfort, as the chief worship of the Gospel is
to desire to receive the forgiveness of sins,
grace, and righteousness. Christ says of this
worship, "For this is the will of My Father,
that everyone who looks on the Son and be-
lieves in Him should have eternal life, and I
will raise him up on the last day" (John 6:40).
And the Father says, "This is My beloved Son,
with whom I am well pleased; listen to Him"
(Matthew 17:5). The adversaries speak of 190
obedience to the Law, but they do not speak [311]
of obedience to the Gospel. We cannot obey
the Law, unless we have been born again
through the Gospel. We cannot love God,
unless we have received the forgiveness of
sins. For as long as we feel that He is angry 191
with us, our human nature runs away from [312]
His anger and judgment. If anyone should
object that this view of faith (which desires

those things offered by the promise) becomes confused with hope, we answer as follows. Hope expects promised things, and hope and faith cannot be separated in reality. Such needless debate takes place in the schools. The Epistle to the Hebrews defines faith as "the assurance (*exspectatio*) of things hoped for" (Hebrews 11:1). Yet if anyone wants a distinction between faith and hope, we say that the object of hope is properly a future event, but that faith is concerned with future and present things. Faith receives the forgiveness of sins offered in the promise in the present.

192 From these statements we hope that it is
[313] clear both what faith is and that we are justi-
fied, reconciled, and regenerated through
faith. We are compelled to hold on to these
teachings because we want to teach the
righteousness of the Gospel, not the righ-
teousness of the Law. For those who teach
that we are justified by love teach the righ-
teousness of the Law. They do not teach us in
justification to trust in Christ as Mediator.
193 These things are also clear. We overcome the
[314] terrors of sin and death not through love, but
through faith. For we cannot set up our love
and fulfilling of the Law against God's wrath,
because Paul says, "Through [Christ] we
have also obtained access [to God] by faith"
(Romans 5:2). We often emphasize this sen-
tence so that we are understood. The sen-
tence shows most clearly our whole argu-
ment and, when carefully considered, can
teach abundantly about the whole matter. It
can console good minds. So, it is helpful to
have it at hand and in sight that we may be
able to set it against the doctrine of our ad-
versaries. They teach that we come to God
not through faith, but through love and
merits, without Christ as Mediator. This sen-
tence also helps us when we fear, so that we
194 may cheer ourselves and exercise faith. This
is also clear. We cannot keep the Law with- [315]
out Christ's aid. He Himself says, "Apart
from Me you can do nothing" (John 15:5).
So, before we keep the Law, our hearts must
be born again through faith.

[Results of the Adversaries' Teaching]

It is clear why we find fault with the ad- 195
versaries' doctrine about good works reward- [316]
ed because of God's generosity (*meritum
condigni*). The decision is very easy.

First. The adversaries do not even men-
tion faith, that we please God through faith
for Christ's sake. Rather, they imagine that
good works, worked by the aid of the habit of
love, make a righteousness worthy to please
God by itself, and also worthy of eternal life.
So they have no need of Christ as Mediator.
What else is this than to transfer Christ's 196
glory to our works? It means we would please [317]
God because of our works, not because of
Christ. But this robs Christ of the glory of
being the Mediator. He is the Mediator for-
ever, and not merely in the beginning of jus-
tification. Paul also says that if one justified
in Christ seeks righteousness elsewhere, he
affirms that Christ is a minister of sin (Gala-
tians 2:17), that is, that He does not fully jus-
tify. What the adversaries teach is most silly. 197
They teach that good works merit grace be- [318]
cause of God's mercy (*de condigno*). They
mean that after the beginning of justifica-
tion, if conscience is terrified (which hap-
pens), grace must be sought through a good
work, and not through faith in Christ.

Second. The doctrine of the adversaries 198
leaves consciences in doubt, so that they [319]
never can be quieted. This is so because the
Law always accuses us, even in good works.
For always "the desires of the flesh are
against the Spirit" (Galatians 5:17). How will
an unbelieving conscience have peace if it
believes that for the sake of one's own work,

it ought now to please God and not for Christ's sake? What work will it find, what will it trust as worthy of eternal life if, in-
199 deed, hope begins from merits? Against these
[320] doubts Paul says, "Therefore, since we have been justified by faith, we have peace with God" (Romans 5:1). We should be firmly convinced that we are granted righteousness and eternal life for Christ's sake. He says about Abraham, "In hope he believed against hope" (Romans 4:18).

200 *Third.* How will a conscience know when
[321] a work was done by the inclination of this habit of love so that it is possible to conclude that the work merits grace in a wholly deserving way (*de condigno*)? This very distinction has been created to dodge the Scriptures. It teaches that people merit grace at one time in a merely agreeable way (*de congruo*) and at another time in a wholly deserving way (*de condigno*). As we have said above, the intention of the one who works does not matter. Hypocrites, in their security, simply think their works are worthy and that they are regarded righteous. On the other hand, terrified consciences have doubts about all works, and for this reason continually seek other works. For this is what it means to merit "in a merely agreeable way" (*de congruo*). It means to doubt and, without faith, to work, until despair takes place. In short, all that the adversaries teach about this matter is full of errors and dangers.

201 *Fourth.* The entire Church confesses that
[322] eternal life is attained through mercy. Augustine speaks this way in *On Grace and Free Will.* There he speaks about the works of the saints completed after justification, "God leads us to eternal life not by our merits, but according to His mercy." He says in his Confessions, Book IX: "Woe to the life of man, however much it may be worthy of praise, if it be judged with mercy removed." And Cyprian, in his treatise on the Lord's Prayer, says this:

> Lest anyone should flatter himself that he is innocent, and by exalting himself, should perish the more deeply, he is instructed and taught that he sins daily, in that he is told to ask forgiveness daily for his sins.

But the subject is well known and has very 202
many and very clear testimonies in Scripture [323]
and in the Church Fathers. They all declare with one mouth that, even though we have good works, yet in these very works we need
mercy. Faith, looking upon this mercy, cheers 203
and consoles us. The adversaries teach [324]
wrongly when they praise merits and add nothing about this faith that takes hold of mercy. For, as we have said before, the promise and faith mutually agree with each other. The promise is grasped only through faith. So we say that the promised mercy agrees with the requirement of faith and cannot be taken hold of without faith. So we justly find fault with the doctrine about wholly deserving merit (*meritum condigni*), since it teaches nothing of justifying faith. It also hides
Christ's glory and office as Mediator. We 204
should not be regarded as teaching anything [325]
new in this matter. The Church Fathers have clearly handed down the doctrine that we need mercy even in good works.

Scripture also often teaches the same. 205
"Enter not into judgment with Your ser- [326]
vant, for no one living is righteous before You" (Psalm 143:2). This passage denies absolutely—even to all saints and servants of God—the glory of righteousness, if God does not forgive, but judges and convicts their hearts. For when David boasts in other places about his righteousness, he speaks about his own cause against the persecutors of God's Word. He does not speak of his

personal purity. He asks that God's cause and glory be defended, "Judge me, O LORD, according to my righteousness and according to the integrity that is in me" (Psalm 7:8) Likewise, in Psalm 130:3, he says that no one can endure God's judgment, if God were to mark our sins:

> "If You, O LORD, should mark iniquities, O Lord, who could stand?"

206 [327]
> I become afraid of all my suffering. (Job 9:28) [Vulgate: *opera*, works]

> If I wash myself with snow and cleanse my hands with lye, yet You will plunge me into a pit. (Job 9:30–31)

> Who can say, "I have made my heart pure; I am clean from my sin"? (Proverbs 20:9)

207 [328]
> If we say we have no sin, we deceive ourselves, and the truth is not in us. (1 John 1:8)

208 [329] In the Lord's Prayer the saints ask for the forgiveness of sins. Therefore, even the saints have sins. The innocent shall not be innocent (Numbers 14:18; [cf. Exodus 34:7]).

> For the LORD your God is a consuming fire, a jealous God. (Deuteronomy 4:24)

> Be silent, all flesh, before the LORD. (Zechariah 2:13)

> All flesh is grass, and all its beauty is like the flower of the field. The grass withers, the flower fades when the breath of the Lord blows on it. (Isaiah 40:6–7)

Namely, flesh and righteousness of the flesh
209 cannot endure God's judgment. Jonah 2:8
[330] also says, "Those who pay regard to vain idols forsake their hope of steadfast love," that is, all confidence is empty, except confidence in mercy. Mercy delivers us; our own merits, our own efforts, do not. So Daniel also prays: 210

> For we do not present our pleas before [331]
> You because of our righteousness, but because of Your great mercy. O Lord, hear; O Lord, forgive. O Lord, pay attention and act. Delay not, for Your own sake, O my God, because Your city and Your people are called by Your name. (Daniel 9:18–19)

So Daniel teaches us in praying to seize mercy, that is, to trust in God's mercy and not to trust in our own merits before God.
We also wonder what our adversaries do in 211
prayer, if the ungodly people ever ask any- [332]
thing of God. If they declare that they are worthy because they have love and good works and ask for grace as a debt, they pray precisely like the Pharisee who says, "I am not like other men" (Luke 18:11). He who prays for grace in this way does not rely upon God's mercy and treats Christ with disrespect. After all, He is our High Priest, who in-
tercedes for us. So prayer relies upon God's 212
mercy, when we believe that we are heard [333]
for Christ's sake. He is our High Priest, as He Himself says, "Whatever you ask in My name, this I will do, that the Father may be glorified in the Son. If you ask Me anything in My name, I will do it" (John 14:13–14). Without this High Priest we cannot approach the Father.

[Salvation Is by God's Mercy]

Here Christ's declaration also applies, 213
"So you also, when you have done all that [334]
you were commanded, say, 'We are unworthy servants; we have only done what was our duty'" (Luke 17:10). These words clearly declare that God saves by mercy and because of His promise, not that it is due because of the
value of our works. But at this point the 214

[335] adversaries play wonderfully with Christ's
words. In the first place, they turn His words
around and then turn them against us. Even
more, they claim it can be said: "If we have
believed all things, say, we are unprofitable
servants." Then they add that works do not
215 profit God, but works do profit us. See how
[336] the childish study of slick logic delights the
adversaries? Although these foolish things do
not deserve a response, we will still reply to
them in a few words. Their reversal of words
216 is defective. In the first place, the adversaries
[337] are deceived regarding the term *faith*. If faith
would signify historical knowledge that the
wicked and the devils also possess, the adver-
saries would correctly argue that faith is un-
profitable when they say: "When we have be-
lieved all things, say, 'We are unprofitable
servants.'" But we are not speaking of histor-
ical knowledge, but of confidence in God's
promise and mercy. This confidence in the
promise confesses that we are unprofitable
servants. Yes, this confession that our works
are unworthy is the very voice of faith, as ap-
pears in this example of Daniel 9:18, which
we cited, "We do not present our pleas before
You because of our righteousness." Faith 217
saves because it takes hold of mercy, or the [338]
promise of grace, even though our works are
unworthy. Understood this way, namely, that
our works are unworthy, the word reversal
does not injure us: "When you shall have be-
lieved all things, say, 'We are unprofitable ser-
vants.'" We teach the same as the entire
Church when we teach that we are saved by
mercy. But if they mean to argue from these 218
similar statements: "When you have done all [339]
things, do not trust in your works," also,
"When you have believed all things, do not
trust in the divine promise," there is no con-
nection. These statements are not alike. The
causes and objects of confidence in the for-
mer statement are very different from those
of the latter. In the former, confidence lies in

Jesus, the Good Shepherd

our own works. In the latter, confidence lies in the divine promise. Christ, however, condemns confidence in our works; He does not condemn confidence in His promise. He does not wish us to lose hope of God's grace and mercy. He attacks our works as unworthy, but does not attack the promise that
219 freely offers mercy. Here Ambrose says well,
[340] "Grace is to be acknowledged; but nature
220 must not be disregarded." We must trust in
[341] the promise of grace and not in our own nature. The adversaries act predictably and distort, against faith, the judgments that have been given on behalf of faith. We leave, how-
221 ever, these thorny points to the schools. The
[342] slick logic is plainly childish when they interpret "unprofitable servant" to mean that works are unprofitable to God, but are profitable to us. Christ does speak about that profit that makes God a debtor of grace to us, although it is out of place to discuss here about what is profitable or unprofitable. For "unprofitable servants" means "insufficient," because no one fears God as much, loves God as much, and believes God as much as he
222 should. Let us overlook these cold jokes of
[343] the adversaries. If they are ever brought to the light, levelheaded people will easily decide what they should conclude. The adversaries have found a flaw in words that are very plain and clear. But everyone sees that confidence in our own works is condemned in this passage.

223 Let us hold on to this confession of the
[344] Church: we are saved by mercy. Let no one think, "Hope will be uncertain if we are to be saved by mercy. It will be unsure without something coming out first that distinguishes those who obtain salvation from those who do not." We must give such a person a satisfactory answer. For the Scholastics, moved by this reason, seem to have invented the doctrine of wholly deserving merit
(*meritum condigni*). Thinking about such a 224
thing can greatly exercise the human mind. [345]
We will, therefore, reply briefly. It is essential to believe that we are saved by mercy so that hope may be sure, so that there may be a resulting distinction between those who obtain salvation and those who do not. When this is expressed in this way without explanation, it seems foolish. For in civil courts and in human judgment, issues about rights or debts are certain, and mercy is uncertain. But the matter is different in God's judgment. Here mercy has a clear and certain promise and command from God. The Gospel is properly the command that directs us to believe that God is reconciled to us for Christ's sake. "For God did not send His Son into the world to condemn the world, but in order that the world might be saved through Him"
(John 3:17). Whenever mercy is spoken of, 225
faith in the promise must be added. This [346]
faith produces sure hope, because it relies upon God's Word and command. If hope would rely upon works, then it would be uncertain, because works cannot quiet the con-
science, as has been said before. Faith makes 226
a distinction between those who obtain sal- [347]
vation and those who do not obtain it. Faith makes the distinction between the worthy and the unworthy, because eternal life has been promised to the justified. Faith justifies.

Here again the adversaries will cry out 227
that there is no need of good works if they do [348]
not merit eternal life. These lies we have refuted above. Of course, it is necessary to do good works. We say that eternal life has been promised to the justified. But those who walk according to the flesh [Galatians 5:19–21] retain neither faith nor righteousness. For this very reason we are justified: being righteous, we may begin to do good works and to obey
God's Law. We are regenerated and receive 228
the Holy Spirit for the very reason that the [349]

new life may produce new works, new dispo-
sitions, the fear and love of God, hatred of
lustful desires (concupiscence), and so on.
229 This faith arises in repentance and should be
[350] established and grow amid good works,
temptations, and dangers. This is so that we
may continually be more firmly persuaded
that God cares for us, forgives us, and hears
us for Christ's sake. This is not learned with-
out many and great struggles. How often is
conscience aroused, how often does it awak-
en even to despair when it shows either old
or new sins, or the impurity of our nature!
This handwriting is not blotted out without a
great struggle [Colossians 2:14]. Experience
230 testifies what a difficult matter faith is. While
[351] we are encouraged in the midst of the terrors
and receive comfort, other spiritual move-
ments grow at the same time: knowledge of
God, fear of God, hope and love of God. We
are "renewed," as Paul says, "in knowledge
after the image of its creator" (Colossians
3:10) and, "Beholding the glory of the Lord,
[we] are being transformed into the same
image" (2 Corinthians 3:18). In other words,
we receive the true knowledge of God, so that
we truly fear Him, we truly trust that we are
cared for by Him, and that we are heard by
231 Him. This regeneration is the beginning of
[352] eternal life as Paul says, "If Christ is in you,
although the body is dead because of sin, the
Spirit is life because of righteousness" (Ro-
232 mans 8:10). And, "Longing to put on our
[353] heavenly dwelling, if indeed by putting it on
we may not be found naked" (2 Corinthians
5:2–3). The honest reader can judge from
these statements that we certainly require
good works, since we teach that faith arises in
repentance and is bound to increase in re-
pentance. We place Christian and spiritual
perfection in these matters, if repentance and
faith grow together in repentance. The godly
can understand this better than the adver-
saries' teaching about contemplation or per-
fection. However, just as justification applies 233
to faith, so also eternal life applies to faith. [354]
Peter says, "Obtaining the outcome [or fruit]
of your faith, the salvation of your souls"
(1 Peter 1:9). For the adversaries confess that
the justified are children of God and coheirs
of Christ. Afterward, because works please 234
God on account of faith, they earn other [355]
bodily and spiritual rewards. For there will be
distinctions in the glory of the saints.

Here the adversaries reply that eternal life 235
is called a reward and that, therefore, it is [356]
merited in a wholly deserving way (*de
condigno*) by good works. We reply briefly
and plainly. Paul calls eternal life a "gift" (Ro-
mans 6:23), because by the righteousness
presented for Christ's sake, we are made at
the same time sons of God and coheirs of
Christ. As John says, "Whoever believes in the
Son has eternal life" (John 3:36). Augustine
says, as also do very many others who follow
him, "God crowns His gifts in us." Elsewhere
it is written, "Your reward is great in heaven"
(Luke 6:23). If these passages seem to conflict
for the adversaries, they themselves may ex-
plain them. But the adversaries are not fair 236
judges. They leave out the word *gift*. They [357]
also leave out the primary teachings of the
entire matter. Further, they select the word
reward and twist its meaning not only against
Scripture, but also against the common use
of language. In this way, they conclude that
because our works are called a reward, there
should be a price paid for eternal life. They
assume they are worthy of grace and life eter-
nal and do not stand in need of mercy or of
Christ as Mediator or of faith. This logic is al- 237
together new. We hear the term *reward* and [358]
are supposed to conclude that there is no
need of Christ as Mediator, or of faith having
access to God for Christ's sake, not for the
sake of our works! Who does not see that

these are unrelated sentences wrongly joined
238 together? We do not argue about the term
[359] *reward.* We argue whether good works are of themselves worthy of grace and of eternal life, or whether they please only on account of faith, which takes hold of Christ as Medi-
239 ator. Our adversaries not only attribute this
[360] to works, namely, that they are worthy of grace and of eternal life, but they also state falsely that works have surplus merits. The adversaries maintain that these merits can be granted to other people to justify them, as when monks sell to others the merits of their orders. They heap up these freakish ideas in the manner of Chrysippus, especially about this one word *reward.*

> It is called a reward; therefore, works are the price paid for it. So works please by themselves, and not for the sake of Christ as Mediator. And since one has more merits than another, some have surplus merits. Those who have earned them can sell them to others.

240 Stop, reader! You don't have the whole chain
[361] of arguments. For certain "sacraments" of this purchase must be added: the hood is placed upon the dead. The blessings brought to us in Christ, and the righteousness of faith, have been hidden by such additions.

241 We are not trying to start a needless word
[362] battle about the term *reward.* But this is a great, exalted, and very important matter about where Christian hearts can find true and certain comfort. It is about whether our works can give consciences rest and peace, whether we are to believe that our works are worthy of eternal life, or whether that is given to us for Christ's sake. These are the real questions regarding these matters. If consciences are not rightly taught about these, they can have no certain comfort. However, we have stated clearly enough that good works do not fulfill the Law, that we need God's mercy, that through faith we are accepted by God, that good works—be they ever so precious, even if they were the works of St. Paul himself—cannot bring rest to the conscience. It makes sense that we are to believe that we receive eternal life through Christ by faith, not because of our works or of the Law. But what do we say of the reward that Scripture mentions? If the adversaries will admit that we are regarded righteous through faith because of Christ, and that good works please God because of faith, we will not afterward argue much about the term *reward.* We confess that eternal life is a reward; it is something due because of the promise, not because of our merits. For the justification has been promised, which we have previously shown to be properly God's gift. To this gift the promise of eternal life has been added, according to Romans 8:30, "Those whom He justified He also glori-
fied." Here belongs what Paul says, "There is 242
laid up for me the crown of righteousness, [363]
which the Lord, the righteous judge, will award to me" (2 Timothy 4:8). The justified are due the crown because of the promise.
Saints should know this promise, not that 243
they may labor for their own profit, for they [364]
ought to labor for God's glory. But saints should know it so they may not despair in troubles. They should know God's will: He desires to aid, to deliver, and to protect them. Although the perfect hear the mention of penalties and rewards in one way, the weak hear it in another way. The weak labor for
the sake of their own advantage. Yet the 244
preaching of rewards and punishments is [365]
necessary. God's wrath is set forth in the preaching of punishments. This applies to the preaching of repentance. Grace is set forth in the preaching of rewards. Just as Scripture, in the mention of good works,

often embraces faith—for it wishes righteousness of the heart to be included with the fruit—so sometimes it offers grace together with other rewards. We find this in Isaiah 58:8–14, and frequently in other
245 places in the Prophets. We also affirm what
[366] we have often said, that although justification and eternal life go along with faith, nevertheless, good works merit other bodily and spiritual rewards and degrees of reward. According to 1 Corinthians 3:8, "Each will receive his wages according to his labor." The righteousness of the Gospel, which has to do with the promise of grace, freely receives justification and new life. But the fulfilling of the Law, which follows faith, has to do with the Law. In it a reward is offered and is due, not freely, but according to our works. Those who earn this are justified before they do the Law. As Paul says, "He has . . . transferred us to the kingdom of His beloved Son," and we are "fellow heirs with Christ" (Colossians
246 1:13; Romans 8:17). But whenever merit is
[367] mentioned, the adversaries immediately transfer the matter from other rewards to justification. Yet the Gospel freely offers justification because of Christ's merits and not of our own. His merits are delivered to us through faith. Works and troubles do not merit justification, but other payments, as the reward is offered for the works in these passages: "Whoever sows sparingly will also reap sparingly, and whoever sows bountifully will also reap bountifully" (2 Corinthians 9:6). Here clearly the measure of the reward is connected with the measure of the work. "Honor your father and your mother, that your days may be long in the land" (Exodus 20:12). Also here the Law offers a reward to a
247 certain work. The fulfilling of the Law earns
[368] a reward, for a reward properly relates to the Law. Yet we should be mindful of the Gospel, which freely offers justification for Christ's sake. We neither obey the Law, nor can obey it, before we have been reconciled to God, justified, and reborn. Nor would fulfilling the Law please God, unless we were accepted because of faith. People are accepted because of faith. For this very reason the initial fulfilling of the Law pleases and has a reward in
this life and in the next. Regarding the term 248
reward, many other remarks, derived from [369]
the nature of the Law, might be made here. Since they are too long, they must be explained in another connection.

[The Adversaries' Other Arguments]

The adversaries insist that good works 249
have the right to merit eternal life, because [370]
Paul says:

> He will render to each one according to his works. (Romans 2:6)
>
> Glory and honor and peace for everyone who does good. (Romans 2:10)
>
> Those who have done good to the resurrection of life. (John 5:29)
>
> I was hungry and you gave Me food, I was thirsty and you gave Me drink, I was a stranger and you welcomed Me. (Matthew 25:35)

In these and all similar passages in which 250
works are praised in the Scriptures, it is nec- [371]
essary to understand not only outward works, but also the faith of the heart. Scripture does not speak of hypocrisy, but of the
righteousness of the heart with its fruit. Fur- 251
thermore, whenever the Law and works are [372]
mentioned, we must know that Christ cannot be excluded as Mediator. He is the end of the Law, and He Himself says, "Apart from Me you can do nothing" (John 15:5). We have said above that all passages about works can be judged according to this rule. When eternal life is granted to works, it is granted to those who have been justified. Only justified people, who are led by the Spirit of

The Last Judgment Depicted as a Harvest

Christ, can do good works. Without faith and
Christ as Mediator, good works do not
please, according to Hebrews 11:6: "Without
252 faith it is impossible to please [God]." When
[373] Paul says, "He will render to each one accord-
ing to his works," not only the outward work
ought to be understood, but all righteousness
or unrighteousness. So, "Glory and honor
and peace for everyone who does good,"
namely, to the righteous. "You gave Me food"
(Matthew 25:35) is cited as the fruit and wit-
ness of the righteousness of the heart and of
faith and, therefore, eternal life is given to
253 righteousness. In this way Scripture, at the
[374] same time with the fruit, embraces the righ-
teousness of the heart. Scripture often names
the fruit, so that the inexperienced under-
stand better. It also names them to show that
a new life and rebirth are required, and not
hypocrisy. But rebirth happens through faith,
in repentance.

254 No sane person can judge otherwise. Nei-
[375] ther do we needlessly attempt to make a fine
distinction, trying to separate the fruit from
the righteousness of the heart. If only the ad-
versaries would have conceded that the fruit
pleases because of faith, and because of
Christ as Mediator, and that by themselves
they are not worthy of grace and of eternal
255 life. We condemn this failure in the doctrine
[376] of the adversaries. In some passages of Scrip-
ture, understood either in a philosophical or
a Jewish manner, they abolish the righ-
teousness of faith and exclude Christ as Me-
diator. From these passages they conclude
that works merit grace, sometimes in a
merely agreeable way (*de congruo*), and at
other times in a wholly deserving way (*de
condigno*), namely, when love is added. They
maintain that works justify, and because
they are righteousness they are worthy of
eternal life. This error clearly abolishes the
righteousness of faith, which believes that
we have access to God for Christ's sake, not
for the sake of our works. It also contradicts
the truth that through Christ, as Priest and
Mediator, we are led to the Father and have a
reconciled Father, as has been said well
enough before. This teaching about the righ- 256
teousness of faith is not to be neglected in [377]
Christ's Church, because without it we can-
not consider Christ's office. Then the doc-
trine of justification that is left is only a doc-
trine of the Law. We should keep the Gospel
and the doctrine about the promise, granted
for Christ's sake.

[Conclusion]

We are not arguing with the adversaries 257
about a small matter. We are not trying to [378]
make a fine distinction when we find fault
with them for teaching that we merit eternal
life by works, while faith that takes hold of
Christ as Mediator is left out. For there is not 258
a syllable in the Scholastics about this faith [379]
that believes the Father is reconciled to us for
Christ's sake. Everywhere they hold that we
are accepted and righteous because of our
works, completed either from reason, or cer-
tainly worked by the inclination of that love
they speak about. Yet they have certain say- 259
ings, proverbs, as it were, of the old writers. [380]
They distort these in interpretation. In the 260
schools it is boasted that good works please [381]
because of grace and that confidence must be
put in God's grace. Here they understand
grace as a habit by which we love God. It is as
though the ancients meant that we should
trust in our love, even though from experi-
ence we know how small and how impure it
is. It is strange how they ask us to trust in
love, since they teach us that we are not able
to know whether it is present. Why do they
not present the grace, the mercy of God to-
ward us? While they are at it, they should add
faith. For the promise of God's mercy, recon-

ciliation, and love toward us is not grasped
unless by faith. With this view they would
rightly say that we should trust in grace, that
good works please because of grace, when
261 faith takes hold of grace. In the schools it is
[382] bragged that our good works work by virtue
of Christ's passion. Well said! But why add
nothing about faith? For Christ is an Atoning
Sacrifice, as Paul says, "by faith" (Romans
3:25). When fearful consciences are comfort-
ed by faith, and are convinced that our sins
have been blotted out by Christ's death, and
that God has been reconciled to us because of
Christ's suffering, then, indeed, Christ's suf-
fering profits us. If the teaching about faith is
left out, saying that works are useful by virtue
of Christ's passion is of no use at all.

262 They corrupt very many other passages in
[383] the schools because they do not teach the
righteousness of faith and because they un-
derstand faith as merely a knowledge of the
history or of dogmas. They do not under-
stand faith to be a virtue, which takes hold of
the promise of grace and of righteousness,
and which enlivens hearts in the terrors of
263 sin and of death. When Paul says, "With the
[384] heart one believes and is justified, and with
the mouth one confesses and is saved" (Ro-
mans 10:10), we think that the adversaries
admit that confession justifies or saves, not
by the outward act, but only because of the
faith of the heart. Paul says that confession
saves in order to show what sort of faith re-
ceives eternal life, namely, that which is firm
264 and active. That faith, however, that does not
[385] present itself in confession is not firm. So
other good works please because of faith, just
as the prayers of the Church ask that all
things may be accepted for Christ's sake
[John 14:13–14]. They likewise ask all things
for Christ's sake. For it is clear that this clause
is always added at the close of prayers:
265 "Through Christ, our Lord." So we conclude
that we are justified before God, are recon- [386]
ciled to God and reborn through faith. In re-
pentance this faith lays hold of the promise
of grace and truly enlivens the terrified mind.
It is convinced that for Christ's sake God
is reconciled and favorable toward us.
"Through" this faith, 1 Peter 1:5 says, "[We]
are being guarded . . . for a salvation ready to
be revealed." The knowledge of this faith is 266
necessary to Christians, brings the most [387]
abundant comfort in all troubles, and shows
us Christ's office. Those who deny that peo-
ple are justified through faith and that Christ
is Mediator and the Atoning Sacrifice, deny
the promise of grace and the Gospel. When it
comes to justification, they teach only the
doctrine either of reason or of the Law. We 267
have shown how this came to be, so far as can [388]
be done here. We have also explained the ob-
jections of the adversaries. Good people will
easily judge these things if they will think in
this way whenever a passage about love or
works is quoted. It is certain that the Law
cannot be kept without Christ and that we
cannot be justified from the Law, but from
the Gospel, that is, from the grace promised
in Christ. We hope that this discussion, al- 268
though brief, will be helpful to good people [389]
for strengthening faith and teaching and
comforting the conscience. For we know that
what we have said is in harmony with the
prophetic and apostolic Scriptures, with the
Holy Fathers, Ambrose, Augustine, and very
many others, and with Christ's whole
Church, which certainly confesses that Christ
is the Atoning Sacrifice and Justifier.

Nor do we immediately conclude that the 269
Roman Church agrees with everything that [390]
the pope or cardinals or bishops or some of
the theologians or monks approve. For it is
clear that most pontiffs consider their own
authority of greater concern than Christ's
Gospel. It has been determined that most of

them are openly mere searchers for pleasure.
Clearly theologians have mingled more of
philosophy with Christian doctrine than was
270 necessary. Their influence should not appear
[391] so great that it will be unlawful to disagree
with their arguments, because at the same
time many clear errors are found among
them. One of these maintains that, from
purely natural powers, we are able to love
God above all things. This preaching, al-
though it is clearly false, has produced many
271 other errors. For the Scriptures, the Holy Fa-
[392] thers, and the judgments of all the godly
everywhere respond. Therefore, popes, or
some theologians, and monks in the Church
have taught us to seek the forgiveness of sins,
grace, and righteousness through our own
works and to invent new forms of worship,
which have clouded over Christ's office and
have made out of Christ not the Atoning Sac-
rifice and Justifier, but only a Legislator. Yet,
the knowledge of Christ has always remained
272 with some godly persons. Scripture, further-
[393] more, has predicted that the righteousness of
faith would be clouded over by human tradi-
tions and the teaching of works in this way.
Paul often complains about this. (See Gala-
tians 4:9; 5:7; Colossians 2:8, 16–19; 1 Timo-
thy 4:2–5; etc.) There were even during his
time those who—instead of the righteousness
of faith—taught that people were reconciled
to God and justified by their own works and
own acts of worship, and not through faith
for Christ's sake. People judge by nature that
273 God should be appeased by works. Nor does
[394] reason see a righteousness other than the
righteousness of the Law, understood in a
civil sense. So there have always been some
who have taught this earthly righteousness
alone to the exclusion of the righteousness of
274 faith. Such teachers will always exist. The
[395] same thing happened among the people of
Israel. The majority of the people thought
that they merited the forgiveness of sins by
their works. Therefore, they piled up sacri-
fices and acts of worship. On the contrary,
the prophets, in condemnation of this opin-
ion, taught the righteousness of faith. What
happened among the people of Israel are il-
lustrations of those things that were to hap-
pen in the Church [1 Corinthians 10:11].
Therefore, let the multitude of the adver- 275
saries, who condemn our doctrine, not dis- [396]
turb godly minds. For the adversaries' spirit
can easily be judged, because in some articles
they have condemned truth that is so clear
and apparent that their godlessness appears
openly. The bull of Leo X condemned a very 276
necessary article, which all Christians should [397]
hold and believe. It stated that we should
trust that we have been forgiven not because
of our sorrow, but because of Christ's word
"Whatever you bind . . ." (Matthew 16:19).
And now, in this assembly, the authors of the 277
Confutation have clearly condemned the fol- [398]
lowing: (a) faith is a part of repentance, (b)
we obtain forgiveness of sins by faith, (c) and
by faith we overcome the terrors of sin, so the
conscience is soothed. Who does not see that
this article—that by faith we obtain the for-
giveness of sins—is most true, most certain,
and especially necessary to all Christians?
Who to all posterity, hearing that such a doc-
trine has been condemned, will judge that
the authors of it had any knowledge of
Christ?

It is possible to make a guess about their 278
spirit based on that inexpressible cruelty, [399]
which it is agreed they exercised among
many good people up to this point. We re-
ceived [news] in this gathering about a cer-
tain reverend father of the imperial senate.
When opinions were stated about our con-
fession, he saw nothing more useful to say to
the council than "to write back with blood"
to what we wrote in ink. Could Phalaris say

anything more cruel? Some princes also have
judged this expression unworthy to be spo-
279 ken in such a meeting. Even though the ad-
[400] versaries claim the name of the Church for
themselves, we know that Christ's Church is with those who teach Christ's Gospel, not with those who defend wicked opinions contrary to the Gospel. As the Lord says, "My sheep hear My voice" (John 10:27). And Augustine says:

> The question is, "Where is the Church?" What, therefore, are we to do? Are we to seek it in our own words or in the words of its Head, our Lord Jesus Christ? I think that we ought to seek it in the words of Him who is Truth, and who knows His own body best.

In this way the judgments of our adversaries will not disturb us, since they defend human opinions contrary to the Gospel, contrary to the authority of the Holy Fathers who have written in the Church, and contrary to the testimonies of godly minds.

ARTICLES VII AND VIII (IV)

The Church

Note: Defining "Church" was naturally one of the more controversial topics during the Reformation. The Medieval Church had developed a massive organizational structure for operating the Church. The foundation of this structure was the papacy. According to Rome, Jesus Christ established the office of the pope, who is Christ's visible representative, or vicar, on earth. All churchly authority resides with the pope, who delegates it to others, primarily the bishops. Obedience to the pope is to be absolute in all matters of faith and morals. Those who deny the pope's authority and teachings as Christ's representative cannot be saved. The Lutherans insisted that the Church cannot be defined by its outward organization. Rather, as the Augsburg Confession had defined earlier, the Church is primarily the gathering of God's people around Christ's Word and Sacraments. Rome accused the Lutherans of saying that even unbelievers were truly part of this Church. The Lutherans were careful not to say this. In Articles VII and VIII of the Apology, Melanchthon speaks of the Church in a wide sense, including all who are seen to gather around Word and Sacraments, and in a narrow sense, that is, all who genuinely have faith in Christ, an aspect of Church that cannot be seen. Fellowship around, in, and through the Word and Sacraments defines unity in the faith. (See also AC VII/VIII; SA III XII; LC II, The Third Article.)

They have condemned Article VII of our 1
Confession, in which we said that the Church
is the congregation of saints. The adversaries
have added a long essay stating that the
wicked are not to be separated from the
Church, since John the Baptist has compared
the Church to a threshing floor on which
wheat and chaff are heaped together
(Matthew 3:12), and Christ has compared it
to a net in which there are both good and bad
fish (Matthew 13:47). This is a true saying: 2
"There is no remedy against the attacks of
the slanderer." Nothing can be spoken with
such care that it can escape ridicule. For this 3
reason we have added Article VIII. Let no one think that we separate the wicked and hypocrites from the outward fellowship of the Church, or that we deny power to Sacraments administered by hypocrites or wicked men. There is no need here of a long defense against this slander. Article VIII is enough to acquit us. For we grant that in this life hypocrites and wicked people have been mingled with the Church, and that they are members of the Church according to the

outward fellowship of the signs of the Church, that is, of Word, profession, and Sacraments (especially if they have not been excommunicated). Neither are the Sacraments powerless because they are administered by wicked men. Yes, we can even be right in using the Sacraments administered
4 by wicked men. For Paul also predicts, "[The antichrist] takes his seat in the temple of God" (2 Thessalonians 2:4). In other words, he will rule and bear office in the Church.
5 But the Church is not only the fellowship of outward objects and rites, as other governments, but at its core, it is a fellowship of faith and of the Holy Spirit in hearts. Yet this fellowship has outward marks so that it can be recognized. These marks are the pure doctrine of the Gospel and the administration of the Sacraments in accordance with the Gospel of Christ. This Church alone is called Christ's body, which Christ renews, sanctifies, and governs by His Spirit. Paul testifies about this when he says, "And gave Him as head over all things to the Church, which is His body, the fullness of Him who
6 fills all in all" (Ephesians 1:22–23). Those in whom Christ does not act are not the members of Christ. The adversaries admit this too. The wicked are "dead" members of the Church. We wonder why the adversaries have found fault with our description that
7 speaks of living members. Neither have we said anything new. Paul has defined the Church precisely in the same way, that it should be cleansed in order to be holy. He adds the outward marks, the Word and Sacraments. For he says:

> Christ loved the Church and gave Himself up for her, that He might sanctify her, having cleansed her by the washing of water with the word, so that He might present the Church to Himself in splendor, without spot or wrinkle or any such thing, that she might be holy and without blemish. (Ephesians 5:25–27)

In the Confession, we have presented this sentence almost word for word. The Church is defined by the Third Article of the Creed, which teaches us to believe that there is a
holy Catholic Church. The wicked indeed are 8
not a holy Church. The words that follow, namely, "the communion of saints," seems to be added in order to explain what the Church signifies: the congregation of saints, who have with each other the fellowship of the same Gospel or doctrine and the same Holy Spirit, who renews, sanctifies, and governs their hearts.

This article has been presented for a nec- 9
essary reason. We see the infinite dangers that threaten the destruction of the Church. In the Church itself, the number of the wicked who oppress it is too high to count. Therefore, this article in the Creed shows us these consolations in order that we may not despair, but may know that the Church will remain ‹until the end of the world›. No matter how great the multitude of the wicked is, we may know that the Church still exists and Christ provides those gifts He has promised to the Church—to forgive sins, to hear
prayer, to give the Holy Spirit. It says *Church* 10
catholic, in order that we may not understand the Church to be an outward government of certain nations. Rather, the Church is people scattered throughout the whole world. They agree about the Gospel and have the same Christ, the same Holy Spirit, and the same Sacraments, whether they have the same or
different human traditions. The explanation 11
appearing in the *Decrees* says, "The Church in its wide sense embraces good and evil." Likewise, it says that the wicked are in the Church only in name, not in fact. The good are in the Church both in fact and in name. To this ef-

fect there are many passages in the Fathers.
For Jerome says, "The sinner, therefore, who
has been soiled with any blotch cannot be
called a member of Christ's Church, neither
can he be said to be subject to Christ."

12 Hypocrites and wicked people are mem-
bers of this true Church according to out-
ward rites ‹titles and offices›. Yet, when the
Church is defined, it is necessary to define
what is the living body of Christ and what is,
in name and in fact, the Church. There are
13 many reasons for this. We should understand
what chiefly makes us members—living
members—of the Church. If we will define
the Church only as an outward political
order of the good and wicked, people will not
understand that Christ's kingdom is righ-
teousness of heart and the gift of the Holy
Spirit [Romans 14:17]. People will conclude
that the Church is only the outward obser-
vance of certain forms of worship and rites.
14 Likewise, what difference will there be be-
tween the people of the Law and the Church
if the Church is only an outward political
order? But Paul distinguishes the Church
from the people of the Law [Israel] in this
way: The Church is a spiritual people. It has
not been distinguished from the pagans by
civil rites ‹its polity and civil affairs›. Instead,
it is God's true people, reborn by the Holy
Spirit. Among the people of the Law [Israel],
apart from Christ's promise, even the earthly
seed had promises about bodily things such
as government. Even though the wicked
among them were called God's people (be-
cause God had separated this earthly seed
from other nations by certain outward ordi-
nances and promises), the wicked did not
15 please God [Deuteronomy 7:6–11]. But the
Gospel brings not merely the shadow of eter-
nal things, but the eternal things themselves:
the Holy Spirit and righteousness. By the
Gospel we are righteous before God.

Only those people who receive this prom- 16
ise of the Spirit receive it according to the
Gospel. Besides, the Church is Christ's king-
dom, distinguished from the devil's king-
dom. It is certain, however, that the wicked
are in the devil's power and members of his
kingdom. Paul teaches this when he says that
the devil "is now at work in the sons of dis-
obedience" (Ephesians 2:2). Christ says to the
Pharisees, who certainly had outward fellow-
ship with the Church, that is, with the saints
among the people of the Law (as officehold-
ers, sacrificers, and teachers), "You are of
your father the devil" (John 8:44). Therefore,
the Church, which is truly Christ's kingdom,
is properly the congregation of saints. For the
wicked are ruled by the devil and are captives
of the devil. They are not ruled by the Spirit
of Christ.

Why say more when the matter is clear? If 17
the Church, which is truly Christ's kingdom,
is distinguished from the devil's kingdom, it
follows necessarily that the wicked are not
the Church, since they are in the devil's king-
dom. It is true that, because Christ's kingdom
has not yet been revealed, the wicked are
mixed in with the Church and hold offices.
But the wicked are not Christ's kingdom, 18
even though that revelation has not yet been
made. For Christ enlivens His true kingdom
by His Spirit, whether it is revealed or is cov-
ered by the cross, just as the glorified Christ is
the same Christ who was afflicted [John
17:1]. Christ's parables clearly agree with 19
this. He says, "The good seed is the children
of the kingdom. The weeds are the sons of
the evil one" (Matthew 13:38). "The field,"
He says, "is the world," not the Church. John
the Baptist speaks about the entire Jewish
people and says that eventually the true
Church will be separated from that people.
Therefore, this passage is more against the
adversaries than in favor of them, because it

shows that the true and spiritual people are to be separated from the earthly people. Christ also speaks of the outward appearance of the Church when He says, "The kingdom of heaven is like a net" (Matthew 13:47), likewise, "ten virgins" (Matthew 25:1). He teaches that the Church has been covered by a lot of evils, so that this stumbling block may not offend the pious, and so that we may know that the Word and Sacraments are powerful even when administered by the wicked. Meanwhile, He teaches that these godless people, although they have fellowship in outward signs, are not Christ's true kingdom and members. They are members of the
20 devil's kingdom. We are not dreaming of a Platonic state, as some wickedly charge. But we do say that this Church exists: truly believing and righteous people scattered throughout the whole world. We add the marks: the pure teaching of the Gospel and the Sacraments. This Church is properly the pillar of the truth (1 Timothy 3:15). For it keeps the pure Gospel as Paul says in 1 Corinthians 3:11. The "foundation" is the true knowledge of Christ and faith. There are also many weak persons, who build upon the foundation stubble that will perish (v. 12), holding certain harmful opinions. Nevertheless, because the weak do not overthrow the foundation, they are both forgiven and corrected.
21 The writings of the Holy Fathers declare that sometimes even they built stubble upon the foundation, but that this did not overthrow their faith. But most of those errors do overthrow faith. Our adversaries defend these errors. Among them is their condemnation of the article about the forgiveness of sins, in which we say that the forgiveness of sins is received through faith. Likewise, it is a clear and deadly error when the adversaries teach that people merit the forgiveness of sins by loving God, before grace. This is an example of removing "the foundation," Christ. Likewise, why do we need faith if the Sacraments justify by the outward act, without a good motive on the part of the one using them?
Just as the Church has the promise that it will 22
always have the Holy Spirit, so it also has warnings that there will be wicked teachers and wolves [Acts 20:29]. Yet, the Church in the proper sense has the Holy Spirit. Although wolves and wicked teachers run rampant in the Church, they are not properly Christ's kingdom. Just as Lyra also testifies when he says:

> The Church does not consist of people in power or ecclesiastical or secular dignity, because many princes and archbishops and others of lower rank have been found to have apostatized from the faith. Therefore, the Church consists of those persons in whom there is a true knowledge and confession of faith and truth.

We have said nothing more in our Confession than what Lyra says here.

The adversaries perhaps require that the 23
Church be defined in the following way. To them, the Church is the supreme outward monarchy of the whole world. In this Church the Roman pontiff's power is unquestioned. No one is allowed to argue against it or criticize it. He sets up articles of faith or abolishes them and abolishes the Scriptures according to his pleasure. He approves worship ceremonies and sacrifices to frame whatever laws he may wish. He dispenses and exempts from whatever laws (divine, canonical, or civil) he may wish. From him, the emperor and all kings receive the power and right to hold their kingdoms according to Christ's command. It must be understood that this right was transferred from Christ (since the Father subjected all things to Him) to the pope. Therefore, the pope must necessarily

Pentecost

be lord of the whole world, of all the kingdoms of the world, of all things private and public. He must have absolute power in earthly and spiritual things and both swords,
24 the spiritual and temporal. Besides, this definition (not of Christ's Church, but of the papal kingdom) has as its authors not only the canon lawyers, but also Daniel 11:36–39.

25 Now, if we would define the Church in this way, we would perhaps have fairer judges. For there exist many excessive and wicked writings about the pope of Rome's power, for which no one has ever been charged. We alone are blamed, because we proclaim Christ's graciousness, that by faith in Christ we obtain forgiveness of sins, and not by worship ceremonies created by the
26 pope. Furthermore, Christ, the prophets, and the apostles define Christ's Church very dif-
27 ferent than the papal kingdom. Neither must we transfer to the popes what belongs to the true Church (as though the popes are pillars of the truth who do not err). How many of the popes care for the Gospel or judge that it is worth being read? Many ‹in Italy and elsewhere› even publicly ridicule all religions. Or, if they approve anything, they approve only things that are in harmony with human reason. They regard the rest like fables and like
28 the tragedies of the poets. According to the Scriptures, we hold that the Church, properly called, is the congregation of saints who truly believe Christ's Gospel and have the Holy Spirit. We confess that in this life many hypocrites and wicked people are mixed in with these. They have the fellowship in outward signs, are members of the Church according to this fellowship in outward signs, and so hold offices in the Church (preach, administer the Sacraments, and bear the title and name of Christians). However, the fact that the Sacraments are administered by the unworthy does not detract from the Sacraments' power. Because of the call of the Church, the unworthy still represent the person of Christ and do not represent their own persons, as Christ testifies, "The one who hears you hears Me" (Luke 10:16). (Even Judas was sent to preach.) When they offer God's Word, when they offer the Sacraments, they offer them in the stead and place of Christ. Those words of Christ teach us not to be offended by the unworthiness of the ministers.

In the Confession, we said clearly enough 29
that we condemn the Donatists and Wycliffites. They thought that people sinned when they received the Sacraments from the unworthy in the Church. These points seem, for the present, to be enough for the defense of our description of the Church. Neither do we see how, when the Church, properly called, is named *the body of Christ*, it should be described differently than we have described it. For it is clear that the wicked belong to the devil's kingdom and body. He drives them on and holds them captive. Such things are clearer than the light of noonday. However, if the adversaries continue to pervert them, we will not hesitate to reply at greater length.

The adversaries also condemn the part of 30
Article VII in which we said that "for the true unity of the Church it is enough to agree about the doctrine of the Gospel and the administration of the Sacraments. It is not necessary that human traditions, that is, rites or ceremonies instituted by men, should be the same everywhere." Here they distinguish between *universal* and *particular* rites. They approve our article if it is understood concerning particular rites; they do not approve it concerning universal rites. We do not com- 31
pletely understand what the adversaries mean. We are speaking of true, spiritual unity. Without faith in the heart, or righ-

teousness of heart before God, such unity cannot exist. Similarity of human ceremonies, whether universal or particular, is not necessary. The righteousness of faith is not a righteousness bound to certain traditions. The righteousness of the Law was bound to the Mosaic ceremonies. But righteousness of the heart is a matter that enlivens the heart. Human traditions, whether they are universal or particular, contribute nothing to this new life. Neither are traditions effects of the Holy Spirit, as are self-control, patience, the fear of God, love for one's neighbor, and the works of love.

32 The reasons why we presented this article were not small. Clearly many foolish opinions about traditions had crept into the Church. Some thought that human traditions were necessary services for earning justification. Afterward, they argued how God came to be worshiped with such variety, as though these observances were acts of worship and not outward and political ordinances. Such ordinances have no connection with the righteousness of heart or the worship of God. These ordinances vary, according to the circumstances, for certain probable reasons, sometimes in one way, and at other times in another. Likewise, some churches have excommunicated others because of such traditions as the observance of Easter, icons, and the like. So the ignorant have imagined that faith (or the righteousness of the heart before God) cannot exist without these ceremonies. Many foolish writings of the Summists and of others exist on this matter.

33 We believe that the true unity of the Church is not injured by dissimilar ceremonies instituted by humans, just as the dissimilar length of day and night does not injure the unity of the Church. However, it is pleasing to us that, for the sake of peace, universal ceremonies are kept. We also willingly keep the order of the Mass in the churches, the Lord's Day, and other more famous festival days. With a very grateful mind we include the beneficial and ancient ordinances, especially since they contain a discipline. This discipline is beneficial for educating and training the people and those
who are ignorant ‹the young people›. We are 34
not discussing now whether it is helpful to keep them because of peace or bodily profit. We speak of something else. The question at hand is whether the observances of human traditions are acts of worship necessary for righteousness before God. This is the point to be judged in this controversy. When this is decided, it can be judged later whether it is necessary that human traditions should everywhere be the same for the true unity of the Church. For if human traditions are not acts of worship necessary for righteousness before God, it follows that those not having the traditions received elsewhere can be righteous and the sons of God as well. For example, if the style of German clothing is not worship of God and necessary for righteousness before God, it follows that people can be righteous and God's sons, and Christ's Church, even though they use a costume that is not German, but French.

Paul clearly teaches this to the Colossians: 35

> Therefore let no one pass judgment on you in questions of food and drink, or with regard to a festival or a new moon or a Sabbath. These are a shadow of the things to come, but the substance belongs to Christ. (2:16–17)

Likewise:

> If with Christ you died to the elemental spirits of the world, why, as if you were still alive in the world, do you

> submit to regulations—"Do not han-
> dle, Do not taste, Do not touch" (re-
> ferring to things that all perish as they
> are used)—according to human pre-
> cepts and teachings? These have in-
> deed an appearance of wisdom in
> promoting self-made religion and as-
> ceticism. (2:20–23)

36 The meaning is this: Righteousness of the
heart is a spiritual matter, a matter of en-
livening hearts. Clearly human traditions do
not enliven hearts and are not effects of the
Holy Spirit. Such efforts are love for one's
neighbor, self-control, and so on. They are
not tools through which God moves hearts
to believe, as are the divinely given Word and
Sacraments. Rather, traditions are customs
that have no connection to the heart. They
perish with the using, and we must not be-
lieve that they are necessary for righteousness
before God. To the same effect Paul says, "For
the kingdom of God is not a matter of eating
and drinking but of righteousness and peace
and joy in the Holy Spirit" (Romans 14:17).
37 But there is no need to cite many testimonies.
For they are everywhere clear in the Scrip-
tures, and we have gathered many of them in
the latter articles of our Confession. In this
controversy the point to be decided must be
repeated, namely, whether human traditions
are acts of worship necessary for righteous-
ness before God. In due course we will discuss
this matter more fully.

38 The adversaries say that universal tradi-
tions should be observed because they were
supposedly handed down by the apostles.
What religious men they are! They wish that
the ceremonies received from the apostles be
kept. Yet, they do not wish the apostles' doc-
39 trine to be kept. They should judge these rites
just as the apostles themselves judge them in
their writings. For the apostles did not want
us to believe that we are justified through
such ceremonies, or that such ceremonies are
necessary for righteousness before God. The
apostles did not want to put such a burden
upon consciences. They did not want to
place righteousness and sin in the observance
of days, food, and the like. Yes, Paul calls such 40
opinions "teachings of demons" (1 Timothy
4:1). Therefore, the apostles' will and advice
should be taken from their writings. It is not
enough to mention their example. The apos-
tles observed certain days, not because this
observance was necessary for justification,
but in order that the people might know at
what time they should gather. They observed
also certain other ceremonies and orders of
lessons whenever they gathered. The people
kept the customs of the Fathers ‹from their
Jewish festivals and ceremonies›. As is com-
monly the case, the apostles adapted to the
history of the Gospel certain things, al-
though somewhat changed. Among these
things were the Passover and Pentecost. The
apostles did this so that not only by teaching,
but also through these examples, they might
hand down to posterity the memory of the
most important subjects. But if these things 41
were handed down as necessary for justifica-
tion, why, afterward, did the bishops change
many things in these very matters? If they
were matters of divine right, it was not lawful
to change them by human authority. Before 42
the Synod of Nicaea, some observed Easter at
one time and others observed it at another
time. Neither did this lack of uniformity
harm faith. Afterward, the plan was adopted
by which our Passover (Easter) did not fall at
the same time as that of the Jewish Passover.
The apostles had commanded the churches
to observe the Passover with the brethren
who had been converted from Judaism.
Therefore, after the Synod of Nicaea, certain
nations held firmly to the custom of observ-

ing the Jewish time. The apostles, by this decree, did not wish to put a demand upon the churches, as the words of the decree testify. For it asks no one to be troubled, even though his brothers and sisters, in observing Easter, do not change the time correctly. The words of the decree are found in Epiphanius:

> Do not calculate, but celebrate it whenever your brethren of the circumcision do; celebrate it at the same time with them, and even though they may have erred, let not this be a care to you.

Epiphanius writes that these are the words presented in a decree about Easter. The wise reader can easily conclude from the decree that the apostles wished to free the people from the foolish opinion of a fixed time, to help them from being troubled, if a mistake
43 should be made in setting the date. However, some in the East, who followed the teaching of Audians, argued that because of this decree of the apostles, the Passover should be observed with the Jews. In refuting them, Epiphanius praises the decree and says that it contains nothing that departs from the faith or rule of the Church. He blames the Audians because they do not correctly understand the expression. Epiphanius interprets it in the sense in which we interpret it, because the apostles thought it unimportant what time the Passover should be observed. Nevertheless, for harmony's sake and because prominent brothers and sisters had been converted from the Jews, who observed their custom, the adversaries wished the rest to follow their
44 example. They wisely warned the reader neither to remove the freedom of the Gospel, nor to burden consciences. The apostles thought that consciences should not be troubled, even though there should be an error in setting the date.

Many things like this can be collected 45
from the historical accounts. In them it appears that a lack of uniformity in human observances does not harm the unity of faith. What need is there of discussion? The adversaries do not at all understand what the righteousness of faith is, what Christ's kingdom is. That is clear when they judge that uniformity of observances in food, days, clothing, and the like (which do not have God's com-
mand) is necessary. Look at these religious 46
men, our adversaries. They require uniform human observances for the unity of the Church. They do this even though they themselves have changed Christ's ordinance in the use of the Supper, which certainly was a universal ordinance before. If universal ordinances are so necessary, why do they themselves change the ordinance of Christ's Supper, which is not human, but divine? We will have to speak about this entire controversy a little later.

Article VIII has been approved entirely, in 47
which we confess that hypocrites and wicked persons have been mixed in with the Church and that the Sacraments are powerful even though given by wicked ministers. Ministers act in Christ's place and do not represent their own persons, according to Luke, "The one who hears you hears Me" (10:16).
Ungodly teachers are to be deserted because 48
they no longer act in Christ's place, but are antichrists. Christ says, "Beware of false prophets" (Matthew 7:15). Paul says, "If anyone is preaching to you a gospel contrary to the one you received, let him be accursed" (Galatians 1:9).

Furthermore, Christ has warned us con- 49
cerning the Church in His parables. When offended by the private sins of priests or people, we should not stir up divisions, as the
Donatists have wickedly done. However, con- 50
cerning those who have stirred up division

because they denied that priests are permitted to hold possessions and property, we hold that they are completely rebellious. To hold property is a civil ordinance. It is lawful, however, for Christians to use civil ordinances, just as they use the air, the light, food, and drink. For as this order of the world and fixed movements of the heavenly bodies are truly God's ordinances and are preserved by God, so lawful governments are truly God's ordinances, preserved and defended by God against the devil.

ARTICLE IX

Baptism

Note: The Pontifical Confutation accepted the Augsburg Confession's teaching on Baptism. Here again, Melanchthon repeats the Lutheran rejection of Anabaptist errors concerning Baptism in general and the Baptism of infants in particular. Baptism is treated more extensively elsewhere in the Book of Concord, most notably in Martin Luther's Large Catechism. (See also AC IX; SA III V; SC IV; LC IV.)

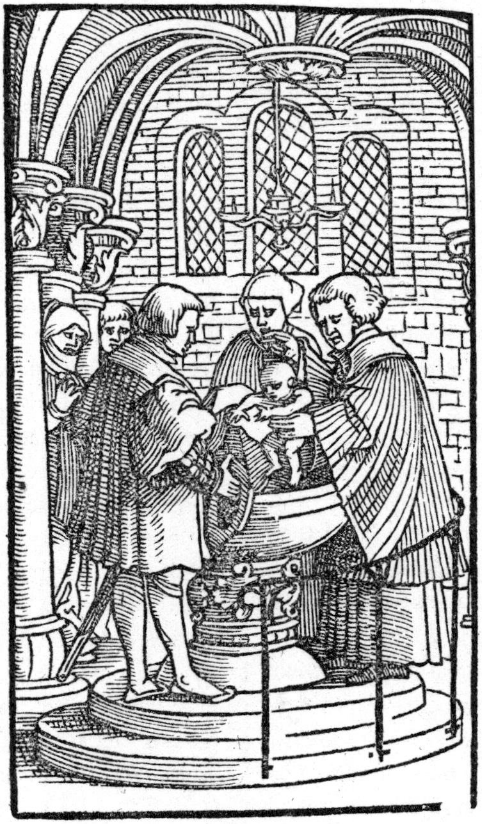

Infant Baptism

51 Article IX has been approved, in which we confess that "Baptism is necessary for salvation," that "children are to be baptized," and that the "Baptism of children is not in vain, but is necessary and effective for salva-
52 tion." Since the Gospel is taught among us purely and diligently, by God's favor we receive also this fruit from it: In our churches no Anabaptists have arisen. This is because the people have been strengthened by God's Word against the wicked and rebellious faction of these robbers. This is also among the distinct errors of the Anabaptists we condemn. They argue that the Baptism of little children is useless. For it is very certain that the promise of salvation also applies to little children. It does not, however, apply to those who are outside of Christ's Church, where there is neither Word nor Sacraments. Christ's kingdom exists only with the Word and Sacraments. Therefore, it is necessary to baptize little children, that the promise of salvation may be applied to them, according to Christ's command to baptize all nations (Matthew 28:19). Just as in this passage salvation is offered to all, so Baptism is offered to all, to men, women, children, infants. It clearly follows, therefore, that infants are to be baptized, because salvation is offered with
53 Baptism. Second, it is clear that God approves of the Baptism of little children. Therefore, the Anabaptists, who condemn the Baptism of little children, believe wickedly. God's approval of the Baptism of little children is shown by this: He gives the Holy Spirit to those baptized [Acts 2:38–39]. For if this Baptism would be empty, the Holy Spirit would be given to no one. No one would be saved. And finally, there would be no Church. This reason, even by itself, can well enough establish good and godly minds against the godless and fanatical opinions of the Anabaptists.

ARTICLE X
The Holy Supper

Note: The Pontifical Confutation approved the Augsburg Confession's statement on the Lord's Supper. The Lutherans clearly rejected the Zwinglian view of the Supper. In a more refined manner, Calvin and Reformed theology would later defend Zwingli's views. Lutheranism maintains the biblical and historic Church doctrine that in the Lord's Supper the body and blood of Jesus Christ are truly present under the bread and wine, distributed, and given into the mouths of all who commune, both worthy and unworthy. This is effected by the institution of Christ who, working through His Word, continues giving what He promises: His body and blood for our forgiveness, life, and salvation, as Luther describes it in his Small Catechism. (See also AC X; SA III VI; SC VI; LC V; FC Ep VII and SD VII.)

Article X has been approved, in which we 54
confess the following: We believe that in the Lord's Supper Christ's body and blood are truly and substantially present and are truly administered with those things that are seen (bread and wine) to those who receive the Sacrament. We constantly defend this belief, as the subject has been carefully examined and considered. Since Paul says, "The bread that we break, is it not a participation in the body of Christ?" (1 Corinthians 10:16), it would follow that if the Lord's body were not truly present, the bread is not a communion
of the body, but only of Christ's spirit. We 55
have determined that not only the Roman Church affirms Christ's bodily presence. The Greek Church also now believes, and formerly believed, the same. Their canon of the Mass testifies to this. In the canon the priest clearly prays that the bread may be changed

and become Christ's very body. Vulgarius, who does not seem to be an unimportant writer to us, says clearly that "bread is not a mere figure, but is truly changed into flesh."

56 There is a long commentary by Cyril on John 15, in which he teaches that Christ is bodily offered to us in the Supper. For he says:

> Nevertheless, we do not deny that we are joined spiritually to Christ by true faith and sincere love. But that we have no way of connection with Him, according to the flesh, this indeed we entirely deny. We say this idea is completely foreign to the divine Scriptures. For who has doubted that Christ is in this manner a vine, and we the branches, deriving life for ourselves from this? Hear Paul saying, "For you are all one in Christ Jesus; so we, though many, are one body in Christ; for we all partake of the one bread" (Galatians 3:28; Romans 12:5; 1 Corinthians 10:17). Does he perhaps think that the virtue of the mystical benediction is unknown to us? Since this is in us, does it not also, by the communication of Christ's flesh, cause Christ to dwell in us bodily? And a little after: Therefore, we must consider that Christ is in us not only according to the habit, which we call love, but also by natural participation.

We have cited these testimonies, not to undertake a discussion here about this subject, 57
for His Imperial Majesty does not disapprove of this article. But we cite them so that all who read them may more clearly discern that we defend the doctrine received in the entire

The Last Supper

Church. In the Lord's Supper, Christ's body and blood are truly and actually present. They are truly administered with those things that are seen, bread and wine. And we speak of the presence of the living Christ, for we know that "death no longer has dominion over Him" (Romans 6:9).

ARTICLE XI

Confession

Note: The Pontifical Confutation accepted the Augsburg Confession's statement about Confession, but insisted that the Church could order people to confess before a priest at least once a year. Melanchthon explains how in Lutheran churches the Sacraments are received often, but no laws are made about how often. Of particular concern is the Roman insistence on the recalling of all sins, or at least the effort to name them all. At no point did the Lutheran Church ever reject private Confession and Absolution. Rather, the Lutherans commended it as a very beneficial practice. (See also AC XI; SA III VIII; SC V; Appendix B, Brief Exhortation to Confession.)

Article XI, "Confession," is approved. But 58
they add a correction in reference to Confession. They say that the regulation called *Omnis utriusque* be observed and annual confession be made. They also say that, although all sins cannot be named, they should be recalled with diligence. Those that can be recalled should be specified. We will speak at greater length about this entire article after a while, when we will explain our entire

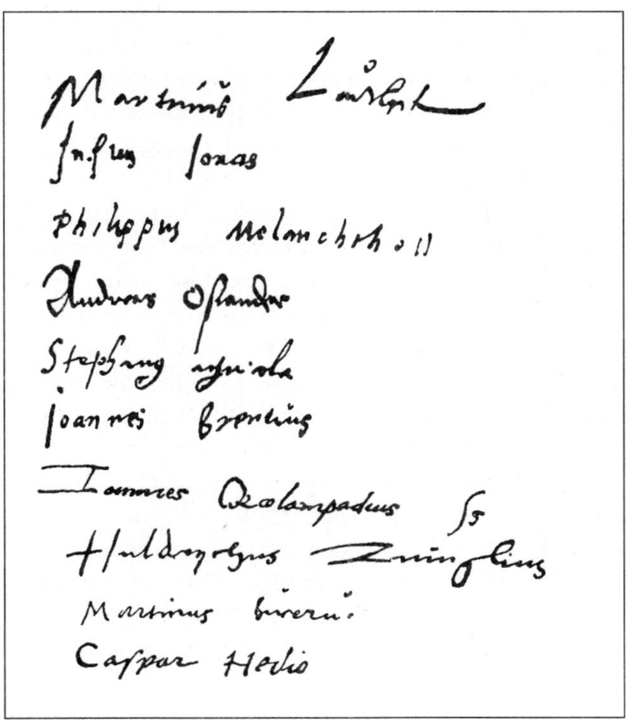

Signatures
on the Marburg Articles

The controversy over the Lord's Supper led to the decisive Marburg Colloquy (1529). Martin Luther, Justas Jonas, and Philip Melanchthon met with representatives of Southern German cities. Here are their signatures (Latin) affixed to the Marburg Articles: Martinus Lutherus, Justus Jonas, Philippus Melanchthon, Andreas Osiander, Stephanus Agricola, Joannes Brentius, Joannes Oecolampadius, Huldrychus Zuinglius, Martinus Bucerus, Caspar Hedio.

59 opinion about repentance. It is well known that we have made clear and praised the benefit of Absolution and the Power of the Keys. Many troubled consciences have derived comfort from our teaching. They have been comforted after they heard that it is God's command, no, rather the very voice of the Gospel, that we should believe the Absolution and regard it as certain that the forgiveness of sins is freely granted to us for Christ's sake. We should believe that through this faith we are truly reconciled to God. This belief has encouraged many godly minds and, in the beginning, brought Luther the highest praise from all good people. This belief shows consciences sure and firm comfort. Previously, the entire power of Absolution had been kept under wraps by teachings about works. For the learned persons and monks taught nothing about faith and free forgiveness.

60 Concerning the time, certainly most people in our churches frequently use the Sacraments (Absolution and the Lord's Supper) during the year. Those who teach about the worth and fruit of the Sacraments speak in a way that invites the people to use the Sacraments frequently. There are many writings by our theologians about this subject that the adversaries, if they are good men, will un-
61 doubtedly approve and praise. Excommunication is also pronounced against the openly wicked and the haters of the Sacraments. These things are done both according to the
62 Gospel and according to the old canons. A fixed time for Confession is not prescribed because all are not ready in the same way at the same time. Yes, if all were to come at the same time, they could not be heard and instructed in order. The old canons and Fathers do not appoint a fixed time. The canon speaks only in this way:

> If any enter the Church and be found never to commune, let them be taught that, if they do not commune, they come to repentance. If they commune ‹if they wish to be regarded as Christians›, let them not be thrown out; if they fail to do so, let them be excommunicated.

Christ [Paul] says that those who eat unworthily eat judgment to themselves (1 Corinthians 11:29). So the pastors do not force those who are not qualified to use the Sacraments.

Concerning the enumeration of sins in 63
Confession, people are taught in such a way as not to trap their consciences. It is helpful to familiarize inexperienced people, to name some things, in order that they may be more readily taught. We are now discussing what is necessary according to divine Law. Therefore, the adversaries should not quote for us the regulation *Omnis utriusque*, which we already know, but they should show from the divine Law that complete naming of sins is necessary for obtaining their forgiveness.
The entire Church, throughout all Europe, 64
knows what sort of snares this point of the regulation has cast upon consciences by commanding that all sins be confessed. The matter was only made worse by the Summists, who collected the circumstances of the sins and added their own ideas. What mazes there were! How great a torture for the best minds! The immoral and ungodly were in no way moved by these instruments of terror.
Afterward, what tragedies did the questions 65
about one's own priest stir up among the pastors and brethren, who then were by no means brethren when they were warring about jurisdiction of confessions! We believe that, according to divine Law, a complete listing of sins is not necessary. This is also pleasing to Panormitanus and very many other learned legal scholars. Nor do we want to

burden the consciences of our people by the regulation *Omnis utriusque*. We judge it to be like any other human tradition. They are not acts of worship necessary for justification. This regulation commands that we do something impossible—that we should confess all sins. However, it is clear that most sins we neither remember nor understand, according to Psalm 19:12, "Who can discern his errors?"

66 If the pastors are good men, they will know to what extent they should examine inexperienced persons. But we do not want to sanction the torture of the Summists. It would have been more tolerable if they had added one word about faith, which comforts and encourages consciences. About this faith, which obtains the forgiveness of sins, there is not a syllable in so great a mass of regulations, commentaries, summaries, or books of confession. Christ is nowhere read there. Only the lists of sins are read. The greater part is occupied with sins against human traditions. This is most useless. This doctrine 67
has forced many to despair. Godly minds were not able to find rest because they believed that by divine Law listing was necessary. Yet they experienced that it was impossible. Other faults of no less importance cling to the doctrine of the adversaries about repentance, which we will now recount.

Confession and Absolution

ARTICLE XIIa (V)

Repentance

Note: The Pontifical Confutation rejected the Lutheran teaching that penance, or repentance, consists only of contrition and faith. God's Law brings about contrition, which is a profound realization of one's sins. The Gospel creates faith, which trusts that God forgives our sins for the sake of Christ. By teaching that repentance consists of three things—contrition, confession, and satisfaction—Rome attributes our forgiveness to human works and denies itself the comforting Gospel.

According to the Roman Church, the eternal penalty of sin is forgiven by Absolution. But in order to escape temporal punishment, one must make satisfaction for sin, either here on earth or later in purgatory. Roman Catholicism still teaches a system of indulgences, which is traditionally associated with the Roman practice of confession. The sale and corresponding abuses of indulgences caused Luther to post his Ninety-five Theses in 1517. Melanchthon carefully demolishes this horrendous error concerning how we are forgiven: "Scripture often teaches that the forgiveness of sins arises freely for Christ's sake, that Christ is the Victor over sin and death [1 Corinthians 15:57]. The merit of satisfaction is not to be patched over this" (Ap XIIB [VI] 60). (See also AC XII; SA III III; SC V; Appendix B, Brief Exhortation to Confession.)

1 In Article XII, the adversaries approve of the first part, in which we present this: those who have fallen after Baptism may obtain the forgiveness of sins whenever and as often as they are converted. They condemn the second part, in which we say that the parts of repentance are contrition and faith. They deny that faith is the second part of repen-
2 tance. O Charles, most invincible Emperor, what should we do? This is the very voice of the Gospel: through faith we obtain the forgiveness of sins. These writers of the Confutation condemn this voice of the Gospel. Therefore, we can in no way agree to the Confutation. We cannot condemn the voice of the Gospel; it is beneficial and full of comfort. What else is the denial that we obtain the forgiveness of sins by faith than contempt
for Christ's blood and death? We beg you, O 3
Charles, most unconquerable Emperor. Patiently and diligently hear and examine this most important subject. It contains the chief topic of the Gospel, the true knowledge of Christ, and the true worship of God. For all good people will determine that especially on this subject we have taught things that are true, godly, beneficial, and necessary for Christ's whole Church. All good people will determine from the writings of our theologians that very much light has been added to the Gospel and many deadly errors have been corrected. By these errors, through the opinions of the Scholastics and canonists, the doctrine of repentance was previously covered up.

Before we defend our position, we must 4
first say this: All good people of all situations, even the theological profession, undoubtedly confess that the teaching of repentance was very much confused before Luther's writings
appeared. Theologians were never able to ex- 5
plain satisfactorily the numberless questions found in the books of the commentaries on the *Sentences*. The people could not grasp the big picture, nor could they see what things were necessary for repentance, in which
peace of conscience could be found. Let any 6
one of the adversaries come forth and tell us when the forgiveness of sins takes place. O good God, there is such darkness! The adversaries do not know whether the forgiveness of sins happens in attrition or contrition. If

forgiveness happens because of contrition,
why do we need Absolution? What does the
Power of the Keys bring about, if sins have
been forgiven already? Here they work even
harder and wickedly divert from the Power of
7 the Keys. Some imagine that guilt is not for-
given by the Power of the Keys, but that eter-
nal punishments are changed into temporal
ones. So the most beneficial power would be
the service, not of life and the Spirit, but only
of God's anger and punishments. The more
cautious imagine that sins are forgiven be-
fore the Church, and not before God, by the
Power of the Keys. This also is a deadly error.
For if the Power of the Keys does not comfort
us before God, what will quiet the con-
8 science? What follows is even more involved.
The adversaries teach that we merit grace by
contrition. In reference to this, if anyone
should ask why Saul, Judas, and similar per-
sons (who were dreadfully contrite) did not
receive grace, here is the answer: We take it
from faith and according to the Gospel, that
Judas did not believe. He did not support
himself by the Gospel and Christ's promise.
For faith shows the distinction between the
contrition of Judas [Matthew 27:3–5] and of
Peter [Matthew 26:75]. But the adversaries
take their answer from the Law, that Judas
did not love God, but feared the punish-
9 ments. When will a terrified conscience be
able to decide whether it fears God for His
own sake or is fleeing from eternal punish-
ments? The Psalms and the Prophets de-
scribe those serious, true, and great terrors,
which the truly converted experience. Such
great emotions can be distinguished in letters
and terms, but they are not separated in fact,
10 as these dear philosophers imagine. Here we
appeal to the judgments of all good and wise
people. Undoubtedly, they will confess that
these discussions in the writings of the ad-
versaries are very confused and intricate.
Still, the most important subject is at stake,
the chief topic of the Gospel, the forgiveness
of sins. In the writings of the adversaries, this
entire doctrine about these questions is full
of errors and hypocrisy and clouds over
Christ's benefit, the Power of the Keys, and
the righteousness of faith.

These things happen in the first act of this 11
play. What about Confession? What a work
there is in the endless listing of sins. Never-
theless, this is in great part devoted to sins
against human traditions! So that good
minds may be more tortured by this, the ad-
versaries falsely assert that this listing is of di-
vine right. They demand this listing under 12
the claim of divine right. In the meantime,
they speak coldly about Absolution, which is
truly of divine right. They falsely assert that
the Sacrament itself bestows grace by the
mere performance of one act (*ex opere oper-
ato*) without a good disposition on the part
of the one using it. They do not mention
faith grasping the Absolution and comfort-
ing the conscience. This is truly what is gen-
erally called departing before the mysteries.

The third act of this play, *concerning satis-* 13
factions, remains. It contains the most con-
fused discussions. The adversaries imagine
that eternal punishments are switched to the
punishments of purgatory and teach that a
part of them is forgiven by the Power of the
Keys and that a part is to be redeemed by
means of satisfactions. Further, they add that 14
satisfactions should be extraordinary works
(supererogation). They make these consist of
most foolish observances, such as pilgrim-
ages, rosaries, or similar observances that do
not have God's command. Then, just as they 15
redeem purgatory by means of satisfactions,
so a scheme was created for redeeming satis-
factions, which was most abundant in rev-
enue. They sell indulgences, which they in-
terpret as the pardon of satisfactions. This

Allegorical Woodcut of Luther Posting the Ninety-five Theses

This woodcut, produced shortly after Luther posted the Ninety-five Theses, is based on a legendary dream that Frederick the Wise had in Schweinitz, the night before Luther posted the Ninety-five Theses. According to the legend, Frederick dreamt that God sent him a monk. The saints came with him to say the monk would do God's will. Right background: Frederick listens as the saints point to Christ. Luther receives a revelation from heaven. On left: Saints ask Frederick to allow Luther to write something on the church door. The words "Concerning Absolution" are large enough for the Elector to read them from Schweinitz. Luther's pen reaches Rome, pierces a lion's ears, and knocks off the pope's threefold crown. Cardinals and princes try to prevent the crown from falling. (Frederick said that he saw himself and his brother, John, reaching out to steady the crown as well.) The lion roars mightily so that Rome and all territories of the Holy Roman Empire run to see what is wrong. The harder Rome tries to break Luther's pen, the stronger it becomes. Other pens pop out of Luther's pen. Lower right: Books burn, with a goose in the middle of the flames. The goose symbolizes John Hus. Top left: The pope, bishops, and cardinals put up a barrier to keep people from Luther. Top center: A monk promotes indulgences. This woodcut shows how printing was used effectively to spread news of the Reformation.

revenue is not only from the living, but is
much more plentiful from the dead. Nor do
they redeem the satisfactions of the dead
only by indulgences, but also by the sacrifice
16 of the Mass. In a word, the topic of satisfac-
tions is infinite. The doctrine of the righ-
teousness of faith in Christ and the benefit of
Christ lies buried among these scandals (for
we cannot list everything) and doctrines of
devils. Therefore, all good people understand
that the doctrine of the learned persons and
canon lawyers about repentance has been
criticized for a useful and godly purpose. For
the following teachings are clearly false and
foreign, not only to Holy Scripture, but also
to the Church Fathers:

17 1. Through good works, apart from grace, we merit grace from the divine covenant.

18 2. We merit grace by attrition.

19 3. Merely hating the crime is enough for the blotting out of sin.

20 4. We obtain forgiveness of sins because of contrition, and not by faith in Christ.

21 5. The Power of the Keys provides the forgiveness of sins before the Church, but not before God.

22 6. Sins are not forgiven before God by the Power of the Keys; rather, the Power of the Keys has been set up to transfer eternal punishments to temporal, to put certain satisfactions upon consciences, to set up new acts of worship, and to put consciences in debt to such satisfactions and acts of worship.

23 7. The listing of offenses in Confession, as taught by the adversaries, is necessary according to divine right.

24 8. Canonical satisfactions are necessary for redeeming the punishment of purgatory, or they benefit as a compensation for blotting out guilt. This is how uninformed persons understand it.

25 9. Without a good disposition on the part of the one using it, that is, without faith in Christ, the reception of the Sacrament of repentance by the outward act (*ex opere operato*) obtains grace.

10. Our souls are freed from purgatory through indulgences by the Power of the Keys. 26

11. In the reservation of cases, not only canonical punishment, but also the guilt, should be reserved for one who is truly converted. 27

[The Two Parts of Repentance]

To deliver godly consciences from these 28
mazes of the learned persons, we have attrib-
uted these two parts to repentance: contri-
tion and faith. If anyone desires to add a
third—fruit worthy of repentance, that is, a
change of the entire life and character for the
better—we will not oppose it. We separate 29
from contrition those useless and endless
discussions regarding grief from loving God
and from fearing punishment. We say that
contrition is the true terror of conscience,
which feels that God is angry with sin and
grieves that it has sinned. This contrition
takes place when sins are condemned by
God's Word. The sum of the preaching of the
Gospel is this: to convict of sin; to offer for
Christ's sake the forgiveness of sins and righ-
teousness, the Holy Spirit, and eternal life;
and that as reborn people we should do good
works. So Christ includes the sum of the 30
Gospel when He says, "Repentance and for-
giveness of sins should be proclaimed in His
name to all nations" (Luke 24:47). Scripture 31
speaks about these terrors:

> For my iniquities have gone over my head; like a heavy burden, they are too heavy for me. I am feeble and crushed; I groan because of the tumult of my heart. (Psalm 38:4, 8)

> Be gracious to me, O LORD, for I am languishing; heal me, O LORD, for my

> bones are troubled. My soul also is greatly troubled. But You, O Lord—how long? (Psalm 6:2–3)
>
> I said, In the middle of my days I must depart; I am consigned to the gates of Sheol for the rest of my years. I calmed myself until morning; like a lion he breaks all my bones. (Isaiah 38:10, 13)

32 In these terrors, conscience feels God's wrath against sin. This is unknown to secure people living according to the flesh. The conscience sees the corruption of sin and seriously grieves that it has sinned. Meanwhile, it also runs away from God's dreadful anger. Human nature, unless sustained by God's
33 Word, cannot endure His anger. So Paul says, "For through the law I died to the law" (Gala-
34 tians 2:19). For the Law only accuses and terrifies consciences. In these terrors our adversaries say nothing about faith. They present only the Word that convicts of sin. When this is taught alone, it is the doctrine of the Law, not of the Gospel. By these griefs and terrors, they say, people merit grace, as long as they love God. But how will people love God in true terrors when they feel God's horrible wrath, which is beyond words? What besides despair do those people teach who, during these terrors, show forth only the Law?

35 As the second part of repentance we add faith in Christ. The Gospel, in which the forgiveness of sins is freely promised concerning Christ, should be presented to consciences in these terrors. They should believe that, for Christ's sake, their sins are freely forgiven.
36 This faith cheers, sustains, and enlivens the contrite, according to Romans 5:1, "Since we have been justified by faith, we have peace with God." This faith obtains the forgiveness of sins. It justifies before God, as the same passage testifies, "since we have been justified by faith." This faith shows the distinction between the contrition of Judas and Peter, of Saul and David. The contrition of Judas or Saul [Matthew 27:3–5; 1 Samuel 31:4–6] is useless because faith is not added. Faith grasps the forgiveness of sins, given as a gift for Christ's sake. So the contrition of David or Peter [2 Samuel 12:13; Matthew 26:75] helps because faith, which takes hold of the forgiveness of sins granted for Christ's sake,
is added to it. Love is not present before rec- 37
onciliation has been made through faith. For without Christ, the Law is not performed, according to Romans 5:2, "Through [Christ] we have also obtained access [to God]." This faith grows gradually and throughout the entire life, struggles with sin, in order to overcome sin and death. Love follows faith,
as we have said above. So childlike fear can 38
be clearly defined as anxiety that has been connected with faith, that is, where faith comforts and sustains the anxious heart. It is slavish fear when faith does not sustain the anxious heart.

Furthermore, the Power of the Keys ad- 39
ministers and presents the Gospel through Absolution, which is the true voice of the Gospel. We also include Absolution when we speak of faith, because "faith comes from hearing," as Paul says in Romans 10:17. When the Gospel is heard and the Absolution is heard, the conscience is encouraged
and receives comfort. Because God truly 40
brings a person to life through the Word, the Keys truly forgive sins before God. According to Luke 10:16, "The one who hears you hears Me." Therefore, the voice of the one absolving must be believed no differently than we
would believe a voice from heaven. Absolu- 41
tion can properly be called a Sacrament of repentance, as even the more learned
scholastic theologians say. Meanwhile, in 42
temptations this faith is nourished in a

variety of ways: through the declarations of the Gospel and the use of the Sacraments. For these are signs of the New Testament, that is, signs of the forgiveness of sins. They offer the forgiveness of sins as the words of the Lord's Supper clearly testify, "This is My body, which is given for you. This is the cup of the New Testament," and so on. (See Matthew 26:26, 28.) So faith is conceived and strengthened through Absolution, through the hearing of the Gospel, through the use of the Sacraments, so that it may not give in to the terrors of sin and death while it struggles.
43 This method of repentance is plain and clear. It increases the worth of the Power of the Keys and of the Sacraments. It illumines Christ's benefit and teaches us to make use of Christ as Mediator and the Atoning Sacrifice.

[Scriptural Proofs]

44 Because the Confutation condemns us for having assigned these two parts to repentance, we must show that Scripture expresses these as the chief parts in repentance or conversion. Christ says, "Come to Me, all who labor and are heavy laden, and I will give you rest" (Matthew 11:28). Here there are two parts. The "labor" and the burden signify the contrition, anxiety, and terrors of sin and death. To "come to" Christ is to believe that sins are forgiven for Christ's sake. When we believe, our hearts are brought to life by the
45 Holy Spirit through Christ's Word. Here, therefore, are these two chief parts: contrition and faith. In Mark 1:15, Christ says, "Repent and believe in the gospel." In the first clause He convicts of sins, and in the second He comforts us and shows the forgiveness of sins. Believing the Gospel is not the general faith that devils also have, but in the proper sense it is believing that the forgiveness of sins has been granted for Christ's sake. This is revealed in the Gospel. You see also here that the two parts are joined: contrition when sins are rebuked; and faith when it is said, "Believe in the gospel." If anyone should say here that Christ also includes the fruit of repentance or the entire new life, we shall not disagree. For this satisfies us, that contrition and faith are named as the chief parts.

When Paul describes conversion or re- 46
newal, he almost everywhere designates these two parts, *making dead and making alive*, as in Colossians 2:11, "In Him also you were circumcised with a circumcision made without hands," namely, "by putting off the body of the flesh." And afterward, "in which you were also raised with Him through faith in the powerful working of God" (2:12). Here are the two parts. One is putting off the body of sins, the other is the rising again through faith. Neither should these terms "making dead," "making alive," "putting off the body of sins," "rising again" be understood in a Platonic way, about a fake change. Rather, "making dead" means true terrors, such as those of the dying, which nature could not sustain unless it were supported by faith. Paul calls that "the putting off the body of sins," which we ordinarily call contrition. In these griefs the natural, lustful desire is purged away. The "making alive" should not be understood as a Platonic fancy, but as comfort that truly sustains life that flickers in
contrition. Here, therefore, are two parts: 47
contrition and faith. For conscience cannot be quieted except through faith. Therefore, faith alone makes alive, according to this declaration: "The righteous shall live by his faith" (Habakkuk 2:4; Romans 1:17).

Colossians 2:14 says, "[Christ canceled] 48
the record of debt that stood against us with its legal demands." Here also there are two parts, the handwriting and the blotting out of the handwriting. The handwriting, how-

ever, is conscience, convicting and condemning us. The Law, furthermore, is the Word that rebukes and condemns sins. Therefore, this voice that says, "I have sinned against the Lord," as David says (2 Samuel 12:13), is the handwriting. Wicked and secure people do not seriously give forth this voice, for they do not see. They do not read the sentence of the Law written in the heart. This sentence is perceived in true griefs and terrors. Therefore, the handwriting that condemns us is contrition itself. To blot out the handwriting is to chisel away the sentence by which we declare that we shall be condemned and to engrave the sentence by which we know that we have been freed from this condemnation. Faith is the new sentence. It reverses the former sentence and gives peace and life to the heart.

49 What need is there to cite many testimonies since they are everywhere clear in the Scriptures?

> The Lord has disciplined me severely, but He has not given me over to death. (Psalm 118:18)

> My soul melts away for sorrow; strengthen me according to Your word! (Psalm 119:28)

Here, contrition is contained in the first
clause, and how we are revived in contrition
is clearly described in the second. We are re-
vived by God's Word, which offers grace.
50 This sustains and enlivens hearts.

> The Lord kills and brings to life; He brings down to Sheol and raises up. (1 Samuel 2:6)

Contrition is meant by one of these; faith is meant by the other.

> 51 [The Lord] will be roused; to do His deed—strange is His deed! and to work His work—alien is His work! (Isaiah 28:21)

He calls it the "strange" work of the Lord
when He terrifies, because to make alive and
comfort is God's own proper work. But He
terrifies, Isaiah says, for this reason—that
there may be a place for comfort and making
alive. For hearts that are secure and do not
feel God's wrath hate consolation. In this 52
manner Scripture is accustomed to join these
two, the terrors and the consolation. It does
this to teach that there are these chief parts in
repentance: contrition and faith that com-
forts and justifies. Neither do we see how the
nature of repentance can be presented more
clearly and simply.

God's two chief works among people are 53
these: to terrify; to justify and make alive
those who have been terrified. Into these two
works all Scripture has been distributed. The
one part is the *Law*, which shows, reproves,
and condemns sins. The other part is the
Gospel, that is, the promise of grace bestowed
in Christ. This promise is constantly repeated
in the whole of Scripture, first having been
delivered to Adam ‹"I will put enmity" in
Genesis 3:15›, afterward, to the patriarchs.
Then, it was still more clearly proclaimed by
the prophets. Lastly, it was preached and set
forth among the Jewish people by Christ and
then spread out over the entire world by the
apostles. All the saints were justified through 54
faith in this promise, and not by their own
attrition or contrition.

The examples also show these two parts. 55
After his sin, Adam is rebuked and becomes
terrified; this was contrition. Then, God
promises grace and speaks of a future seed
(the blessed seed, that is, Christ) by which the
devil's kingdom, death, and sin will be de-
stroyed [Genesis 3:15]. There He offers the
forgiveness of sins. These are the chief things.
For although the punishment is added after-
ward, it does not merit the forgiveness of sin.

We will speak about this kind of punishment a little later.

56 David is rebuked by Nathan in this way.
Terrified, he says, "I have sinned against the
LORD" (2 Samuel 12:13). This is contrition.
Afterward, he hears the Absolution, "The
LORD also has put away your sin; you shall
not die." This voice encourages David, and
through faith it sustains, justifies, and en-
livens him. A punishment is also added, but
this punishment does not merit the forgive-
57 ness of sins. Nor are special punishments al-
ways added. In repentance these two things
ought always to exist, namely, contrition and
faith, as in Luke 7. The woman, who was a
sinner, came to Christ weeping. By these tears
the contrition is recognized. Afterward, she
hears the Absolution, "Your sins are forgiven.
Your faith has saved you; go in peace" (vv. 48,
50). This is the second part of repentance,
namely, faith that encourages and comforts
58 her. From all these it is clear to godly readers
that we assign to repentance those parts that
properly belong to it in conversion, or the
new birth, and the forgiveness of sin. Worthy
fruit and punishments follow rebirth and the
forgiveness of sin. For this reason we have
mentioned these two parts so that the faith
required in repentance might be seen better,
and so that faith, which the Gospel pro-
claims, can be better understood when it is
contrasted with contrition and making dead.

[Forgiveness of Sins Received by Faith]

59 Since the adversaries clearly condemn our statement that people obtain the forgiveness of sins by faith, we shall add a few proofs. From these it will be understood that the forgiveness of sins is received not by the outward deed (*ex opere operato*) because of contrition, but by that special faith by which an individual believes that sins are pardoned for him. For this is the chief article that we are debating with our adversaries and the knowledge we regard is necessary to all Christians. However, we have said enough already about the same subject and will be brief. For the doctrine of repentance and justification are very closely related.

When the adversaries speak of faith, say- 60
ing that it comes before repentance, they understand faith this way: not that faith justifies, but that, in a general way, it believes that God exists, that punishments have been threatened to the wicked, and so on. In addition to this faith, we require that each one believe that his sins are pardoned. We are arguing about this specific faith, and we contrast it to the opinion that asks us to trust not in Christ's promise, but in the outward act (*opus operatum*) of contrition, confession, satisfactions, and so on. This faith follows terrors in such a way as to overcome them and make the conscience peaceful. We attribute justification and regeneration to this faith, since it frees from terrors and produces not only peace and joy, but also a new life in the heart. ‹With God's help,› we shall defend ‹to eternity and against all the gates of hell› that this faith is truly necessary for the forgiveness of sins, and so place it among the parts of repentance. Nor does Christ's Church believe otherwise, although our adversaries contradict us.

Furthermore, we ask the adversaries 61
whether or not Absolution is a part of repentance. If they separate it from Confession (they are clever in making the distinction), we do not see what benefit Confession has without Absolution. If, however, they do not separate Absolution from Confession, it is necessary for them to hold that faith is a part of repentance, because Absolution is not received except through faith. However, that Absolution is received only through faith is proven from Paul, who teaches that the

promise cannot be received *except by faith* (Romans 4:16). Absolution is the promise of the forgiveness of sins. Therefore, it necessar-
62 ily requires faith. Neither do we see how the person who does not yield to Absolution may be said to receive Absolution. What else is the refusal to yield to Absolution but charging God with falsehood? If the heart doubts, it regards those things that God promises as uncertain and of no account. So, it is written, "Whoever does not believe God has made Him a liar, because he has not believed in the testimony that God has borne concerning His Son" (1 John 5:10).

63 Second, we think that the adversaries recognize that the forgiveness of sins is either a part of repentance or its end (the *terminus ad quem*). Therefore, whatever receives the forgiveness of sins is correctly added to the parts of repentance. However, it is very certain that even though all the gates of hell contradict us, the forgiveness of sins cannot be received except by faith alone. This faith believes that sins are pardoned for Christ's sake, according to Romans 3:25, "whom God put forward as a propitiation by His blood, to be received by faith." Likewise, "Through Him we have also obtained access by faith into this grace" (Romans 5:2). For a terrified conscience cannot 64
set our works or our love against God's wrath. It is eventually quieted when it takes hold of Christ as Mediator and believes the promises given for His sake. For those who imagine that hearts become quieted without

The Good Shepherd and False Shepherds

faith in Christ do not understand what the
65 forgiveness of sins is or how it came to us. So
1 Peter 2:6 cites from Isaiah 49:23 and 28:16,
"Whoever believes in Him will not be put to
shame." It is necessary, therefore, that hyp-
ocrites be puzzled. They are confident that
they receive the forgiveness of sins because of
their own works, and not because of Christ.
Peter also says, "To Him all the prophets bear
witness that everyone who believes in Him
receives forgiveness of sins" (Acts 10:43).
What he says, through His name, could not
be expressed more clearly. He adds, "every-
one who believes in Him." So we receive the
forgiveness of sins only through Christ's
name, that is, for Christ's sake, and not for
the sake of any merits and works of our own.
This happens when we believe that our sins
are forgiven for Christ's sake.

66 Our adversaries cry out that they are the
Church, that they are following the general
agreement of the Church. But Peter also cites
here in our issue the consensus of the
Church, "To Him all the prophets bear wit-
ness that everyone who believes in Him re-
ceives forgiveness of sins" (Acts 10:43). The
general agreement of the prophets is certain-
ly to be judged as the general agreement of
the Church universal. We admit neither to
the pope nor to the Church the power to
make decrees against this general agreement
67 of the prophets. But the bull of Leo openly
condemns this article, "Repentance," and the
adversaries condemn it in the Confutation. It
is clear what sort of a Church we must judge
these men to be. By their decrees they not
only condemn the doctrine that we obtain
the forgiveness of sins through faith (not on
account of our works, but because of Christ),
but they also give the command to abolish it
by force and the sword and by every kind of
cruelty to put to death good people who be-
lieve this way.

They have famous authors, Scotus, 68
Gabriel Biel, and the like, and passages of the
Fathers that are quoted in a butchered form
in the decrees. Certainly, if the quotations are
to be counted, they win. For there is a very
great crowd of most silly writers on the *Sen-
tences*. As though they had worked together,
they defend these fables about the merit of
attrition and of works and other things that
we have mentioned previously. But let no 69
one be moved by the multitude of citations.
There is no great weight in the testimonies of
the later writers. They did not create their
own writings, but only, by compiling from
the writers before them, transferred these
opinions from some books into others. They
have exercised no judgment. Just like petty
judges they have silently approved the errors
of their superiors, which they have not un-
derstood. Therefore, let us not hesitate to use 70
this saying of Peter, which summarizes the
Prophets and opposes ever so many legions
of the commentators on the *Sentences*. The 71
Holy Spirit's testimony is added to this state-
ment of Peter. For the text speaks in this way,
"While Peter was still saying these things, the
Holy Spirit fell on all who heard the word"
(Acts 10:44). Therefore, let godly consciences 72
know that God's command is this: They are
to believe that they are freely forgiven for
Christ's sake, and not for the sake of our
works. Let them sustain themselves against
despair and against the terrors of sin and of
death by this command of God. Let them 73
know that this belief has existed among
saints from the beginning of the world. For
Peter clearly cites the general agreement of
the Prophets, and the writings of the apostles
confirm that they believe the same thing. Nor
are testimonies of the Fathers lacking. For
Bernard says the same thing in words that are
in no way hidden:

> It is necessary first of all to believe that you cannot have forgiveness of sins except by the indulgence of God, but add yet that you believe also this, namely, that through Him sins are forgiven to you. This is the testimony that the Holy Spirit asserts in your heart, saying: "Your sins are forgiven you." For so the apostle concludes that a person is justified freely through faith.

74 These words of Bernard shed a wonderful light upon our cause, because he not only requires that we believe in a general way that sins are pardoned through mercy, but he also asks us to add special faith, by which we believe that our sins are forgiven. He teaches how we can be sure about the forgiveness of sins, namely, when our hearts are encouraged through faith and become peaceful through the Holy Spirit. What more do the adversaries require? Do they still dare deny that we receive the forgiveness of sins through faith or that faith is a part of repentance?

75 Third, the adversaries say that sin is pardoned because an attrite or contrite person brings forth an act of love to God, and by this act deserves the forgiveness of sins. This is nothing but teaching the Law, the Gospel being blotted out, and the promise about Christ being abolished. For they require only the Law and our works because the Law demands love. Besides, they teach us to be confident that we obtain forgiveness of sins because of contrition and love. What else is this than to put confidence in our works, not in God's Word and promise about Christ? But if the Law is enough for receiving the forgiveness of sins, what need is there of the Gospel? What need is there of Christ if we receive forgiveness of sins because of our own work?
76 We, on the other hand, call consciences away from the Law to the Gospel, and from confidence in their own works to confidence in the promise and Christ. We do so because the Gospel presents Christ to us and freely promises the forgiveness of sins for Christ's sake. In this promise it asks us to trust, namely, that we are reconciled to the Father for Christ's sake, not for the sake of our own contrition or love. For there is no other Mediator or Atoning Sacrifice than Christ. Neither can we do the works of the Law unless we have first been reconciled through Christ. If we would do anything, we must believe that for Christ's sake, as Mediator and Atoning Sacrifice, we receive the forgiveness of sins, and not for the sake of these works.

Yes, it is a disgrace to Christ and a repeal 77
of the Gospel to believe that we receive the forgiveness of sins because of the Law, or any way other than through faith in Christ. We discussed this before in the article on justification. There we declared why we confess that people are justified through faith, not
through love. The doctrine of the adversaries 78
is merely the doctrine of the Law, when they teach that by their own contrition and love people receive the forgiveness of sins and trust in this contrition and love. Even so, it is not understood ‹they do not understand the kind of love toward God it demands›, just as the Jewish people looked upon Moses' veiled face [2 Corinthians 3:15]. Let us imagine that love is present, and let us imagine that works are present. Yet neither love nor works can be an atoning sacrifice for sin. The adversaries cannot even be opposed to God's wrath and judgment, according to Psalm 143:2, "Enter not into judgment with Your servant, for no one living is righteous before You." Neither should Christ's honor be transferred to our works.

For these reasons Paul argues that we are 79
not justified by the Law. He contrasts the Law to the promise of the forgiveness of sins,

which we freely receive and which is granted
for Christ's sake. Paul calls us away from the
Law to this promise. Upon this he asks us to
look. The promise certainly will be void if we
are justified by the Law before we are justified
through the promise, or if we receive the for-
giveness of sins because of our own righ-
80 teousness. Clearly the promise was given to
us and Christ was offered to us because we
cannot do the works of the Law. Therefore, it
is necessary that we are reconciled by the
promise before we do the works of the Law.
The promise, however, is received only
through faith. It is necessary for contrite per-
sons to take hold of the promise of the for-
giveness of sins granted for Christ's sake
through faith and to be confident that they
have a reconciled Father freely for Christ's
81 sake. This is Paul's meaning when he says,
"That is why it depends on faith, in order
that the promise may rest on grace and
be guaranteed" (Romans 4:16). And, "The
Scripture imprisoned everything under sin,
so that the promise by faith in Jesus Christ
might be given to those who believe" (Gala-
tians 3:22). This means that all are under sin,
neither can they be freed except by grasping
the promise of the forgiveness of sins
82 through faith. Therefore, we must accept the
forgiveness of sins through faith before we do
the works of the Law. Although, as has been
said before, love follows faith because the re-
born person receives the Holy Spirit and so
begins to do the works of the Law.

83 We would cite more testimonies if they
were not clear in the Scriptures to every
godly reader. We do not wish to be too
wordy, so that we may bring this case to a
84 conclusion. Neither is there any doubt that
we are defending Paul's meaning. He teaches
that through faith we receive the forgiveness
of sins for Christ's sake, and that through
faith we should set Christ as Mediator
against God's wrath, and not our works. Nor
should godly minds be disturbed when the
adversaries find fault with Paul's judgments.
Nothing is said so simply that it cannot be
distorted by objecting. We know that we have
mentioned Paul's true and genuine meaning.
We know that our belief brings sure comfort
to godly consciences, without which no one
can stand in God's judgment.

Let these legalistic opinions of the adver- 85
saries be rejected. Among these are that we do
not receive the forgiveness of sins by faith, but
that it should be merited by our love and
works. Another opinion is that we should set
our love and our works against God's wrath.
This doctrine is not of the Gospel, but of the
Law. It wrongly teaches that a person is justi-
fied by the Law before he has been reconciled
through Christ to God. Christ says, "Apart
from Me you can do nothing"; likewise, "I am
the vine; you are the branches" (John 15:5).
But the adversaries wrongly teach that we are 86
branches not of Christ, but of Moses. For they
want to be justified by the Law and to offer
their love and works to God before they are
reconciled to God through Christ, before they
are branches of Christ. On the other hand,
Paul argues that the Law cannot be obeyed
without Christ. We must receive the promise
first so that through faith we may be recon-
ciled to God on account of Christ. Then we
can do the works of the Law. Those who truly
feel and have experienced sin and anguish of
conscience must cling to the promise of
grace. We think that these things are clear 87
enough to godly consciences. In this way they
will understand why we have declared before
that people are justified through faith, not
through love. We must set against God's
anger not our love or works (or trust in our
love or works), but Christ as Mediator. We
must grasp the promise of the forgiveness of
sins before we do the works of the Law.

88 Finally, when will conscience be quieted if we receive forgiveness of sins on the ground that we love, or that we do the works of the Law? The Law will always accuse us, because we never satisfy God's Law. Just as Paul says, "The law brings wrath" (Romans 4:15). Chrysostom asks about repentance, "Where are we made sure that our sins are forgiven?" The adversaries also, in their *Sentences,* ask about the same subject. This cannot be explained; consciences cannot be made at peace unless they know it is God's command and the very Gospel that they should be firmly confident that sins are forgiven freely for Christ's sake, and that they should not doubt this. If anyone doubts, he charges the divine promise with falsehood, as 1 John 5:10 says. We teach that the Gospel requires this certainty of faith. The adversaries leave con-
89 sciences uncertain and wavering. Consciences, however, do nothing by faith when they constantly doubt whether they have forgiveness. In this doubt how can they call upon God? How can they be confident that they are heard? So the entire life would be without God and without the true worship of God. This is what Paul says, "Whatever does not proceed from faith is sin" (Romans 14:23). Because they are constantly occupied with this doubt, they never experience what faith is. So finally they rush at last into despair. Such is the doctrine of the adversaries, the doctrine of the Law, the setting aside of
90 the Gospel, the doctrine of despair. We are glad to refer judgment about this subject of repentance (for it is clear) to all good people. They can decide whether we or the adversaries have taught those things that are more godly and healthful to consciences. Indeed, these disagreements in the Church do not delight us. If we did not have great and necessary reasons for disagreeing with the adversaries we would, with the greatest pleasure, be silent. But since they condemn the clear truth, it is not right for us to abandon what is not our own cause, but the cause of Christ and the Church.

[Faith and Repentance]

We have declared why we assigned these 91
two parts, contrition and faith, to repentance. We have done this willingly. Many writings about repentance are published that cite the Fathers in a butchered way. The adversaries have distorted these to put faith out of sight. Among these are, "Repentance is to lament past evils, and not to commit again deeds that ought to be lamented." Again, "Repentance is a kind of vengeance of him who grieves, thus punishing in himself what he is sorry for having committed." In these passages, no mention is made of faith. Not even in the schools, when they interpret them, is anything added about faith.
Therefore, in order that the doctrine of 92
faith might be clearer, we have named it among the parts of repentance. For experience shows that those passages are dangerous that require contrition or good works, and make no mention of justifying faith.
Caution can justly be desired in those who 93
have collected these centos of the *Sentences* and decrees. Since the Fathers speak in some places about one part of repentance, and in other places about another part, it would have been good to select and combine their judgments not only about one part but about both, that is, about contrition and faith.

Tertullian speaks very well about faith, 94
discussing the oath in the prophet Ezekiel, "As I live, declares the Lord God, I have no pleasure in the death of the wicked, but that the wicked turn from his way and live" (33:11). As God swears that He does not want the death of a sinner, He shows that

faith is required, in order that we may believe the one swearing and be firmly confident that He forgives us. In our estimation, the authority of the divine promises should be great by itself. But this promise has also been confirmed by an oath. Therefore, if anyone is not confident that he is forgiven, he denies that God has sworn what is true. A more horrible blasphemy cannot be imagined. For Tertullian says this:

> He invites by reward to salvation, even swearing. Saying, "I live," He desires that He be believed. Oh, blessed we, for whose sake God swears! Oh, most miserable if we believe not the Lord even when He swears!

95 Here we must know that this faith should be confident that God freely forgives us for Christ's sake, for the sake of His own promise, not for the sake of our works, contrition, confession, or satisfactions. For if faith relies upon these works, it immediately becomes uncertain, because the terrified conscience
96 sees that these works are unworthy. So Ambrose speaks well about repentance:

> Therefore, it is proper for us to believe both that we are to repent, and that we are to be pardoned, but in such a way as to expect pardon from faith, which obtains pardon as from a handwriting.

Again,

> It is faith that covers our sins.

97 Therefore, there are sentences written by the Fathers not only about contrition and works, but also about faith. But the adversaries, since they understand neither the nature of repentance nor the language of the Fathers, select passages about a part of repentance, namely, about works. They overlook the declarations made elsewhere about faith, since they do not understand them.

ARTICLE XIIb (VI)

Confession and Satisfaction

Note: The Roman Church transformed the great blessing of Confession and Absolution into a legalistic burden on the back of every Christian. In addition to requiring every sin to be confessed, Rome demanded satisfaction, or meritorious works, in order to "make up" for confessed sins. Absolution, the sweet announcement of forgiveness of sins through Christ, became tangled in the web of indulgences, satisfactions, and other human works that Rome required from her faithful. Melanchthon makes it clear that Lutherans cherish private Absolution, which is God's forgiveness in Christ applied personally to the believer burdened with guilt and sorrow over sin. He writes that those who despise Absolution understand neither forgiveness nor the Office of the Keys.

When death confronts a human being, he must face it with Christ alone, not with human works and satisfactions. We receive God's forgiveness freely because Christ Jesus is the Victor over sin, death, and Satan. Melanchthon discusses this extensively, because the teaching pointed to Luther's evangelical breakthrough in recovering the centrality of Christ and the Gospel in the Church. Lutherans never denied that good works follow the gift of faith and the blessings of the Gospel. But these gifts are not earned, merited, or deserved. By teaching that our participation with God's grace is what brings about eternal life, Roman theology horribly distorted and obscured the Gospel and robbed Christ of His place as our only Mediator, who makes satisfaction for our sin. (See AC XI and XXV; SA III VIII; SC V; Appendix B, Brief Exhortation to Confession.)

Good people can easily conclude that it is 1
very important that the true doctrine be pre- [98]
served about the above-mentioned parts: contrition and faith. Therefore, we have al-

ways been busier with making these topics
clear and have argued nothing as yet about
2 confession and satisfaction. We also keep
[99] Confession, especially because of the Absolu-
tion. Absolution is God's Word which, by di-
vine authority, the Power of the Keys pro-
3 nounces upon individuals. Therefore, it
[100] would be wicked to remove private Absolu-
4 tion from the Church. If anyone despises pri-
[101] vate Absolution, he does not understand
what the forgiveness of sins or the Power of
5 the Keys is. Regarding the complete listing of
[102] offenses in Confession, we have said above
that we hold that it is not necessary by divine
6 right. Some object to this, saying that a judge
[103] should investigate a case before he rules on it,
which has nothing to do with this subject.
The ministry of Absolution is favor or grace;
7 it is not a legal process or law. Ministers in
[104] the Church have the command to forgive sin.
They do not have the command to investi-
8 gate secret sins. Indeed, they absolve us
[105] from those sins that we do not remember.
For that reason Absolution, which is the voice of the Gospel forgiving sins and comforting consciences, does not require judicial examination.

9 It is ridiculous to apply to this discussion
[106] the saying of Solomon, "Know well the con-
dition of your flocks" (Proverbs 27:23). For Solomon says nothing about Confession. He gives to the father of a family a domestic precept, that he should use what is his own and refrain from what is another's. Solomon commands the father to take good care of his own property. Yet he should do so in such a way that, with his mind occupied with the increase of his resources, he should not cast away the fear of God or faith or care in God's Word. But our adversaries, by a wonderful change, transform Scripture passages to whatever meaning they please. Here to "know" means to them hearing confessions, "the condition," not the outward life, but the secrets of conscience. And "your flocks" mean people. The interpretation is truly neat and is worthy of these haters of pursuing eloquence. If anyone desires to transfer by analogy a precept from a father of a family to a pastor of a Church, he should certainly interpret "the condition" as applying to the outward life. This comparison will be more consistent.

Let us skip such matters as these. Confes- 10
sion is mentioned at different times in the [107]
Psalms. "'I will confess my transgressions to the LORD,' and You forgave the iniquity of my sin" (32:5). Such confession of sin, which is made to God, is contrition itself. When confession is made to God, it must be made with the heart, not only with the voice, like actors on the stage. Confession is contrition in which, feeling God's anger, we confess that God is justly angry and that He cannot be reconciled by our works. Yet, we seek for
mercy because of God's promise. Such is the 11
following confession, "Against You, You only, [108]
have I sinned . . . so that You may be justified in Your words and blameless in Your judgment" (Psalm 51:4). This means, "I confess that I am a sinner and have merited eternal wrath. Nor can I set my righteousnesses, my merits, against Your wrath. So I declare that You are just when You condemn and punish us. I declare that You are clear when hypocrites judge You to be unjust in punishing them or in condemning the well-deserving. Yes, our merits cannot satisfy Your judgment. But we will be justified in this way, namely, if You justify us, if through Your mercy You
count us righteous." Perhaps someone may 12
also cite James 5:16, "Confess your sins to [109]
one another." But here the reference is not to confession made to priests, but is the reconciliation of brothers to each other. Confession should be mutual.

13 Our adversaries will condemn many well-
[110] respected teachers if they will agree that in
Confession a listing of offenses is necessary
according to divine Law. We approve of Con-
fession, and conclude that some examination
is helpful, so that people may be instructed
better. Yet, Confession must be done in such
a way that consciences are not entrapped.
They never will be quieted if they think that
they cannot receive the forgiveness of sins
14 unless this precise listing is made. What the
[111] adversaries have expressed in the Confuta-
tion is certainly most false: A full confession
is necessary for salvation. This is impossible.
What traps they lay for the conscience when
they require a full confession! When will a
conscience be sure that the confession is
15 complete? Church writers mention Confes-
[112] sion. However, they do not speak about this
listing of secret offenses, but about the rite of
public repentance. The fallen or notorious
sinners were not received [into fellowship]
without fixed satisfactions. They confessed to
the presbyters, so that satisfactions might be
prescribed to them according to the degree of
their guilt. This type of confession has noth-
ing similar to the listing about which we are
arguing. This kind of confession was made,
not because the forgiveness of sins before
God could not happen without it, but be-
cause satisfactions could not be prescribed
unless the kinds of offense were first known.
Different offenses had different rules.

[The Church Fathers on Satisfaction]

16 The word *satisfaction* has been left from
[113] this rite of public repentance. The Holy Fa-
thers were unwilling to welcome back the
fallen or the notorious sinners unless, as far as
it was possible, their repentance had been first
examined and shown publicly. There seem to
have been many causes for this. To discipline
those who had fallen served as an example, as
the gloss upon the decrees reminds us. Also, it
was improper to admit notorious people im-
mediately to Communion. These customs
have long since grown obsolete. It is not nec-
essary to restore them, because they are not
necessary for the forgiveness of sins before
God. The Fathers did not maintain that peo- 17
ple merit the forgiveness of sins through such [114]
customs or works. These spectacles ‹outward
ceremonies› usually lead astray the igno-
rant, who thought that they merited the
forgiveness of sins before God by these
works. If anyone believes this, he has the
faith of a Jewish person and a pagan. For
even the pagans had certain remedies for
offenses through which they imagined they
were reconciled to God. Now, even though 18
the custom has been cast aside, the word *sat-* [115]
isfaction still remains. A small part of the cus-
tom also remains of prescribing in confession
certain satisfactions, which they define as
works that are not required. We call them
canonical satisfactions. Like the complete list- 19
ing of sins, we hold that canonical satisfac- [116]
tions are not necessary by divine Law for the
forgiveness of sins. Neither were those ancient
displays of satisfactions in public repentance
necessary by divine Law for the forgiveness of
sins. The teaching about faith must be kept,
that we receive the forgiveness of sins for
Christ's sake through faith, not for the sake of
our works that precede or follow. This is why
we have discussed especially the question
of satisfactions—the righteousness of faith
should not be clouded over in submitting to
them. Nor should people think that they re-
ceive the forgiveness of sins for the sake of
these works. Many current sayings in the 20
schools aid the error. Among these are those [117]
that give the definition of satisfaction, namely,
that it is done to reconcile divine displeasure.

Nevertheless, the adversaries admit that 21
satisfactions do not help in the pardon of [118]

guilt. They imagine that satisfactions help in
delivering one from punishment, whether
of purgatory or other punishments. They
teach that God pardons guilt in the forgive-
ness of sins. Yet, because divine justice re-
quires sin to be punished, He transfers eter-
nal punishment into temporal punishment.
Further, they add that a part of this tempo-
ral punishment is pardoned by the Power of
the Keys, but that the rest is delivered by
means of satisfactions. It cannot be under-
stood which punishments the Power of the
Keys partially forgive, unless the adversaries
say that a part of the punishments of purga-
tory is forgiven. That would mean that sat-
isfactions are only punishments delivering
from purgatory. They say satisfactions ben-
efit, even though they are presented by
those who have fallen again into mortal sin,
as though indeed the divine displeasure
could be appeased by those who are in mor-
22 tal sin. This entire matter is fake and recently
[119] made up without Scriptural authority and
the old writers of the Church. Not even
Lombard speaks of satisfactions in this way.
23 The Scholastics saw that there were satisfac-
[120] tions in the Church. They did not notice
that these displays had been set up both for
the purpose of example and for testing
those who desired to be welcomed back
by the Church. In a word, they did not see
that it was a discipline and entirely a secular
matter. So they superstitiously imagined
that these [displays] benefit not for disci-
pline before the Church, but for reconciling
God. In other places, they frequently, with
great incompetence, have confused spiritual
and civil matters. The same happens also re-
24 garding satisfactions. But at various places
[121] the explanation of the canons confirms that
these observances were set up for the sake of
Church discipline.

[Misuses of Scripture]

In the Confutation, the adversaries had 25
the nerve to impose on His Imperial Majesty. [122]
Let us see how they prove these fables of theirs. They cite many passages from the Scriptures to impress the inexperienced. They do this as though this subject—unknown even in the time of Lombard—had authority from the Scriptures. They promote such passages as these: "Bear fruit in keeping with repentance" (Matthew 3:8; see also Mark 1:15). "Present your members as slaves to righteousness" (Romans 6:19). Christ preaches repentance, "Repent" (Matthew 4:17). Again, Christ commands the apostles to preach repentance (Luke 24:47), and Peter preaches repentance (Acts 2:38). Afterward, the adversaries quote certain passages of the Fathers and the canons, and conclude that satisfactions in the Church are not to be set aside. This is contrary to the plain Gospel and the decrees of the councils and Fathers. They even claim that those who have been absolved by the priest should finish the repentance that has been directed. They base this on Paul's declaration, "Who gave Himself for us to redeem us from all lawlessness and to purify for Himself a people for His own possession who are zealous for good works" (Titus 2:14).

May God confuse these godless philoso- 26
phers. They wickedly distort God's Word to [123]
their own most empty dreams! What good person is not moved by such insult? "Christ says, 'Repent,' the apostles preach repentance; therefore, eternal punishments are relieved by the punishments of purgatory; therefore, the Keys have the power to pardon part of the punishments of purgatory; therefore, satisfactions deliver from the punishments of purgatory!" Who has taught these asses such logic? Yet this is neither logic nor slick

thinking, but deceitful trickery. They appeal to the expression "repent" in such a way that, when the inexperienced hear such a passage cited against us, they may come to the opinion that we deny repentance in its entirety. By these moves they try hard to turn away minds and to stir up hatred. They do this so that the inexperienced may cry out against us, that the deadly heretics that disapprove of repentance should be removed from their midst.

27 We hope that these lies may make little
[124] headway among good people. We also hope that God will not put up with such rudeness and wickedness much longer. The pope of Rome has not become any more dignified using such patrons, because he has entrusted a very important matter of the greatest importance to the judgment of these philosophers. Since we include almost all of the Christian doctrine in the Confession, judges should have been appointed to declare about important and various matters. Their learning and faith would have been more acceptable than the learning of these philosophers
28 who have written this Confutation. It was
[125] very fitting of you, O Campegius, according to your wisdom, to have made sure that they should write nothing about important matters that, either now or later, might appear to lower respect for the Roman See. If the Roman See determines that all nations should recognize her as mistress of the faith, she should try very hard to have educated and godly people investigate religious matters. What will the world conclude if at any time the adversaries' writing is brought to light? What will future generations think about these disgraceful judicial investiga-
29 tions? You see, O Campegius, that these are
[126] the last days. Christ predicted that the greatest danger to religion would happen in them [Matthew 24:9–28]. You, who should sit on the watchtower [Hosea 9:8] and control religious matters, should in these times also use unusual wisdom and diligence. Unless you heed them, there are many signs that threat-
en a change to the Roman state. And you 30
make a mistake if you think that churches [127]
should be kept only by force and arms. The people are asking to be taught about religion. How many do you suppose there are, not only in Germany, but also in England, in Spain, in France, in Italy, and finally even in the city of Rome? Since controversies have come up about subjects of the greatest importance, they are beginning to doubt here and there, to be silently insulted that you refuse to investigate and rightly judge such weighty subjects. They doubt and are insulted that you do not help wavering consciences, that you only ask us to be over-
thrown and destroyed by arms. To many 31
good people this doubt is more bitter than [128]
death. You do not think enough about how great a subject religion is, if you think that good people are in anguish for little reason when they doubt any teaching. This doubt can have no other effect than to produce the greatest bitterness of hatred against those who hinder the explanation of the subject
when they should heal consciences. We are 32
not saying here that you should fear God's [129]
judgment. The religious leaders think that they can easily ensure against this since they hold the Keys. Of course, they can open heaven for themselves whenever they want. We are speaking of the judgments of people and the silent desires of all nations. At this time they require that these matters be investigated and decided so that good minds may be healed and freed from doubt. For, according to your wisdom, you can easily decide what will happen if at any time this hatred should break out against you. By this favor you will be able to bind all nations to yourself.

All sane people regard it as the highest and most important matter if you heal doubting
33 consciences. We have said these things not be-
[130] cause we doubt our Confession. For we know
that it is true, godly, and useful to godly consciences. It is likely that there are many in many places who waver about matters of no small importance. Yet they do not hear teachers that are able to heal their consciences.

34 Let us return to the main point. The
[131] Scriptures cited by the adversaries do not
speak of canonical satisfactions and of the opinions of the Scholastics, since it is clear that the latter were born only recently. Therefore, it is pure slander when they distort Scripture to their own opinions. We say that good fruit, good works in every kind of life, should follow repentance, that is, conversion or regeneration. Neither can there be true conversion or true contrition where the putting to death of the flesh and bearing good fruit do not follow. True terrors, true griefs of mind, do not allow the body to satisfy itself in sensual pleasures, and true faith is not ungrateful to God. Neither does true faith hate God's commandments. In a word, there is no inner repentance unless it also produces the
35 outward putting to death of the flesh. We say
[132] that this is John's meaning when he says,
"Bear fruit in keeping with repentance" (Matthew 3:8). Likewise of Paul when he says, "Present your members as slaves to righteousness" (Romans 6:19); just as he likewise says elsewhere, "Present your bodies as a living sacrifice" (Romans 12:1), and so forth. When Christ says, "Repent" (Matthew 4:17), He certainly speaks of repentance in its entirety, of the entire newness of life and its fruit. He does not speak of those hypocritical satisfactions that the Scholastics imagine benefit by delivering from the punishment of purgatory or other punishments when they are made by those in mortal sin.

Many arguments, likewise, can be 36
brought together to show that these Scrip- [133]
ture passages have nothing to do with scholastic satisfactions. [First,] these men imagine that satisfactions are works that are not due. However, Scripture, in these passages, requires works that are due. For this word of Christ, "Repent," is the word of a
commandment. Likewise, the adversaries 37
write that if anyone who goes to Confession [134]
should refuse to undertake satisfactions, he does not sin, but will pay these penalties in purgatory. Now the following passages are, without controversy, rules having to do with this life: "repent," "bear fruit in keeping with repentance," "present your members as slaves to righteousness." Therefore, they cannot be twisted to the satisfactions that are permitted to be refused. Refusing God's command-
ments is not permitted. Third, indulgences 38
pardon these satisfactions, as is taught in [135]
the article "Repentance" (beginning *Quum ex eo*), and so on. But indulgences do not free us from these commandments: "repent," "bear fruit in keeping with repentance." Clearly these Scripture passages have been wickedly twisted to apply to canonical satisfactions.
See further what follows. If the punishments 39
of purgatory are satisfactions, or "satispas- [136]
sions," or if satisfactions are a pardoning of the punishments of purgatory, do the passages also command that souls be punished in purgatory? Since this must follow from the opinions of the adversaries, these passages should be interpreted in a new way: "bear fruit in keeping with repentance," "repent," that is, suffer the punishments of purgatory
after this life. But we do not care to respond 40
any further to the silly points of the adver- [137]
saries. Clearly, Scripture speaks of works that are required, of the entire newness of life, and not of these observances of works that are not required, of which the adversaries

speak. Yet, by these fables they defend orders
of monks, the sale of Masses, and endless ob-
servances, calling them works that, if they do
not make satisfaction for guilt, can still make
satisfaction for punishment.

41 The Scripture passages cited do not say
[138] that eternal punishments are to be paid by
works that are not required. So the adver-
saries are rash to assert that these satisfactions
are paid by canonical satisfactions. The Keys
do not have the command to transfer some
punishments and, likewise, to pardon a part
of the punishments. For where are such
things read in the Scriptures? Christ speaks of
the forgiveness of sins when He says, "What-
ever you loose . . ." (Matthew 18:18). He
means sin being forgiven, eternal death taken
away, and eternal life bestowed. "Whatever
you bind" does not speak of requiring pun-
ishments, but of retaining the sins of those
42 who are not converted. Furthermore, the dec-
[139] laration of Lombard about pardoning a part
of the punishments has been taken from the
canonical punishments; the pastors forgave a
part of these. We hold that repentance should
produce good fruit for the sake of God's glory
and command. Good fruit, true fastings, true
prayers, true alms, and so forth, have God's
commands. Yet in the Holy Scriptures we find
nowhere that eternal punishments are only
pardoned because of the punishment of pur-
gatory or canonical satisfactions, that is, be-
cause of certain works not required, or that
the Power of the Keys has the command to
transfer their punishments or to forgive a
portion. The adversaries were going to prove
these things.

43 Besides, Christ's death is a satisfaction not
[140] only for guilt, but also for eternal death, ac-
cording to Hosea 13:14, "O Death, where are
your plagues?" It is freakish to say that the
satisfaction of Christ redeemed from the
guilt, but our punishments redeem from
eternal death. The expression "I will be your
death" does not get understood about Christ,
but about our works and, indeed, not about
the works commanded by God, but about
some dull observances created by men!
These are said to abolish death, even when
they are completed in mortal sin. It is with 44
incredible grief we recite these foolish points [141]
of the adversaries. They only cause one who
considers them to be enraged against such
demonic teachings. The devil has spread
these teachings in the Church to hinder the
knowledge of the Law and Gospel, of repen-
tance and being made alive, and of Christ's
benefits. For of the Law they speak this way: 45

> God, deferring to our weakness, [142]
> has given to people a measure of those
> things that necessarily binds them.
> This is obeying laws, so that from
> what is left, that is, from works of
> supererogation, he can present satis-
> faction with reference to offenses that
> have been committed.

Here people imagine that they can keep
God's Law in such a way that they do
even more than the Law requires [Romans
3:10–20]. But Scripture shouts everywhere
that we are far away from the perfection that
the Law requires. Still these people imagine
that God's Law affects only outward and
civil righteousness. They do not see that it re-
quires true love for God "with all your heart"
[Deuteronomy 6:4] and that it condemns all
lustful desires in human nature. Therefore, no
one does as much as the Law requires. Their
imagination that we can do more is ridicu-
lous. We *can* perform outward works not
commanded by God's Law. Yet confidence
that satisfaction has accomplished God's Law
is empty and wicked. True prayers, true alms, 46
and true fastings have God's command. [143]
Where they have God's command, they can-
not be left out without sin. But because these

other works have not been commanded by God's Law, but have a fixed form derived from human rule, they are works of human traditions. Christ says about such works, "In vain do they worship Me, teaching as doctrines the commandments of men" (Matthew 15:9). Such works include certain fasts appointed not for restraining the flesh, but so that honor may be given to God, as Scotus says, and so that eternal death be made up for. Likewise, such works include a fixed number of prayers, a fixed measure of alms when they are offered in worship by the outward act (*ex opere operato*), giving honor to God, and making up for eternal death. For they assign satisfaction to these works by the outward act because they teach that they benefit even
47 those who are in mortal sin. There are works
[144] that depart still farther from God's commands, such as pilgrimages. There is a great variety of these. One makes a journey ‹to St. Jacob› clothed in metal armor, and another with bare feet. Christ calls these "vain acts of worship." They do not serve to reconcile God's displeasure, contrary to what the adversaries say. Yet they decorate these works with magnificent titles. They call them works of supererogation. To these works the honor is assigned of being a price paid instead of
48 eternal death. They are preferred over the
[145] works of God's commandments. So God's Law is clouded over in two ways. One, because satisfaction is thought to be rendered to God's Law by means of outward and civil works. The other, because human traditions are added, whose works are preferred over the works of the divine Law.

49 In the second place, repentance and grace
[146] are clouded over. Eternal death is not atoned for by this payment of works because it is idle and does not taste of death in the present life. Something else must be set up against death when it tests us. For just as God's anger is overcome through faith in Christ, so death is overcome through faith in Christ. Just as Paul says, "But thanks be to God, who gives us the victory through our Lord Jesus Christ" (1 Corinthians 15:57). He does not say, "Who gives us the victory if we set up our satisfactions against death." The adversaries foster 50
needless debates about the pardon of guilt. [147]
They do not see how, in the pardon of guilt, the heart is freed through faith in Christ from God's anger and eternal death. Christ's death is a satisfaction for eternal death. The adversaries themselves confess that these works of satisfactions are works that are not required, but are works of human traditions, of which Christ says that they are vain acts of worship (Matthew 15:9). Therefore, we can safely affirm that canonical satisfactions are not necessary by divine Law for the pardon of guilt or eternal punishment or the punishment of purgatory.

[Additional False Teachings]

The adversaries object that revenge or 51
punishment is necessary for repentance, be- [148]
cause Augustine says that "repentance is revenge punishing" and so on. We grant that revenge or punishment is necessary in repentance. Yet it is not necessary as merit or price, as the adversaries imagine that satisfactions are necessary. But revenge is in repentance formally, that is, because rebirth itself happens by a continuous putting to death of the oldness of life. The saying of Scotus may indeed be very beautiful, that penitence (*poenitentia*) is so called because it is "holding to punishment" (*poenae tenentia*). But what punishment, what revenge, does Augustine speak about? Certainly true punishment, true revenge, namely, contrition, true terrors. Nor do we exclude here the outward putting to death (mortification) of the body, which fol-
lows true grief of mind. The adversaries 52

[149] make a great mistake if they imagine that
canonical satisfactions are more truly punish-
ments than are true terrors in the heart. It is
most foolish to twist the name of punishment
to these dull satisfactions, and not to refer
people to those horrible terrors of conscience
of which David says, "The cords of death en-
compassed me" (Psalm 18:4; see also 2 Sam-
uel 22:5). Who would not rather, clad in
metal armor and equipped, seek the Church
of James, the basilica of Peter, and so on, than
bear that violence of grief that is beyond
words and exists even in persons of ordinary
lives, if there be true repentance?

53 They say that it belongs to God's justice to
[150] punish sin. He certainly punishes it in con-
trition, when in these terrors He shows His
wrath. Just as David shows when he prays, "O
LORD, rebuke me not in Your anger" (Psalm
6:1). And Jeremiah, "Correct me, O LORD, but
in justice; not in Your anger, lest You bring
me to nothing" (10:24). Here, indeed, the
most bitter punishments are spoken of. The
adversaries admit that contrition can be so
great that satisfaction is not required. Con-
trition is, therefore, more truly a punishment
54 than is satisfaction. Besides, saints are subject
[151] to death and all general afflictions, as 1 Peter
4:17 says, "For it is time for judgment to
begin at the household of God; and if it be-
gins with us, what will be the outcome for
those who do not obey the gospel of God?"
Although these afflictions are for the most
part the punishments of sin, yet in the godly
they have a better end, namely, to exercise
them, that they may learn amid trials to seek
God's aid, to acknowledge the distrust of their
own hearts, and so forth. As Paul says of him-
self, "Indeed, we felt that we had received the
sentence of death. But that was to make us
rely not on ourselves but on God who raises
the dead" (2 Corinthians 1:9). Isaiah says,
"They poured out a whispered prayer when
Your discipline was upon them" (26:16), that
is, afflictions are a discipline by which God
exercises the saints. Likewise, afflictions are 55
inflicted because of present sin, since in the [152]
saints they put to death and extinguish lustful
desires, so that they may be renewed by the
Spirit, as Paul says, "The body is dead because
of sin" (Romans 8:10). The body is put to
death (mortified) because of present sin that
is still left in the flesh. Death itself serves this 56
purpose, namely, to abolish this flesh of sin, [153]
that we may rise absolutely new [1 Corinthi-
ans 15:42]. Since by faith the believer has
overcome death's terrors, there is no longer
in the believer's death that sting and sense
of anger of which Paul says, "The sting of
death is sin, and the power of sin is the law"
(1 Corinthians 15:56). This strength of sin,
this sense of wrath, is truly a punishment as
long as it is present. Without this sense of
wrath, death is not properly a punishment.
Furthermore, canonical satisfactions do not 57
belong to these punishments. The adversaries [154]
wrongly say that by the Power of the Keys a
part of the punishments is forgiven. Likewise,
according to these very men, the Keys pardon
the satisfactions and the punishments be-
cause of which the satisfactions are made. But
it is clear that common troubles are not re-
moved by the Power of the Keys. If the adver-
saries wish to be understood regarding these
punishments, why do they add that satisfac-
tion is to be accomplished in purgatory?

They object to Adam's example, and also 58
to David's, who was punished for his adul- [155]
tery. From these examples they get the uni-
versal rule that peculiar temporal punish-
ments in the forgiveness of sins correspond
to individual sins. It has been said before that 59
saints suffer punishments, which are God's [156]
works. They suffer contrition or terrors; they
also suffer other common troubles. So, for
example, some suffer punishments of their

Life in the Sixteenth Century

Job's Misfortune

own that have been applied by God. These punishments have nothing to do with the Keys, because the Keys can neither apply nor pardon them. But God, without the ministry of the Keys, applies and pardons them.

Neither does their universal rule follow. A peculiar punishment was put upon David [2 Samuel 12:11–14]. Therefore, in addition to common troubles, [they say] there is another punishment of purgatory, in which
60 each degree corresponds to each sin. Where
[157] does Scripture teach that we cannot be freed
from eternal death except by the payment of certain punishments in addition to common troubles? On the other hand, Scripture often teaches that the forgiveness of sins arises freely for Christ's sake, that Christ is the Victor over sin and death [1 Corinthians 15:57]. The merit of satisfaction is not to be patched over this. Although troubles still remain, Scripture interprets these as the putting to death of present sin, and not as the payments of eternal death or as prices for eternal death.

61 Job is excused though he was not trou-
[158] bled by past evil deeds [Job 2:3–10]. There-
fore, troubles are not always punishments or signs of wrath. Indeed, terrified consciences should be taught that there are more important purposes for afflictions [2 Corinthians 12:9], so that they do not think God is rejecting them when they see nothing but God's punishment and anger in troubles. The other more important purposes are to be considered, that is, that God is doing His strange work so that He may be able to do His own work, as Isaiah 28 teaches in a long
62 speech. When the disciples asked about the
[159] blind man who sinned, Christ replies that the
cause of his blindness is not sin, but that "the works of God might be displayed in him" (John 9:2–3). In Jeremiah it is said, "If those who did not deserve to drink the cup must drink it . . ." (49:12). So the prophets, John the Baptist, and other saints were killed
[Matthew 5:11]. Therefore, troubles are not 63
always punishments for certain past deeds, [160]
but they are God's works, intended for our benefit, and that God's power might be made more apparent in our weakness.

So Paul says God's strength "is made perfect in weakness" (2 Corinthians 12:9). Because of God's will, our bodies should be sacrifices, to declare our obedience, and not to pay for eternal death. God has another price
for that: the death of His own Son. Gregory 64
interprets David's punishment in this sense, [161]
when he says:

> If God had threatened that David would be humbled this way by his son because of that sin, why did He fulfill that which He had threatened against him when the sin was forgiven? The reply is that this forgiveness was made so that man might not be hindered from receiving eternal life. The example of the threatening followed, in order that the piety of humanity might be exercised and tested even in this humility. So because of sin, God inflicted upon humanity the death of the body. After the forgiveness of sins, He did not remove the affliction for the sake of exercising justice, namely, so that the righteousness of those who are sanctified might be exercised and tested.

Nor are common disasters, properly speak- 65
ing, removed by these works of canonical sat- [162]
isfactions, that is, by these works of human traditions. The adversaries say that these satisfactions benefit by the outward work (*ex opere operato*) in such a way that, even though they are done in mortal sin, they still
deliver from the punishments. When the pas- 66
sage of Paul is cited against us, "But if we [163]
judged ourselves truly, we would not be judged [by the Lord]" (1 Corinthians 11:31),

"to judge" should be understood to include
all of repentance and required fruit, not
works that are not required. Our adversaries
pay the penalty for hating grammar when
they understand "to judge" to equal making a
pilgrimage dressed in armor to the Church of
St. James, or similar works. "To judge" means
all of repentance; it means to condemn sins.
67 This condemnation truly happens in contri-
[164] tion and the change of life. All of repen-
tance—contrition, faith, and good fruit—
receives the reduction of public and private
punishments and disasters, as Isaiah 1:16–19
teaches, "Cease to do evil, learn to do good.
. . . Though your sins are like scarlet, they
shall be as white as snow. . . . If you are will-
ing and obedient, you shall eat the good of
68 the land." Neither should a most important
[165] and beneficial meaning be transferred from
all of repentance, and from works required
or commanded by God, to the satisfactions
and works of human traditions. It is benefi-
cial to teach the following: common evils are
reduced by our repentance and by the true
fruit of repentance, by good works complet-
ed from faith, not, as these men imagine,
69 completed in mortal sin. Here belongs the
[166] example of the Ninevites (Jonah 3:10), who
by their repentance (all of repentance) were
reconciled to God and received the favor that
their city was not destroyed.

70 Furthermore, the mentioning of satisfac-
[167] tion by the Fathers, and the framing of
canons by the councils, was a matter of
Church discipline set up as an example, as we
have said before. Nor did the councils hold
that this discipline is necessary for the par-
don either of the guilt or of the punishment.
If some of them mention purgatory, they in-
terpret it neither as payment for eternal pun-
ishment nor as satisfaction, but as purifica-
tion of imperfect souls. Just as Augustine says
that "venial offenses are consumed," that is,
distrust toward God and other similar ten-
dencies are destroyed. Now and then the 71
writers transfer the term *satisfaction* from the [168]
rite itself or spectacle, to illustrate true put-
ting to death (mortification). So Augustine
says:

> True satisfaction is to cut off the causes of sin, that is, to put the flesh to death, likewise to hold the flesh in check, not in order that eternal punishments may be paid for, but so that the flesh may not be drawn to sin.

About repayment, Gregory says that repen- 72
tance is false "if it does not satisfy those [169]
whose property we have taken." For the per-
son who still steals does not truly grieve that
he has stolen or robbed. He is a thief or rob-
ber as long as he is the unjust possessor of the
property of another. This civil satisfaction is
necessary, because it is written, "Let the thief
no longer steal" (Ephesians 4:28). Likewise, 73
Chrysostom says, "In the heart, contrition; in [170]
the mouth, confession; in the work, entire
humility." This amounts to nothing against
us. Good works should follow repentance. It
should be repentance (not a show), a change
of the entire life for the better.

Likewise, the Fathers wrote that it is 74
enough if once in life this public or ceremo- [171]
nial penitence happens, for which the canons
about satisfactions have been made. Clearly,
they held that these canons are not necessary
for the forgiveness of sins. In addition to this
ceremonial penitence, they frequently want
penitence to be done another way, in which
canons of satisfactions were not required.

The composers of the Confutation write 75
that the setting aside of satisfactions (which [172]
are contrary to the plain Gospel), is not to be
tolerated. So far we have shown that these
canonical satisfactions, that is, unrequired
works performed to pay for punishment, do

76 not have the command of the Gospel. The
[173] subject itself shows this. If works of satisfaction are works that are not required, why do they cite the plain Gospel? For if the Gospel would command that punishments be paid for by such works, the works would already be required. But they speak in this way in order to burden the inexperienced, and they cite testimonies that speak of required works, although they themselves in their own satisfactions prescribe works that are not required. Indeed, in their schools they themselves admit that satisfactions can be refused without sin. Therefore, they write here falsely that we are compelled by the plain Gospel to undertake these canonical satisfactions.

[True Repentance Produces Good Works]

77 We have already frequently testified that
[174] repentance should produce good fruit. These good fruit are what the commandments teach: prayer, thanksgiving, the confession of the Gospel, teaching the Gospel, obeying parents and rulers, and being faithful to one's calling. We should not kill, not hold on to hatred, but we should be forgiving and give to the needy, so far as we can according to our means. We should not commit sexual sins or adultery, but should hold in check, bridle, and chastise the flesh, not for a repayment of eternal punishment, but so as not to obey the devil or offend the Holy Spirit. Likewise, we should speak the truth. These fruit have God's command and should be produced for the sake of God's glory and command. They have their rewards also. But Scripture does not teach that eternal punishments are only pardoned through the payment offered by
78 certain traditions or by purgatory. Indul-
[175] gences used to be pardon for these public observances, so that people should not be burdened excessively. But if, by human authority, satisfactions and punishments can be pardoned, this payment is not necessary by divine Law. A divine Law is not set aside by human authority. Further, since the custom is no longer used and the bishops ignore it in silence, these pardons are not necessary. Yet the word *indulgences* remained. Satisfactions were understood not referring to outward discipline, but referring to the payment of punishment. So indulgences were incorrectly understood to free souls from purgatory. But 79
the Keys have the power of binding and [176]
loosing only upon earth [not in purgatory], according to Matthew 16:19, "Whatever you bind on earth shall be bound in heaven, and whatever you loose on earth shall be loosed in heaven." As we have said before, the Keys do not have the power to impose penalties or to institute rites of worship, but only the command to forgive sins [John 20:23] to those who are converted and to convict and excommunicate [1 Corinthians 5] those who are unwilling to be converted. For just as to *loose* means to forgive sins, so to *bind* means not to forgive sins. Christ speaks of a spiritual kingdom, and God's command is that ministers of the Gospel should absolve those who are converted, according to 2 Corinthians 10:8, "our authority, which the Lord gave for building you up." Therefore, the 80
reservation of cases is a secular affair. It is a [177]
reservation of canonical punishment. It is not a reservation of guilt before God in those who are truly converted. The adversaries judge rightly when they confess that in the matter of death the reservation of cases should not hinder Absolution.

We have presented all of our doctrine 81
about repentance. We certainly know it is [178]
godly and beneficial to good minds. If good people will compare our doctrine with the very confused discussions of our adversaries, they will see that the adversaries have left out

the doctrine about faith justifying and comforting godly hearts. They will also see that the adversaries invent many things about the merits of attrition, about the endless listing of offenses, and about satisfactions. They say things that agree neither with human law nor divine Law, and which not even they themselves can explain clearly enough.

ARTICLE XIII (VII)

The Number and Use of the Sacraments

Note: The Pontifical Confutation demanded that Lutherans teach that there are exactly seven Sacraments. Melanchthon's approach was to emphasize that the word *sacrament* is somewhat fluid in its meaning. The term is not strictly biblical (though it does appear in the Latin Vulgate as a translation for the Greek term *mysterion*; e.g., 1 Corinthians 4:1). As such, the term is capable of different uses in the Church. If the Church chooses to consider the Sacraments rites that God has commanded, to which the promise of grace is added, then there would be three: Baptism, the Lord's Supper, and Absolution or Repentance. Martin Luther generally spoke of Holy Baptism and the Sacrament of the Altar as Sacraments and regarded Confession and Absolution to be an extension of Baptism. Quibbling over the number of the Sacraments is unproductive and is to be avoided. It is better to focus on the gifts of God given in and through the Sacraments. Melanchthon is even willing in this article to regard ordination to the Church's ministry as a Sacrament, but only in relation to the ministry of the Word. Melanchthon makes the number of Sacraments an issue only because Rome did. He was forced to respond in more detail. What is important is receiving God's gracious gifts through faith, making sure that we never regard Sacraments as works to appease God or to merit His favor. (See AC XIII.)

In Article XIII, the adversaries approve our 1
statement that the Sacraments are not just marks of profession among people, as some imagine. Rather, they are signs and testimonies of God's will toward us. Through
them God moves hearts to believe. But here 2
they ask us to count seven Sacraments. We hold that the matters and ceremonies instituted in the Scriptures, whatever the number, should not be neglected. Neither do we believe it to be of any consequence. However, for teaching purposes, different people do count differently, provided they still rightly keep the matters handed down in Scripture. The ancients also did not count in the same way.

If we call Sacraments "rites that have the 3
command of God, and to which the promise of grace has been added," it is easy to decide what are true Sacraments. For rites instituted by human beings will not be called true Sacraments. For human authority cannot promise grace. Therefore, signs set up without God's command are not sure signs of grace, even though signs perhaps instruct the unlearned or admonish about something.
Therefore, Baptism, the Lord's Supper, and 4
Absolution (which is the Sacrament of Repentance) are truly Sacraments. For these rites have God's command and the promise of grace, which is peculiar to the New Testament. When we are baptized, when we eat the Lord's body, when we are absolved, our hearts must be firmly assured that God truly for-
gives us for Christ's sake. At the same time, by 5
the Word and by the rite, God moves hearts to believe and conceive faith, just as Paul says, "Faith comes from hearing" (Romans 10:17). But just as the Word enters the ear in order to strike our heart, so the rite itself strikes the eye, in order to move the heart. The effect of the Word and of the rite is the same. It has been well said by Augustine that a Sacrament is a visible Word, because the rite is received

by the eyes and is, as it were, a picture of the
Word, illustrating the same thing as the Word.
The result of both is the same.

6 Confirmation and extreme unction are
rites received from the Fathers that not even
the Church requires as necessary to salvation,
because they do not have God's command.
Therefore, it is useful to distinguish these
rites from the former, which have God's di-
rect command and a clear promise of grace.

7 The adversaries understand priesthood
not about the ministry of the Word, and giv-
ing out the Sacraments to others, but as re-
ferring to sacrifice. This is as though there
should be a priesthood like the Levitical one
[Leviticus 8–9] to sacrifice for the people and
merit the forgiveness of sins for others in the
8 New Testament. We teach that the sacrifice of
Christ dying on the cross has been enough
for the sins of the whole world. There is no
need for other sacrifices, as though Christ's
sacrifice were not enough for our sins. So
people are justified not because of any other
sacrifices, but because of this one sacrifice of
Christ, if they believe that they have been re-
9 deemed by this sacrifice. So they are called
priests, not in order to make any sacrifices for
the people as in the Law, that by these they
may merit forgiveness of sins for the people.
Rather, they are called to teach the Gospel
and administer the Sacraments to the people.
10 Nor do we have another priesthood like
the Levitical, as the Epistle to the Hebrews
11 teaches well enough [Hebrews 8]. But if or-
dination is understood as carrying out the
ministry of the Word, we are willing to call
ordination a Sacrament. For the ministry of
the Word has God's command and has glori-
ous promises, "The gospel . . . is the power of
God for salvation to everyone who believes"
(Romans 1:16). Likewise, "So shall My word
be that goes out from My mouth; it shall not
return to Me empty, but it shall accomplish
that which I purpose" (Isaiah 55:11). If ordi- 12
nation is understood in this way, neither will
we refuse to call the laying on of hands a
Sacrament. For the Church has the com-
mand to appoint ministers, which should be
most pleasing to us, because we know that
God approves this ministry and is present in
the ministry ‹that God will preach and work
through men and those who have been cho-
sen by men›. It is helpful, so far as can be 13
done, to honor the ministry of the Word with
every kind of praise against fanatical people.
These fanatics imagine that the Holy Spirit is
given not through the Word, but through
certain preparations of their own. For exam-
ple, they imagine He is given if they sit unoc-
cupied and silent in far-off places, waiting for
illumination, as the Enthusiasts formerly
taught and the Anabaptists now teach.

Marriage was not first instituted in the 14
New Testament, but in the beginning, imme-
diately after the creation of the human race
[Genesis 1:28]. Furthermore, it has God's
command. It has also promises, not truly
having to do with the New Testament, but
rather having to do with bodily life. There-
fore, if anyone wishes to call it a Sacrament,
he or she should still distinguish it from
those preceding ones. They are truly signs of
the New Testament and testimonies of grace
and the forgiveness of sins. But if marriage 15
has the name "Sacrament" because it has
God's command, other states or offices also,
which have God's command, may be called
Sacraments, as, for example, the government.

Finally, if among the Sacraments every- 16
thing should be numbered that has God's
command, and to which promises have been
added, why do we not add prayer, which
most truly can be called a Sacrament? For it
has both God's command and very many
promises. If numbered among the Sacra-
ments, although in a more prominent place,

17 it would encourage people to pray. Alms
could also be counted here and, likewise,
troubles. These are themselves signs to which
God has added promises. But let us leave out
these things. For no levelheaded person will
labor greatly about the number or the term,
if only those things are still kept that have
God's command and promises.

18 It is more important to understand how
the Sacraments are to be used. Here we con-
demn the whole crowd of scholastic doctors,
who teach that the Sacraments give grace by
the outward act (*ex opere operato*), without a
good frame of mind on the part of the one
using them, provided he does not place a
hindrance in the way. This is absolutely a
Jewish opinion, to hold that we are justified
by a ceremony, without a good tendency of
the heart, that is, without faith. Yet this un-
godly and deadly opinion is taught with great
authority throughout the entire realm of the
19 pope. Paul contradicts this, and denies (Ro-
mans 4:9) that Abraham was justified by cir-
cumcision. He asserts that circumcision was
an illustration presented for exercising faith.
So we teach that in the use of the Sacraments,
faith should be added. Faith should believe
these promises and receive the promised
20 things offered in the Sacrament. The reason
is plain and thoroughly grounded. The
promise is useless unless it is received by
faith. The Sacraments are the signs of the
promises. Therefore, faith should be added in
the use of the Sacraments. If anyone uses the
Lord's Supper, he should use it by faith. This
is a Sacrament of the New Testament, as
Christ clearly says (Luke 22:20). For this very
reason he should be confident that the free
forgiveness of sins promised in the New Tes-
tament is offered. Let him receive this by
faith, let him comfort his alarmed conscience
and know that these testimonies are not false.
They are as sure as though ‹and still surer
than if› God by a new miracle would declare
from heaven that it was His will to grant for-
giveness. What advantage would these mira-
cles and promises be to an unbeliever? Here 21
we speak of special faith that believes the
present promise that the forgiveness of sins is
offered. This use of the Sacrament consoles 22
godly and alarmed minds. We are not speak-
ing of a faith that only in general believes that
God exists.

It is beyond words what abuses the fanat- 23
ical opinion about outward works (*opus op-
eratum*) has produced in the Church (with-
out a good disposition on the part of the one
using the Sacraments). From it has come the
endless profanation of the Masses. We shall
speak about this later. A single letter cannot
be produced from the old writers that sup-
ports the Scholastics in this matter. On the
contrary, Augustine says the faith that uses
the Sacrament, and not the Sacrament, justi-
fies. And the declaration of Paul is well-
known, "With the heart one believes and is
justified" (Romans 10:10).

ARTICLE XIV

Order in the Church

Note: Here Melanchthon affirms Lutheranism's desire to maintain whatever best contributes to good order, peace, and harmony in the Church. Therefore, Lutherans have insisted on a rightly ordered call and ordination for those who will serve the Church as ministers of Word and Sacrament. For the sake of human order, Lutherans are willing for bishops to continue serving in the Church. However, bishops are nowhere given authority to impose nonbiblical teachings on the Church. After Luther's death, Lutherans in Germany established local clergy groups called consistories, with one of the pastors named as superintendent. These groups usually included learned laymen. In other Lutheran countries such as Sweden, the office of bishop was continued. The external order of the Church was left free. Lutheranism has never insisted on one form of Church government over another, like the Roman Catholic or Reformed Churches. Melanchthon makes clear that the important thing is the Word of God being purely taught and the Sacraments being properly given to the people. (See AC XIV; SA III X.)

---

24 In Article XIV, we say that no one should administer the Word and Sacraments unless he is rightly called. The adversaries accept the article, but on the condition that we use canonical ordination. About this subject we have often testified in this assembly that it is our greatest desire to keep Church orders and ranks, even though they have been made by human authority. We know that Church discipline in the manner laid down in the ancient canons was set up by the Fathers for a
25 good and useful purpose. But the bishops either urge our priests to reject and condemn the doctrine we have confessed or, by a new and unheard-of cruelty, they put the poor innocent men to death. These causes hinder our priests from recognizing such bishops. The cruelty of the bishops is the reason why the canonical government, which we greatly desired to keep, is dissolved in some places. Let them see how they will answer to God for
26 tearing apart the Church. In this matter our consciences are not in danger. Since we know that our Confession is true, godly, and catholic, we should not approve the cruelty
27 of those who persecute this doctrine. We know that the Church is among those who teach God's Word rightly and administer the Sacraments rightly. The Church it is not with those who try hard to wipe out God's Word by their orders and also put to death those who teach what is right and true. Toward them even the very canons are gentler, even though they do something contrary to the canons. Furthermore, we want to declare 28
again that we will gladly keep Church and canonical government, so long as the bishops stop attacking our churches. Our request will acquit us, both before God and among all nations forever, from the charge that we have undermined the authority of the bishops. People will acquit us when they read and hear that, although protesting against the unrighteous cruelty of the bishops, we could not obtain justice.

ARTICLE XV (VIII)

Human Traditions in the Church

Note: The Pontifical Confutation accepted Article XV of the Augsburg Confession, in which the Lutherans affirmed that traditions contributing to peace and order should be observed. But the Confutation opposed the Augsburg Confession's statement that any traditions created to appease God, merit His grace, and earn forgiveness be rejected. Melanchthon expresses surprise that Rome would demand anything contrary to this. Once more he returns to the constant refrain throughout the Apology: Anything that obscures the Gospel is to be rejected. This article provides more reasons why suggesting, implying, or teaching that human traditions merit God's grace is contrary to the Gospel of free and full forgiveness of sins in Christ alone. In this article Melanchthon states that the "chief service of God is to preach the Gospel." Preaching enables hearers to receive good things from God (Ap V 189). This turns on its ear the Roman notion that worship is primarily what we do to please or placate God. Worship is most essentially gathering to receive, through faith, God's gifts in Christ, by means of His Gospel and Sacraments. Our praise and thanksgiving for God's gifts is a response to

His grace, not a condition for receiving it. (See also AC XV; SA III XV; FC Ep X and FC SD X.)

---

1 In Article XV, the adversaries accept the
first part, in which we say that ecclesiastical
rites are to be kept that can be observed with-
out sin and are beneficial in the Church for
peace and good order. They completely con-
demn the second part, in which we say that
human traditions (set up to reconcile God, to
merit grace, and make satisfactions for sins)
2 are contrary to the Gospel. In the Confession
itself, we spoke long enough about traditions
such as the distinction of meats. Yet certain
things should be briefly reviewed here.

3 We supposed that the adversaries would
defend human traditions on other grounds.
Yet we did not think that this would happen,
that they would condemn this article: We do
not merit the forgiveness of sins or grace by
celebrating human traditions. Since this arti-
cle has been condemned, we have an easy and
4 straightforward case. The adversaries are
now openly Judaizing [Acts 15:1]; they are
openly hindering the Gospel by the doctrines
of demons (1 Timothy 4:1). For Scripture
calls traditions *doctrines of demons* when it is
taught that religious rites serve to merit the
forgiveness of sins and grace. For they are
then clouding over the Gospel, Christ's ben-
5 efit, and the righteousness of faith. The
Gospel teaches that through faith we receive
freely, for Christ's sake, the forgiveness of sins
and are reconciled to God. The adversaries,
on the other hand, appoint another media-
tor: these traditions. By these they want to
gain forgiveness of sins; by these they want to
reconcile God's anger. But Christ clearly says,
"In vain do they worship Me, teaching as
doctrines the commandments of men"
(Matthew 15:9).

6 We have already discussed at length that
people are justified through faith when they
believe that they have a reconciled God, not
because of our works, but freely, for Christ's
sake. It is certain that this is the doctrine of
the Gospel because Paul clearly teaches, "By
grace you have been saved through faith.
And this is not your own doing; it is the gift
of God, not a result of works" (Ephesians
2:8–9). Now these men say that people merit 7
the forgiveness of sins by these human cele-
brations. What else is this than to appoint
another justifier, a mediator other than
Christ? Paul says to the Galatians, "You are 8
severed from Christ, you who would be justi-
fied by the law" (5:4). This means, if you hold
that by obeying the Law you merit righ-
teousness before God, Christ will benefit you
nothing. Why do they need Christ who hold
that they are righteous by their obeying the
Law? God has presented Christ with the 9
promise that, because of this Mediator, and
not because of our righteousness, He wishes
to be gracious to us. But these men hold that
God is reconciled and gracious because of
the traditions, not because of Christ. There-
fore, they take the honor of Mediator away
from Christ. So far as this matter is con- 10
cerned, there is not any difference between
our traditions and Moses' ceremonies. Paul
condemns Moses' ceremonies [Galatians
3:10–12], just as he condemns traditions, be-
cause they were regarded as works that merit
righteousness before God. So the office of
Christ and the righteousness of faith were
clouded over. With the Law and traditions
removed, he argues that the forgiveness of
sins has been promised not because of our
works, but freely, because of Christ, if only
we receive it through faith. For the promise is
not received except through faith. Since we 11
receive the forgiveness of sins through faith,
since we have a merciful God for Christ's sake
by faith, it is an error and sin to declare that

George, Duke of Saxony
(1471–1539) c. 1533

Duke George was Luther's most bitter opponent among the rulers of Germany. He ruled Albertine Saxony. Around George's neck hangs a symbol of the Order of the Golden Fleece, established to support the Roman Church and to honor the knightly virtues of courage, honor, loyalty, and kindness to others—virtues not extended by George to his Lutheran opponents. George persecuted all Lutherans in his territory and refused Christian burial to them. He reimbursed people who turned over Luther's books for burning. His efforts to stamp out Lutheranism did not succeed. His son-in-law Philip of Hesse became one of the most energetic Lutheran princes.

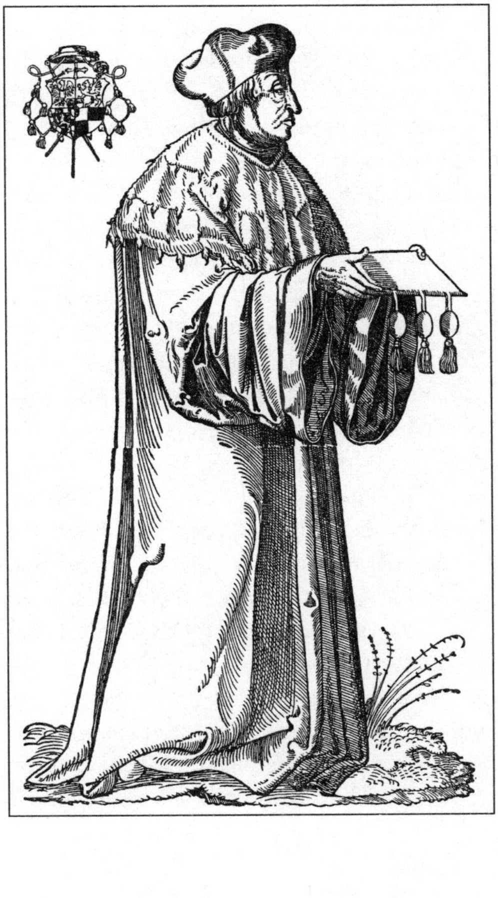

Albert, Archbishop of Mainz
(1490–1545)

Pope Leo X permitted Albert to publish an indulgence (1514) to help pay for the construction of St. Peter's Basilica, Rome. Albert became a leading bishop in Germany by paying the papacy to waive the canon law preventing one person from holding more than one office. Albert ardently supported the new Jesuit order, which was established to exterminate Lutheranism and other "heresies" threatening the Roman Church.

we merit the forgiveness of sins because of
12 these observances. If anyone should say that
we do not merit the forgiveness of sins, but
that those who have already been justified by
these traditions merit grace, Paul again
replies, "Christ [is] then a servant of sin"
(Galatians 2:17). The same would be true if
we were to hold that, after justification, we
were not counted righteous for Christ's sake,
but we should first, by other observances,
merit that we are counted righteous. Like-
wise, "Even with a man-made covenant, no
one annuls it or adds to it once it has been
ratified" (Galatians 3:15). We should not add
to God's covenant, for God promises that He
will be merciful to us for Christ's sake. Nor
should we add that we must first get such
merit in order to be regarded as accepted and
righteous through these observances.

13 Why do we need a long discussion? No
tradition was set up by the Holy Fathers for
the purpose of meriting the forgiveness of
sins, or righteousness. Rather, they were in-
stituted for the sake of good order in the
14 Church and for the sake of peace. When any-
one wants to set up certain works to merit
the forgiveness of sins, or righteousness, how
will he know that these works please God
since there is no testimony of God's Word?
How, without God's command and Word,
will he make people certain of God's will?
Doesn't God forbid people everywhere in the
Prophets from setting up peculiar rites of
worship without His commandment? In
Ezekiel it is written, "Do not walk in the
statutes of your fathers, nor keep their rules,
nor defile yourselves with their idols. I am
the LORD your God; walk in My statutes, and
15 be careful to obey My rules" (20:18–19). If
people are allowed to set up religious rites,
and through these rites merit grace, the reli-
gious rites of all the pagans will have to be
approved. The rites instituted by Jeroboam
(1 Kings 12:26–33) and by others, apart from
the Law, will have to be approved. What dif-
ference does it make? If we have been al-
lowed to institute religious rites that help
merit grace, or righteousness, why were the
pagans and the Israelites not allowed the
same? The religious rites of the pagans and 16
the Israelites were rejected for the very rea-
son that they believed they merited forgive-
ness of sins and righteousness by these rites.
Yet they did not know the righteousness of
faith. Finally, where are we made certain that 17
rites instituted by men justify without God's
command, since nothing can be affirmed of
God's will without His Word? What if God
does not approve these services? How, there-
fore, do the adversaries affirm that they jus-
tify? Without God's Word and testimony,
this cannot be affirmed. Paul says, "Whatev-
er does not proceed from faith is sin" (Ro-
mans 14:23). Since these services have no
testimony of God's Word, conscience must
doubt if they please God.

Why do we need words on a subject so 18
clear? If the adversaries defend these human
services as meriting justification, grace, and
the forgiveness of sins, they simply set up the
kingdom of Antichrist. The kingdom of An-
tichrist is a new service of God, devised by
human authority rejecting Christ [2 Thessa-
lonians 2:3–4], just as the kingdom of
Muhammad has services and works through
which it wishes to be justified before God. It
does not hold that people are freely justified
before God through faith, for Christ's sake.
So the papacy will also be a part of the king-
dom of Antichrist if it defends human serv-
ices as justifying in this way. For honor is
taken away from Christ when they teach that
we are not justified freely through faith, for
Christ's sake, but by such services. This is
especially true when they teach that such
services are not only useful for justification,

but are also necessary, as they maintain in
Article VII. There they condemn us for say-
ing that for true unity of the Church it is
not necessary that rites instituted by human
19 beings should be alike everywhere. Daniel
11:38 indicates that new human services
will be the very form and basic principle of
the kingdom of Antichrist. He says this, "He
shall honor the god of fortresses instead of
these. A god whom his fathers did not know
he shall honor with gold and silver, with
precious stones." Here Daniel describes new
services, because he says that the fathers
were ignorant of the god that shall be wor-
20 shiped. Although the Holy Fathers them-
selves had both rites and traditions, they did
not maintain that these are useful or neces-
sary for justification. They did not cloud
over Christ's glory and office, but taught
that we are justified by faith for Christ's
sake, and not for the sake of these human
services. The Fathers celebrated human rites
for the body's benefit. For example, by such
rites the people would know what time they
should gather so that, for the sake of exam-
ple, all things might be done in order and
properly in the churches [1 Corinthians
14:40] and that the common people might
receive a sort of training. Distinctions of
times and the variety of rites help in re-
21 minding the common people. The Fathers
maintained the rites for these reasons. We
also conclude it is proper for these reasons
to keep traditions ‹good customs›. We are
greatly surprised that the adversaries argue
for another design of traditions, that they
may merit the forgiveness of sins, grace, or
justification. What else is this than to honor
God *with gold and silver, with precious stones*
‹as Daniel 11:38 says›, that is, to hold that
God becomes reconciled by a variety in
clothing, ornaments, and by similar rites,
which are countless in human traditions?

Paul writes to the Colossians that tradi- 22
tions have "an appearance of wisdom"
(2:23). Indeed, they have. Good order is very
fitting in the Church, and is for this reason
necessary. Human reason, because it does
not understand the righteousness of faith,
naturally imagines that such works justify
people because they reconcile God. Among 23
the Israelites the common people thought
this, and by this opinion increased such cer-
emonies. Among us ceremonies have grown
in the monasteries. Human reason also 24
thinks this about bodily exercises, such as
fasts. Although the purpose of these bodily
exercises is to hold the flesh in check, reason
falsely adds that they are services that justify.
As Thomas writes, "Fasting avails for the ex-
tinguishing and the prevention of guilt."
These are Thomas's words. The look of wis-
dom and righteousness in such works tricks
people. The examples of the saints are
added. When people want to imitate these,
they imitate, for the most part, the outward
exercises. They do not imitate their faith.

After this look of wisdom and righ- 25
teousness has deceived people, then count-
less evils follow. The Gospel about the righ-
teousness of faith in Christ is clouded over,
and empty confidence in such works suc-
ceeds. Then God's commandments are
clouded over. These human works assume
the title of a perfect and spiritual life. They
are preferred more than the works of God's
commandments (works of one's own calling,
the administration of the state, the manage-
ment of a family, married life, and the bring-
ing up of children). Compared with those 26
ceremonies, the latter are judged to be un-
godly, so that they are exercised by many
with doubting consciences. For it is known
that many have left the administration of the
state and married life to welcome these
human ceremonies as better and holier.

27 Nor is this enough. When the belief has possessed minds that such ceremonies are necessary for justification, consciences are in miserable anxiety because they cannot exactly perform all ceremonies. How many are there who could list all these ceremonies? There are immense books, indeed, whole libraries, containing not a syllable about Christ, about faith in Christ, about the good works of one's own calling. They only collect the traditions and interpretations by which
they are sometimes made quite strict and
28 sometimes relaxed. How that most excellent
man Gerson is tortured while he searches for the steps and extent of the rules! Yet, he is not able to fix mitigation (*epieikeian*) in a definite grade. Meanwhile, he deeply regrets the dangers to godly consciences that this strict interpretation of the traditions produces.

29 Against this look of wisdom and righteousness in human rites, which tricks people, let us strengthen ourselves by God's Word. Let us know, first of all, that these rites neither merit the forgiveness of sins or justification before God, nor are they necessary
30 for justification. We have mentioned some
testimonies above. Paul is full of them. To the Colossians he clearly says:

> Therefore let no one pass judgment on you in questions of food and drink, or with regard to a festival or a new moon or a Sabbath. These are a shadow of the things to come, but the substance belongs to Christ. (2:16–17)

Here he welcomes both Moses' Law and human traditions at the same time, so that the adversaries may not dodge these testimonies, according to their custom, on the ground that Paul speaks only about Moses' Law. He clearly testifies here that he is speaking of human traditions. However, the adversaries do not see what they are saying. If the Gospel says that Moses' ceremonies—which were divinely instituted—do not justify, how much less do human traditions justify!

Neither do the bishops have the power to 31
institute services, as though they justified, or were necessary for justification. Yes, the apostles say, "Why are you putting God to the test by placing a yoke" (Acts 15:10), and so forth, where Peter declares this effort to burden the Church a great sin. Paul forbids the Galatians, "Do not submit again to a yoke of slav-
ery" (5:1). Therefore, it is the will of the apos- 32
tles that this freedom remain in the Church, that no services of the Law or of traditions be considered necessary (just as ceremonies were necessary for a time in the Law), lest the righteousness of faith be clouded over. This would be the case if people judged that these services merited justification or are necessary
for justification. Many seek various mitiga- 33
tions (*epieikeias*) in traditions to heal consciences. Yet they do not find any sure steps by which to free consciences from these
chains. Just as Alexander solved the Gordian 34
knot once for all by cutting it with his sword when he could not disentangle it, so the apostles free consciences from traditions once for all, especially if they are taught to merit justification. The apostles drive us to oppose this doctrine by teaching and examples. They drive us to teach that traditions do not justify, that they are not necessary for justification, and that no one should invent or receive traditions with the opinion that
they merit justification. Then, even if anyone 35
should celebrate them, let them be celebrated as civil customs without superstition, just as soldiers are clothed in one way and scholars
in another without superstition. The apostles 36
violate traditions and are excused by Christ. The example was shown to the Pharisees that
these services do not benefit. If our people 37
neglect some traditions that are of little help, they are now excused well enough, when

these are required as though they merit justi-
fication. For such an opinion regarding tra-
ditions is ungodly.
38 We cheerfully maintain the old traditions
made in the Church for the sake of useful-
ness and peace. We interpret them in a more
moderate way and reject the opinion that
39 holds they justify. Our enemies falsely accuse
us of setting aside good ordinances and
Church discipline. We can truly declare that
the public form of the churches is more fit-
ting with us than with the adversaries. If any-
one will consider it in the right way, we con-
form to the canons more closely than the
40 adversaries. Among the adversaries, unwill-
ing celebrants, and those hired for pay, and
very frequently only for pay, celebrate the
Masses. They sing psalms, not that they may
learn or pray, but for the sake of the service
(as though this work were a service) or, at
least, for the sake of reward. Among us many
use the Lord's Supper every Lord's Day. They
do so after they have been first instructed, ex-
amined, and absolved. The children sing
psalms in order that they may learn. The
people also sing so that they may either learn
41 or pray. Among the adversaries there is no
catechizing of the children whatever, about
which even the canons give commands.
Among us the pastors and ministers of the
churches are encouraged publicly to instruct
and hear the youth. This ceremony produces
42 the best fruit. Among the adversaries, in
many regions, no sermons are delivered
during the entire year, except during Lent.
Yet the chief service of God is to preach the
Gospel. When the adversaries do preach,
they speak of human traditions, of the wor-
ship of saints and similar trifles, which the
people justly hate. Therefore, they are imme-
diately deserted in the beginning, after the
reading of the Gospel text. A few better ones
begin now to speak of good works; but
about the righteousness of faith, faith in
Christ, and the comfort of consciences, they
say nothing. Indeed, this most wholesome
part of the Gospel they rail at with their re-
proaches. On the contrary, in our churches 43
all the sermons are filled with such topics as
these: repentance; the fear of God; faith in
Christ, the righteousness of faith, the com-
fort of consciences by faith; the exercises of
faith; prayer, what its nature should be, and
that we should be fully confident that it is
powerful, that it is heard; the cross; the au-
thority of officials and all civil ordinances;
the distinction between the kingdom of
Christ, or the spiritual kingdom, and politi-
cal affairs; marriage; the education and in-
struction of children; chastity; all the offices
of love. From this condition of the churches 44
it may be determined that we earnestly keep
Church discipline, godly ceremonies, and
good Church customs.

We teach this about the putting to death 45
of the flesh and discipline of the body. Just as
the Confession states, a true and not a false
putting to death [mortification] happens
through the cross and troubles, by which God
exercises us. In them we must obey God's will,
as Paul says, "Present your bodies as a living
sacrifice" (Romans 12:1). They are the spiri-
tual exercises of fear and faith. In addition to 46
this putting to death, which happens through
the cross, there is also a necessary, voluntary
exercise. Christ says, "But watch yourselves
lest your hearts be weighed down with dis-
sipation" (Luke 21:34). And Paul says, "I dis-
cipline my body and keep it under control"
(1 Corinthians 9:27), and so on. These exer- 47
cises are to be accepted not because they are
services that justify, but because they are as-
sumed to control the flesh, should overindul-
gence overpower us, and make us secure and
unconcerned. This results in people indulging
and obeying the tendencies of the flesh. This

effort [at mortification] should be constant because it has God's permanent command.
48 The required order of certain meats and times does nothing toward controlling the flesh. For it is more overflowing and costly than other feasts. Not even the adversaries obey the order given in the canons.

49 This topic about traditions contains many and difficult controversial questions. We have actually experienced that traditions are truly traps of consciences. When traditions are required as necessary, they torture in terrible ways the conscience, leaving out any ceremony. The repeal of ceremonies has
50 its own evils and its own questions. But we have an easy and plain case because the adversaries condemn us for teaching that human traditions do not merit the forgiveness of sins. Likewise, the adversaries require universal traditions, as they call them, as necessary for justification. Here we have Paul as a constant champion, who argues everywhere that these ceremonies neither justify nor are they necessary additions to
51 the righteousness of faith. Still, we teach that freedom should be so controlled that the inexperienced may not be offended and, because of freedom's abuse [Romans 14:13–23], may not become more opposed to the true doctrine of the Gospel. Nothing in customary rites should be changed without a reasonable cause. So to nurture unity, old customs that can be kept without sin or
52 great inconvenience should be kept. In this very assembly we have shown well enough that for love's sake we do not refuse to keep adiaphora with others, even though they may be burdensome. We have judged that such public unity, which could indeed be produced without offending consciences, should be preferred. We shall speak about this entire subject later, when we present on vows and Church authority.

ARTICLE XVI
Political Order

Note: To clearly move away from the Anabaptists and other radical reformers, the Augsburg Confession states very plainly that Lutherans support the role of government. Christians have the freedom and the duty to participate in proper political order. The Lutheran understanding of God's work in the Church and in the world has come to be known as the doctrine of the two kingdoms. Here Melanchthon articulates the distinction between the kingdom of Christ, which is spiritual and a matter of faith and the righteousness of Christ, and the kingdom of the world. Lutheranism confesses firmly that Christ came to set up no particular external government. God has, can, and will work through a variety of political organizations and forms to enact His will in the world. The Church, as Church, is not to interfere, as Rome clearly and often did, with the rule of the state. Today the Roman Catholic Church no longer makes grand claims of possessing all authority in both the realms of the Church and secular authority. (See also AC XVI.)

The adversaries accept Article XVI with- 53
out exception. In it we have confessed that it is lawful for the Christian to hold public office, sit in judgment, determine matters by the imperial laws and other laws currently in force, set just punishments, engage in just wars, act as a soldier, make legal contracts, hold property, take an oath (when public officials require it), and contract marriage. Finally, we have confessed that legitimate public ordinances are good creations of God and divine ordinances, which a Christian can
safely use. This entire topic about the distinc- 54
tion between the spiritual kingdom of Christ and a political kingdom has been explained in the literature of our writers. Christ's king-

dom is spiritual [John 18:36]. This means
that the knowledge of God, the fear of God
and faith, eternal righteousness, and eternal
life begin in the heart. Meanwhile, Christ's
kingdom allows us outwardly to use legiti-
mate political ordinances of every nation in
which we live, just as it allows us to use med-
icine or the art of building, or food, drink,
55 and air. Neither does the Gospel offer new
laws about the public state, but commands
that we obey present laws, whether they have
been framed by heathens or by others. It
commands that in this obedience we should
exercise love. Carlstadt was crazy to impose
56 on us Moses' judicial laws. Our theologians
have written more fully about these subjects.
They have done so because the monks spread
many deadly opinions in the Church. They
called holding property in common the gov-
ernance of the Gospel. They said that not
holding property, or not acquitting oneself at
law, were evangelical counsels. These opin-
ions greatly cloud over the Gospel and the
spiritual kingdom and are dangerous to the
57 commonwealth. For the Gospel does not
destroy the state or the family, but rather
approves them and asks us to obey them as
a divine ordinance, not only because of pun-
ishment, but also because of conscience.

58 Julian the Apostate, Celsus, and very many
others objected to Christians that the Gospel
would tear states apart because it forbade
legal remedy and taught certain other things
ill-suited to political association. Origen,
Nazianzus, and others wonderfully worked
on these questions. However, they can be eas-
ily explained if we keep this in mind: The
Gospel does not introduce laws about the
public state, but is the forgiveness of sins and
the beginning of a new life in the hearts of be-
lievers. Besides, the Gospel not only approves
outward governments, but also subjects us to
them (Romans 13:1). In a similar way we have
been necessarily placed under the laws of sea-
sons, the changes of winter and summer, as
divine ordinances. The Gospel forbids private 59
remedy. Christ instills this often so that the
apostles do not think they should seize the
governments from those who held otherwise,
just as the Jewish people dreamed about the
kingdom of the Messiah. Christ did this so
that the apostles might know they should
teach that the spiritual kingdom does not
change the public state. Therefore, private
remedy is prohibited not by advice, but by a
command (Matthew 5:39; Romans 12:19).
Public remedy, made through the office of the
public official, is not condemned, but is com-
manded and is God's work, according to Paul
(Romans 13). Now the different kinds of
public remedy are legal decisions, capital
punishment, wars, and military service.
Clearly, many writers have thought wrongly 60
about these matters. They were in the error
that the Gospel is an outward, new, and
monastic form of government. Also, they
did not see that the Gospel brings eternal
righteousness to hearts, while it outwardly
approves the public state.

It is also a most empty myth that Chris- 61
tian perfection consists in not holding prop-
erty. For Christian perfection does not con-
sist in contempt for public ordinances, but in
the inclinations of the heart, in great fear of
God, and in great faith. Abraham, David, and
Daniel, even in great wealth and while exer-
cising public power, were no less perfect than
any hermits. But the monks have spread this 62
outward hypocrisy before the eyes of the
people. They have done this so that the
things in which true perfection exists could
not be seen. How they have praised holding
property in common, as though it were evan-
gelical! But these praises are very dangerous, 63
especially since they are very different than
the Scriptures. Scripture does not command

Wise King Solomon

that we hold property in common. The Law of the Ten Commandments, when it says, "You shall not steal" (Exodus 20:15), distinguishes rights of ownership and commands each one to hold what is his own. Clearly Wycliffe was speaking madness when he said that priests were not allowed to hold
64 property. There are countless discussions about contracts. Good consciences can never be satisfied about them unless they know the rule that it is lawful for a Christian to make use of public ordinances and laws. This rule protects consciences. It teaches that contracts are lawful before God just to the extent that the public officials or laws approve them.

65 This entire topic about public affairs has been clearly set forth by our theologians. Very many good people working in the state and in business have declared that they have been greatly benefited by it. Before, troubled by the opinion of the monks, they doubted whether the Gospel allowed these public offices and business. As a result, we have repeated these things so that outsiders may also understand that the doctrine we follow does not wreck the authority of magistrates and the dignity of all public ordinances. Rather, they are strengthened even more. Previously the importance of these matters was greatly clouded over by those silly monastic opinions. They preferred the hypocrisy of poverty and humility to the state and the family. The latter have God's command, while this Platonic community ‹monasticism› does not.

ARTICLE XVII

Christ's Return for Judgment

Note: During the Reformation, radical groups made numerous predictions about the end of the world. Such foolishness still plagues the Church today. The vast majority of Christians agree on the basics of this important article of faith. These are also beautifully summarized in the Apostles' Creed. (See AC XVII.)

66 The adversaries accept Article XVII without qualification. In it we confess that Christ will appear at the consummation of the world. He will raise up all the dead and will give eternal life and eternal joys to the godly [2 Timothy 4:8], but He will condemn the ungodly to endless punishment with the devil [Matthew 25:46].

ARTICLE XVIII

Free Will

Note: A key discussion in the Apology is found here. Melanchthon exposes Rome's Pelagian attitudes about a person's ability, under his own powers, to bring himself to love God. This remains Rome's view of free will. The 1994 Catholic Catechism teaches that we cooperate with the power and action of the Holy Spirit for our justification. In other words, since we have been given free will, that is, the ability to choose good and evil, we seek to do what is good.

Melanchthon explains that we have free will in earthly matters, but not in spiritual matters (in that which is beneath us, not in what is above us, as Luther explained in *The Bondage of the Will*). We are able to apply ourselves to temporal concerns, but not matters of divine revelation. Rome is now careful to speak of God's grace as being responsible for initiating the relationship between God and man, but also still maintains that man's response to grace is, in fact, what causes justification. Lutherans still maintain that mankind has no free will in spiritual matters, having lost it in the fall into sin. (See also AC XVIII; FC Ep II and FC SD II.)

The adversaries accept Article XVIII, 67
"Free Will," although they add some references having nothing to do with this case.
They also add a speech that neither should
the free will be granted too much, like the
Pelagians, nor should all freedom be denied
it, like the Manichaeans. Very well, but what 68
difference is there between the Pelagians and
our adversaries, since both hold that people
can love God and perform His commandments with respect to the substance of the
acts and can merit grace and justification by
works that reason performs by itself, without the Holy Spirit? How many foolish 69
things follow from these Pelagian opinions,
which are taught with great authority in the
schools! Augustine, following Paul, disapproves of these with great emphasis. We have
repeated his opinion in the article "Justification." We do not deny freedom to the human 70
will. The human will has freedom in the choice of works and things that reason understands by itself. To a certain extent reason can display public righteousness or the righteousness of works. It can speak of God, offer to God a certain service by an outward work, and obey public officials and parents. In choosing an outward work, it can hold back the hand from murder, adultery, and theft. Because human nature has been left with reason and judgment about objects subjected to the senses, choice between these things, the liberty and power to produce public righteousness are also left.

Scripture calls this the righteousness of the flesh, which the carnal nature (that is, reason) produces by itself, without the Holy
71 Spirit. However, the power of lustful desire is such that people more often obey evil inclinations than sound judgment. The devil, who is powerful in the godless, does not cease to stir up this weak nature to various offenses, as Paul says in Ephesians 2:2. For these reasons even public righteousness is rare among people. Not even the philosophers, who seem to have hoped for this
72 righteousness, achieved it. But it is false to say whoever performs the works of the commandments without grace does not sin. The adversaries add further that such works also merit the forgiveness of sins and justification in merely an agreeable way (*de congruo*). For without the Holy Spirit, human hearts lack the fear of God. Without trust toward God, they do not believe that they are heard, forgiven, helped, and preserved by God. Therefore, they are godless. For "a diseased tree [cannot] bear good fruit" (Matthew 7:18). And "without faith it is impossible to please [God]" (Hebrews 11:6).

73 Although we admit that free will has the freedom and power to perform the extreme works of the Law, we do not assign spiritual matters to free will. These are to truly fear God, believe God, be confident and hold that He cares for us, hears us, and forgives us. These are the true works of the First Table, which the heart cannot produce without the Holy Spirit, as Paul says, "The natural person [namely, a person using only natural strength] does not accept the things of the Spirit of God" (1 Corinthians 2:14).
74 People can determine this if they consider what their hearts believe about God's will, whether they are truly confident God cares for and hears them. Even the saints find keeping this faith difficult (which is not possible in unbelievers). But, as we have said before, it begins when terrified hearts hear the Gospel and receive comfort.

Their distinction is helpful. Civil righ- 75
teousness is assigned to free will, and spiritual righteousness is assigned to the governing of the Holy Spirit in the reborn. In this way, outward discipline is kept, because all people should know that God requires this civil righteousness and that, to some extent, we can achieve it. And yet a distinction is shown between human and spiritual righteousness, between philosophical teaching and the teaching of the Holy Spirit. It can be understood why the Holy Spirit is needed.
We did not invent this distinction; Scripture 76
clearly teaches it. Augustine also presents it, and recently William of Paris has presented it very well. But those who dream that people can obey God's Law without the Holy Spirit, and that the Holy Spirit is given so that obeying the Law may be considered meritorious, have wickedly hindered the distinction.

ARTICLE XIX

The Cause of Sin

Note: (See also AC XIX; SA III I.)

The adversaries accept Article XIX. In it 77
we confess that only God and He alone has created all nature and preserves all things that exist. Yet the cause of sin is the will of the devil and people turning away from God, according to the saying of Christ about the devil, "When he lies, he speaks out of his own character" (John 8:44).

ARTICLE XX
Good Works

Note: The Confutation rejected the Lutheran insistence that we do not merit the forgiveness of sins by good works. On this point, more so perhaps than on any other, Roman Catholic doctrine is revealed to be, at its essence, deeply anti-Gospel. Melanchthon puts it this way: "What is more certain in the Church than that the forgiveness of sins happens freely for Christ's sake, that Christ, and not our works, is the Atoning Sacrifice for sins?" Melanchthon makes it plain that the writers of the Confutation are blaspheming Christ by suggesting otherwise. Rome has considerably toned down its teaching on the merit of human good works. Now it carefully asserts that God's grace is responsible for man's response, but still attributes merit to that response, thus contradicting and obscuring the full and sufficient grace of God. (See also AC XX; SA III XIII; FC Ep IV and FC SD IV.)

78 In Article XX, they clearly state that they reject and condemn our statement that people do not merit the forgiveness of sins by good works. ‹Mark this well!› They clearly declare that they reject and condemn this article. What more can be said on a subject so
79 clear? Here the framers of the Confutation display what spirit leads them. What is more certain in the Church than that the forgiveness of sins happens freely for Christ's sake, that Christ, and not our works, is the Atoning Sacrifice for sins, as Peter says, "To Him all the prophets bear witness that everyone who believes in Him receives forgiveness of sins" (Acts 10:43)? We would rather give agreement to this Church of the prophets than to these godless writers of the Confutation, who
80 so rudely blaspheme Christ. There were writers who held that after the forgiveness of sins, people are righteous before God, not by faith, but by works themselves. Yet, they did not hold that the forgiveness of sins happens because of our works, not freely for Christ's sake.

The blasphemy of assigning Christ's 81
honor to our works cannot be tolerated. These theologians are now entirely shameless if they dare to bring such an opinion into the Church. Nor do we doubt that His Most Excellent Imperial Majesty and many of the princes would not have allowed this passage to remain in the Confutation had they been
advised about it. Here we could cite count- 82
less passages from Scripture and from the Fathers. But we have said enough about this subject before. One who knows why Christ has been given to us, and who knows that Christ is the Atoning Sacrifice for our sins, needs no further proof. Isaiah says, "The LORD has laid on Him the iniquity of us all" (53:6). The adversaries, on the other hand, teach that God does not lay our offenses on Christ, but on our works. Neither are we inclined to mention here the sort of works that
they teach. We see that a horrible decree has 83
been prepared against us, which would terrify us still more if we were arguing about doubtful or silly subjects. Our consciences understand that the adversaries condemn the clear truth, whose defense is necessary for the Church and increases Christ's glory. Therefore, we easily look down on the terrors of the world, and we will bear with a strong spirit all suffering for Christ's glory
and the Church's benefits. Who would not 84
joyfully die in the confession of these articles, that we receive the forgiveness of sins through faith freely for Christ's sake, and that we do not merit the forgiveness of sins
by our works? The consciences of the pious 85
will not have sure enough comfort against

Faith [*Glaub*] Produces Love [*Lieb*] and Works [*Werck*]

the terrors of sin and of death, and against
the devil tempting with despair, if they do
not know that their confidence lies in the
forgiveness of sins freely for Christ's sake.
This faith sustains and enlivens hearts in
that most violent conflict with despair.

86 The cause is so worthy that we should re-
fuse no danger. To every one of you who has
agreed to our Confession, "Do not yield to
the wicked, but, on the contrary, go forward
the more boldly." Do not yield when the ad-
versaries, by means of terrors and tortures
and punishments, try hard to drive away
from you that comfort presented to the en-
87 tire Church in our article. Those seeking
Scripture passages to settle their minds will
find them. As the saying goes, at the top of
his voice, Paul cries out that sins are freely
forgiven for Christ's sake. "It depends on
faith," he says, "in order that the promise may
rest on grace and be guaranteed" (Romans
4:16; see also Romans 3:24–25). If the prom-
ise were to depend upon our works, it would
not be sure. If forgiveness of sins were to be
given because of our works, when would we
know that we had received it? When would a
terrified conscience find a work that it would
consider enough to reconcile God's anger?
88 We spoke fully about this entire matter before.
The reader can get the references there. The
unworthy presentation of the subject has
forced us not to discuss, but complain. They
have clearly gone on record as disapproving of
our article, that we receive forgiveness of sins
not because of our works, but through faith
and freely because of Christ.

89 The adversaries also add references to
their own condemnation, and it is worth-
while to provide several of them. They quote
from 2 Peter 1:10, "Be all the more diligent to
make your calling and election sure." Now
you see, reader, that our adversaries have not
wasted any effort in learning logic, but have
the art of concluding whatever pleases them
from the Scriptures. For they conclude,
"Make your calling sure by good works."
Therefore, they think that works merit the
forgiveness of sins. This is a very nice way of
thinking, if one would argue this way about a
person whose death sentence had been par-
doned: "The judge commands that from now
on you stop stealing from others. Therefore,
you have earned the pardon from the pun-
ishment, because you no longer steal from
others." To argue in this way makes a cause 90
out of no cause. Peter speaks of works fol-
lowing the forgiveness of sins and teaches
why they should be done. They should be
done so that the calling may be sure, that is,
should they fall from their calling if they sin
again. Do good works in order that you may
persevere in your calling, in order that you
do not lose the gifts of your calling. They
were given to you before, and not because of
works that follow, and which now are kept
through faith. Faith does not remain in those
who lose the Holy Spirit and reject repen-
tance. As we have said before (Article XII 1),
faith exists in repentance.

They add other references that make no 91
more sense. Finally, they say that this opinion
was condemned a thousand years before, in
Augustine's time. This also is quite false. For
Christ's Church always held that the forgive-
ness of sins is received freely. Indeed, the
Pelagians were condemned. They argued that
grace is given because of our works. Besides, 92
we have shown above well enough that we
hold that good works should follow faith.
"Do we then overthrow the law?" asks Paul.
"On the contrary, we uphold the law" (Ro-
mans 3:31), because when we have received
the Holy Spirit through faith, the fulfilling of
the Law necessarily follows. Patience, chasti-
ty, and other fruit of the Spirit gradually
grow by this love.

ARTICLE XXI (IX)

The Invocation of Saints

Note: Melanchthon says that after numerous protests all the Confutation has done is prove that the saints should be honored and that living saints may pray for others, which is all the Lutherans said to begin with. In Roman Catholicism, then and still today, the saints take on a nonbiblical role. The saints are said to have a storehouse of merits that they use to intercede for us. Melanchthon provides a careful discussion of what a propitiator (atonement maker) is and is not. Only Christ may be called a propitiator. Only the merit of Christ is counted as meritorious for us in God's eyes. This Lutheran assertion, then as well as now, stands in stark contrast to what Rome teaches about these things. Melanchthon rightly points out how, in popular devotion and practice, Mary has completely replaced Christ in the minds of many. This is still very much a problem in Roman Catholicism today. (See also AC XXI; SA II II.)

1 They absolutely condemn Article XXI be-
cause we do not require the invocation of
saints. On no other topic do they speak more
smoothly or wordily. Yet they are not able to
prove anything other than that the saints
should be honored, or that living saints pray
for others, as though invoking dead saints
2 were necessary for that reason. They cite
Cyprian because he asked Cornelius, while
he was still alive, to pray for his brothers after
his death. By this example they prove the in-
vocation of the dead. They quote also Jerome
against Vigilantius. "On this field," they say,
"eleven hundred years ago, Jerome overcame
Vigilantius." So the adversaries triumph, as
though the war had already ended. Nor do
those asses see that in Jerome, against Vigi-
lantius, there is not a syllable about invoca-
tion. He speaks about honors for the saints,
not about invocation. Before Gregory, none 3
of the other ancient writers mentioned invo-
cation. Certainly this kind of invocation, and
the opinions that the adversaries now teach
about the application of merits, are not con-
firmed by the ancient writers.

Our Confession approves honoring the 4
saints in three ways. The first is thanksgiving.
We should thank God because He has shown
examples of mercy, because He wishes to save
people, and because He has given teachers
and other gifts to the Church. These gifts,
since they are the greatest, should be ampli-
fied. The saints themselves, who have faith-
fully used these gifts, should be praised just
as Christ praises faithful businessmen
(Matthew 25:21, 23). The second service is 5
the strengthening of our faith. When we see
Peter's denial forgiven, we also are encour-
aged to believe all the more that grace truly
superabounds over sin (Romans 5:20). The 6
third honor is the imitation, first of faith,
then of the other virtues. Everyone should
imitate the saints according to his calling.
The adversaries do not require these true 7
honors. They argue only about invocation,
which, even if it were not dangerous, still is
not necessary.

Besides, we also grant that the angels pray 8
for us. For there is a passage in Zechariah
1:12, where an angel prays, "O LORD of hosts,
how long will You have no mercy on
Jerusalem?" We admit that, just as the saints 9
(when alive) pray for the Church universal in
general, so in heaven they pray for the
Church in general. However, no passage
about the praying of the dead exists in the
Scriptures, except the dream taken from the
Second Book of Maccabees (15:14).

Furthermore, even if the saints do pray 10
for the Church, that does not mean they

should be invoked. Our Confession affirms only this: Scripture does not teach the invocation of the saints, or that we are to ask the saints for aid. Since neither a command nor a promise nor an example can be produced from the Scriptures about the invocation of saints, it makes sense that conscience remains uncertain about this invocation. Since prayer should be made from faith, how do we know that God approves this invocation? Without the testimony of Scripture, how do we know
that the saints know about the prayers of
11 each one? Some plainly ascribe divinity to
the saints, namely, that they discern the silent thoughts of our minds. They argue about morning and evening knowledge, perhaps because they doubt whether the saints hear us in the morning or the evening. They in-
vent these things, not to honor the saints, but
12 to defend profitable services. The adversaries
cannot produce anything against this argument. Since the invocation of saints does not have a testimony from God's Word, it cannot be affirmed that the saints understand our
invocation or, even if they understand it, that
13 God approves it. Therefore, the adversaries
should not force us into an uncertain matter, because a prayer without faith is not prayer. For when they cite the Church's example, it is clear that this is a new custom in the Church. Although the old prayers mention the saints, they do not invoke the saints. This new invocation in the Church is unlike the invocation of individuals.

14 Further, the adversaries not only require invocation in worshiping the saints, but also apply the merits of the saints to others. They make the saints not only intercessors, but also people who make atonement. This cannot be tolerated. Here honor that belongs to Christ alone is completely transferred to the saints. The adversaries make them mediators and atonement makers. Although they distinguish between mediators of intercession and mediators ‹the Mediator› of redemption,
they plainly make the saints mediators of re-
demption. Without the testimony of Scrip- 15
ture, they declare that the saints are mediators of intercession. This, be it said ever so reverently, still clouds over Christ's office and transfers to the saints the confidence of mercy belonging to Christ. People imagine that Christ is stricter and the saints more easily appeased. They trust the saints' mercy rather than Christ's mercy. They flee from Christ and seek the saints. So they actually make the saints mediators of redemption.

Therefore, we will show that the adver- 16
saries truly make the saints not just intercessors, but atonement makers, that is, mediators of redemption. Here we will not describe the abuses of the common people. We are still speaking about the opinions of the doctors. Regarding the rest, even the inexperienced can judge.

In a person who makes atonement, two 17
things are required. First, there should be a Word of God from which we certainly know that God wants to pity, and listen to, those calling upon Him through this atonement maker. There is such a promise about Christ, "Whatever you ask of the Father in My name, He will give it to you" (John 16:23). There is no such promise about the saints. Therefore, consciences cannot be completely confident that we are heard by the invocation of saints.
This invocation, therefore, does not spring
from faith. We also have the command to call 18
upon Christ:

> "Come to Me, all who labor. (Matthew 11:28)
>
> In that day the root of Jesse, who shall stand as a signal for the peoples—of Him shall the nations inquire. (Isaiah 11:10)

> The people of Tyre will seek Your favor with gifts, the richest of the people. (Psalm 45:12)
>
> May all kings fall down before Him. (Psalm 72:11)
>
> May prayer be made for Him continually. (Psalm 72:15)
>
> That all may honor the Son, just as they honor the Father. (John 5:23)
>
> Now may our Lord Jesus Christ Himself, and God our Father . . . comfort your hearts and establish them. (2 Thessalonians 2:16–17)

What commandment, what example, can the adversaries produce from the Scriptures
19 about the invocation of saints? The second requirement for an atonement maker is that his merits are shown to make satisfaction for other people. They are divinely given to others, so that through them, just as by their own merits, other people may be regarded righteous. For example, when any friend pays a debt for a friend, the debtor is freed by the merit of another, as though it were by his own. So Christ's merits are given to us so that, when we believe in Him, we may be regarded righteous by our confidence in Christ's merits as though we had merits of our own.

From both of these—the promise and the 20
giving of merits—arises confidence in mercy. Such confidence in the divine promise, and likewise in Christ's merits, should be promoted when we pray. For we should be truly confident, both that for Christ's sake we are heard and that by His merits we have a reconciled Father.

Here the adversaries ask us first to invoke 21
the saints, although they have neither God's

The Rich Man and Lazarus

promise nor a command nor an example from Scripture. Yet they incite greater confidence in the saints' mercy than in Christ's mercy, although Christ asked us to come to
22 Him and not to the saints. Second, they apply the saints' merits, just as Christ's merits, to others. They ask us to trust in the saints' merits as though we were regarded righteous because of their merits, just as we are regarded righteous by Christ's merits. We are making
23 none of this up. In indulgences, the adversaries say that they apply the saints' merits. And Gabriel Biel, the interpreter of the canon of the Mass, confidently declares, "According to the order instituted by God, we should betake ourselves to the aid of the saints, in order that we may be saved by their merits and vows." These are Gabriel's words. Nevertheless, still more silly things are read here and there in the adversaries' books and sermons. What is this other than creating people who make atonement? If we must trust that we are saved by their merits, they are made completely equal to Christ.

24 Where has this arrangement, to which Gabriel refers when he says that we should resort to the aid of the saints, been instituted by God? Let him produce an example or command from the Scriptures. Perhaps they get this arrangement from the courts of kings, where friends must be used as intercessors. But if a king has appointed a certain intercessor, he will not want cases brought to him through others. So, since Christ has been appointed Intercessor and High Priest, why do we seek others?

25 Here and there this form of Absolution is used:

> The passion of our Lord Jesus Christ, the merits of the most blessed Virgin Mary and of all the saints, be to you for the forgiveness of sins.

Here the Absolution is pronounced on the theory that we are reconciled and regarded righteous not only by Christ's merits, but
also by the merits of the other saints. Some of 26
us have seen a doctor of theology dying. A certain theologian, a monk, was enlisted to comfort him. He pressed on the dying man nothing but this prayer, "Mother of grace, protect us from the enemy; receive us in the hour of death."

Granted, the blessed Mary prays for the 27
Church. Does she receive souls in death? Does she conquer death? Does she make alive? What does Christ do if the blessed Mary does these things? Although she is most worthy of the most plentiful honors, yet she does not want to be made equal to Christ. Instead she wants us to consider and
follow her example. The very subject reveals 28
that in public opinion the blessed Virgin has taken over Christ's place. People have invoked her, have trusted in her mercy, and through her have wished to appease Christ, as though He were not an Atoning Sacrifice,
but only a dreadful judge and avenger. We 29
believe, however, we must not trust that the saints' merits are applied to us, that because of these God is reconciled to us, regards us just, or saves us. For we receive forgiveness of sins only by Christ's merits when we believe in Him. Of the other saints it has been said, "Each will receive his wages according to his labor" (1 Corinthians 3:8), that is, they cannot mutually give their own merits, one to the other, as the monks sell the merits of
their orders. Even Hilary says of the foolish 30
virgins (cf. Matthew 25:1–13):

> As the foolish virgins could not go forth with their lamps extinguished, they sought those who were prudent to lend them oil; to whom they replied that they could not give the oil because there might not be enough

for all. In other words, no one can be aided by the works and merits of another, because it is necessary for every one to buy oil for his own lamp.

31 The adversaries teach us to place confidence in the invocation of saints, although they have neither God's Word nor the example of Scripture. They apply the saints' merits on behalf of others in the same way they apply Christ's merits, and they transfer to the saints the honor belonging only to Christ. Therefore, we cannot accept their opinions about the worship of the saints, nor the practice of invocation. For we know that confidence is to be placed in Christ's intercession, because this alone has God's promise. We know that Christ's merits alone atone for us. Because of His merits we are regarded righteous when we believe in Him, as the text says, "Whoever believes in Him will not be put to shame" (1 Peter 2:6; see also Romans 9:33; Isaiah 28:16). Neither are we to trust that we are regarded righteous by the merits of the blessed Virgin or of the other saints.

32 The following error persists also among
the educated. Each saint has been given a par-
ticular duty: Anna gives riches, Sebastian
wards off disease, Valentine heals epilepsy,
George protects horsemen. These opinions
have clearly sprung from pagan examples.
Among the Romans, Juno was thought to give
wealth, Febris to ward off fever, Castor and
33 Pollux to protect horsemen, and so on. If the
invocation of saints were taught with the
greatest caution, even such speculation is
dangerous. Why defend it when it has no
command or testimony from God's Word?
Indeed, it does not even have the testimony of
34 the ancient writers. First, as I have said before,
when other mediators are sought in addition
to Christ, and confidence is put in others, the
entire knowledge of Christ is hindered. The
subject shows this. In the beginning, mention
of the saints seems to have been permitted. It
was viewed as tolerable, as in the ancient
prayers. Afterward, invocation followed, and
abuses that are unnatural and more than
pagan followed invocation. From invocation
the next step was to images. These also were
worshiped. A force was supposed to exist in
them, just as magicians imagine that a force
exists in images of the heavenly bodies carved
at a particular time. In a certain monastery we
have seen a statue of the blessed Virgin. It
moved automatically by a trick, seeming to
turn away ‹from those who did not make a
large offering› or to nod to those making a re-
quest.

The incredible stories about the saints, 35
which are taught with great authority in pub-
lic, go beyond the marvelous tales of the stat-
ues and pictures. While being tormented,
Barbara asks for the reward that no one in-
voking her should die without the Eucharist.
Standing on one foot, another recited the
whole Psalter daily. Some wise man painted
Christopher. He did so to illustrate that there
should be great strength of mind in those
who bear Christ, that is, those who teach or
confess the Gospel. It is necessary for them
to undergo the greatest dangers. Then the
foolish monks taught the people that they
should invoke Christopher, as though such a
Polyphemus had once existed. The saints per- 36
formed very great deeds, either useful to the
state or providing private examples. Re-
membering these acts would go far toward
strengthening faith and following their exam-
ple in the administration of affairs. However,
no one has searched for these from true sto-
ries. Indeed, it is helpful to hear how holy
men ruled governments, what disasters and
dangers they underwent, how holy men
helped kings in great dangers, how they
taught the Gospel, what encounters they had
with heretics. Examples of mercy help as well,

such as when we see Peter forgiven his denial [Mark 16:7], when we see Cyprian forgiven for having been a magician, when we see Augustine, having experienced faith's power in sickness, steadily affirming that God truly hears believers' prayers. It was beneficial that these examples, which contain reminders for either faith or fear or the rule of the state, be
37 repeated. But certain silly persons, having knowledge neither of faith nor for governing states, have invented stories sounding like poems. They contain superstitious models for certain prayers, fastings, and additional works for bringing in gain. These are the miracles that have been invented about rosaries and similar ceremonies. There is no need to recite further examples here. For the legends, as they call them, the mirrors of examples, and the rosaries, in which there are very many things not unlike the true stories of Lucian, are still in existence.

38 The bishops, theologians, and monks praise these freakish and wicked stories because they help them get their daily bread. They do not put up with us. So that Christ's honor and office may be more evident, we do not require the invocation of saints, and we condemn the abuses in the worship of saints.
39 All good people everywhere greatly wanted the bishops' authority or the preachers' diligence to help correct these abuses. Yet in the Confutation our adversaries completely overlook other apparent sins. They do so as though they wish, by receiving the Confutation, to push us to accept even the most scandalous abuses.

40 The Confutation has been written untruthfully, not only on this topic, but almost everywhere. There is no passage in the Confutation in which they distinguish between apparent abuses and their teachings. Nevertheless, if any of them can think, they confess that many false opinions are contained in the teaching of the Scholastics and canon lawyers. Besides, they keep many abuses that crept into the Church due to the pastors' ignorance and negligence. For Luther 41
was not the first to complain about public abuses. Long before these times, many educated and excellent men greatly regretted the abuses of the Mass, confidence in monastic observances, services to the saints intended to gain a profit, and the confusion of the doctrine about repentance. The latter should be as clear and plain in the Church as possible. We ourselves have heard that excellent theologians desire moderation in the scholastic teaching. It contains much more for philosophical quarrels than for piety. Nevertheless, the older theologians are generally closer to Scripture than are the recent theologians. Their theology has worsened more and more. Many good men, who at the beginning were friendly to Luther, saw that he was freeing people's minds from these mazes of most confused and countless discussions held by the scholastic theologians and canon lawyers. They saw that Luther was teaching things beneficial for godliness.

When they wanted us to agree to the 42
Confutation, the adversaries were not honest in overlooking the abuses. If they wanted to help the Church, they should encourage our most excellent emperor to take measures to correct abuses. We see plainly enough that the emperor wants the healing and well establishing of the Church. But the adversaries do not act to help the emperor's most honorable and most holy will, but they act in every way to crush us. Many signs show that they 43
have little anxiety about the state of the Church. They make no effort to see that the people have a summary of the Church's teachings. They defend clear abuses by new and unusual cruelty. They continue every day to shed innocent blood. They do not allow

suitable teachers in the churches. Good people can easily decide if these things help. In this way they care neither for their own authority nor for the Church. After the good teachers have been killed and sound teaching hindered, fanatical spirits will rise up. The adversaries will not be able to restrain them. They will disturb the Church with godless teachings and will overthrow the entire Church government. We wish very much to keep this government.

44 Most excellent Emperor Charles, for the sake of Christ's glory, which doubtlessly you wish to praise and magnify, we beg you not to agree to the violent advice of our adversaries. Rather, we beg you to seek other honorable ways of establishing harmony so that godly consciences are not burdened, that no cruelty is exercised against innocent people (as we have seen before) and that sound teaching is not hindered in the Church. To God above all you owe the duty to preserve sound teaching and hand it down to future generations, to defend those who teach what is right. For God demands this when He honors kings with His own name, calling them gods, saying, "I said, 'You are gods' " (Psalm 82:6). They should work toward the preservation and growth of divine things, that is, the Gospel of Christ on the earth [Acts 12:24]. As God's representatives, they should defend the life and safety of the innocent.

ARTICLE XXII (X)

Both Kinds in the Lord's Supper

Note: The Pontifical Confutation rejected the Lutheran request that the laity receive both the consecrated bread and wine in the Lord's Supper. It said that insistence on such a thing "is an abuse and disobedience," and that the layperson should be content receiving the Lord's Supper under one kind, since Christ is completely present in both the bread and the wine. This remains the view of Rome, though today it is stated more gently, and in some parishes communicants may receive both bread and wine. Melanchthon chides the Roman theologians in the Apology and again insists that there is no legitimate biblical reason to withhold the consecrated wine, the blood of Christ, from the laity. (See also AC XXII; SA III VI; FC Ep VII and FC SD VII.)

There is no doubt that using both parts in 1
the Lord's Supper is godly and in agreement with Christ's institution and Paul's words. For Christ instituted both parts, not for a portion of the Church, but for the whole Church. Not only the presbyters, but the entire Church uses the Sacrament by Christ's authority, and not by human authority. We
suppose the adversaries recognize this. If 2
Christ has instituted the Supper for the entire Church, why is one kind denied to a part of the Church? Why is the use of the other kind prohibited? Why is Christ's ordinance changed, especially when He Himself calls it His testament? If it is unlawful to set aside a man's testament, it is more unlawful to set
aside Christ's testament. Paul says, "For I re- 3
ceived from the Lord what I also delivered to you" (1 Corinthians 11:23). He had delivered the use of both kinds, as the text, 1 Corinthians 11, clearly shows. He says, "Do this" (11:24), first about His body; afterward, Paul repeats the same words about the cup ‹Christ's blood›. And then, "Let a person examine himself, then, and so eat of the bread and drink of the cup" (11:28). These are the words of Him who has instituted the Sacrament. Indeed, He says before that those who will use the Lord's Supper should use both.

4 It is clear, therefore, that the Sacrament was
instituted for the whole Church. The custom
still remains in the Greek churches, and was
once also observed in the Latin churches, as
Cyprian and Jerome testify. For Jerome says
on Zephaniah: "The priests who administer
the Eucharist, and distribute the Lord's blood
to the people," and so on. The Council of
Toledo gives the same testimony. Nor would
it be difficult to gather a great multitude of
5 references. We are not exaggerating. We will
allow the levelheaded reader to determine
what should be held about the divine ordi-
nance.

6 In the Confutation, the adversaries do not
try hard to relieve the Church, to which one
part of the Sacrament has been denied. This
would have been fitting to good and religious
men. A strong reason for relieving the
Church should have been sought, and con-
sciences, which would have received only a
part of the Sacrament, should have been in-
structed. Now these very men maintain that
it is right to ban the other part of the Sacra-
7 ment and forbid the use of both parts. First,
they imagine at the Church's beginning, it
was customary at some places to give out
only one part of the Sacrament. However,
they are not able to produce any ancient ex-
ample for this. They quote the passages men-
tioning bread, as Luke 24:35, where it is writ-
ten that the disciples recognized Christ in the
breaking of bread. They quote also other pas-
sages (Acts 2:42, 46; 20:7) about the breaking
of bread. Although we do not object if some
interpret these passages as referring to the
Sacrament, it does not make sense that only
one part of the Sacrament was given. Accord-
ing to the ordinary usage of language, nam-
8 ing one part also means the other. They also
refer to lay Communion, which was not the
use of only one kind, but of both. Whenever
priests are commanded to use lay Commu-
nion, it is meant that they have been removed
from the ministry of consecration. The ad-
versaries are not ignorant of this, but they
abuse the ignorance of the uneducated.
When the uneducated hear of lay Commu-
nion, they imagine the custom of our time,
by which only a part of the Sacrament is
given to laypeople.

Consider the adversaries' rudeness. 9
Gabriel Biel recalls among other reasons why
both parts are not given: to distinguish be-
tween laymen and presbyters. It is credible
that the chief reason why one part is prohib-
ited is this: the clerical order may be more
dignified by a religious rite. To say nothing
more extreme, this is a human design. It can
easily be judged whether this helps. In the 10
Confutation they also mention Eli's sons.
After the loss of the high priesthood, they
were to seek the one part applying to the
priests. (See 1 Samuel 2:36.) Here they say
that the use of one kind was meant. They
add: "So, our laypeople should also be con-
tent with one kind, with only the priests re-
ceiving the other." The adversaries are clearly
being silly when they transfer the history of
Eli's descendants to the Sacrament. Eli's pun-
ishment is described there. Will they also say
that, as a punishment, laypeople have been
separated from the other part? The Sacra-
ment was instituted to comfort terrified
minds. This happens when they believe that
Christ's flesh is given as food for the life of
the world [John 6:51] and when they believe
that, being joined to Christ, they are made
alive. But the adversaries argue that laypeople
are separated from the other part as a pun-
ishment. "They should," they say, "be con-
tent." This is enough for a dictator. Why 11
should they [withhold both parts of the
Sacrament]? "The reason must not be asked,
but let whatever the theologians say be law."
This is Eck's doing. We recognize those

proud words. If we wanted to criticize, there would be no lack of words. You see how great the rudeness is. He commands, as a tyrant in the tragedies: "Whether they will or not, they
12 must be content." Will the reasons that he cites excuse, in God's judgment, those who ban a part of the Sacrament and attack peo-
13 ple using an entire Sacrament? If they make the prohibition in order that there may be a distinguishing mark between priests and laity, this very reason should move us not to agree with the adversaries, even though we could go along with their custom, but for other reasons. There are marks that distinguish the order of priests from the people, but it is clear why they defend this distinction so earnestly. We do not want to ridicule the value of the order, so we will not say more about the adversaries' real intent.

14 They also bring up the danger of spilling (the wine) and certain similar things. These are not serious enough to change Christ's
15 ordinance. Certainly, if we assume that we are free to use either one part of the Sacrament or both, how can prohibiting ‹the use of both kinds› be defended? The Church does not allow itself to change Christ's ordi-
16 nances into unimportant matters. We certainly excuse the Church that has suffered since it could not receive both parts. But we do not excuse the writers who maintain that using the entire Sacrament is justly banned and who now not only ban, but even excommunicate and violently persecute, those using the entire Sacrament. Let them figure out how they will answer God for their de-
17 cisions. It should not be immediately judged that the Church decides or approves whatever the pontiffs decide, especially since Scripture prophesies about the bishops and pastors in this regard, as Ezekiel 7:26 says, "The law perishes from the priest."

ARTICLE XXIII (XI)

The Marriage of Priests

Note: In this article, Melanchthon rebuts the Confutation's argument that priests should not marry. He anchors his argument in the institution of marriage at creation. Marriage is a divine ordinance that the Church cannot contradict. Melanchthon is not saying that a minister who chooses to remain celibate should be married; rather, he insists that the Church cannot command men to be celibate who want to be ministers in the Church, when clearly the gift of celibacy is reserved only for a very few. Nowhere in the Bible is forced celibacy, or forced marriage, tied to ministry. The apostles were both married and single. Priestly celibacy is yet another example of antiscriptural traditions in the Roman Church. (See also AC XXIII; SA III XI.)

In spite of the great scandal about their filthy celibacy, the adversaries arrogantly defend pontifical law under the wicked and false excuse of the divine name. They even encourage the emperor and princes, to the disgrace and scandal of the Roman Empire, to not allow the marriage of priests. This is how they speak. 1

Where in any history can one read of greater rudeness than this of the adversaries? We will review their arguments later. Now let the wise reader consider how shameful these good-for-nothing men are. They claim that marriages produce scandal and disgrace to the government, as though this public scandal of criminal and unnatural lusts glowing among these very Holy Fathers were a great ornament to the Church, while they pretend that they are Curii and live like bacchanals! Most things done with the greatest license by these men cannot even be named without a 2

3 breach of modesty. These are their lusts, which they ask you to defend with your chaste right hand, Emperor Charles. (Certain ancient predictions name you as the king of modest face, for the saying appears about you, "One modest in face shall reign everywhere.") Contrary to divine Law, the law of nations, and the canons of the councils, they ask you to break apart marriages, to punish innocent men horribly merely for the sake of marriage, to put priests to death, whom even barbarians reverently spare, to exile banished women and fatherless children. They bring such laws to you, most excellent and most chaste Emperor, to which no barbarity, however monstrous and cruel, could lend its ear.

4 But because disgrace or cruelty does not stain your character, we hope that you will deal with us mildly in this matter, especially when you have learned that we have the weightiest reasons for our belief, taken from God's Word, which the adversaries reject with the most silly and vain opinions.

5 Nevertheless, they do not seriously defend celibacy. They are not ignorant of how few there are who practice chastity. They create a counterfeit religion for their domain, which they think that celibacy helps. So we understand that Peter was right to advise that "there will be false teachers among you, who will secretly bring in destructive heresies" (2 Peter 2:1). The adversaries say, write, or do nothing truly, frankly, and candidly in this entire case. They actually argue only about the domain they falsely think is in danger, and which they try hard to support with a wicked excuse of godliness.

6 We cannot approve this law about celibacy that the adversaries defend, because it conflicts with divine and natural law and disagrees with the very canons of the councils. It is clearly superstitious and dangerous. It produces countless scandals, sins, and corruption of public morals. Our other disagreements need some discussion by the doctors. But in this matter the subject is so clear to both parties that it requires no discussion. It only requires as judge a man who is honest and fears God. Although we defend the clear truth, the adversaries still have created certain reproaches for mocking our arguments.

[Arguments for the Marriage of Priests]

First, Genesis 1:28 teaches that people were created to be fruitful, and that one sex should desire the other in a proper way. We are not speaking about lustful desire, which is sin, but about that appetite that was in nature in its perfection. They call this physical love. This love of one sex for the other is truly a divine ordinance. But since this ordinance of God cannot be removed without an extraordinary work of God, it makes sense that statutes or vows cannot remove the right to contract marriage. 7

The adversaries object to these arguments. They say that in the beginning, the commandment was given to populate the earth. Now that the earth has been populated, marriage is not commanded. See how wisely they judge! Human nature is so formed by God's Word that it is fruitful not only in the beginning of creation, but as long as this nature of our bodies exists. Humanity is fruitful just as the earth becomes fruitful by the Word, "Let the earth sprout vegetation, plants yielding seed" (Genesis 1:11). Because of this ordinance, the earth not only started to produce plants in the beginning, but as long as this natural order exists, the fields are covered every year. Therefore, just as human laws cannot change the nature of the earth, so, without God's special work, neither vows nor a human law can change a human being's nature. 8

9 Second, because this creation, or divine
ordinance, in humanity is a natural right,
jurists have said wisely and correctly that
the union of male and female belongs to
natural right. Natural right is unchangeable.
Therefore, the right to contract marriage
must always remain. Where nature does not
change, that ordinance which God gave na-
ture does not change. It cannot be removed
10 by human laws. Therefore, it is ridiculous
for the adversaries to babble that marriage
was commanded in the beginning, but is
not now. This is the same as if they would
say, "Formerly, when people were born, they
were born with gender; now they are not.
Formerly, when they were born, they
brought with them natural right; now they
do not." No craftsman (*Faber*) could pro-
duce anything more crafty than these fool-
ish things. They were created to dodge a
11 natural right. Therefore, let this point re-
main, that both Scripture teaches and the
jurist says wisely: the union of male and fe-
12 male belongs to natural right. Furthermore,
a natural right is truly a divine right because
it is an ordinance divinely imprinted on na-
ture. Because this right cannot be changed
without an extraordinary work of God, the
right to contract marriage remains, the nat-
ural desire of one sex for the other sex is an
ordinance of God in nature, and for this
reason is a right. Otherwise, why would
13 both sexes have been created? As it has been
said before, we are not speaking of lustful
desires, which is sin, but of that desire called
physical love. Lustful desire has not re-
moved this physical love from nature, but
inflames it, so that now physical love has
greater need of a cure. Marriage is necessary
not only for the sake of procreation, but also
as a cure. These things are clear and so well
established that they cannot be disputed.

14 Third, Paul says, "Because of the tempta-
tion to sexual immorality, each man should
have his own wife" (1 Corinthians 7:2). This
is a clear command having to do with every-
one unfit for celibacy. The adversaries ask to 15
be shown a commandment that commands
priests to marry, as though priests are not
men! We certainly judge that the things we
hold about human nature in general also
have to do with priests. Does not Paul in this 16
passage command marriage for those who
do not have the gift of chastity? Paul inter-
prets himself a little later when he says, "It is
better to marry than to be aflame with pas-
sion" (7:9). And Christ has clearly said, "Not
everyone can receive this saying, but only
those to whom it is given" (Matthew 19:11).
Since Adam's fall into sin, these two things
agree: natural appetite and lustful desire.
Lustful desire inflames the natural appetite,
so that now there is more need of marriage
than in nature in its perfection. So Paul
speaks of marriage as a cure, and because of
these flames he commands marriage. Nei-
ther can any human authority, law, or vows
remove this declaration, "It is better to
marry than to be aflame with passion," be-
cause they do not remove the nature or lust-
ful desire. Therefore, all who burn keep the 17
right to marry. By this commandment of
Paul, "Because of the temptation to sexual
immorality, each man should have his own
wife" [1 Corinthians 7:2], all are held bound
who do not truly keep themselves chaste.
The decision about chastity is one of indi-
vidual conscience.

Here the adversaries command seeking 18
chastity from God, weakening the body
through labor and hunger. Why do they not
proclaim these magnificent commandments
to themselves? As we have said before, the
adversaries are only playing; they are doing
nothing seriously. If chastity were possible to 19
all, it would not require a peculiar gift. But

Christ shows that it needs a peculiar gift. Therefore, not everyone has it. God wishes the rest to use the common law of nature, which He has instituted. He does not wish His ordinances, His creations, to be hated. He wishes people to be chaste in this way, that they use the remedy divinely presented, just as He wishes that we use food and drink
20 so that our life is nourished. Gerson also testifies that there have been many good men who tried very hard to subdue the body, and yet made little progress. So, Ambrose is right in saying, "Virginity is only a thing that can be recommended, but not commanded; it is
21 a matter of vow rather than of precept." If anyone here would object that Christ praises those "who have made themselves eunuchs for the sake of the kingdom of heaven" (Matthew 19:12), let him also consider that He praises those having the gift of chastity. Because of this He adds, "Let the
22 one who is able to receive this receive it." For an impure chastity does not please Christ. We also praise true chastity. But now we are arguing about the law, and about those who do not have the gift of chastity. The matter should be left free, and traps should not be cast upon the weak through this law.

23 Fourth, the pontifical law differs also from the canons of the councils. The ancient canons do not ban marriage. Neither do they dissolve marriages that have been contracted, even though they remove from clerical office those who contracted marriage during their ministry. At those times this dismissal was an act of kindness. The new canons, which have not been framed in the synods, but have been made according to the private judgment of the popes, both ban the contraction of marriages and dissolve them when contracted. This is to be done openly, contrary to Christ's command, "What therefore God has joined together, let not man separate" (Matthew
19:6). In the Confutation the adversaries ex- 24
claim that the councils command celibacy. We do not find fault with the councils' decrees. Under a certain condition they allow marriage. However, we do find fault with the laws enacted since the ancient synods, which the popes of Rome have created contrary to the authority of the synods. The popes hate the authority of the synods, just as much as they want that authority to appear holy to
others. Therefore, this law about permanent 25
celibacy is peculiar to this new pontifical tyranny. Nor is it without a reason. For Daniel 11:37 attributes this mark to the kingdom of Antichrist: hatred for women.

Fifth, the adversaries do not defend the 26
law because of superstition. For they see that it is not generally obeyed. Yet, they spread superstitious opinions, while giving an appearance of religion. They claim that they require celibacy because it is purity, as though marriage were impure and a sin, or as though celibacy merited justification more than
marriage! To this end they cite the cere- 27
monies of the Mosaic Law, because under the Law at the time of ministering, the priests were separated from their wives. The priest in the New Testament, because he should always pray, should always practice chastity. This silly comparison is presented as a proof that should urge priests to permanent celibacy, although in this very comparison marriage is allowed. Only during the time of ministry was its use prohibited. It is one thing to pray; it is another to minister. The saints prayed even when they did not exercise the public ministry. Conjugal intercourse did not hinder them from praying.

We will reply to these daydreams in an or- 28
derly way. In the first place, the adversaries should acknowledge that in believers, marriage is pure because it has been sanctified by God's Word. That is to say, it is a matter that

is permitted and approved by God's Word, as
29 Scripture testifies abundantly. Christ calls
marriage a divine union when He says,
"What therefore God has joined together"
30 (Matthew 19:6). And Paul says of marriage,
of meats and similar things, "It is made holy
by the word of God and prayer"
(1 Timothy 4:5), that is, "by the Word," by
which consciences become certain that God
approves, and "by prayer," that is, by faith,
which uses it with thanksgiving as God's gift.
31 Likewise, "The unbelieving husband is made
holy because of his wife" (1 Corinthians
7:14), that is, the use of marriage is permitted
and holy because of faith in Christ, just as it
32 is permitted to use meat, and so on. Likewise,
"She will be saved through childbearing," and
so on (1 Timothy 2:15). If the adversaries
could produce such a passage about celibacy,
then certainly they would celebrate a wonderful triumph. Paul says that woman is saved by childbearing. What more honorable thing could be said against the hypocrisy of celibacy than that woman is saved by the conjugal works themselves, by conjugal intercourse, by bearing children and the other duties? But what does St. Paul mean? Let the reader observe that faith is added, and that domestic duties without faith are not praised. "If they continue," he says, "in faith." For he speaks of the whole class of mothers. Therefore, he requires especially faith, through which a woman receives the forgiveness of sins and justification. Then he adds a particular work of the calling, just as in every person a good work of a particular calling should follow faith. This work pleases God because of faith. So the duties of the woman please God because of faith, and the believing woman is saved who devoutly serves her calling in such duties.

33 These references teach that marriage is a
lawful thing. Therefore, if purity illustrates
that which is allowed and approved before
God, marriages are pure, because they have
been approved by God's Word. Paul says 34
about lawful things, "To the pure, all things
are pure" (Titus 1:15), to those who believe in Christ and are righteous by faith. Therefore, as virginity is impure in the godless, so in the godly, marriage is pure because of God's Word and faith.

Again, if purity is properly opposed to 35
lustful desires, it illustrates purity of heart, that is, lustful desires put to death [mortified]. For the Law does not prohibit marriage, but lustful desires, adultery, fornication. Therefore, celibacy is not purity. There may be greater purity of heart in a married man, as in Abraham or Jacob, than in most of those who are even truly chaste.

Finally, if they understand that celibacy is 36
pure in the sense that it merits justification
more than marriage does, we most forcefully
deny it. We are justified neither because of
virginity nor because of marriage, but freely
for Christ's sake, when we believe that for His
sake God is merciful to us. Here perhaps they 37
will cry out that, like Jovinian, marriage is
made equal to virginity. But, because of such
racket, we will not reject the truth about the
righteousness of faith, which we explained
before. Yet, we do not make virginity and 38
marriage equal. For just as one gift excels an-
other, as prophecy excels power of speech,
the science of military affairs excels agricul-
ture, and power of speech excels architecture,
so virginity is a more excellent gift than mar-
riage. Just as a public speaker is not more 39
righteous before God because of his ability to speak than an architect because of his skill in architecture, so a virgin does not merit justification by virginity any more than a married person merits it by conjugal duties. Each person should faithfully serve in his own gift and believe that for Christ's sake he receives

the forgiveness of sins and through faith is regarded righteous before God.

40 Neither Christ nor Paul praise virginity because it justifies, but because it is freer and less distracted by domestic occupations in praying, teaching, and serving. For this reason Paul says, "The unmarried man is anxious about the things of the Lord" (1 Corinthians 7:32). Virginity, therefore, is praised because of meditation and study. So Christ does not simply praise those "who have made themselves eunuchs," but adds, "for the sake of the kingdom of heaven," that is, they may have freedom to learn or teach the Gospel. He does not say that virginity merits the forgiveness of sins or salvation.

41 To the examples of the Levitical priests we
have replied that they do not establish the
duty of demanding permanent celibacy from
the priests. Furthermore, the Levitical impu-
rities are not to be transferred to us. Then in-
tercourse contrary to the Law was an impuri-
ty. Now it is not an impurity because Paul
says, "To the pure, all things are pure" (Titus
1:15). The Gospel frees us from these Leviti-
42 cal impurities. If anyone defends the law of
celibacy with the intent to burden con-
sciences by these Levitical commands, we
must labor against this, just as the apostles in
Acts 15:10 labored against those who re-
quired circumcision and tried to force
Moses' Law upon Christians.

43 In the meantime, good people will know
how to control the use of marriage, espe-
cially when they occupy public offices.
These often give good people so much labor
that all domestic thoughts are expelled from
their minds. Good people know this also,
that Paul commands everyone "to control
his own body in holiness" (1 Thessalonians
4:4). They also know that they must rest
sometimes, so that there may be freedom
for prayer. Paul does not wish this to be per-
manent (1 Corinthians 7:5). Such chastity is 44
easy to those who are well occupied. But the
great crowd of unemployed priests in the
fraternities cannot afford, in this sensuality,
even this Levitical chastity, as the facts
show. The lines are well known, "The boy
used to pursuing a lazy life hates those who
are busy."

Many heretics misunderstand the Law of Moses and have treated marriage with contempt. Yet they admire celibacy very much. Epiphanius complains that, especially by this approval, the Encratites captured the minds of the gullible. They refrained from wine even in the Lord's Supper. They refrained from eating the flesh of all animals, in which they excelled the Dominican brethren, who live upon fish. They refrained also from marriage, and this in particular gained the chief admiration. They thought that these works and services merited grace more than the use of wine, flesh, and marriage. To them those things appeared to be profane and unclean and could scarcely please God, even though they were not condemned. 45

In Colossians 2:18, Paul greatly disap- 46
proves these angelic forms of worship. For
when people believe that they are pure and
righteous because of such hypocrisy, they
hinder the knowledge of Christ and the
knowledge of God's gifts and command-
ments. God wishes us to use His gifts in a
godly way. We might mention examples 47
where certain godly consciences were greatly
disturbed because of the lawful use of mar-
riage. This evil was taken from the opinions
of monks superstitiously praising celibacy.
Yet, we do not find fault with self-control or 48
chastity. We have said before that spiritual
exercises and putting the flesh to death are
necessary. Certainly we deny that confidence
should be placed in certain ceremonies, as

49 though they made one righteous. Epiphanius
has said elegantly that these ceremonies
should be praised "for restraining the body
or because of public morals," just as certain
rites were set up for instructing the ignorant,
and not as services that justify.

50 Our adversaries do not require celibacy
through superstition. They know that
chastity is not ordinarily practiced. The ad-
versaries fake superstitious opinions to fool
the ignorant. They should be hated more
than the Encratites, who seem to have erred
by a show of religion. These Sardanapali
‹Epicureans› willingly misuse the appear-
ance of religion.

51 Sixth, we have many reasons for disap-
proving the law of permanent celibacy. Be-
sides these, there are also dangers to souls
and public scandals. Even if the law were just,
these should discourage good people from
approving such a burden that has destroyed
countless souls.

52 For a long time, good people have com-
plained about this burden, either for them-
selves or for others whom they saw to be in
danger. But the popes do not listen to these
complaints. It is beyond doubt that this law is
injurious to public morals, and has produced
vices and shameful lusts. The Roman
comedic plays still exist. Rome still recog-
nizes and reads its own morals in them.

53 So God punishes the hatred of His own
gift and ordinance in those who ban mar-
riage. For other laws the custom was that if a
benefit could clearly be shown, they were
changed. Why isn't the same done with this
law? There are weighty reasons to support
such a change, especially now. Nature is
growing old and is gradually becoming
weaker. Vices are increasing. Therefore, the
54 divine cures should be used. We see what vice
God condemned before the flood and before
the burning of the five cities. Similar vices
have come before the destruction of many
other cities, such as Sybaris and Rome. These
illustrate what it will be like in the end times.
So now, marriage should be strongly defend- 55
ed by the strictest laws and warning exam-
ples. People should be encouraged to marry.
This duty belongs to public officials, who
should maintain public discipline. Mean-
while, the teachers of the Gospel should do
both of these things: encourage unchaste
people to marry; encourage others not to
hate the gift of chastity.

The popes daily enact and change other 56
excellent laws. However, when it comes to
the law of celibacy, they are as hard and cold
as iron, even though it is clear that this is
simply a human right. They are now mak- 57
ing this law more burdensome in many
ways. The canon asks them to suspend
priests. These rather unfriendly interpreters
suspend them not from office, but from
trees. They cruelly kill many men for noth-
ing but marriage. These very murders of 58
close relatives show that this law is a doc-
trine of demons [1 Timothy 4:1]. Since the
devil is a murderer [John 8:44], he defends
his law by these murders.

We know that there is some offense re- 59
garding schism. We seem to have separated
from those who are considered regular bish-
ops. But our consciences are very secure. We
know that, though we earnestly desire to es-
tablish harmony, we cannot please the adver-
saries unless we cast away clear truth and
then willingly agree with these very men to
defend this unjust law, to dissolve marriages
that have been contracted, to put priests to
death if they do not obey, and to drive poor
women and fatherless children into exile. But
since these conditions clearly displease God,
we cannot feel sorry that we are not allied
with the multitude of murderers among the
adversaries.

[Conclusion]

60 We have explained why we cannot with a
good conscience agree with the adversaries
when they defend the pontifical law about
permanent celibacy. It conflicts with divine
and natural law, and it varies from the
canons themselves. It is superstitious and full
of danger. Finally, the whole affair is insin-
cere. For the law is enacted not for the sake of
religion. It was enacted for the sake of con-
trol, and this is wickedly given the appear-
ance of religion. No sane person can produce
anything against these most firmly estab-
61 lished reasons. The Gospel allows marriage
for those to whom it is necessary. Neverthe-
less, it does not compel marriage for those
who can be chaste, provided they are truly
chaste. We hold that the priests should be al-
lowed this freedom also. We do not wish to
compel anyone to be celibate by force, nor do
we want to break up marriages that have
been contracted.

62 We have also shown on the side how the
adversaries object to several of our argu-
ments while we presented them. We have ex-
plained away these false accusations. As
briefly as possible, we will now relate what
important reasons they claim to have for de-
63 fending the law. First, they say that it has
been revealed by God. You see the extreme
rudeness of these sorry fellows. They dare to
affirm that the law of permanent celibacy has
been divinely revealed, although it is con-
trary to clear Scripture passages. These pas-
sages command that "because of the tempta-
tion to sexual immorality, each man should
have his own wife" (1 Corinthians 7:2). Like-
wise, they forbid breaking up marriages that
have been contracted. (See Matthew 5:32;
19:6; 1 Corinthians 7:27.) Paul reminds us
what kind of author such a law has when he
calls it "teachings of demons" (1 Timothy
4:1). Fruit show their author; many mon-
strous lusts and murders are now committed
under the appearance of that law.

The second argument of the adversaries is 64
that the priests should be pure, according to
Isaiah 52:11, "Purify yourselves, you who
bear the vessels of the LORD." And they cite
many things to this effect. We have dealt with
this particularly false reason before. We have
said that virginity without faith is not purity
before God, and marriage is pure because of
faith, according to Titus 1:15, "To the pure,
all things are pure." We have also said that
outward purity and the ceremonies of the
Law are not to be demanded today, because
the Gospel requires purity of heart. A hus-
band's heart, as in the case of polygamists
Abraham or Jacob, may be purer and burn
less with lusts than that of many virgins who
are truly chaste. What Isaiah says, "Purify
yourselves, you who bear the vessels of the
LORD," should be understood as referring to
the cleanness of heart and to the whole of re-
pentance. Besides, in the exercise of marriage 65
the saints will know to what extent it is ben-
eficial to restrain its use, and as Paul says, "to
control his own body in holiness" (1 Thessa-
lonians 4:4). Finally, since marriage is pure, 66
those who are not chaste in celibacy are
rightly told that they should marry wives to
be pure. So the same law, "Purify yourselves,
you who bear the vessels of the LORD," com-
mands that impure celibates become pure
husbands.

The third argument is horrible: the mar- 67
riage of priests is the heresy of Jovinian. Fine-
sounding words! This is a new crime, that
marriage is a heresy! In the time of Jovinian
the world did not as yet know the law about
permanent celibacy. Therefore, it is a rude lie
that the marriage of priests is the heresy of
Jovinian, or that such marriage was then
condemned by the Church. In such passages 68

we can see what plan the adversaries had in writing the Confutation. They determined that the ignorant would be the most easily excited if they would hear frequently the charge of heresy, and if they pretend that our cause had been condemned and executed by many previous decisions of the Church. So they frequently cite falsely the Church's judgment. Because they knew about this, they were unwilling to show us a copy of their Apology, lest this lie and these charges be ex-
69 posed. We have already expressed our opinion, however, regarding Jovinian, which concerns the comparison of virginity and marriage. We do not make marriage and virginity equal, although neither virginity nor marriage merits justification.

70 The adversaries defend a law that is godless and destructive to good morals by such false arguments. By such reasons they set the minds of princes firmly against God's judgment. God will call them to explain why they have broken apart marriages and why they have tortured and killed priests. For do not doubt that, as the blood of dead Abel cried out (Genesis 4:10), so the blood of many good men, whom they have unjustly attacked, will also cry out. God will punish this cruelty. There you will discover how worthless are these reasons of the adversaries. You will discern that in God's judgment no lies against God's Word remain standing, as Isaiah says, "All flesh is grass, and all its beauty is like the flower of the field" (40:6).

Whatever may happen, our princes will be 71
able to comfort themselves with the consciousness of right counsels. Even if the priests had done wrong in contracting marriages, this disruption of marriages, these prohibitions, and this cruelty are clearly contrary to God's will and Word. Neither novelty nor dissent delights our princes. Especially in an undoubted matter more regard had to be paid to God's Word than to anything else.

Katharina von Bora (1499–1552)

Before her marriage to Martin Luther, Katharina von Bora, the daughter of German nobility, was a nun of the Marienthron convent. Far from being the "unseen partner" in the *Lutherhaus,* she was a talented and knowledgeable wife, mother, and advocate for evangelical reforms. Katharina exhibited a deep spirituality in her private and family life as she encouraged her husband in times of desperation and doubt and provided for the numerous students and guests to Wittenberg and the parsonage.

EDITORIAL EXCURSUS: THE DIVINE SERVICE

Unlike other reformers, Luther's revisions to the medieval Roman Mass were quite conservative. Calvin and Zwingli threw out all traditional services; enthusiasts substituted spiritualism for Word and Sacrament. But for Luther, true reform did not equal total rejection. He restored the Gospel to its proper place in the life of the Church and purged the liturgy of false teaching and practice. Below, compare the medieval Mass with Luther's Divine Service for the Church at Wittenberg. Other than the unscriptural Canon of the Mass, the two services are strikingly similar.

Luther's Form of the Mass, 1523

1. Introit
2. Kyrie, "*Lord have mercy upon us.*"
3. Gloria, "*Glory be . . .*" (may be omitted)
4. Collect (only one permitted)
5. Epistle
6. Gradual/Alleluia
7. Sequences (only one of three permitted)
8. Gospel (candles and incense optional)
9. Nicene Creed (may be sung)
10. Sermon
11. Order for Holy Communion
    a. Sursum Corda, "*The Lord be with you . . .*" and Preface
    b. Words of Institution (preferably sung)
    c. Sanctus, "*Holy, Holy, Holy . . .*" and Benedictus, "*Blessed is He who comes . . .*" (with elevation of body and blood)
    d. Lord's Prayer
    e. Pax, "*The peace of the Lord . . .*"
    f. Agnus Dei, "*Lamb of God . . .*" (sung by choir during administration)
    g. Communion (antiphonal Psalm, during which priest communes first, then people)
    h. Benedicamus, "*Let us bless the Lord*" (optional Alleluia in place of "Ite missa est," "*Go; it is the dismissal*")
    i. Aaronic Benediction, "*The Lord bless you and keep you . . .*"

Medieval Roman Mass

1. Introit
2. Kyrie
3. Gloria (may be omitted)
4. Collects
5. Epistle
6. Gradual/Alleluia
7. Sequences (all but four later rejected by Council of Trent)
8. Gospel/Sermon
9. Nicene Creed
10. Offertory and Secret (inaudible prayer; only conclusion heard)
11. Order for Holy Communion
    a. Sursum Corda and Preface
    b. Sanctus and Benedictus
    c. Canon of the Mass (numerous prayers referencing the Mass as a sacrifice for the living and dead; commemoration of angels and saints; numerous genuflections and sign of the cross; includes Words of Institution)
    d. Lord's Prayer
    e. Pax
    f. Agnus Dei
    g. Communion
    h. Post-Communion prayer (and Benedicamus when Gloria is omitted at beginning of service)
    i. Deacon: "Ite missa est." Response: "*Thanks be to God.*"

ARTICLE XXIV (XII)

The Mass

Note: Melanchthon asserts that Lutherans keep all the traditional forms of worship that do not conflict with the Gospel. The Zwinglian and Calvinistic branches of the Reformation tended toward "iconoclasm," that is, the rejection of pictures and statues of Christ and the saints, traditional clerical vestments, and other liturgical items. This same attitude prevailed when it came to the historic liturgy, whereby even what is perfectly biblical was stripped away. Unlike Zwinglianism and Calvinism, Lutheranism retained the historic aesthetic and liturgical forms of the Western Church, which had developed through pious use over the centuries.

In the Western Church, many abuses had become associated with the primary worship service, the Mass. Melanchthon rejects these abuses and explains how the Bible clearly declares that Christ's sacrifice on the cross was once-for-all-time. The Mass is a "sacrifice," Melanchthon maintains, but in the sense that we offer to God prayer, praise, and thanksgiving for what He has already done for us in Christ. While we do receive Christ's true body and blood in the Sacrament, the priest does not re-sacrifice Christ in the Mass. This is one of the most important articles in the Apology because it so clearly explains the two kinds of sacrifice and since many of Rome's false teachings and quite lucrative religious practices were connected with the Mass. (See also AC XXIV; SA II II; FC Ep X and FC SD X.)

1 At the outset, we must again make this preliminary statement: we do not abolish the Mass, but religiously keep and defend it. Masses are celebrated among us every Lord's Day and on the other festivals. The Sacrament is offered to those who wish to use it, after they have been examined and absolved. And the usual public ceremonies are observed, the series of lessons, of prayers, vestments, and other such things.

The adversaries have a long speech 2
about the use of the Latin language in the Mass. In this speech, they joke about how it benefits an unlearned hearer to hear, in the faith of the Church, a Mass that he does not understand [cf. 1 Corinthians 14:9–12]. They clearly imagine that the mere work of hearing is a service, that it benefits without
being understood. We are unwilling to rebel- 3
liously pursue these things, but we leave them to the judgment of the reader. We mention them only for the purpose of stating, in passing, that we keep also the Latin lessons and prayers.

However, ceremonies should be celebrated to teach people Scripture, that those admonished by the Word may conceive faith and godly fear, and may also pray. (This is the intent of ceremonies.) So, we keep the Latin language to aid those who are learning and understand Latin. We mix with it German hymns so that the people also may have something to learn, and by which faith and
godly fear may be produced. This custom has 4
always existed in the churches. Some more frequently, and others more rarely, introduced German hymns into the service. Yet almost everywhere the people sang something
in their own tongue. However, it has never 5
been written or presented that people benefit from hearing lessons they cannot understand or that ceremonies benefit, not because they teach or admonish, but by the outward act (*ex opere operato*) because they are performed that way or are looked upon. Away with such pharisaic opinions!

The fact that we hold only public or com- 6
mon Mass is no offense against the Church catholic. For even today private Masses are not held in the Greek churches. There is only

a public Mass, and that on the Lord's Day and festivals. In the monasteries daily Mass is held, but this is only public. These are the traces of former customs. Before Gregory no ancient
7 writer mentions private Masses. We no longer recognize how they got started. Clearly after the begging monks came to power, mostly from false opinions and because of financial gain, private Masses increased to the point that for a long time all good people desired to set some limit on private Masses. St. Francis wished to correct this matter, so he decided that each fraternity should be content with a single, daily, common Mass. Later this was changed, either by superstition or for the sake
8 of financial gain. So, where it is advantageous to them, they themselves change the institutions of the Fathers. Later they cite the Fathers' authority against us. Epiphanius writes that in Asia Communion was celebrated three times a week, and that there were no daily Masses. Indeed, he says that this custom was handed down from the apostles. For he says, "Assemblies for Communion were set up by the apostles to be held on the fourth day, on the evening of the Sabbath, and on the Lord's Day."

9 The adversaries compile many references on this topic to prove that the Mass is a sacrifice. Yet this great war of words will be quieted when the single reply is put forward that this line of authorities, reasons, and references, however long, does not prove that the Mass bestows grace by the outward act (*ex opere operato*) or that, when applied on behalf of others, it merits the forgiveness of venial and mortal sins, of guilt and punishment for them. This one reply overthrows all objections of the adversaries, not only in this Confutation, but in all writings about the Mass that they have published.

10 This is the issue our readers are to be reminded about. Aeschines reminded the judges that, just as boxers struggle with one another for their position, so they should labor with their adversaries about the disputed point and not permit him to wander beyond the discussion. In the same way our adversaries should be compelled to speak on the subject as presented. When the disputed point has been thoroughly understood, a decision about the arguments on both sides will be very easy.

We showed in our Confession our belief 11
that the Lord's Supper does not give grace by the outward act (*ex opere operato*) and that, when applied on behalf of others, alive or dead, it does not merit for them the forgiveness of sins, guilt, or punishment by the outward act. This position is supported by a 12
clear and firm proof. It is impossible to receive the forgiveness of our sins because of our own work by the outward act. The terrors of sin and death must be overcome through faith when we comfort our hearts with the knowledge of Christ and believe that for His sake we are forgiven and that His merits and righteousness are granted to us, "since we have been justified by faith, we have peace" (Romans 5:1). These things are so sure and so firm that they can stand against all the gates of hell [Matthew 16:18].

If we are to say only as much as is neces- 13
sary, the main point has already been stated. No sane person can accept that pharisaic and pagan opinion about the outward act (*opus operatum*). Yet, this opinion still exists among the people and has increased countlessly the number of Masses. For Masses are purchased to reconcile God's anger, and by this work they want to receive the forgiveness of guilt and of punishment. They want to obtain whatever is necessary in every kind of life. They even want to free the dead. Monks and philosophers have taught this pharisaic opinion in the Church.

14 Although our main point has already
been stated, because the adversaries foolishly
pervert many Scripture passages to defend
their errors, we will add a few things on this
topic. In the Confutation, they said many
things about "sacrifice," although we pur-
posely avoided this term in our Confession
because of its ambiguity. We have presented
what those persons (whose abuses we now
condemn) understand by "sacrifice." To ex-
plain the Scripture passages that have been
wickedly perverted, we must first present
15 what a sacrifice is. For ten years the adver-
saries have published many volumes about
sacrifice, and yet not one of them so far has
defined sacrifice. They only grab the word
sacrifices either from the Scriptures or the
Fathers. Afterward, they add their own
thoughts, as though a sacrifice means what-
ever they please.

What Is a Sacrifice, The Kinds of Sacrifice

16 In the *Phaedrus* of Plato, Socrates says
that he is especially fond of distinctions, be-
cause without these nothing in speech can ei-
ther be explained or understood. If he dis-
covers anyone skilful in making distinctions,
he says that he pays attention and follows his
footsteps as those of a god. (He instructs the
one to separate the parts of speech in their
very joints. So like an inept cook, he breaks
some part of speech to pieces.) But the ad-
versaries truly hate these basic rules and, ac-
cording to Plato, are truly poor butchers. For
they break the parts of "sacrifice." This can be
understood when we have listed the kinds of
17 sacrifice. Theologians are rightly familiar
with distinguishing between a Sacrament
and a sacrifice. Therefore, let them be subdi-
vided into either a ceremony or a sacred
18 work. A Sacrament is a ceremony or work in
which God presents to us what the promise
of the ceremony offers. Baptism is not a work
that we offer to God. It is a work in which
God baptizes us. In other words, a minister
baptizes us on God's behalf. God here offers
and presents the forgiveness of sins, and so
forth, according to the promise "Whoever
believes and is baptized will be saved" (Mark
16:16). A sacrifice, on the contrary, is a cere-
mony or work that we give to God in order to
provide Him honor.

Furthermore, there are two kinds of sac- 19
rifice and no more. One is the atoning sacri-
fice, that is, a work that makes satisfaction for
guilt and punishment. It reconciles God, or
reconciles His wrath and merits the forgive-
ness of sins for others. The other kind is the
eucharistic sacrifice, which does not merit
the forgiveness of sins or reconciliation. It is
practiced by those who have been reconciled,
so that we may give thanks or return grati-
tude for the forgiveness of sins that has been
received, or for other benefits received.

In this controversy, as well as in many 20
other discussions, we should especially have
these two kinds of sacrifice in view and pre-
sent them. Special care must be taken lest
they should be confused. (If the limits of this
book would permit it, we would add the rea-
sons for this distinction. It has many refer-
ences in the Epistle to the Hebrews and else-
where.) All Levitical sacrifices can be referred 21
to either of these two distinctions as if [they
were] their own homes. In the Law certain
sacrifices were named *atoning* because of
their meaning or by comparison. They were
not called sacrifice because they merited the
forgiveness of sins before God, but because
they merited the forgiveness of sins accord-
ing to the righteousness of the Law, so that
those for whom they were made might not
be excluded from that commonwealth ‹from
the people of Israel›. Therefore, for a trespass,
the sacrifices were called sin offerings and

The Last Supper

burnt offerings. But the eucharistic sacrifices were the grain offering, the drink offering, thank offerings, firstfruits, tithes [Leviticus 1–7].

22 In fact there has been only one atoning sacrifice in the world, namely, Christ's death, as the Epistle to the Hebrews teaches, "It is impossible for the blood of bulls and goats to take away sins" (10:4). A little later, of the will of Christ, "By that will we have been sancti-
fied through the offering of the body"
23 (10:10). Isaiah interprets the Law, so that we
may know Christ's death is truly a satisfaction for our sins, or remedy, and that the ceremonies of the Law are not. He says, "When his soul makes an offering for sin, he shall see his offspring," and so on (Isaiah 53:10). The word used here means a victim for transgression (*asham*). In the Law this illustrated that a certain Victim was to come to make satisfaction for our sins and reconcile God. This was so that people might know that God wishes to be reconciled to us, not because of our own righteousnesses, but because of another's merits: Christ. Paul interprets the same word (*asham*) as *sin*, "For sin, he condemned sin" (Romans 8:3), that is, He punished sin for sin, that is, by a Victim for sin. The meaning of the word is more easily understood from pagan customs. These were adopted from their misunderstanding of statements by the Fathers. The Latins called a victim a *piaculum*, which was offered to reconcile God's anger in great calamities, where He seemed to be especially enraged. Sometimes they sacrificed human victims, perhaps because they had heard that a human victim would reconcile God for the entire human race. The Greeks sometimes called them cleansing (*katharmata*)and sometimes wiping away (*peripsemata*). Isaiah and Paul, therefore, mean that Christ became a victim, that is, a remedy, that by His merits, and not
by our own, God might be reconciled. Let 24
this remain the case: Christ's death alone is truly an atoning sacrifice. For the Levitical atoning sacrifices were so called only to illustrate a future remedy. Because of a certain resemblance they were satisfactions delivering the righteousness of the Law and preventing those persons who sinned from being excluded from the commonwealth. But after the revelation of the Gospel, those sacrifices had to end. Since they had to end in the revelation of the Gospel, they were not true atoning sacrifices, for the Gospel was promised specifically to present an atoning sacrifice.

Now the rest are eucharistic sacrifices, 25
which are called sacrifices of praise (Leviticus 3; 7:11[–18]; Psalm 56:12). These are the preaching of the Gospel, faith, prayer, thanksgiving, confession, the troubles of saints, yes, all good works of saints. These sacrifices are not satisfactions for those making them, nor can they be applied to others to merit the forgiveness of sins or reconciliation by the outward act (*ex opere operato*). They are made by those who have been reconciled.
These are the sacrifices of the New Testa- 26
ment, as Peter teaches, "a holy priesthood, to offer spiritual sacrifices" (1 Peter 2:5). Spiritual sacrifices, however, are contrasted not only with those of cattle, but even with human works offered by the outward act, because *spiritual* refers to the movements of the Holy Spirit in us. Paul teaches the same thing, "Present your bodies as a living sacrifice, holy and acceptable to God, which is your spiritual worship" (Romans 12:1). "Spiritual worship" means, however, a service in which God is known and is grasped by the mind. This happens in the movements of fear and trust toward God. Therefore, it contrasts not only with the Levitical service, in which cattle are slain, but also with a service

in which a work is imagined to be offered by the outward act. The Epistle to the Hebrews teaches the same thing, "Through Him then let us continually offer up a sacrifice of praise to God" (13:15). He adds the interpretation, that is, the fruit of our lips, giving thanks to His name. He asks us to offer praises, that is, prayer, thanksgiving, confession, and the like. These benefit not by the outward act, but because of faith. This is taught by the clause "Through Him then let us continually offer," that is, by faith in Christ.

27 In short, the worship of the New Testament is spiritual. It is the righteousness of faith in the heart and the fruit of faith. New Testament worship sets aside Levitical services. Christ says, "True worshipers will worship the Father in spirit and truth, for the Father is seeking such people to worship Him. God is spirit, and those who worship Him must worship in spirit and truth" (John 4:23–24). This passage clearly condemns opinions about sacrifices that, as the adversaries imagine, benefit by the outward act (*ex opere operato*). In contrast, it teaches that people should worship in spirit, that is, with the in-
28 clinations of the heart and by faith. So, even in the Old Testament, the prophets condemn the opinion of the people about the outward act (*opus operatum*) and teach the righteousness and sacrifices of the Spirit. "I did not speak to your fathers or command them concerning burnt offerings and sacrifices. But this command I gave them: 'Obey My voice, and I will be your God,'" and so on (Jeremiah 7:22–23). How do we suppose that the Jews received this charge, which seems to conflict openly with Moses? God clearly gave the fathers commands about burnt offerings and victims. But Jeremiah condemns the opinion about sacrifices that God had not delivered, namely, that these services please Him by the outward act. Concerning faith, he adds that God had commanded this: "Hear Me," that is, "believe Me that I am your God, and that I wish to be known when I care for you and help you. I do not need your sacrificial victims. Believe that I want to be God the Justifier and Savior, not because of works, but because of My Word and promise. Truly seek and expect help from Me from the heart."

Psalm 50:13–15, which rejects sacrificial 29
victims and requires prayer, also condemns the opinion about the outward act (*opus operatum*): "Do I eat the flesh of bulls . . .?" "Call upon Me in the day of trouble; I will deliver you, and you shall glorify Me." The psalmist testifies that this is true service and true honor if we call upon Him from the heart.

Likewise, "Sacrifice and offering You have not desired, but You have given me an open ear" (Psalm 40:6), that is, "You have offered me Your Word that I may hear it, and You do require that I believe Your Word and Your promises. You truly desire to care for me and to help," and so on. Likewise, "You will not be pleased with a burnt offering. The sacrifices of God are a broken spirit; a broken and contrite heart, O God, You will not despise" (Psalm 51:16–17). "Offer right sacrifices, and put your trust in the LORD" (Psalm 4:5). He asks us to hope, and says that this is a righteous sacrifice, meaning that other sacrifices are not true and righteous sacrifices. And, "I will offer to You the sacrifice of thanksgiving and call on the name of the LORD" (Psalm 116:17).

Scripture is full of such references that 30
teach that sacrifices by the outward act (*ex opere operato*) do not reconcile God. Since Levitical services have been repealed, the New Testament teaches that new and pure sacrifices will be made: faith, prayer, thanksgiving, confession, the preaching of the

Gospel, troubles on account of the Gospel, and the like.

31 Malachi speaks about these sacrifices, "For from the rising of the sun to its setting My name will be great among the nations, and in every place incense will be offered to My name, and a pure offering" (1:11). The adversaries perversely apply this passage to the Mass and quote the authority of the Fathers. A reply, however, is easy. Even if this passage spoke most particularly about the Mass, it would not make sense that the Mass justifies by the outward act (*ex opere operato*) or that, when applied to others, it merits the forgiveness of sins. The prophet says nothing about those things that the monks and
32 philosophers rudely make up. Besides, the very words of the prophet express his meaning. First, his words say this: the name of the Lord will be great. This is accomplished by the preaching of the Gospel. Through this preaching, Christ's name is made known and the Father's mercy, promised in Christ, is recognized. The preaching of the Gospel produces faith in those who receive the Gospel [Romans 10:17]. They call upon God, give thanks to God, bear troubles for their confession, and produce good works for Christ's glory. So the name of the Lord becomes great among the Gentiles [Malachi 1:11]. Therefore, *incense* and a *pure offering* means not a ceremony by the outward act, but all those sacrifices through which the name of the Lord becomes great: faith, invocation, the preaching of the Gospel, confession, and so
33 on. If anyone would have this term include the ceremony ‹of the Mass›, we readily concede it, provided he neither understands the ceremony alone nor teaches that the ceremony benefits by the outward act. We include the preaching of the Word among the sacrifices of praise, that is, among the praises of God. So the reception itself of the Lord's Supper can be praise or thanksgiving. But it does not justify by the outward act, neither is it to be applied to others to merit the forgiveness of sins for them. Later we will explain how even a ceremony is a sacrifice. Malachi speaks about all the services of the New Testament, and not only about the Lord's Supper. Likewise, since he does not favor the pharisaic opinion of the outward act (*opus operatum*), he is not against us, but rather helps us. He requires services of the heart, through which the name of the Lord becomes truly great.

Another passage also is cited from 34
Malachi, "He will purify the sons of Levi and refine them like gold and silver, and they will bring offerings in righteousness" (3:3). This passage clearly requires the sacrifices of the righteous, and so does not favor the opinion about the outward act (*opus operatum*). But the sacrifices of the sons of Levi, that is, of those teaching in the New Testament, are the preaching of the Gospel and the good fruit of preaching. About this Paul says, "To be a minister of Christ Jesus to the Gentiles in the priestly service of the gospel of God, so that the offering of the Gentiles may be acceptable, sanctified by the Holy Spirit" (Romans 15:16). He means that the Gentiles may be offerings acceptable to God through faith. In the Law the slaying of victims illustrated both Christ's death and the preaching of the Gospel, by which this old flesh should be put to death and new and eternal life be begun in us.

But everywhere the adversaries wrongly apply the name *sacrifice* to the ceremony alone. They leave out the preaching of the Gospel, faith, prayer, and similar things, although the ceremony has been established because of these. The New Testament should have sacrifices of the heart, not ceremonies for sin that are to be performed like the Levitical priesthood.

35 They cite also the daily sacrifice. (See Exodus 29:38–39; Daniel 8:11; 12:11.) Just as there was a daily sacrifice in the Law, so the Mass should be a daily sacrifice of the New Testament. The adversaries have made out well if we allow ourselves to be overcome by allegories. Clearly allegories do not produce firm proofs. We readily allow the Mass to be understood as a daily sacrifice, as long as that includes the entire Mass: the ceremony with the preaching of the Gospel, faith, invocation, and thanksgiving. Joined together, these are a daily sacrifice of the New Testament because the ceremony ‹of the Mass, or the Lord's Supper,› was set up because of these things. The Mass is not to be separated from them. So Paul says, "For as often as you eat this bread and drink the cup, you proclaim the Lord's death until He comes" (1 Corinthians 11:26). But it cannot be shown from this Levitical type that a ceremony justifying by the outward work (*ex opere operato*) is necessary, or should be applied on behalf of others, that it may merit the forgiveness of sins for them.

36 The type represents appropriately not only the ceremony, but also the preaching of the Gospel. In Numbers 28:4–8, three parts of that daily sacrifice are represented: the burning of the lamb, the drink offering, and the offering of wheat flour. The Law had pictures or shadows of future things [Colossians 2:17]. So Christ and the entire worship of the New Testament are shown in this picture. The burning of the lamb illustrates Christ's death. The drink offering illustrates that everywhere in the entire world, by the preaching of the Gospel, believers are sprinkled with the blood of that Lamb, that is, sanctified. Peter says, "In the sanctification of the Spirit, for obedience to Jesus Christ and for sprinkling with His blood" (1 Peter 1:2). The offering of wheat flour means faith,
prayer, and thanksgiving in hearts. There- 37
fore, in the Old Testament, the shadow is dis-
cerned. In the New, the thing illustrated
should be sought, and not another type, as
sufficient for a sacrifice.

Although a ceremony is a memorial of 38
Christ's death, it alone is not the daily sacri-
fice. The memory itself is the daily sacrifice,
that is, preaching and faith. Faith truly believes that, by Christ's death, God has been reconciled. A drink offering is required, that is, the effect of preaching, in order that, being sprinkled by the Gospel with the blood of Christ, we may be sanctified, as those put to death and made alive. Offerings also are required, that is, thanksgiving, confessions, and troubles.

The pharisaic opinion of the outward act 39
(*opus operatum*) being cast aside, let us un-
derstand that spiritual worship and a daily sacrifice of the heart are meant, because in the New Testament the substance of good things should be sought for. This means the
Holy Spirit, putting the flesh to death, and
new life. These things should make it clear 40
that the type of the daily sacrifice declares
nothing against us, but rather for us, because we look for all the parts illustrated by the daily sacrifice. The adversaries falsely imagine that the ceremony alone is meant, and not also the preaching of the Gospel, putting the flesh to death, and enlivening of heart, and so forth.

Now, good people, it can easily be deter- 41
mined that the complaint against us—that we abolish the daily sacrifice—is entirely false. Experience shows what sort of Antiochi they are who hold power in the Church. Under the appearance of religion, they assume to themselves the kingdom of the world. They rule without concern for religion and the teaching of the Gospel. They wage war like kings of the world, and they set

42 up new services in the Church. The adver-
saries keep only the ceremony in the Mass
and publicly apply this to sacrilegious gain.
Afterward, they misrepresent that this work,
as applied for others, merits grace and all
43 good things for them. They do not teach the
Gospel in their sermons, they do not com-
fort consciences, they do not show that sins
are freely forgiven for Christ's sake. Rather,
they present the worship of saints, human
satisfactions, and human traditions, and
they affirm that people are justified before
God by these. Although some of these tradi-
tions are clearly godless, they still defend
them by violence. If any preacher wants to
be regarded as more learned, he presents
philosophical questions, which neither the
people nor even those who propose them
understand. Lastly, those who are more tol-
erable teach the Law and say nothing about
the righteousness of faith.

44 In the Confutation, the adversaries fuss
over the desertion of churches. Altars stand
unadorned, lacking candles and images. They
regard these trifles as ornaments to churches.
45 It is a far different desertion that Daniel
means (11:31; 12:11), namely, ignorance of
the Gospel. Overwhelmed by the multitude
and variety of traditions and opinions, the
people were in no way able to welcome the
46 sum of Christian doctrine. Among the peo-
ple, who ever understood the doctrine of re-
pentance as presented by the adversaries? Yet
this is the chief topic of Christian doctrine.

Consciences were tormented by the list-
ing of offenses and by satisfactions. The ad-
versaries never mention faith, by which we
freely receive the forgiveness of sins. All the
books and all the sermons of the adversaries
were silent about the exercises of faith, strug-
gling with despair, and the free forgiveness of
47 sins for Christ's sake. To these, the horrible
profanation of the Masses and many other
godless services in the churches were added.
This is the desertion described by Daniel.

On the contrary, by God's favor, our 48
priests attend to the ministry of the Word,
teach the Gospel about Christ's blessings, and
show that the forgiveness of sins happens
freely for Christ's sake. This doctrine brings
sure comfort to consciences. The doctrine of
good works that God commands is also
added. The worth and use of the Sacraments
are declared.

If the daily sacrifice was the proper use of 49
the Sacrament, we would keep the sacrifice.
The adversaries would not. For their priests
use the Sacrament to make money. There is a
more frequent and more conscientious use.
The people use it after having first been in-
structed and examined. People are taught
about the true use of the Sacrament. It was
set up to be a seal and testimony of the free
forgiveness of sins, and so that it should re-
mind alarmed consciences to be truly confi-
dent and believe that their sins are freely for-
given. Since we keep both the preaching of
the Gospel and the lawful use of the Sacra-
ment, the daily sacrifice remains with us.

If we must speak of outward appearances, 50
Church attendance among us is better than
among the adversaries. The audiences are
held by useful and clear sermons. (Neither
the people nor the teachers have ever under-
stood the doctrine of the adversaries.) ‹There
is nothing that keeps people at church more
than good preaching.›The true adornment 51
of the churches is godly, useful, and clear
doctrine, the devout use of the Sacraments,
fervent prayer, and the like. Candles, golden
vessels, and similar adornments are fitting,
but they are not the specifically unique
adornment belonging to the Church. If the
adversaries make these things the focus of
worship, and not the preaching of the
Gospel, in faith (and the struggles of faith)

they are to be numbered among those whom Daniel describes as worshiping their god with gold and silver [Daniel 11:38].

52 They quote also from the Epistle to the Hebrews, "For every high priest chosen from among men is appointed to act on behalf of men in relation to God, to offer gifts and sacrifices for sins" (5:1). They conclude that, since there are high priests and priests in the New Testament, that means there is also a sacrifice for sins. This passage particularly impresses the unlearned, especially when the showiness of the priesthood and the sacrifices of the Old Testament are spread before the eyes. This resemblance deceives the ignorant, so that they decide that a ceremonial sacrifice should also exist among us in the same way, which should be applied for the sins of others, like in the Old Testament. The service of the Mass and the rest of the polity of the pope is nothing more than false zeal for the misunderstood Levitical order.

53 The main proofs for our belief are in the Epistle to the Hebrews. Yet, the adversaries twist mutilated passages from this Epistle against us, as in this very passage, where it is said that every high priest is ordained to offer sacrifices for sins. Scripture immediately adds that Christ is the High Priest (Hebrews 5:5–6, 10). The preceding words speak about the Levitical priesthood and show that the Levitical priesthood was an image of Christ's priesthood. The Levitical sacrifices for sins did not merit the forgiveness of sins before God. They were only an image of Christ's sacrifice, which was to be the one atoning
54 sacrifice, as we said before. To a great extent the Epistle speaks about how the ancient priesthood and the ancient sacrifices were set up not to merit the forgiveness of sins before God or reconciliation, but only to illustrate
55 the future sacrifice of Christ alone. In the Old Testament, saints had to be justified by faith, which receives the promise of the forgiveness of sins granted for Christ's sake, just as saints are also justified in the New Testament. From the beginning of the world all saints had to believe that Christ would be the promised offering and satisfaction for sins, as Isaiah 53:10 teaches, "when His soul makes an offering for sin."

In the Old Testament, sacrifices did not 56
merit reconciliation, except as a picture (for they merited civil reconciliation), but they illustrated the coming sacrifice. This means that Christ is the only sacrifice applied on behalf of the sins of others. Therefore, in the New Testament, no sacrifice is left to be applied for the sins of others, except the one sacrifice of Christ upon the cross.

Those who imagine that Levitical sacri- 57
fices merited the forgiveness of sins before God, and by this example require sacrifices in the New Testament that are to be applied on behalf of others in addition to Christ's death, are completely mistaken. This imagination absolutely destroys the merit of Christ's passion and the righteousness of faith, and it corrupts the doctrine of the Old and New Testaments. Instead of Christ, it makes for us other mediators and atonement makers out of the priests and sacrificers, who daily sell their work in the churches.

If anyone argues that in the New Testa- 58
ment a priest is needed to make offering for sins, this can only be said about Christ. The entire Epistle to the Hebrews confirms this explanation. In addition to Christ's death, if we were to look for any other satisfaction that applies to the sins of others and so to reconcile God, this would be nothing more than to make other mediators in addition to Christ.
The priesthood of the New Testament 59
is the Spirit's ministry, as Paul teaches (2 Corinthians 3:6). So it has only Christ's one sacrifice, which is enough and applies to

the sins of others. Besides, this priesthood has no sacrifices like the Levitical order, which could be applied by the outward act (*ex opere operato*) to others. Rather, it offers the Gospel and the Sacraments to others, so that they may conceive faith and the Holy Spirit through them and be brought from death to life. So the Spirit's ministry conflicts with the application of an outward act (*opus operatum*). The Spirit's ministry is that through which the Holy Spirit is powerful in hearts. Therefore, this ministry is beneficial to others when it is powerful in them and regenerates and enlivens them. This does not happen by applying someone's work to another.

60 We have shown why the Mass does not justify by the outward act (*ex opere operato*) and why, when applied to others, it does not merit forgiveness. This is because both conflict with the righteousness of faith. For it is impossible that sins should be forgiven and the terrors of death and sin be overcome by anything other than faith in Christ, according to Romans 5:1, "Since we have been justified by faith, we have peace."

61 Also, we have shown that the Scriptures, which are quoted against us, do not approve the godless opinion of the adversaries about the outward act (*opus operatum*). Every per-
62 son everywhere can determine this. Therefore, Thomas's error is to be rejected. He wrote:

> That the body of the Lord, once offered on the cross for original debt, is continually offered for daily offenses on the altar, in order that, in this, the Church might have a service by which to reconcile God to herself.

63 The other common errors are also to be rejected, such as that the Mass by the outward act (*ex opere operato*) gives grace to the one using it. Or, that when the Mass is applied for others (even wicked persons, provided they do not introduce an obstacle), it merits the forgiveness of sins, guilt, and punishment for them. All these things are false and godless and are recently invented by unlearned monks. They cloud over the glory of Christ's passion and the righteousness of faith.

From these errors sprang countless oth- 64
ers, such as Masses benefit when applied for many, just as much as when applied individually. The philosophers have particular degrees of merit, just as moneychangers have varying weights for gold or silver. Besides, they sell the Mass as the cost for receiving what each one seeks. Merchants pay so that business may be prosperous, hunters so that hunting may be successful, and countless other things. Finally, they also apply it to the dead. By applying the Sacrament, they free souls from the pains of purgatory, even though the Mass does not even help the liv-
ing without faith. The adversaries are unable 65
to produce even one syllable from the Scriptures to defend these fables, which they teach with great authority in the Church. They do not have the testimonies of the ancient Church or of the Fathers.

What the Fathers Thought about Sacrifice

Since we have explained the Scripture 66
passages that are quoted against us, we must also reply about the Fathers. We know well that the Fathers call the Mass a sacrifice. Yet, they do not mean that the Mass gives grace by the outward act (*ex opere operato*) and that, when applied to others, it merits the forgiveness of sins, guilt, and punishment for them. Where can such freakish stories be found in the Fathers? The adversaries openly declare that they speak about thanksgiving.
So they call it a eucharist. However, we have 67

said before that a eucharistic sacrifice does not merit reconciliation, but is made by those who have been reconciled, just as troubles do not merit reconciliation, but are eucharistic sacrifices when those who have been reconciled tolerate them.

In general, this reply to the sayings of the Fathers defends us well enough against the adversaries. Certainly these daydreams about the merit of the outward act (*opus operatum*) cannot be found in the Fathers. But so that the whole matter may be better understood, we will also state those things that actually agree with the Fathers and Scripture about the use of the Sacrament.

The Use of the Sacrament and of the Sacrifice

68 Some clever men imagine that the Lord's Supper was set up for two reasons. First, that it might be a mark and reference of profession, just as a particular shape of a hood is the sign of a particular monastic profession. Second, they think that such a mark was especially pleasing to Christ, namely, a feast to illustrate mutual union and friendship among Christians, because banquets are signs of covenant and friendship. But this is a secular view. It does not show the chief use of the things delivered by God. It speaks only about the exercise of love, which people, however profane and worldly, understand. It does not speak of faith, the nature of which few understand.

69 The Sacraments are signs of God's will toward us and not merely signs of people among one another. Those who define Sacraments in the New Testament as signs of grace are correct. There are two things in a Sacrament: a sign and the Word. In the New Testament, the Word is the promise of grace added. The promise of the New Testament is the promise of the forgiveness of sins, "This is My body, which is given for you. This [cup] is My blood of the new testament, which is shed for you for the forgiveness of sins." [See Matthew 26:26–28; Mark 14:22–24; Luke
22:19–20; 1 Corinthians 11:24–25.] So the 70
Word offers the forgiveness of sins. A ceremony is a sort of picture, or seal, as Paul (Romans 4:11) calls it, the Word making known the promise. Therefore, just as the promise is useless unless it is received through faith, so a ceremony is useless unless faith, which is truly confident that the forgiveness of sins is here offered, is added. This faith encourages penitent minds. Just as the Word has been given to excite this faith, so the Sacrament has been set up so that what meets the eyes might move the heart to believe. The Holy Spirit works through these: Word and Sacrament.

Such a use of the Sacrament, in which 71
faith enlivens terrified hearts, is a service of the New Testament. That is because the New Testament requires spiritual inclinations, making dead and alive. Christ instituted the Sacrament for this use, since He commanded the disciples to do this in remembrance of
Him. Remembering Christ is not the useless 72
celebration of a show. It is not something set up for the sake of example, as the memory of Hercules or Ulysses is celebrated in tragedies. Rather, it is remembering Christ's benefits and receiving them through faith, to be enlivened by them. So Psalm 111:4–5 says, "He has caused His wondrous works to be remembered; the Lord is gracious and merciful. He provides food for those who fear Him." The Sacrament illustrates that God's will and mercy should be discerned in the
ceremony. Faith that grasps mercy enlivens. 73
This is the chief use of the Sacrament. It is clear who are fit for the Sacrament (namely, terrified consciences) and how they should use it.

74 The sacrifice also is added. For there are several reasons with one purpose. After a conscience encouraged through faith has determined from what terrors it is freed, it fervently gives thanks for Christ's benefit and passion. It also uses the ceremony itself to God's praise, to show its gratitude by this obedience. It declares that it holds God's gifts in high esteem. So the ceremony becomes a sacrifice of praise.

75 The Fathers certainly speak of a twofold effect: the comfort of consciences and thanksgiving, or praise. The former of these effects has to do with the nature of the Sacrament; the latter has to do with the sacrifice. Ambrose says about comfort:

> Go to Him and be absolved, because He is the forgiveness of sins. Do you ask who He is? Hear Him when He says, "I am the bread of life; whoever comes to Me shall not hunger, and whoever believes in Me shall never thirst" (John 6:35).

This passage declares that the forgiveness of sins is offered in the Sacrament. It also declares that this should be received through faith. Countless references with this meaning are found in the Fathers, all of which the adversaries pervert to the outward act (*opus operatum*) and to a work applied to others. Yet the Fathers clearly require faith and speak of the comfort belonging to everyone, and not of the application.

76 Besides these, expressions are also found about thanksgiving. One beautiful expression by Cyprian is about those communing in a godly way. "Piety, in thanking the Bestower of such abundant blessing, makes a distinction between what has been given and what has been forgiven." This means piety regards both what has been given and what has been forgiven, that is, it compares the greatness of God's blessings and the greatness of our evils, sin and death, with each other, and gives thanks, and so on. In this way the term *eucharist* arose in the Church. Certainly the 77
ceremony itself—the giving of thanks by the outward act (*ex opere operato*)—does not apply to others. It does not merit the forgiveness of sins for others and free souls of the dead. These opinions conflict with the righteousness of faith. Without faith, a ceremony cannot benefit either the one performing it or others.

The Term *Mass*

The adversaries also refer us to linguistics. 78
They get arguments from the names of the Mass, which do not require a long discussion. For even though the Mass is called a sacrifice, it does not make sense that it must give grace by the outward act (*ex opere operato*) or, when applied to others, merits the forgiveness of sins for them. *Leitourgia*, they say, 79
means a sacrifice, and the Greeks call the Mass *liturgy*. (Why do they leave out here the old name *synaxis*, which shows that the Mass used to be the communion of many?) Let us discuss the word *liturgy*. This word 80
does not properly mean a sacrifice, but rather the public ministry. Liturgy agrees well with our belief that one minister who consecrates gives the Lord's body and blood to the rest of the people, just as one minister who preaches offers the Gospel to the people. As Paul says, "This is how one should regard us, as servants of Christ and stewards of the mysteries of God" (1 Corinthians 4:1), that is, of the Gospel and the Sacraments. And, "We are ambassadors for Christ, God making His appeal through us. We implore you on behalf of Christ, be reconciled to God" (2 Corinthians 5:20). So the term *leitourgia* agrees well 81
with the ministry. For it is an old word, ordinarily used in public civil administrations. To

the Greeks it meant public burdens, such as tribute, the expense of equipping a fleet, or similar things. *For Leptines*, the oration of Demosthenes, speaks about such things, discussing at length public duties and exemptions: "He will say that some unworthy men, having found an exemption, have withdrawn from public burdens." And so they spoke in the time of the Romans, as the reply of Pertinax, *On the Law of Exemption*, shows: "Even though the number of children does not liberate parents from all public burdens." And the Commentary on Demosthenes states that *leitourgia* is a kind of tribute, the expense of the games, the expense of equipping vessels, of attending to the gymnasia and similar
82 public offices. In 2 Corinthians 9:12, Paul uses it for a collection. Taking a collection not only supplies those things that the saints lack, but also causes them to give more thanks abundantly to God. In Philippians 2:25, he calls Epaphroditus a "minister to my need," where certainly a sacrificer cannot be
83 understood. Further references are not needed, since examples are understandable for those reading the Greek writers, in whom *leitourgia* is used for public civil burdens or ministries. Because of the pair of vowels, grammarians do not get this term from *lite*, which means prayers, but from public goods, which they call leita, so that *leitourgeo* means "I pay attention to," or "I administer public goods."

84 Their argument that, since the Holy Scriptures mention an altar, the Mass must be a sacrifice, is ridiculous. Paul refers to the
85 figure of an altar only by comparison. They invent the idea that the Mass was named from an altar (*midzbeah*). Why do they need such far-fetched sources for words unless they want to show their knowledge of the Hebrew language? Why seek the sources for words from a distance when the term *Mass* is found in Deuteronomy 16:10, where it means the collections or gifts of the people, not the offering of the priest? Individuals coming to the celebration of the Passover were obliged to bring some gift as a contribution. Early Christians also kept this cus- 86
tom. Coming together, they brought bread, wine, and other things, as the canons of the apostles declare. From there a portion was taken to be consecrated; the rest was given out to the poor. With this custom they also kept *Mass* as the name of the contributions. Because of such contributions, it appears also that in other places the Mass was called *agape*, unless one would prefer that it was so called because of the common feast. Let us 87
leave out these silly things. It is ridiculous that the adversaries should produce such trifling guesses about such an important matter. Although the Mass is called an offering, how does the term favor the dreams about the outward act (*opus operatum*), and their application, which merits the forgiveness of sins for others? Can it be called an offering because prayers, thanksgivings, and the entire worship are offered there, as it is also called a eucharist? Neither ceremonies nor prayers benefit by the outward act (*ex opere operato*) without faith. We are not arguing here about prayers, but particularly about the Lord's Supper.

The Greek canon also says many things 88
about the offering, but it plainly shows that it is not speaking properly of the body and blood of the Lord, but of the whole service, of prayers and thanksgivings. For it says this, "Make us worthy to bring to You prayers and requests and bloodless sacrifices on behalf of all people." When this is rightly understood, it is not offensive. It prays that we be made worthy to *offer prayers* and supplications and bloodless sacrifices for the people. He calls even prayers "bloodless sacrifices." Just as

also a little afterward, "We offer," he says, "this reasonable and bloodless service." Those who would rather interpret this as a reasonable sacrifice, and transfer it to Christ's very body, do so inappropriately. The canon speaks of the entire worship, and in opposition to the outward act (*opus operatum*) Paul has spoken of reasonable service (*logike latreia;* Romans 12:1), namely, of the worship of the mind, of fear, of faith, of prayer, of thanksgiving, and so on.

[The Mass for the Dead]

89 Our adversaries have no references and no command from Scripture for defending the use of the ceremony for freeing the souls of the dead. Yet they receive unlimited revenue from this. Certainly it is no light sin to establish such services in the Church without God's command and without the example of Scripture and to apply the Lord's Supper to the dead. (It was set up for commemoration and preaching among the living.) This violates the Second Commandment by abusing God's name.

First, it dishonors the Gospel to hold that a ceremony by the outward act (*ex opere operato*), without faith, is a sacrifice reconciling God and making satisfaction for sins. It is a horrible saying to assign as much importance to the work of a priest as to Christ's death. Again, sin and death cannot be overcome except by faith in Christ, as Paul teaches, "Since we have been justified by faith, we have peace with God" (Romans 5:1). Therefore, the punishment of purgatory cannot be overcome by applying to one person the work of another.

90 Now we will leave out the sort of references about purgatory that the adversaries have, what kinds of punishments they think there are in purgatory, what grounds the doctrine of satisfactions has, which we have shown above to be most empty. We will only present the following in opposition. Certainly the Lord's Supper was set up because of the pardon of guilt. It offers the forgiveness of sins, where it is necessary that guilt be truly understood. Yet, it does not make satisfaction for guilt; otherwise, the Mass would be equal to Christ's death. The pardon of guilt can be received only through faith. Therefore, the Mass is not a satisfaction, but a promise and Sacrament that require faith.

Certainly all godly persons should be 91
seized with the bitterest grief if they consider that the greater portion of the Mass has been transferred to the dead and to satisfactions for punishments. This banishes the daily sacrifice from the Church. This is the kingdom of Antiochus, who transferred the most beneficial promises about the pardon of guilt and about faith to the emptiest opinions about satisfactions. This pollutes the Gospel and corrupts the use of the Sacraments. Paul said that these persons are "guilty of profaning the body and blood of the Lord" (1 Corinthians 11:27). They have hindered the doctrine about faith and the forgiveness of sins and, under the appearance of satisfactions, have devoted the Lord's body and blood to sacrilegious profit. At some time they will pay the penalty for this sacrilege. Therefore, we and all godly consciences should guard against approving the abuses of the adversaries.

Let us return to the matter. The Mass is 92
not a satisfaction, either for punishment or for guilt, without faith (*ex opere operato*). Therefore, applying it to the dead is useless. There is no need here of a longer discussion. Clearly these applications for the dead have no references from the Scriptures. Neither is it safe, without the authority of Scripture, to set up forms of worship in the Church. If it is ever necessary, we will speak at greater length

about this entire subject. Why should we now argue with adversaries who misunderstand sacrifice, Sacrament, the forgiveness of sins, and faith?

93 The Greek canon does not apply the offering as a satisfaction for the dead because it applies it equally for all the blessed patriarchs, prophets, and apostles. Apparently the Greeks make an offering as thanksgiving and do not apply it as satisfaction for punishments. Furthermore, they do not speak of offering solely the Lord's body and blood, but of the other parts of the Mass, namely, prayers and thanksgiving. After the consecration they pray that it may benefit those who partake of it; they do not speak of others. Then they add:

> Yet we offer to you this reasonable service for those having departed in faith, forefathers, fathers, patriarchs, prophets, apostles.

"Reasonable service" [Romans 12:1], however, does not mean the offering itself, but prayers and all things that are preferred there.
Regarding the adversaries' quoting the Fa- 94
thers about the offering for the dead, we know that the ancients speak of prayer for the dead, which we do not ban. We disapprove of applying the Lord's Supper for the dead by the outward act (*ex opere operato*). The ancients do not favor the adversaries regarding the outward act (*opus operatum*). Even though they have the references especially of

Elijah versus the Prophets of Baal

Gregory or the moderns, we hold up to
them the most clear and certain Scriptures.
95 There is a great diversity among the Fathers.
They were men and could err and be de-
ceived. If they were alive now and would see
their sayings assigned as falsehood for the
scandalous lies that the adversaries teach
about the outward act (*opus operatum*), they
would interpret themselves far differently.

96 The adversaries also falsely quote against
us the condemnation of Aerius, who, they
say, was condemned for denying that an of-
fering is made for the living and the dead in
the Mass. They often use this clever turn:
quote the ancient heresies and falsely com-
pare our cause with them to crush us by this
comparison. Epiphanius declares that Aerius
maintained prayers for the dead are useless.
He finds fault with this. We do not favor
Aerius either, but we do argue with you be-
cause you defend a heresy that clearly con-
flicts with the prophets, apostles, and Holy
Fathers. This heresy is that the Mass justifies
by the outward act (*ex opere operato*), that
when applied it merits the pardon of guilt
and punishment even for the unjust if they
do not present an obstacle. We object to
these deadly errors, which divert people
from the glory of Christ's passion and en-
tirely overthrow the doctrine about the
97 righteousness of faith. In the Law, the god-
less had a similar belief. That is, they be-
lieved they merited the forgiveness of sins,
not freely through faith, but through sacri-
fices by the outward act. Therefore, they in-
creased these services and sacrifices, set up
the worship of Baal in Israel, and even sacri-
ficed in the groves in Judah. Therefore, the
prophets condemn this belief and war
against not only the worshipers of Baal, but
also other priests who made sacrifices or-
dained by God with this godless belief
[cf. 1 Kings 18:1–40]. This belief, that such
services and sacrifices atone, remains and
always will remain in the world. Carnal peo-
ple cannot tolerate that the honor of an
atoning sacrifice belongs solely to Christ's
sacrifice because they do not understand
the righteousness of faith. Rather, they as-
sign equal honor to the rest of the services
and sacrifices. The godless priests in Judah 98
held a false belief about such sacrifices; Baal
worship even continued in Israel. Neverthe-
less, a Church of God was there that objected
to these godless services [1 Kings 19:18]. Baal
worship remains in the realm of the pope:
the abuse of the Mass. By it they think they
can merit the pardon of guilt and punish-
ment for the unrighteous. It seems that this
Baal worship will persist as long as the reign
of the pope. It will continue until Christ
comes to judge and by the glory of His return
destroy the reign of the Antichrist [2 Thessa-
lonians 2:1–8]. Meanwhile, all who truly be-
lieve the Gospel should condemn these
wicked services. Against God's command,
they were created to cloud over Christ's glory
and the righteousness of faith.

We have briefly said these things about 99
the Mass for the following reasons. First, we
hope that all good people everywhere un-
derstand that we keep the dignity of the
Mass and show its true use with the greatest
zeal. Second, our reasons for disagreeing
with the adversaries are most just. Further,
we would encourage all good people not to
help the adversaries in the profanation of
the Mass, burdening themselves with other
people's sin. This is an important cause and
an important subject, no less important
than the work of the prophet Elijah, who
condemned the worship of Baal. We have
presented this important discussion with
the greatest restraint and now reply without
using abusive words. But if the adversaries
push us to collect all kinds of abuses of the

Mass, we will not present the discussion with such toleration.

ARTICLE XXVII (XIII)

Monastic Vows

Note: The Pontifical Confutation, as one would have expected, rejects the Augsburg Confession's position on monasticism. Melanchthon's additional comments explain the biblical reasons why Lutheranism does not, and cannot, condone or support the view that monasticism is a "higher calling" than other vocations. The key point again is the Roman assertion that monasticism and the practices, promises, and customs associated with it are means by which people can merit God's grace and forgiveness. Lutheranism restored to the Church a proper regard for how men and women should, can, and do serve God in all the various callings and stations in life. (See also AC XXV and XXVII; SA III VIII and XIV; SC Table of Duties.)

1 To our knowledge there was a monk named John Hilten in the Thuringian town of Eisenach. Thirty years ago, he was thrown into prison by his religious order because he had condemned certain scandalous abuses. We have seen his writings, which clearly explain the nature of his doctrine. Those who knew him declare that he was mild in his old
2 age and serious indeed, but not gloomy. He predicted many things, some of which have already happened. Others still seem close at hand, but we do not want to repeat them, lest it may be inferred that they are told either from hatred toward one or from preference toward another. Finally, either because of his age or the foulness of the prison, he became ill. He sent for the guard to tell him of his sickness. Inflamed with pharisaic hatred, the guard began to rebuke the man harshly because of his kind of doctrine, which seemed to interfere with the work of the kitchen. Without mentioning his sickness, Hilten said with a sigh that he was patiently bearing these injuries for Christ's sake, since he had neither written nor taught anything that could undermine the monastic life, but had only criticized some well-known abuses.
"Another one," he said, "will come in AD 3
1516. He will destroy you, and you will be unable to resist him." Later, his friends found this very prediction about the declining influence of the monastic orders and the very date written in his surviving commentaries
dealing with certain passages of Daniel. The 4
outcome will show how much emphasis should be given to this declaration, yet there are other signs that threaten a change in the monks' power, no less certain than oracles. It is clear how much hypocrisy, ambition, and greed there are in the monasteries, how much ignorance and cruelty exists among all the unlearned, what pride there is in their sermons, and how they continually create new ways of making money. There are other faults, which we do not care to mention.
Monasteries were schools for Christian in- 5
struction; now they have deteriorated, as though from a golden to an iron age (or as Plato says, the cube deteriorates into bad harmonies bringing destruction). All the most wealthy monasteries support only a lazy crowd, which gorges itself upon the public
alms of the Church. Christ, however, teaches 6
that the salt that has lost its savor should be cast out and be trodden underfoot (Matthew 5:13). By such morals the monks are singing their own fate ‹a requiem, and it will soon be
over with them›. Now another sign is added, 7
because in many places, they are the instigators of the death of good men. No doubt, God
will soon avenge these murders. Certainly we 8
do not accuse every one of them, for here and

Martin Luther, 1520

Lucas Cranach the Elder portrays Luther as he appeared in 1520, with Augustinian monk's hood (cowl) and haircut (tonsure). Luther dressed as a monk until October 9, 1524, when he first appeared in public in Wittenberg wearing secular clothing. A week later he discarded his cowl permanently. He had continued to dress and live as a monk for the sake of the weak, but realized that old believers interpreted his behavior as uncertainty about his teachings. His friend James Propst, former Augustinian monk, challenged him to practice his teachings. After 1524 Luther dressed as a doctor of theology [see color plate 9] and appeared that way until his death (1546).

there some good men in the monasteries decide fairly about human and "factitious" services, as some writers call them, and do not approve the cruelty exercised by the hypocrites among them.

9 Now we are discussing the kind of teaching that the writers of the Confutation defend, not the question of whether vows should be kept. We hold that legitimate vows should be kept. However, we are discussing different questions: Can these services merit the forgiveness of sins and justification? Are they satisfactions for sins? Are they equal to Baptism? Are they the obedience to basic rules and counsels? Are they evangelical perfection? Do they have the merits of superabundance? Do these merits, when applied to others, save them? Are vows made with these beliefs legitimate? Are vows legitimate that are made under the appearance of religion, merely for the sake of the belly and laziness? Are those true vows that have been forced either from the unwilling or from those who because of age were not able to understand this kind of life, whom parents or friends thrust into the monasteries so that they might be supported at public expense, without the loss of their private inheritance? Are vows legitimate that openly come to a bad end, either because they are not kept due to weakness, or because those in the monastic orders are pushed to approve and help the abuses of the Mass, the godless worship of saints, and the counsels attacking good peo-
10 ple? We have said many things in the Confession about such vows that even the canons of the popes condemn. Yet, the adversaries command that everything we have produced must be rejected. They have used these words.

It is worthwhile to hear how they distort our reasoning and what they mention to support their own case. So we will briefly review a few of our arguments. In passing, we will explain away the adversaries' slick logic in reference to them. However, this entire case has been carefully and fully discussed by Luther in his book *On the Vows of the Monks* [LW 44:243–400]. We wish to be seen as repeating that case here.

First, it is very clear that a vow is illegiti- 11
mate if the person who makes the vow thinks that the forgiveness of sins before God is merited by it or satisfaction is made before God for sins. This opinion clearly insults the Gospel, which teaches that the forgiveness of sins is freely granted to us for Christ's sake, as has been said at some length before. Therefore, we have quoted correctly Paul's declaration to the Galatians, "You are severed from Christ, you who would be justified by the law; you have fallen away from grace" (5:4). Those who seek the forgiveness of sins, not through faith in Christ, but through monastic works, divert people from Christ's honor and crucify Christ again. Listen, listen how the writers of the Confutation look for a way
out! They explain this passage of Paul only in 12
relation to Moses' Law, and they add that the monks obey all things for Christ's sake. They try hard to live nearer to the Gospel in order to merit eternal life. They add a horrible conclusion in these words, "Therefore, those things are wicked that are here alleged
against monasticism." O Christ, how long 13
will You bear these accusations with which our enemies present Your Gospel? In the Confession we said that the forgiveness of sins is received freely for Christ's sake, through faith. O Christ, who is in the bosom of the Father, You revealed the Gospel to the world. If our teaching is not the very voice of the Gospel, if it is not the eternal Father's judgment, we are rightly blamed. But Your death is a witness, Your resurrection is a witness, the Holy Spirit is a witness, Your entire Church is a witness of this: the true meaning

of the Gospel is that we receive forgiveness of sins, not because of our merits, but because of You, through faith.

14 When Paul denies that by Moses' Law people merit the forgiveness of sins, he withdraws this praise much more from human traditions. He clearly presents this in Colossians 2:16. If Moses' Law, which was divinely revealed, did not merit the forgiveness of sins, how much less do these silly observances, hostile to the civil custom of life, merit the forgiveness of sins!

15 The adversaries wrongly claim that Paul abolishes Moses' Law and that Christ follows in such a way that He does not freely grant the forgiveness of sins, but forgives because of the works of other laws, if any are now cre-
16 ated. By this godless and fanatical imagination they bury Christ's benefit. Then they wrongly claim that among those who obey this "Law of Christ," the monks obey it better than others, because of their hypocritical poverty, obedience, and chastity, since indeed all these things are full of sham. They brag about poverty most of all. No class of men has greater license than the monks; they boast of obedience. We do not like to speak about celibacy. Gerson indicates how pure this is in most of those who desire to be sexually pure. How many of them do desire to be chaste?

17 Of course, in this sham life the monks live more closely according to the Gospel! Christ does not follow Moses in such a way as to forgive sins because of our works, but to set His own merits and His own atoning sacrifice against God's wrath for us, so that we may be freely forgiven. Now, apart from Christ's atoning sacrifice, whoever applies his own merits to God's wrath and tries to receive the forgiveness of sins because of his own merits (whether the works of Moses' Law or of the Ten Commandments or of the rule of Benedict or of the rule of Augustine or of other rules) *does away with Christ's promise, has cast away Christ, and has fallen from grace.* This is Paul's verdict [Galatians 5:4].

Look, most merciful Emperor Charles. 18
Look, you princes. Look, all you ranks, how great is the impudence of the adversaries! Although we have quoted Paul's declaration to this effect, they have written, "Wicked are those things that are here cited against monasticism." What is more certain than 19
that men receive the forgiveness of sins through faith for Christ's sake? And these wretches dare to call this a wicked belief! We do not doubt that if you had been advised about this passage, you would have taken care that such blasphemy be removed from the Confutation.

It has been fully shown above that this 20
belief is wicked: We receive the forgiveness of sins because of our works. Therefore, we shall be briefer here. For the levelheaded reader will easily determine that we do not merit the forgiveness of sins by monastic works. Therefore, this blasphemy, which appears in Thomas, also cannot be tolerated, "The monastic profession is equal to Baptism." It is insane to make human tradition, which has neither God's command nor promise, equal to Christ's ordinance. Baptism has both God's command and promise, which contains the covenant of grace and of eternal life.

Second, religious exercises, obedience, 21
poverty, and celibacy—provided the latter is not impure—are adiaphora. Therefore, the saints can use them without impiety, just as Bernard, Francis, and other holy men used them. They used them to restrain the body, so that they might have more freedom to teach and to perform other godly offices, not that these works themselves are, by them-

selves, works that justify or merit eternal life.
Finally, these exercises are of the type that
Paul says, "Bodily training is of some value"
22 (1 Timothy 4:8). It is believable that in some
places there are also currently good men, en-
gaged in the ministry of the Word, who use
23 these exercises without wicked opinions. But
to hold that these exercises are [justifying]
services because they are counted just before
God, and through which they merit eternal
life, conflicts with the Gospel about the righ-
teousness of faith. This Gospel teaches that
for Christ's sake righteousness and eternal
life are granted to us. It conflicts also with
Christ's saying, "In vain do they worship Me,
teaching as doctrines the commandments of
men" (Matthew 15:9). It conflicts also with
this statement, "Whatever does not proceed
from faith is sin" (Romans 14:23). But how
can the adversaries affirm that God approves
these services as righteousness before Him
when they have no testimony of God's Word?

24 See how impudent the adversaries are!
Not only do they teach that these exercises
are justifying services, but they add that these
services are more perfect, that is, meriting
more the forgiveness of sins and justification
than do other kinds of life. Here many false
and deadly beliefs agree. The adversaries
imagine that they observe basic rules and
counsels. Afterward, these generous men,
dreaming that they have the merits of super-
25 abundance, sell these to others. These things
are full of pharisaic pride. It is the height of
ungodliness to hold that these merits satisfy
the Ten Commandments in such a way that
merits remain, while such basic rules as
these accuse all the saints, "You shall love the
Lord your God with all your heart"
(Deuteronomy 6:5). Likewise, "You shall not
covet" (Romans 7:7). The prophet says, "All
mankind are liars" (Psalm 116:11), that is,
not thinking rightly about God, not fearing
God enough, not believing Him enough.
Therefore, the monks falsely brag that the
commandments are fulfilled in the obedi-
ence of a monastic life, and more is done
than what is commanded.

This is also false: monastic observances 26
are works of the counsels of the Gospel. The
Gospel does not advise about distinguishing
clothing and meats and the giving up of
property. These are human traditions, about
which it has been said, "Food will not com-
mend us to God" (1 Corinthians 8:8). There-
fore, they are neither justifying services nor
perfection. Indeed, when they are presented
covered with these titles, they are mere
"teachings of demons" [1 Timothy 4:1].

Virginity is recommended, but to those 27
who have the gift, as has been said before.
However, it is a most deadly error to hold that
evangelical perfection lies in human tradi-
tions. In this way even the monks of the Mus-
lims could brag that they have evangelical per-
fection. Neither is virginity part of the things
called adiaphora. Because God's kingdom is
righteousness and life in hearts (Romans
14:17), perfection is growth in the fear of God,
growth in confidence in the mercy promised
in Christ, and growth in devotion to one's call-
ing. Paul also describes perfection this way,
"[We] are being transformed into the same
image from one degree of glory to another.
For this comes from the Lord who is the Spir-
it" (2 Corinthians 3:18). He does not say, "We
are continually receiving another hood or
other sandals or other girdles." It is regrettable
that such pharisaic, indeed, Muslim, expres-
sions should be read and heard in the Church.
For they say the perfection of the Gospel and
Christ's kingdom (which is eternal life) should
be wed along with these foolish observances
about vestments and similar trifles.

Now hear our Areopagites ‹excellent 28
teachers› on what an unworthy declaration

they have recorded in the Confutation. They say:

> It has been clearly declared in the Holy Scriptures that the monastic life merits eternal life if maintained by a due observance, which by the grace of God any monk can maintain. And, indeed, Christ has promised this much more abundant to those who have left home or brothers, and so on (Matthew 19:29).

29 These are the words of the adversaries, in which it is first said most rudely that the Holy Scriptures say that a monastic life merits eternal life. Where do the Holy Scriptures speak of a monastic life? The adversaries plead their case this way, so men of no account quote the Scriptures. Although no one is ignorant that the monastic life is a recent creation, yet they quote the authority of Scripture and say, too, that their decree has been clearly declared in the Scriptures.

30 Besides, they dishonor Christ when they
say that men merit eternal life by monasticism. Not even to His Law has God assigned
the honor that it should merit eternal life, as
He clearly says in Ezekiel, "I gave them
statutes that were not good and rules by
31 which they could not have life" (20:25). First,
it is certain that a monastic life does not
merit the forgiveness of sins, but we receive
this freely through faith, as has been said be-
32 fore. Second, for Christ's sake, through
mercy, eternal life is granted to those who through faith receive forgiveness and do not apply their own merits against God's judgment, as Bernard also says with very great force:

> It is necessary first of all to believe that you cannot have the forgiveness of sins except by God's good will. Second, you cannot have any good work, unless He has given it. Finally, you cannot merit eternal life by works, unless this also is freely given.

We have quoted above the rest of the passage, which speaks in the same way. Furthermore, Bernard adds at the end, "Let no one deceive himself, because if he will reflect well, he will undoubtedly find that with ten thousand he cannot meet Him ‹namely, God› who comes
against him with twenty thousand." We do 33
not merit the forgiveness of sins or eternal life by the works of the divine Law, but it is necessary to seek the mercy promised in Christ. The honor of meriting the forgiveness of sins or eternal life cannot be assigned to monastic observances, since they are mere human traditions.

Those who teach that the monastic life 34
merits the forgiveness of sins or eternal life, and transfer the confidence owed Christ to these foolish observances, completely suppress the Gospel about the free forgiveness of sins and the promised mercy in Christ, which is to be grasped. Instead of Christ they worship their own hoods and their own filth. But since even they need mercy, they act wickedly by inventing works of supererogation and selling them to others.

We speak more briefly here about these 35
subjects, because from what we have said before about justification, repentance, and human traditions, it is clear that monastic vows are not rewarded with the forgiveness of sins and eternal life. Since Christ calls traditions useless services, they are in no way evangelical perfection.

The adversaries deceitfully wish to appear 36
as if they modify the common opinion about perfection. They say that a monastic life is not perfection, but that it is a state in which one acquires perfection. What a pretty phrase! We remember that this change is

found in Gerson. Clearly levelheaded people, although they did not risk removing monastic life from being praised as perfection, were offended by its excessive praise. So they made the change that monasticism is a state
37 in which one acquires perfection. If we follow this logic, monasticism will be no more a state of perfection than the life of a farmer or mechanic. For these are also states in which one acquires perfection. All people, in every vocation, should seek perfection, that is, grow in the fear of God, in faith, in love toward one's neighbor, and similar spiritual virtues.

38 In the accounts of the hermits there are stories of Anthony and others that make the various stations in life equal. It is written that when Anthony asked God to show him how he was progressing in this kind of life, he was shown in a dream a certain shoemaker in the city of Alexandria for comparison. The next day Anthony came into the city and went to the shoemaker to determine his exercises and gifts, and he spoke with the man. He heard nothing except that early in the morning the shoemaker prayed a few words for the entire state and then worked his trade. Here Anthony learned that justification is not to be assigned to the kind of life that he had entered.

An Augustinian Monk
(Luther was an Augustinian)

Although the adversaries now lessen their 39
praises about perfection, they actually think otherwise. They sell and apply merits to others under the appearance that they are obeying basic rules and counsels. So they actually maintain that they possess surplus merits. What is this other than assuming perfection to oneself? The Confutation states that the monks try hard to live more closely in line with the Gospel. So it assigns perfection to human traditions if they are living more clearly in line with the Gospel by not having property, being unmarried, and obeying the monastic rule regarding clothing, meats, and similar silly things.

The Confutation also says that the monks 40
merit eternal life more abundantly and quotes Scripture, "everyone who has left houses," and so on (Matthew 19:29). So here it claims perfection also for man-made religious rites. But this Scripture passage in no way favors monastic life. Christ does not mean that leaving parents, wife, and siblings is a work that must be done because it merits the forgiveness of sins and eternal life. Indeed, such leaving is cursed. Anyone who leaves parents or wife to merit the forgiveness of sins or eternal life by this work dishonors Christ.

There are two kinds of leaving. One hap- 41
pens without a call, without God's command, which Christ does not approve (Matthew 15:9). The works we choose are useless services. When Christ speaks about

leaving wife and children, it becomes clear that He does not approve this kind of leaving. We know that God's commandment forbids leaving wife and children. God's command to leave is different, that is, when power or tyranny pushes us either to leave or to deny the Gospel. Here we are commanded to bear injury and should rather allow not only wealth, wife, and children, but life to be taken from us. Christ approves of this kind of leaving, and so He adds for the Gospel's "sake" [Mark 10:29]. He does so to illustrate that He is speaking not of those who injure wife and children, but who bear injury be-
42 cause of the confession of the Gospel. For the
Gospel's sake we should even leave our body. Here it would be ridiculous to hold that it would serve God to kill oneself and to leave the body without God's command. So, too, it is ridiculous to hold that it is a service to God without His command to leave possessions, friends, wife, and children.

43 Clearly, they wickedly twist Christ's word into a monastic life. Unless perhaps the declaration that they "receive a hundredfold in this life" is in place here. Many become monks not because of the Gospel, but because of extravagant living and laziness. They find the most plentiful riches instead of slen-
44 der inheritances. Because the entire subject
of monasticism is full of shams, they deceptively quote Scripture passages. So they sin doubly. They trick people and that, too, under the appearance of the divine name.

45 They also quote another passage about perfection, "If you would be perfect, go, sell what you possess and give to the poor, and you will have treasure in heaven; and come, follow Me" (Matthew 19:21). This passage has stirred up many who have imagined that casting away possessions and the control of
46 property is perfection. Let us allow the
philosophers to praise Aristippus, who cast a great weight of gold into the sea. Such stories have nothing to do with Christian perfection. The division, control, and possession of property are civil ordinances, approved by God's Word in the commandment "You shall not steal" (Exodus 20:15). The abandonment of property has no command or advice in the Scriptures. Evangelical poverty does not come from the abandonment of property, but from not being greedy, from not trusting in wealth, just as David was poor in a most wealthy kingdom.

Since the abandonment of property is 47
merely a human tradition, it is a useless service. The praises in the *Extravagante* are also excessive. This papal bull says that abandoning ownership of all things for God's sake gains merit, is holy, and is a way of perfection. It is very dangerous to praise so excessively a matter that conflicts with political
order. But ‹they say› Christ speaks about per- 48
fection here. Indeed, those who quote the text in a butchered way violate it. Perfection is found in what Christ adds, "Follow Me"
[Matthew 19:21]. Here He presents an ex- 49
ample of obedience to one's calling. Because not all callings are the same, this calling does not belong to everyone, but only to that person with whom Christ speaks. In the same way we are not to imitate the call of David to the kingdom [1 Samuel 16] or of Abraham to slay his son [Genesis 22]. Callings are personal, just as business matters themselves vary with times and persons. However, the example of obedience is
general. Perfection would have belonged to 50
that young man if he had believed and obeyed this vocation. So with us perfection is that everyone with true faith should obey his own calling.

Third, chastity is promised in monastic 51
vows. We have said above, however, about the marriage of priests, that the law of nature in

human beings cannot be removed by vows or enactments. Because not everyone has the gift of chastity [Matthew 19:12], many are not successful at it because of weakness. Neither, indeed, can any vows or any enactments set aside the Holy Spirit's command: "Because of the temptation to sexual immorality, each man should have his own wife" (1 Corinthians 7:2). Therefore, this vow is illegitimate in those who do not have the gift of chastity, but who are polluted because of
52 weakness. We have already said enough about this topic. Regarding this, it certainly is strange that the adversaries still defend their traditions contrary to God's clear command, since the dangers and scandals are clearly visible to all. Not even Christ's voice moves them. He scolded the Pharisees (Matthew 23:13[–36]), who had made traditions contrary to God's command.

53 Fourth, those who live in monasteries are released from their vows by godless ceremonies such as these: the Mass applied to the dead for profit and the worship of saints. In the latter, there are two faults. First, the saints are put in Christ's place, and they are wickedly worshiped, just as the Dominicans invented the rosary of the Blessed Virgin, which is mere babbling, as foolish as it is wicked, and nourishes the most empty arrogance. Then, too, these very impieties are applied only for
54 profit. Likewise, they neither hear nor teach the Gospel about the free forgiveness of sins for Christ's sake, the righteousness of faith, true repentance, or works having God's command. They are occupied with philosophic discussions or preserving ceremonies that conceal Christ.

55 We will not discuss here the entire service of ceremonies, the lessons, singing, and similar things. They could be tolerated if they were regarded simply as exercises, such as school lectures. Their purpose is to teach the hearers and, while teaching, to move some to fear or faith. But now the adversaries wrongly describe these ceremonies as services of God that merit the forgiveness of sins for themselves and for others. Because of this they increase the number of these ceremonies. However, if they would use them to teach and encourage the hearers, brief and pointed lessons would be more profitable
than these limitless babblings. So, the entire 56
monastic life is full of hypocrisy and false beliefs. Further, there is this danger: some in these monastic communities are driven to yield to those persecuting the truth. Therefore, there are many important and compelling reasons that free good people from the obligation to this kind of life.

Finally, the canons themselves release 57
many who either without discretion made vows when seduced by the tricks of monks or when compelled by friends. Not even the canons declare such vows to be legitimate. Consider all these things. Clearly there are many reasons showing that monastic vows made in the past are illegitimate. Because of this, a life full of hypocrisy and false beliefs can be safely abandoned.

The adversaries object to this and present 58
an argument taken from the Law of the Nazirites (Numbers 6:2[–21]). However, the Nazirites did not make their vows with the same opinion of the monks, which we condemn. The rite of the Nazirites was an exercise or a declaration of faith before the people. It did not merit the forgiveness of sins before God and did not justify before God. Further, just as circumcision or slaying victims would not be a service of God now, so the rite of the Nazirites should not be presented now as a service. It should be regarded simply as an adiaphoron. It is not right to compare (a) monasticism, created without God's Word, as a service that should merit

the forgiveness of sins and justification with (b) the rite of the Nazirites, which had God's Word and was not taught for the purpose of meriting the forgiveness of sins. The rite of the Nazirites was an outward exercise, just as other ceremonies of the Law. The same can be said about other ceremonies required in the Law.

59 The Rechabites are also quoted. They did not have any possessions and did not drink wine, as Jeremiah 35:6–10 says. Indeed, the example of the Rechabites agrees beautifully with our monks, whose monasteries excel the palaces of kings and who live most extravagantly! Yet the Rechabites, in their poverty of all things, were married. Our monks, although overflowing with self-indulgence, profess celibacy.

60 Besides, examples should be interpreted according to the rule, that is, according to certain and clear Scripture passages, not contrary to the rule, that is, contrary to the
61 Scriptures. Certainly our observances do not merit the forgiveness of sins or justification. Therefore, when the Rechabites are praised, it is necessary [to point out] that they have observed their custom, not because they believed (a) they merited forgiveness of sins by it or (b) that the work was itself a justifying service or (c) that it was a service by which they obtained eternal life instead of by God's mercy, for the sake of the promised Seed [Genesis 3:15; Galatians 3:16]. Their obedience is praised because they had their parents' command. One of God's commandments relates to this, "Honor your father and your mother" [Exodus 20:12].

62 The custom also had a particular purpose. Because they were foreigners, not Israelites, it is clear that their father wanted to distinguish them from their fellow citizens by certain marks so that they might not relapse into the impiety of their countrymen. By these marks he wanted to encourage them in the doctrine of faith and immortality. That is a legitimate reason. Far different reasons are given for monasticism. They pretend that monastic works are a [justifying] service; they pretend that they merit
the forgiveness of sins and justification. The 63
Rechabites' example is, therefore, different from monasticism. (We leave out the other evils in monasticism, which still continue.)

The adversaries also quote from 64
1 Timothy 5 about widows. As widows served the Church, they were supported at public expense, where it is said, "They desire to marry and so incur condemnation for having abandoned their former faith" (5:11–12).
First, let us suppose that the apostle speaks 65
here of vows. Still, this passage will not support monastic vows, which are made for godless services and with the opinion that they merit the forgiveness of sins and justification. With ringing voice, Paul condemns all services, all laws, all works if they are obeyed to merit the forgiveness of sins. Or he condemns the idea that because of them, instead of through Christ's mercy, we receive forgiveness of sins. Therefore, the vows of widows, if there were any, must have been different from monastic vows.

Besides, if the adversaries do not stop 66
misapplying the passage to vows, the prohibition "Let a widow be enrolled if she is not less than sixty years of age" (1 Timothy 5:9)
must be misapplied in the same way. So vows 67
made before this age will be of no account. The Church did not know this kind of vows. So Paul condemns widows, not because they marry, for he commands the younger to marry. But he condemns because, when supported at the public expense, they became unchaste, thus casting off faith. He calls this "former faith," clearly not in a monastic vow, but in Christianity. In this sense he understands faith in the same

chapter, "But if anyone does not provide for his relatives, and especially for members of his household, he has denied the faith and is
68 worse than an unbeliever" (5:8). Paul speaks of faith differently than the philosophers. He does not assign faith to those who have mortal sin. So he says that people cast off faith who do not care for their relatives. In the same way he also says that unchaste women cast off faith.

69 We have repeated some of our reasons and, in passing, have dismissed the adversaries' objections. We have collected these matters, not simply because of the adversaries, but much more because of godly minds, that they may see the reasons why they should condemn hypocritical and fictitious monastic services. All such things certainly are done away with by this one saying of Christ, "In vain do they worship Me, teaching as doctrines the commandments of men" (Matthew 15:9). Therefore, the vows themselves and the observances of meats, lessons, chants, vestments, sandals, girdles are useless services in God's sight. All godly minds should certainly know that the following opinions are simply pharisaic and condemned: (a) these observances merit the forgiveness of sins, (b) we are regarded righteous because of them, (c) we receive eternal life because of them, and not through mercy because of Christ. The holy people who have lived this kind of life must have learned—having rejected confidence in such observances—that they had the forgiveness of sins freely. They must have learned that for Christ's sake through mercy they would receive eternal life, and not for the sake of these services. God only approves services set up by His Word, which are of benefit when used in faith.

ARTICLE XXVIII (XIV)
Church Authority

Note: This topic would be covered in more detail six years later in Melanchthon's Treatise on the Power and Primacy of the Pope for the Smalcaldic League. The issue in this article is whether the Church, through its bishops, has the authority to command man-made regulations and impose them on people. Whether the Church has the duty to assign certain persons to carry out supervisory responsibilities is not at issue. All who are called and ordained to the office of preaching and administering the Sacraments share the same biblical authority or "power." This power is the Gospel ministry of Word and Sacrament in the Church and the authority to excommunicate persons and withhold the Sacrament of the Altar from them. The Church's ministers are not tyrants who can do whatever they want. Regulations must be in place to provide order and peace, but they must never suggest that anyone receives forgiveness from God by following them. (See also AC XXVIII; SA II IV; The Power and Primacy of the Pope; SC Table of Duties.)

The adversaries cry out violently here 1
about the privileges and immunities of the Church estate, and they add these concluding remarks, "All things are vain which are stated in the present article against the immunity
of the churches and priests." This is mere 2
trickery, for we have argued about other things in this article. Besides, we have testified frequently that we do not find fault with political ordinances and the gifts and privileges granted by princes.

If only the adversaries would hear, on the 3
other hand, the complaints of the churches and of godly minds! The adversaries courageously guard their own dignities and wealth. Meanwhile, they neglect the condi-

Preaching the Word and Administering the Sacraments

tion of the churches. They do not care that
the churches are rightly taught and that the
Sacraments are duly administered. They let
all kinds of men into the priesthood without
proper selection. Afterward, they impose in-
tolerable burdens, as though they delighted
in the destruction of their fellows. They de-
mand that their traditions be observed far
4 more accurately than the Gospel. In the most
important and difficult controversies, in
which people urgently desire instruction, so
that they can with certainty follow some-
thing, the adversaries do not relieve minds
tortured with doubt. Rather, they only call
people to arms. Besides, in matters ‹against
clear truth› they present decrees written in
blood, which threaten horrible punishments
against people unless they clearly act against
5 God's command. On the other hand, you
should see the tears of the poor and hear the
pitiful complaints of many good people. God
undoubtedly considers and regards them,
and one day you will give an account of your
stewardship.

6 Although we have in this article em-
braced various topics in the Confession, the
adversaries do not reply, except to say that
the bishops have the power of rule and force-
ful correction to direct their subjects to the
goal of eternal blessedness, and that the
power of ruling requires the power to judge,
to define, to distinguish, and to fix those
things that are serviceable or lead to the re-
sults just mentioned. These are the Confuta-
tion's words, by which the adversaries teach
us that the bishops are authorized to enact
laws useful for receiving eternal life. The con-
troversy is about this article.

7 We must keep in the Church the doctrine
that we receive the forgiveness of sins freely
for Christ's sake, through faith. We must also
keep the doctrine that human traditions are
useless services and, therefore, neither sin
nor righteousness should be placed in meat,
drink, clothing, and like things. Christ
wished the use of such things to be left free,
since He says, "It is not what goes into the
mouth that defiles a person" (Matthew
15:11); and Paul says, "The kingdom of God
is not a matter of eating and drinking" (Ro-
mans 14:17). Therefore, the bishops have no 8
right to enact traditions in addition to the
Gospel, so that people must merit the for-
giveness of sins, or that they think are servic-
es that God approves as righteousness. They
must not burden consciences (as though it
were a sin to leave such observances un-
done). All this is taught by that one passage
in Acts 15:9, where the apostles ‹Peter› say
that hearts are cleansed through faith. Then
they prohibit the imposing of a yoke and
show how great a danger this is, and multiply
the sin of those who burden the Church.
"Why do you tempt God?" they say. Our ad-
versaries are not terrified even by this thun-
derbolt. They defend traditions and godless
opinions with violence.

The adversaries also condemned Article 9
XV, in which we stated that traditions do not
merit the forgiveness of sins. They here say
that traditions lead to eternal life. Do they
merit the forgiveness of sins? Are they servic-
es that God approves as righteousness? Do
they enliven hearts? Writing to the Colos- 10
sians (2:20[–23]), Paul says that traditions do
not help with respect to eternal righ-
teousness and eternal life, because food,
drink, clothing, and the like are things that
perish through use. Eternal life is worked in
the heart by eternal things, that is, by God's
Word and the Holy Spirit. Therefore, let the
adversaries explain how traditions lead to
eternal life.

The Gospel clearly testifies that traditions 11
should not be imposed upon the Church to
merit the forgiveness of sins, to be services

that God approves as righteousness, to burden consciences, so that leaving them out is regarded as sin. The adversaries will never be able to show that the bishops have the power to set up such services.

12 Besides, we have declared in the Confession what kind of power the Gospel assigns to bishops. Those who are now bishops do not perform the duties of bishops according to the Gospel. Indeed, they may be bishops according to canonical polity, which we do not condemn. But we are speaking of a bishop
13 according to the Gospel. We are pleased with the ancient division of power into (a) power of the order and (b) power of jurisdiction. Therefore, the bishop has the power of the order, that is, the ministry of the Word and Sacraments. He also has the power of jurisdiction. This means the authority to excommunicate those guilty of open crimes and again to absolve them if they are converted
14 and seek absolution [John 20:23]. But their power is not to be tyrannical, without a fixed law. Nor is it to be regal, above the law. Rather, they have a fixed command and a fixed Word of God, according to which they should teach and exercise their jurisdiction. Even though they should have some temporal jurisdiction, it does not mean that they are able to set up new services. Spiritual services have nothing to do with temporal jurisdiction. They have the Word, the command, and how far they should exercise jurisdiction, if anyone did anything contrary to that Word they have received from Christ.

15 In the Confession we also have discussed to what extent they may legitimately enact traditions, not as necessary services, but only for the sake of order in the Church and for peace. These traditions should not entrap consciences, as though to require necessary services. Paul teaches when he says, "Stand firm therefore, and do not submit again to a yoke of slavery" (Galatians 5:1). The use of 16
such ordinances should be left free, so long as offenses are avoided and they are not determined to be necessary services. In the same way the apostles themselves ordained many things that have been changed with time. Neither did they hand them down in such a way that they never could be changed. They did not depart from their own writings, in which they greatly labored should the Church be burdened with the opinion that human rites are necessary services.

This is the simple way of interpreting tra- 17
ditions: they are services that are not necessary. Yet, for the sake of avoiding offense, we should observe them in the proper place.
Many learned and great people in the 18
Church have understood it this way. Nor do we see what can be said against this. Clearly, the expression "the one who hears you hears Me" (Luke 10:16) is not speaking about traditions, but is directed primarily against traditions. It is not a bestowal of unlimited authority (*a mandatum cum libera*), as they call it, but it is a caution about something prescribed (*a cautio de rato*). Regarding the special command [Luke 10:16], that is, the testimony given to the apostles that we believe them with respect to the word of another, not their own. Christ wishes to assure us, as was necessary, that we should know that the Word delivered by human beings is powerful, and that no other Word should be sought
from heaven. "The one who hears you hears 19
Me" cannot be understood of traditions. Christ requires that they teach in such a way that He Himself is heard because He says, "The one . . . hears Me." Therefore, He wishes His own voice, His own Word, to be heard, not human traditions. So a saying that clearly supports us and contains the most important comfort and doctrine is distorted by these stupid men into the most

silly matters: the distinctions of food, vestments, and the like.

20 The adversaries also quote Hebrews 13:17, "Obey your leaders." This passage requires obedience to the Gospel. It does not establish a dominion for the bishops apart from the Gospel. Neither should the bishops enact traditions contrary to the Gospel or interpret their traditions contrary to the Gospel. When they do this, obedience is prohibited, according to Galatians 1:9, "If anyone is preaching to you a gospel contrary to the one you received, let him be accursed."

21 We make the same reply to Matthew 23:3, "So practice and observe whatever they tell you," because clearly a universal command is not given that we should receive all things, since elsewhere Scripture asks us to "obey God rather than men" (Acts 5:29). Therefore, they teach wicked things; they should not be heard. These are wicked things: human traditions are services of God, they are necessary services, and they merit the forgiveness of sins and eternal life.

22 The adversaries object, arguing that pub-
lic offenses and turmoil have arisen under
23 the appearance of our doctrine. We briefly
reply to these. If all the scandals were com-
bined, still the one article about the forgive-
ness of sins—that for Christ's sake through
faith we freely receive the forgiveness of
sins—brings so much good it hides all evils.
In the beginning, this gained for Luther not 24
only our approval, but also that of many
who are now fighting against us. "Former
favor ceases, and mortals are forgetful," says
Pindar. Yet, we neither desire to desert truth
necessary for the Church, nor can we agree
with the adversaries in condemning it. For 25
"we must obey God rather than men" [Acts
5:29]. Those who earlier condemned clear
truth, and are now persecuting it with the
greatest cruelty, will give an account for the
schism that has arisen [Matthew 12:36]. Are
there no scandals among the adversaries?
How much evil is there in the sacrilegious 26
profanation of the Mass performed for prof-
it! What a disgrace is celibacy! But let us
leave out comparisons. For now, this is our
response to the Confutation. Now we leave it 27
to the discernment of all the godly whether
the adversaries are right in bragging that
they have actually, from the Scriptures, re-
futed our Confession.

Luther's Exhortation to the Clergy in Augsburg, 1530

Editorial Introduction

The Exhortation to the Clergy Assembled at the Diet at Augsburg was Martin Luther's first work from the Coburg Fortress after he arrived there, where he stayed during the Diet of Augsburg. It was as far as Luther could go in Saxony without leaving it. And since Luther was still both a public criminal and a heretic, as a result of the Imperial and papal edicts against him, leaving Saxony would have been risky, since it was only in Saxony that his prince, the elector John the Steadfast, would be able to protect him from arrest, trial, and quite probably, execution.

On April 15, 1530, the elector of Saxony arrived at Coburg, with his retinue, on his way to the Diet of Augsburg. One of the major purposes of this diet, as announced by the emperor, was to reconcile religious differences and bring Germany to religious unity. With this end in view, he had called upon the "estates" to be ready to express their views on the religious questions then dividing the empire. The elector of Saxony, therefore, took with him as advisers the leaders of religious thought in his dominions—Luther, Melanchthon, Spalatin, Justus Jonas, and Agricola. They had already discussed a confession of faith that might be presented at the diet and had agreed upon a part, at least, of its contents, though its final form had not been determined and the Augsburg Confession was not finished until immediately before its presentation, on June 25. The elector's party remained at Coburg for a week, and then it moved on toward Augsburg, leaving Luther behind. He was under the ban of the empire, and it was not safe to take him farther. On April 23, he took up his residence at the castle—Feste Coburg—where he remained while the diet was in session. During this period of enforced retirement, he had leisure for writing. He began work on the Exhortation as soon as he was settled in the castle.

On April 29, he wrote to Melanchthon that the work was growing under his hands. On May 12, he sent the manuscript to Wittenberg to be printed. Before the end of the month, it was off the press, and before June 7, it was on sale in Augsburg, where one bookseller disposed of five hundred copies in a few days; "Everybody is reading it," wrote Justus Jonas to Luther on June 12. Cardinal Campeggio ordered it translated into Latin, though we do not know whether the work was ever done. The man who had been commissioned to make the translation wrote to a friend on June 21, "It is a summary of all Lutheranism. If you would know the whole Luther, you would better buy it."

This treatise may be regarded as Luther's own Augsburg Confession. Not only was it written at the same time as the Confession presented at Augsburg, but it deals with many of the subjects that the Confession treats, especially in the section that deals with abuses in the Church. It reveals Luther's mind on those subjects far more plainly than does the work of the more diplomatic and careful Melanchthon. The material is quite evidently suggested by the Torgau Articles, which had been agreed upon as a basis of a confession of faith by Luther, Melanchthon, and others at a conference held at Torgau on March 20. The latter part of the work is based on notes that Luther apparently made in connection with the conference at Torgau.

To All the Clergy Assembled in Augsburg at the Diet in the Year 1530.

Exhortation of Martin Luther

Grace and peace from God our Father and the Lord Jesus Christ.

It is not fitting, Dear Sirs, that I should appear in person at this diet; and even though I had to appear, or were to do so, it would serve no useful purpose, for it would make no difference amid all the splendor and bustle.

Nevertheless, beside my spiritual presence (which I will prove with all my heart and with God's help, through my diligent and earnest prayers and supplications to my God) I have undertaken to be among you with this mute and feeble written message.

The reason is that my conscience drives me to pray, beseech, and exhort each and all of you, in the kindliest way and from the heart, that you will not pass this diet by or use it to vain purposes. For God, through our most gracious Emperor Charles, is giving you grace, chance, time, and cause to accomplish much that is great and good by means of this diet, if only you have the will to do so. He is speaking now as Paul speaks in 2 Corinthians 6:1: "I exhort you that ye receive not the gift of God in vain."

For He says, "I have heard thee in an accepted time, and helped thee on the day of salvation." "Behold, now is an accepted time and a day of salvation," especially for you. And we see and hear how the hearts of all men are set upon this diet, and expect, with high hope, that good will come out of it.

If, however, this diet shall break up without result (which may God graciously forbid!) and nothing worthwhile be accomplished, after all the world has for a long while been fed with false hopes and put off by diets and councils, and that hope has all been false and vain, it is to be feared that despair will be bred, and everyone will become overtired of false hopes and delays, and the long, fruitless waiting will produce impatience and make bad blood. For things cannot longer stay as they now are, especially with you and your class; you know and feel that better than I can tell you. I am therefore doing what now I do, for your own good and for the sake of peace and unity.

Certain ones, perhaps, will look with evil eyes on my presumption, and say, "Who needs you? Whoever asked for your exhortation or your writing? There are many learned and pious people here who can give better advice in this matter than a fool like you." Ah, well! I shall willingly believe this.

God help that it may all be true! I am quite willing that my presumption shall be criticized and condemned. But it is also true that one cannot do too much of a good thing, and a fool has often given better counsel than many wise men, while the greatest wrongs on earth have usually been done by wise people, especially when they relied on their own wisdom and did not act in the fear of God, and did not pray with humble hearts for divine help and grace.

All the histories are full of illustrations of this, both in the Scriptures and out of them; but even though there were no other illustration of it, we could find a good one in yourselves. For ten years now, you have tried your wisdom on this matter, with so many diets, with so many proposals, with so many wiles and tricks, with so much holding out of false hopes, nay, even with force and wrath, with murder and punishment, so that I have seen in you a cause for wonder and woe; and yet the matter has never gone the way you wanted it. That is the whole thing! Wisdom has wanted to control such high and great matters by itself, without fear of God and humble prayer, and has come to shame in its presumption. And if you do not come to fear God and to humble yourselves before Him, so that you cease from threatening and vengefulness and ask God earnestly for help and counsel, you shall still accomplish nothing, though you were as wise as King Solomon; for there stands the Scripture, 1 Peter 5, "God resists the proud, but to the humble He gives His grace."

We, for our part, pray with diligence; we also know the right way to pray for God's grace, and we are certain, too, that our prayer is acceptable and is heard. This, I fear, only few of your party can do. Moreover, we have now begun to pray earnestly for you, that God Almighty may for once enlighten your hearts and move them to fear His Word and to walk humbly with Him. Such prayer is accepted for us—that we know; but may God grant that you do not set yourselves stubbornly against it, so that our prayer must return again into our bosom because it has been lost and despised among you! For we see that the devil is trying to bring on the Turks, and is stirring up one disturbance after another, and would like to smash everything. If, then, you were still to be hard of heart and continue to be as stubborn as heretofore, that would be too much and altogether intolerable.

To begin with, then, you need not take any action because of me or the likes of me. The true Helper and Counselor has brought us and our cause so far, and has put it where it is to stay and where we want to leave it, so that for ourselves we need no diet, no counsel, no settling of the matter; and we would not have these things come from you, because we know that you can do no better than we; nay, not so well as we. For whether we come under Turks or Tartars, under pope or devil, our cause is secure; so that we know how to believe and live, how to suffer and pray, how to get well and to die, where we are to look for and get and find everything, and where we are at last to abide, according to the word of St. Paul in Romans 8:28: "To the elect the Spirit does all things for the best."

These things God has given us in rich measure through Jesus Christ our Lord, and they have already been proclaimed and confirmed (Philippians 3:16) by the blood and anguish of many godly people who have been put to death by your party. Not that we are perfect or that we have yet attained all things! But we have the right "rule," as St. Paul calls it, the right way, the right beginning; nay, so far as doctrine is concerned, we have no lack at all, no matter how it is with life.

But we have compassion upon you and the poor people under you, who are altogether uninstructed, or at least uncertain; and we would gladly help you, by means of our prayers and exhortations, as best we might. For I greatly fear that you have forgotten your office and the humility that you owe to God, and are going to draw the reins too tight and ride the willing horse too hard, so that another revolt will occur and both we and you will come to grief and distress, as happened the other time. For without doubt you remember how, before the revolt, the diet had been called to meet at Spires with such glorious and comforting hopes that all the world looked forward to it eagerly and heartily awaited the good that would come out of it. But your counsels were full of wisdom and managed to have that diet called off without result and shamefully. The rod—that is Müntzer and the revolt—came quickly and gave you a blow from which you have not yet recovered; and sad to say, we have been hurt by it even more than you. That is what comes of doing everything with force and according to your own notions.

At Worms, too, our dear Emperor Charles, that noble youth, had to do what you wanted, and condemned me and all my teachings, parts of which you yourselves had before then secretly accepted and made use of.

Even now, your preachers would have no sermons were it not for Luther's books. For they are now leaving their sermon books under the bench, together with the things that used to be all the rage in the pulpit, and are beginning to preach about faith and good works and subjects of that kind, about which nothing used to be heard or known. At that time, also, you extorted from him a decree for the slaying of Lutherans so horrible that you yourselves could not keep it or tolerate it, and it had to be changed at the diet at Nürnberg; indeed, some of the princes had of their own accord to forbid the edict so that they might not place themselves and their lands and peoples in danger. I am reciting these things not to scoff at you or mock you, for I am already amply revenged upon you; but in order that I may earnestly beg you and faithfully admonish you to learn from your own experience and misfortune to give up henceforth your swaggering and threatening, your force and boasting, and to deal with God in fear and humility, and laying aside your presumption, to seek His help and grace with earnest prayer. This is certain—if you keep on with your swaggering and boasting, you will find that Müntzer's spirit still lives and is, I fear, mightier and more dangerous than you can now believe or conceive. It is more your affair than ours, though he is more hostile to us than to you, but (God be thanked eternally!) we have a defense against him. Would God that you had the same defense!

It is the pure Word and honest prayer.

You know, too, the strong and firm stand that we have taken against all the fanatics. If I wanted to boast, I might also say that we had been your protectors and that it was our doing that you have remained what you still are. If it had not been for us, your scholars would, I fear, have been too weak for the case, and the fanatics and rebels would have taught you something that you did not know. Therefore, they hate us more than they hate you, and blame us when they have to creep to the cross and recant.

We have to put up with that and learn by experience that the proverb is true—"If you help a man down from the gallows, he tries to put you on it." The rebellious knaves would not have known the first thing about attacking the pope; but now that, by our help, they have got free and eat our bread, they lift up their heel against us, as Christ says of Judas, the betrayer.

But some will say here—"Yes, it is all your fault; you began it, and these are the fruits of your teaching." Ah, well! I must suffer that, knowing full well that I am accused of it; but, on the other hand, I know many godly people among you who know that it is not true. The work is there in broad daylight, and it is my strong witness. The fanatics have always despised and persecuted my doctrine more than yours, and I have had to set myself against them more strongly and defend myself more harshly than I ever did against the pope. How then, can it have come out of my teaching? Or why did not this disturbance arise among my followers, where I was preaching and teaching every day, and where the first and worst evil should have happened, if this kind of dissension was to come out of my doctrine?

Have you forgotten that at Worms the German nobility laid before His Imperial Majesty some hundred and four statements in which they made complaints against the clergy, and boldly declared that if His Imperial Majesty did not abolish the things complained of, they would do it themselves, because they could no longer endure them? If that had been started (as the rebels afterward did start it), and a single preacher had arisen to advise that it be done, where would you clergy be now? In hell. And yet my teaching was then in full course and had given rise to no revolt, and was not tending that way, but was teaching the people to keep the peace and obey their rulers. Had it not been for that, the complaints of the clergy would surely have started a pretty game. But now it must be my teaching that has done it. This is the thanks I deserve! To be sure, I desire no other, for so it went with all the prophets and apostles, and with Christ Himself.

In the second place, have you also forgotten how at the first my teaching was so welcome to almost all of you? Were not all the bishops glad to see that the tyranny of the pope—who was going too hard after the endowed positions—was checked a little? They could look on and listen and sit quiet and wait for the opportunity to get all of their episcopal jurisdiction back again. A fine teacher was this Luther, who attacked indulgences so honestly! For in those days, the bishops and pastors had to put up with it when a monk or a rascal from outside came into their chapters and their parishes and drove a scandalous trade with letters of indulgence, and no one dared to peep. There was no doctor or professor in all the universities or monasteries who could have known how to oppose this miserable business or have dared to do it. Luther was "dear son"; he cleansed the chapters and parishes of this huckstering and held the bishops' stirrups to help them back into the saddle and threw a stumbling block in the pope's road; why did you not call that revolt?

Afterward, when I attacked the monastic life and the monks became fewer, I heard neither bishop or pastor weeping over it, and I know that no greater service has ever been done the bishops and pastors than ridding them of the monks. Indeed, I fear that there will be no one now at Augsburg to take the part of the monks and ask that they be restored to their old place. Nay, the bishops will not allow these bedbugs and lice to be put back in their fur. They are glad that their fur is so clean rid of them, though, to tell the truth, the monks had to rule the Church under the pope, for the bishops did nothing except bear the titles of nobility. I destroyed the monks, not with revolution, but with my teaching, and the bishops were glad; they could not have done it with the force of all the kings and the learning of all the universities; why, then, did they not consider that revolutionary? Oh, they are too glad that the monks are down and that the pope has almost lost a hand thereby; and yet they give no thanks to Luther, this part of whose doctrine they use so gloriously.

Because I am now discussing the fact that people have forgotten what the world was like before my teaching began, and are not now willing to admit that anyone did anything wrong, I must bring out again the old pretenses and picture to the clergy their forgotten virtue, so that they may see or recollect what the world would be like if our Gospel had not come. We, too, may see, to our comfort, what great and glorious fruit the Word of God has produced. We shall begin at the point where my doctrine began, that is, with the indulgences.

Concerning Indulgences

If our Gospel had done nothing else than release men's consciences from the shameful abomination and idolatry of the indulgences, that alone would be enough to show that it was the Word and power of God. For the whole world must admit that no human wisdom could have done this, since no bishop, no chapter, no monastery, no doctor, no university, not I myself, in short, no human reason, understood or knew this abomination. Still less did any know how to check it or attack it; everyone had to approve it and let it pass as good and wholesome doctrine; and the dear bishops and the pope got money out of it, and let it go on richly.

1. They sold the indulgence as the divine grace that forgives sin, and thereby Christ's blood and death were denied and blasphemed, together with the Holy Ghost and the Gospel.
2. They falsely sold souls out of purgatory by it; it was an insult to God's majesty, but it brought in a lot of money.
3. They made of the pope a god in heaven, with power to command the angels to carry to heaven the souls of pilgrims who died on the way to Rome.

4. The Gospel, which is the only true indulgence, had to be silent in the churches in the presence of the indulgence.
5. The whole world was cheated and skinned out of immeasurable amounts of money, with the most shameless avarice and lies, on the pretext of war against the Turks.
6. They gave up earlier indulgence letters for the sake of new ones, and abrogated the old indulgence in the churches for the new one's sake, and played with the Golden Year according as they wanted money. (The Golden Year is the Jubilee year, in which special indulgences were granted.) Oh yes, for war against the Turks!
7. But the pretense of the Golden Year is pure fiction and a baseless lie; to corrupt the faith of Christ and Christ's daily Golden Year; but countless thousands of souls have been misled by it and the people shamefully deceived into taking pilgrimages to Rome and cheated out of their money, having their pains and their expense for nothing.
8. In the indulgence, they sold the good works of the whole Church and also, as a special thing, the absolution the Gospel forever gives to the whole world free of charge; thus souls were seduced from the Gospel and from Christ to the works of men.
9. They praised the indulgence above all works of love.
10. They made the merits of the saints, beyond what they needed for themselves, the indulgence treasure, as though Christ's Passion was not sufficient for the forgiveness of all sins; this, too, corrupts faith in Christ.
11. At last, they so exalted the indulgence as to teach that if one had even committed a sin of lust with the Mother of God, it would be forgiven him through the indulgence.
12. They taught that when the penny rang in the money box, the soul rose to heaven.
13. One had no need of penitence and regret in order to get the indulgence; it was enough that one invested his money.
14. St. Peter could not give a grace that was greater than the indulgence.
15. What has now become of the immeasurable money, treasure, and wealth that was so long stolen and so shamefully acquired by means of the indulgence?

In a word, who can tell all the abominations that the indulgence, as a true and mighty idol, has caused in all the chapters, cloisters, churches, chapels, hermitages, altars, pictures, tables, nay, in almost all the houses and chambers, so long as there was money in them? One would have to read again the books that were written against them ten years ago or so. Now speak up, dear sirs! For this unspeakable thievery and robbery of money, and for this inconceivable number of deceived hearts and consciences, and for this terrible and abominable lie, this blasphemy of Christ's Passion, of the Gospel, of grace, nay, of God Himself, which have been committed by indulgences, all of you clergy are together to blame; not only you who have got money by them, but also you who were silent about it and looked on willingly at this raging of the devil. You talk of rebellion, of confiscation of monasteries, of the Turks! What are all these things together compared to you indulgence vendors, when one thinks about it? It was a real Turkish army against the true Christian faith.

But which of you has ever once repented for this terrible abomination, or even sighed over it, or had a wet eye? And now, like hardened, unrepentant sinners, you will have it that you never did anything wrong; therefore, you come together in Augsburg and want to persuade us that the Holy Ghost is with you and will accomplish great things through you, though all your life long you have done the Church nothing but harm, and that afterward He will lead you straight to heaven with all these unrepented abominations—nay, with the abominations that you have defended—as though He must rejoice that you have served your god Belly so gloriously and laid waste God's Church so pitifully. This is why you have no good luck; and you will have none until you repent and amend your ways.

Well, that is one of the pretenses! That is the way things went in this matter before my teaching came. That it is no longer so is the fault of my rebellious Gospel.

It is right that the indulgences should be followed by that other bargain trade called *confessionalia*.

Concerning Confessionals

These were the butter letters, in which the pope sold liberty to eat butter, cheese, milk, and eggs; to hear Mass at home; to marry within the forbidden degrees; and to choose a father confessor, to be released from penalty and guilt as often as one desires in life and in the article of death, and the like.

Dear, was not this a vicious bargain trade throughout the world, all invented for the sake of money? As if God had not before given all such things as these freely to all the world through the Gospel. Or as if God had forbidden these things, and they were the giants who could sell God's commandments for money! The Gospel must be nothing, and God must be their merchandise! This skinning, trading, and blaspheming, too, has been overthrown by the rebellious Gospel, but now it is all forgotten and there is no bishop or cleric who is sorry, or who needs forgiveness for it before God. Here was another thing that no bishop or doctor attacked, but all kept silence and consented to it. Well, we shall see whether God will let Himself be aped, as they think to do.

Concerning Confession

Your books are still extant in which you have set down your teaching about Confession, which I count one of the greatest plagues on earth, whereby you have confused the conscience of the whole world, cast so many souls into despair, and weakened and deadened all men's faith in Christ. For you have told us nothing of the comfort of the Absolution, which is the main thing and the best thing in Confession and which strengthens faith and confidence in Christ; but you have made a work of it, extorted it by force from unwilling hearts in order to strengthen your tyranny; then you have made them worry and torture and scourge themselves by the relation of all their sins; that is, you have disturbed forever the rest and peace of their hearts by laying upon them an impossible task. When will you bring all these souls back again and make up for the deadly, baseless injury you have done them? This kind of Confession, too, my Gospel has set to rights, and has given new strength to weak consciences. No bishop, doctor, or university knew anything about this; and even now they have neither sorrow nor pity for this misery.

Concerning Penance

This is the dregs! It is a very hell! If all the other abominations were forgiven, this one could never be forgiven you. This has filled hell; it has injured Christ's kingdom more cruelly than the Turk or the whole world could ever do. You taught us that by our works we ought to make satisfaction for sin, even for sin against God; and that was called repenting of sin! You never laid so much importance on contrition and confession, though you made works of them too. What is it to say, "You must render satisfaction for your sins," except to say, "You must deny Christ, renounce your Baptism, blaspheme the Gospel, call God a liar, disbelieve the forgiveness of sins, trample Christ's blood and death underfoot, dishonor the Holy Ghost, and go to heaven with these virtues by your own efforts"?

Where are there tongues and voices with which to say enough about this?

How does this faith differ from the faith of Turks and heathen and Jews?

All of them, too, would make satisfaction by their works. But how can a soul do anything else than despair if it has no other confidence against sin than its own works? You cannot deny this charge; your books are extant in which nothing is taught concerning faith in the treatment of either penitence or confession, but all the teaching is about our own works. And yet there is neither bishop nor cleric to shed a tear over this horrible, hellish blasphemy of Christ. They are pure and safe. They call us rebels and slay the married priests, contrary to their own law. They are offended because the Lutherans do not make a pretense of fasting, as they do, and do not wear tonsures. They defy the eternal God with their inhuman wickedness.

Out of this abomination have come (nay, they had to come; there was no way to prevent it!) all the other abominations; namely, the self-righteousness of so many of the monasteries and chapters, with their services of worship, their sacrifices, masses, purgatory, vigils, brotherhoods, pilgrimages, indulgences, fasts, worship of saints, relics, evil spirits, and the whole parade of the hellish procession. What else is possible? If conscience is to stand and build on its own works, it stands on sand, which slips and slides continually. It must be looking for works, one after another, and the longer it seeks, the more works it must seek. At last, they put cowls on the dead so that the dead might go to heaven. Dear Lord God! What were poor consciences to do? They had to build on works; therefore, they had to seek them so wretchedly, and snatch whatever they could find, and fall into this deep folly.

By these shameful doctrines, too, all the real good works that God has established and ordered were despised and brought to naught. Such are the works of rulers, subjects, fathers, mothers, sons, daughters, servants, maids. These were not called good works, and no account was taken of them in repentance. They were known as "a worldly life," "a perilous state," "lost works." Thus this doctrine trod underfoot both the Christian and the worldly life and gave neither God nor Caesar his due. Instead, it invented a new and peculiar life that is neither Christian nor worldly; indeed, they do not know themselves what it is, because they have no word of God for it; but as Moses says, they serve gods whom they know not.

This was no wonder. For at that time, no one knew how to preach the Gospel otherwise than to teach out of it examples of good works, and no one of us ever heard a Gospel that aimed to give comfort to the conscience and to lead to faith and trust in Christ. That is how it ought to be preached, and—praise God!—it is now preached that way again. Thus, the world was in the Gospel, and yet it was without the Gospel.

They ought to have made a wise distinction between two kinds of satisfaction for sin, namely, that for sins against men, which can be made, and that for sins against God, which cannot be made, as Christ shows in Matthew 7:12 and Matthew 18:15. The Holy Fathers made use of it and caused Christians who had sinned to render satisfaction before the Church and their brethren. This is apparent from the words with which they imposed two or three or seven years of penance. Thus, Christ and His satisfaction would have remained in heaven. But in that way, the services in the chapters and monasteries would not have come up, likewise the indulgences of which I spoke above, and the great god Belly would not have got so much. Therefore, they had to confuse the two kinds of satisfaction, and at last make satisfaction avail before God only. To be sure, this error attacked the Church from the beginning, and through great men, at that, such as Origen and Jerome and Gregory; but it never reached the government of the Church, nay, the very throne of God, as it has done under the pope. For this is the oldest of errors and goes back to the beginning of the world; it will also remain the newest, clear down to the world's end. We will now tell of some of the things that have come in later.

Concerning the Sale of Masses, or Private Masses

You yourselves know, dear sirs, what a scandalous huckstering you have made of the Sacrament. That is the handiwork of all of you, because every day, throughout the world, you have bought and sold so many thousand masses for money, one for a groschen, one for eight pence, one for six pence, and so on. You can neither excuse yourselves for this nor lie out of it. For though you have not called this a regular trade, it has been, in fact, nothing else than a trade. It has been done for money; no money, no masses! This sin alone is so horrible that it would be no wonder if God had let the whole world become Turks because of it, or had allowed the world to sink into the abyss; one of the things I marvel at is that God has suffered it so long.

His patience has been inconceivable, though His wrath has not been absent.

You did it, and it was your practice, before our Gospel came. You cannot put on airs; it is so plain that you yourselves shuddered at it, and yet you let it go on and would not have it called an innovation.

Now your scholars want to be so fine that they bring out the ancient canons and the sayings of the Fathers to prove that they called the Mass a sacrifice. Shine yourself up, kitty-cat; you need to! You quote lengthy canons and sayings, but what good does that do? We are talking of private masses, and the canons speak of common masses, or communicants' masses, and they lay great importance to the communing. This the private masses do not do. They compare with the common, or communicants' masses, as a priest's secret mistress compares with a pious, honest, acknowledged wife. That shows what these great scholars know about quoting the canons. But they do even better than that! The ancient canons distinguish between the sacrifice and the Communion, but they scramble the two together. For in the early days of the Church, when Mass was held, it was after the fashion of the old law, the Christians brought to the altar all kinds of firstfruits—milk, honey, apples, pears, and so on. The priest then offered this, as Moses commanded the Jews; therefore, the service was known for a long while as a sacrifice. This was followed by the Communion, or Sacrament. They did not call that sacrifice, but Communion. But our private masses make a sacrifice out of the Sacrament and let the Communion go.

Right here, dear sirs, I must talk with you who cry out that no innovations ought to be allowed. Tell me, is not the private Mass a shameful innovation? Why did they allow it to be introduced, and why do they now defend it? Nay, if no innovations had been allowed, how much would we now find among you that was found in the ancient canons and the Fathers?

Why, I could almost get it in a nutshell, while your innovations have filled the world. I will say even more. What was your church life before our Gospel came but daily innovations? They broke in, one after another; nay, they poured in like a cloudburst. One set up St. Anne, another St. Christopher, another St. George, another St. Barbara, another St. Bastian, another St. Catherine, another the Fourteen; and who can tell the whole story of these new kinds of saint worship? Are not these innovations? Where were the bishops then, and the people who cry out that there must be no innovations? No, even more! One set up the rosary, another the crown of Mary; one the Psalter of Mary, another the Paternoster stones on the church doors, another the prayers to St. Bridget; one this prayer, another that prayer. It was all without number or measure, and there were whole books full of it. Where was there a bishop or doctor who would even look slightly disapproving at these innovations?

It was the same way with the pilgrimages. Every day, there was some new place of pilgrimage—our Lady at Grimmathal, at Eicha, at Birnbaum, at Regensburg, and so many other "our Ladies." There was scarcely a chapel or an altar but there was a pilgrimage to it, and the people ran to them like crazy, neglecting their work and their obedience, so that it was plainly a delusion of the devil; but the bishops and the monasteries and the universities kept silence. If our Gospel had not come, there would soon have been no place left to which pilgrims could go. And was not that a particularly masterly deception with our Lord's coat at Trier, which was afterward exposed as a shameful lie? What have all the Lutheran innovations done when compared with this one rascally deception alone?

Here again, there was no one who cried out against the novelty or exposed it; but Luther, who exposes and rebukes these new things, is an innovator!

Again, how are the indulgences multiplied every day? How many new brotherhoods do the priests and monks set up, through all the guilds, in the names of all the saints? Every day, they sold letters of brotherhood and gave their good works and holy lives in exchange for money. They sold vigils, anniversary masses, masses for the dead, with ceremonies around the bier. Some invented the golden masses, others the "five-masses," still others masses of this kind and that, till they could not be counted. Nothing is found about these masses in the ancient Fathers.

I shall say nothing about the relics. God help us, how one new one followed another! Among them were gross and palpable lies about the Holy Cross, about many whole bodies of one and the same saint, about many fingers of a single saint. It went so far as that they revered even the drawers of St. Francis, and some woman's hair as the hair of St. Catherine. In a word, it was without end or measure, so that you yourselves made a jest of it; and yet it went along unrebuked, and no bishop saw in it anything new.

If I were to come to the pulpits, then things would really be beyond all bounds. Every day, the monks were preaching their new visions and dreams and ideas, new miracles and illustrations, and that without measure. There was scarcely a monk who had been a preacher for two or three years who did not make a new sermon book that was to rule the pulpit for a while.

The world was full of these books, and there was nothing in them about Christ and faith, but they were all about our own works and merits and devotion, with many false and shameful examples of these things. Even when they did their best in this, it was to call upon the saints—not forgetting their own order—until, at last, they pictured to all the world that holy and noble woman, the Virgin Mary, as the mediator for poor sinners, even with her Son, Christ Himself. For we all know—and I was as deep in it as all the rest—that we had taught that Mary was to be held in Christ's place; we held Christ to be our angry judge and Mary to be our throne of grace, in whom must be all our confidence and refuge, if we were not to despair. Was that not a horrible novelty? Where were the bishops who rebuked these new blasphemers and betrayers of Christ, who took Christ's office from Him and gave it to Mary, who taught us to flee from Christ and fear Him as though He were master of a whipping post, and place in someone else the confidence that we owe Him as our true service of God? Sheer idolatry is what we learned from these betrayers!

The doctors in the universities helped it along. They had nothing else to do except invent new "opinions," one after another, and no one could get a doctor's degree with special honors unless he had brought out something new. Their best work, however, was in despising the Holy Scriptures and letting them lie under the bench! "Bible, Bible?" said they. "The Bible is a heretics' book! You must read the doctors! There you find what is what!" I know that I am not lying about this, for I grew up among them and have heard and seen all this from them. Scotus says that the article "He descended into hell" cannot be proved from the Scriptures.

Occam, my dear master, writes that it cannot be proved from the Scriptures that man needs the grace of God in order to do a good work.

These are the best of them; what are we to expect from the rest? Thomas Aquinas ("teacher of teachers," the Dominicans call him!) goes them all one better, for he says that to become a monk is as good as to be baptized.

This is the way to honor the blood and the death of Christ! But this is not an innovation! And besides, the pope and all the bishops have made him a saint!

In a word, the condition of the preaching and the teaching was sad and pitiful; but the bishops were all silent; they saw no innovations, though now they can see a new gnat in the sun. Everything was so upside down with discordant doctrines and strange new opinions that no one knew any more what was certain or uncertain, what it was to be a Christian or an un-Christian. The old doctrine of the faith of Christ, of love, of prayer, of the Cross, of comfort in affliction was overthrown; nay, in all the world there was not a doctor who knew the whole catechism—that is, the Lord's Prayer, the Ten Commandments and the Creed—to say nothing of understanding and teaching it as (praise God!) it is now taught, and learned even by the young children. In proof of this, I call to witness all the books of both the theologians and the jurists. If you can rightly learn from them one part of the catechism, I shall let myself be hooked on the wheel and let the flesh be picked from my bones. And yet in all this, there can have been no innovations! But this must be an innovation! "Nay," say you, "these things are now accepted and in daily use; but your teaching is altogether new." Tell me, then, dear friend, how old is that idol St. Anne? How old is the rosary, or the crown of Mary? How old are the barefoot friars' Paternoster stones on the doors and the gates and in every corner? How old is the pilgrimage to Grimmathal, to Regensburg, to the coat at Trier, and all the rest? Were they not new ten, twenty, forty years ago? But who was opposed to innovations then? Let my Gospel go that long and it too will become old. "Well, your new Gospel may be right, but it has about it a peculiar novelty that cannot be endured." What is that? The canons of Magdeburg say it works harm to purse and kitchen. "'There's sense in that,' said the servant." That would at least be good German;

we could understand it; I wish I had known it before! Why have we been wasting so many words? Well, then, let us resolve here, in privy council, that "new doctrine" is that which hurts purse and kitchen, and "old doctrine" is that which fills purse and kitchen. Write that down and seal it; we shall send it to the diet at Augsburg and hear what the lords have to say to it!

God knows I do not say this to your dishonor; your destruction would help me not at all; I would rather things were better with you. But you yourselves may well consider that, if you forget these abominations and preen yourselves into the bargain, there will be people who do not forget, and who will perhaps deal with them foully enough. For such a shameless procedure cannot be endured, that you should give the name of innovation to whatever you please, and that whatever you choose not to call innovation cannot be such. You are suppressing the truth and doing so against your own consciences. This would bring us back to the beginning of the whole matter, and we would be harsher with you than before. It is a terrible thing when one undertakes to conceal such a wretched state of affairs, and justify it, and slander and persecute others. That will be a sign of a hardened and unrepentant heart and will show that you must soon go to destruction, for no other sin insults and angers God more than denying, adorning, and concealing open wickedness. This was the sin of Cain and of Saul. Not so, dear sirs! Do not so! Some of you do honor God! Confess that in these matters you have done wrong. Humble yourselves, and He will exalt you; pray, and He will forgive you; amend your ways, and He will help you.

But if you will not humble yourselves, but prefer to bury these matters in silence, and leave them unrepented and unpunished, and rather persecute the poor Lutherans because of them, and take it in mind to suppress them, well, we shall watch you. If a plague comes upon you (and it cannot but come), remember that you had warning enough; you will not be the first to boast yourselves above God; this I know for sure. My mind toward you is kindly and true; I would that I might move some of you, because I hope that there may still be a Lot or two in your Sodom. The rest, who remain unrepentant, will not only not acknowledge these abominations, by which they have deserved death more than a thousandfold, but they will, because of them, kill, drown, hang, and burn the innocent ones who will not praise this vice and shame; as, indeed, they are now doing.

But too many things are coming to my mind! I shall return to the private masses, and spare the abominations that I am now thinking about until I see how you amend your ways, or how you adorn and excuse yourselves, at this diet; then we shall come with your right color, and bid you *proficiat*, if God will.

Let this be enough, for the present, about the traffic in paid masses! But even when they are not sold, but are said, at their best, for God's sake, nevertheless you teach and hold them as a sacrifice and a work whereby one serves God and makes satisfaction for sin, both for ourselves and for others, whether living or dead, and especially for the dead, as we all know that the Mass has almost to fight for the dead against purgatory. The suffragan bishop who made me a priest and put the cup in my hand said these very words, "Receive power to sacrifice for the living and the dead." That the earth did not swallow us both was wrong, and was due to God's too-great patience. The living had this benefit from it—they believed that he who witnessed one Mass a day was safe and sound and blessed. This was the best and commonest use of the Mass; you cannot deny it. Ask the merchants about it and those who have to make journeys, and the pious burghers of the cities, at least at the Rorate Mass. Is not this a horrible innovation? Do not your ancient Apostolic Canons say, "No one shall be present at Mass who does not desire to communicate or receive the Sacrament"? Did not Christ institute it in order that it might be received, and that He might be remembered, and that faith in Him might be strengthened, when He said, "This do in remembrance of me"? But you keep silent about this remembrance, allow people neither to remember Him nor receive the Sacrament, and do not teach or exhort men to faith according to Christ's institution; but you are satisfied to let the bystanders see the Mass, which you, meanwhile, are secretly offering. Thus, you allow the poor onlookers to keep in their hearts the lie and the false confidence that by their onlooking they have done a good work, though they have had none of the blessing of the Sacrament, either physical or spiritual, as willed by Christ and His apostles after Him. I say it again! You complain that the endowments and the monastic property are being taken away; because of this abomination and vicious abuse of the Mass, they ought to do to the endowments and the monasteries what Josiah, king of Judah, did to the altar at Bethel—not leave one stone upon another. That would be fair and just, if you were not to amend your ways in this respect.

You cry out, "What good has come out of Luther's new doctrine?" I must ask you a question in reply, "What good is left among you?" You have left not one thing incorrupt. The Mass, our peculiar and highest treasure, you have put to shame with countless abominations and idolatries, as I have said; and you have trampled its right Christian usage underfoot, disturbed faith, and silenced the Word. Baptism has remained for the children, though it has been used clumsily and carelessly enough; but as soon as the child has grown up and come to the use of reason, you have straightway killed him, worse than the Turk does, and have taken his Baptism away again with your miserable doctrine of penance and works, whereby he learns to despise his Baptism, as now lost by sin and become of no value, and henceforth to seek salvation by his own works. As though Baptism were a temporary human work, as the Anabaptists teach, and not an everlasting covenant of God! Tell me here, what good have you left? I shall not ask what good would have come if we had been unable to maintain, in spite of you, our Baptism, Sacrament, Gospel, faith, and Christ; for you have taught nothing that was right, but all your teaching has been against Baptism, the Sacrament, and repentance. That is plain as day.

Those who live among the Turks have this advantage, that if a man is baptized, he is not taught doctrines that are against his Baptism, though the evil Turkish life and example is perilous and offensive. And even though there were teaching against Baptism, it would be easy to resist, because the Turk is not a Christian and is held in contempt among Christians, along with his doctrine. But among you, not only are life and example dangerous, but you also teach against Baptism and storm against it with words and works, and do this under the name of Christ, as the dear fathers of souls, and the friends of Baptism. That cuts like a sharp razor, as the Psalm says, and St. Peter, too, laments over you in 2 Peter 2:18, "They utter swelling words though there is nothing back of them, and entice by lasciviousness to fleshly lust those who had just escaped, and now must walk in error."

The good that has come out of my doctrine is that all this abomination and blasphemy of yours has been brought to light and condemned; and this is a great good and more than enough, though more good comes out of it every day, as will appear later. Among you, however, all good is corrupted and none has remained.

On the Ban

You know, to begin with, that it is a great robbery and outrage that you have snatched for yourselves the great ban, called *Excommunicatio major*, which properly belongs to the secular authorities. It has gone so far that popes have undertaken to depose emperors, kings, and princes, and make themselves temporal emperors. Let me tell you, dear sirs, that this is not right! Your ban should be called the small ban, which shuts the doors, not of earth, but of heaven, and separates from the Church and from the Sacrament, as Christ says in Matthew 18:17, "Hold him as a heathen." and St. Paul in 1 Corinthians 5:12, "What have I to do with them that are without?" If other matters are to be amended, this too must be amended, for God is not pleased with any sacrifice or service that comes from robbery, as Isaiah [61:8] says.

The use of the ban is another thing. It should be for the punishment of public offenses, such as robbery, adultery, fornication, murder, hate, usury, drunkenness, also heresy, blasphemy, and the like, for our Lord Christ teaches in Matthew 18:17 that the ban shall be put upon those who will not hear the Church or congregation. Thus the Church teaches in harmony with God's Word.

Now tell me, what is good and ancient about the ban that has remained among you? What new and mischievous abuses have not arisen around it? I shall not bring in the fact that you have banned, cursed, damned, and slain innocent and pious people as heretics. The ban is used for nothing else than to collect taxes and debts and cause great misery to poor people. For the arbitrary power that the knaves, officials, and commissaries have exercised in this matter is already known to you in part; and if you do nothing about it at this diet, we shall hereafter put out a calendar of these virtues that will convince you that we have understood your abuse of the ban and will make it plain to the whole world.

But in the place where the ban should rightly have its power and use, it has been a mere indulgence and a very benediction, and has lost its cutting edge.

The place I mean is among the bishops and canons, nay, among the popes and the cardinals themselves. On this point, I would like to hear a doctor of canon law who would show me how often, according to the canons and the spiritual law, the pope, cardinals, bishops, priests, endowed livings, and monasteries have been put under the ban and cursed because of simony and other vices. Who holds them excommunicate? The declaration is in their hand and runs as follows: "He is under the ban whom we will to be under the ban; whom we will not have under the ban, he is not under the ban." Go on, dear sirs; if your will is to be law, the Church can get rid of such bishops and popes!

I wish I knew what we are to take you for anyhow. You do not want to be Christians, for you will not endure Christ's word and ordinance; and you do not want to be papists, for you keep the canons and the spiritual law even less; though, to be sure, they are much harder to keep than the Gospel. But is it not a strange piece of news that papists will not be papists, and yet will give themselves out to be papists; will hold the goods of the Church and the rule over it, but only for their own sweet will, not for the good of the churches? These things do not fit together. Well then, keep on being Epicurean and Turkish, for that is certainly what you are!

But just because the goods of the monasteries and the endowments are being seized, I must have a private and friendly talk with you.

It is a fact—and it does not please me either—that these goods are seized and scattered. The un-Lutherans are doing most of it, and they get more of the profits than those who are accused of being Lutherans, as can easily be proved. I am especially ill-pleased when knaves get hold of them, of whom I know that they have not earned it; for my conscience does not trouble me when those who work and render honest service get some of them. But there is one question that I would like to have answered. Because there are plainly two kinds of endowment thieves and monastery robbers: those, namely, who are outside and those who are inside—and I would like to be told who are the worse of the two. Those on the outside are the wicked and unworthy of whom I spoke; those on the inside are the bishops, the canons, and the monks themselves, who sit in the houses. They misuse the property for all kinds of vice and unchastity, and shamelessly overstep the bounds of their order, and send great sums to Rome to knaves that are still greater. Thus they plunder the endowed places shamefully!

Think you not that if the emperors, kings, and princes who have endowed these monasteries and bishoprics had wanted to found brothels or churches for the Romans to rob, they would have had sense enough to act differently and not hand over their money and property to harlots and knaves or to Roman thieves and robbers? Because then, such fellows sit in the endowed houses and monasteries, and their property is used by people whom the founders neither intended nor willed. And these fellows, therefore, hold it contrary to the will of the founders, consume it in vicious ways, and employ it shamefully. They are, on this account, under the ban and accursed as irregulares—since all these things are true, tell me, who are the greatest endowment robbers and church thieves? You will see the pope sitting in the highest place among them, with cardinals, bishops, canons, abbots, and monks; for they do none of that for which their positions were founded, but exactly the opposite, as though they were crazy; nevertheless, they take the property and use it as they please. Ah, good friend, if you can see the splinter in another's eye and cry out about the theft of spiritual goods, you must be shown the beam in your own eye, which you do not want to see. If you can say the one, you must also hear the other, so that you may know that other people, too, have eyes, and feel and smell and hear.

You allege that what is yours should not be taken from you. Of course, what is yours should not be taken. Nevertheless, I would play your canon law with you. The canon law condemns, bans, curses, and deposes you, and says, "It is not yours." It is called *deponatur*. For you do not keep the rule and law of the foundation, and you have deposed yourself thereby.

Thus, according to your own law, you lost your property long ago and have so far held it unlawfully like damned robbers. If one were to decline and conjugate the word *deponatur* through all its persons, where would pope, cardinals, bishops, and canons be? It would surely become an impersonal verb; no person would be left. But if you think it proper that people have patience with you for not keeping your own law, then you should also think it proper to have patience with those who take property from you as unrepentant simonists and outlawed robbers, or who forbid you to succeed to it, because you do not keep your own law; that is *deponatur*.

May your request be granted, then, that what is yours be left to you, that is, your harlotry and knavery; but that what is not yours, that is, the taxes and the goods, be not left to you, but be taken from you, as from robbers and thieves!

I do not wish this to be a defense for anyone. Let everyone see to it for himself for what service or purpose he needs the property. But against the complainants I make a distinction in the use of spiritual goods. I say that if the goods of the foundations and monasteries are to be knavishly stolen and sent to Rome and shamefully consumed out there with harlots and knaves, and the intention of the founders is to be defeated, I would far rather that the emperors, kings, princes and lords kept them and put them to better use. For it is sure that the founders entrusted them to pious, chaste, Christian persons, not to men who stood and bellowed, or who went a-falconing, but to men who studied and read and prayed, so that learned men could be chosen from among them to be bishops, pastors, preachers, schoolteachers, chancellors, secretaries, and so on; and this was the case long ago, at the beginning. Now, however, they neglect and despise these works and duties; nay, they mock at them and persecute them, and are under the ban many times over; therefore, I should not weep if they were to lose the profit and the income. There is a saying, "*Beneficium propter officium*,"[6] but not, "*Beneficium propter maleficium*."[7] Your own canon law teaches that, and punishes it most cruelly with the ban, and calls it simony.

Tell me now, what pope, bishop, foundation, or monastery has ever known sorrow or repentance because it has allowed the officia to go down, or has ever seriously considered how they might be restored again? Nevertheless, they have used

6 benefit for the job

7 benefit for the wrongdoing

the beneficia and lived on them. Thus, they are twofold church thieves and double monastery robbers; for they have not only possessed the goods that were given for a different kind of people from themselves, but they have also stolen and robbed from the whole Church and prevented it from having pious, learned, Christian bishops, pastors, preachers, and like necessary persons whom the Church cannot do without, and whom it was their duty to give it, according to the intention of the founders. Dear friend, the founders did not intend the officia to be the weaving of a long cloak, an alb, and a tonsure, or the putting on of chasubles and consecrated clothes. Sticks and stones can wear these things! Their will was to train people for the comfort and welfare of the Church.

If, then, you would make such a great disturbance about the restoration of the endowments and the monasteries, the proper answer to you is this: Dear sirs, first make good your double robbery of persons and property. You have robbed the Church of the persons; you have stolen the property from the foundations. Give these back, so that the officia may go on again, and then you may rightly acquire the beneficia. Such persons are more important to the Church than all the property and all the glory of all the clergy. If not, it will be bad accounting for you to give account of the expenditures only, and merely estimate the income. You must be told to keep your books differently and look better to your work. You have received the property of the lords in order to support and train persons.

Where are these persons? Give an account of them! Nay, it is you who have let the boys' schools go down, so that the whole Church everywhere is, through you, corrupted to the very bottom, for no other purpose than that your Epicurean belly may be well off.

I have said this so that it may be seen what the condemners of motes gain by stirring up filth. Therefore, remember God, and ask Him to help you accomplish some good at this diet. These matters are great and weighty, and, unfortunately, they are so deep rooted that human power and wit can do nothing with them. The ban is necessary, but—Lord God!—it must not strain out gnats and swallow camels, or nothing will come of it.

The subjects of penance, Mass, Baptism, faith, and works are, I fear, too high for you. Therefore, I have small hope that you will reach pure decisions about them, for even your scholars have no understanding of them, and these things must be maintained and practiced only through Christ Himself and His Holy Spirit, without human aid. Then too, except for the first of them, only one or two of the councils have dealt with them.

Therefore, I shall confine my further petitions, supplications, and exhortations to the subjects about which we do not need the special illumination of the Holy Spirit, but which all Christians can comprehend and be sure of, and which can almost be known by the reason. And first:

On Two Kinds in the Sacrament

On this point, you well know that the one kind is an offensive innovation, contrary to the clear, plain words of Christ and against the long, ancient usage of the whole Church. All this has been mightily demonstrated to you by much Scripture; nevertheless, you great enemies of all innovation have not only accepted and maintained this blasphemous innovation but have also defended it arbitrarily with cruel ragings and persecutions, whereby you have tempted God to the uttermost, and blasphemed and condemned His Word. God grant that you may repent it and submit your idea to His Word! You could not support it with any Scripture; and if you maintain it with outrage and force against the Scriptures, no good will come out of it in the end. It does not help you to allege that we are to do nothing new and alter nothing; for you have heard that this thing is new, and that it is you who, without ceasing, have brought innovation and alteration into the Church. What is altered according to God's Word is no innovation, for all customs must give way to the Word of God; so your own law says. God and His Word are older than you are; they will also be younger and newer than you and us, for they are eternal. Therefore, the Word must alter and rule both old and new, and not be altered or ruled either by new or old.

You allege that without the consent of the Church, nothing should be changed, and nothing introduced. Who, then, is the Church? Are you? Then show your seals and credentials; or prove it, without them, in some other way, by means of your deeds and your fruits. Why are not we, too, the Church? We are baptized as well as you; and we teach, preach, have the Sacraments, believe, pray, love, hope, and suffer more than you. Or are you the Church because you bring in innovations, and in so doing, change, blaspheme, persecute, and slay God's Word and, as church robbers, hold possession of the foundations and monasteries? Yes, you are the Church—the devil's church! She is a liar against God's Word and a murderess, because she sees that her god, the devil, is a liar and a murderer. The true Church must be the one that holds to God's Word and suffers for it, as (praise God!) we do, and murders no one and leads no one away from God's Word. You ought not, therefore, say to us so much "Church, Church, Church." You ought rather make us certain that you are the Church; that is the important thing. The devil, too, can say, "I am God; worship me." The wolf can say, "I am the shepherd." We know very well that we must listen to the Church; but we ask, "Who and where is it?"

God help you to a reformation on this point! If you do not reform, we shall continue, by God's grace, to do as we have done heretofore. Nay, I shall go further, and say: If God wills that at this diet you make some concessions, we shall not accept them from you with the thought that by your concessions things that were wrong before are now made right. No, we count you far too small for us to think that it is in your arbitrary power to say when and how long God is truthful or a liar, and when and how long His Word is right or wrong. That would be too much! It would be putting you, with the pride of Antichrist, above God and His Word, and taking back all that we have taught and done. On the contrary, we want to have this forced from you by God's Word, and have you blasphemers, persecutors and murderers compelled to it, so that you humble yourselves before God, confess your sins, your murders, and your blasphemy against God's Word, and reform, as men who have hitherto done wrong, persecuted God's Word, and shed innocent blood. We want this sin and wickedness of yours to be unconcealed, and we are not willing to consent to it by keeping quiet and covering things up, thus making ourselves partakers in these abominations. We are willing to stake everything on this, and fight this out with you on the basis of God's Word, which you persecute. For, as I said at the beginning, we do not need your diet and your resolutions. We stand where we do stand, without your help; nay, we stand there against your raging and raving. But for your own sakes, and for the poor people's sakes, we are doing what we do, on the chance that we may help you, or some of you, and that we may give the people good advice, to the honor of God and the welfare of Christendom.

On the Unmarried State

Coelibatus, that is, the unmarried state or prohibited marriage, is another of your papal innovations contrary to the eternal Word of God and to the ancient blessed usage of the Church; contrary also to God's creation. But in it is fulfilled the prophecy of Daniel 11:37, where the prophet says of your king, "Neither shall he regard any god, nor the desire of women." It must be a great sin not to love women, for the prophet indicates here that it is a peculiar abomination of Antichrist, and puts it next after the denial of God. The old translation has, "*Erit in concupiscentiis foeminarum,*" "He shall be in desire of women"; but that would not be an anti-Christian "virtue"; it would have to be "*Erit in concupiscentiis masculorum,*" though that is what he means when he says "*Affectum erga mulieres non curabit,*" which is the correct text.

Now, dear sirs, if you would be pious and do a good deed, compel yourselves to repentance for all the miserable and unspeakable wretchedness of all kinds of vice throughout the world that has grown out of this accursed papal innovation. It hangs about the necks of all of you, and it will stay there, unless you do something about it and remove it.

You have heard that to despise the love of women, that is, to forbid marriage, is an abomination and plague of Antichrist, for God made woman to be held in honor and to be the helper of man. Therefore, He would have this love unforbidden and undespised. It is the flesh and the devil that teach us to use women only for dishonor by putting one after another of them to shame, as your new, highly praised, unmarried (I had almost said dishonorable) state has done and still does. That is not loving women but loving unchastity, and loving shame done to women, and holding them not as women but as harlots, whom no one can thenceforth love or honor. But it is God's will that they be regarded as women, and that this be done gladly and with love; that is to say, we are to have them in marriage and dwell with them in marital love. That pleases God, but it takes knowledge and grace.

Or do you know that the Sixth Commandment says, "Thou shalt not break the marriage vow?" This commandment, like all the rest, makes no distinction of persons, spiritual or temporal, priests or laymen. They are not to break the marriage vow, that is, not to touch another's wife. But it is certain that the commandment, in forbidding everyone another's wife, permits everyone a wife of his own; nay, in order that no one may touch another's wife, it compels him to have his own wife. If it were true, as the dear canons wickedly declare, that a pastor cannot serve God if he has a wife of his own, then this Sixth Commandment would have to be entirely abolished and would not apply generally to persons of all kinds, and permit them to have their own wives.

Right here, I would like to speak of other commandments also. For example, "Thou shalt have no money or property of thine own, otherwise thou canst not serve God." And yet the Seventh Commandment, "Thou shalt not steal," allows one to have one's own money and property, and only forbids one to have another's property; nay, in order that one may not steal, it commands that one have one's own property. Therefore, I do not yet know whether there is more danger of sin from one's own money or one's own wife. Avarice, mammon, and company are indeed mighty! It is a great knavery of the canon law that it declares that God cannot be served if one has one's own wife, and that He can be well served if one has one's own mammon, money, property, castles, and cities. The opposite is true! It is better to serve God having a wife than having property, though neither is a hindrance to a Christian. For a wife one already has, and the worry of how to get her is over, and she can take care of herself; but of money, one can never get enough, and one worries incessantly how to increase it and keep it. It is this worry and love that are the real hindrances to the service of God, and such worry a wife can well take from a pastor by doing the worrying herself and letting him serve God entirely.

Again, one might easily play the fool with the Fifth Commandment and say, "Thou canst not have weapons, guns, and other arms and serve God at the same time, for thou mightest kill, do injury, or be hindered thereby." And yet, the Fifth Commandment forbids only killing, but permits weapons and arms; nay, in order that murder may be prevented, it commands to have weapons and arms. Why have our marriageless saints both their own money and their own arms, and do their farming and their fighting with a clear conscience? Does not that hinder them in the service of God? No, but a little wife must hinder them! It was a dolt that made this canon and a dolt that made the other. Nevertheless, he has blinded the whole world, even the great scholars!

The devil, however, wanted so to fix things, by means of this canon, that his celibates should have no wives of their own but should have instead the wives, daughters, and maids of everybody else, and Sodom into the bargain. This would not have been the case had they been married. It was also his will that instead of having their own property, which is hard to acquire, they should swallow up the property of all the world and consume it in idleness, which would not happen if they had to seek and acquire property for themselves. In like manner they have forbidden weapons, so that they might lay hands on the swords of all the kings and do with them what they would; this, too, would not be the case if they had their own swords. It is a wonder of wonders that these three things—all sorts of free unchastity, all sorts of avarice and splendor, all sorts of weapons and war—do not prevent these unmarried saints from serving God, and yet, one pious wife prevents them!

If everything were to fail, and pope, bishops, canons, and even the people were to remain in their unmarried, knavish state—since even the heathen poet admits that pimps and procurers take wives unwillingly—I hope, nevertheless, that you will have pity on the poor parish priests and pastors, and allow them to marry; and that you will not be such shameful, murderous, crazy canonists and jurists as you have been in the past. For your canons decree that a married priest is to be suspended, that is, put out of office; and you, with your dull asses and bacchantes, have interpreted that to mean that they are to be hanged, drowned, run through, murdered, and hunted. So utterly bloodthirsty and murderous are you bloodhounds that you are not ashamed to rage as you will even against and beyond your own law. If you will not have pity—and I fear that so much innocent blood, so many horrible sins, and such enormous wickedness hang on your necks and press so hard upon you that God will hardly give you grace to do otherwise than you are doing, except to bring your own destruction upon you, as St. Peter says in his second epistle—well, God's will shall be done, nevertheless, and not your pleasure.

For the monks, I know not what to ask. It is well known that you wish them all to the devil, whether they take wives or not. And not without reason, for two roosters on the same dunghill cannot endure one another.

They want to have the life that you have and that you would like to have all to yourselves; and that you cannot suffer. Therefore, let them go, the rascals! They must not lead the lives of bishops or canons; that befits only the Church and the servants of God—and that means you. God Almighty will do more and better than you intend and than we expect of you. Amen!

Else, I fear, the devil will be abbot and his dam will be abbess. And yet, I have one hope and comfort; you cannot live here forever, and we must always be training up new parish priests and pastors, and (God willing!) the young fellows who are coming on will not allow themselves to be tied up with your crazy, wicked vows and obligations to the unhonored state and other abominations. But if the parish clergy become corrupt and the people are without the Word, and if the monks go down, you will see how long bishops and canons, foundations and monasteries will remain. There must be pastors, even if there are no bishops, canons, or monks.

Christendom was maintained for many hundred years without these endowment bishops and canons, and it can henceforth be maintained without them. At the Last Judgment, no Christian soul will be able to boast or testify that, in all these centuries, a single one of them had ever heard or learned from his endowment bishop the Lord's Prayer, the Ten Commandments, the Creed, or one of the Gospels, or ever had or enjoyed from him a single episcopal duty or work. "We ourselves lived, before Luther, as though we had no bishops, and so we must continue to live." I know for sure that the whole world must say that, before Luther's doctrine, they received no more from their bishops than they do now, and they receive no less now than they received before, except that they suffer from extortion and assessment. They cannot feel or notice whether they used to have bishops or have none now; so little experience have they had of episcopal offices and duties! This is called watching diligently over souls; and this is the way they want to watch over them again! "Nay," say they, "we consecrate and ordain others to do these things in our stead." Even this they do not do; it is the suffragan who does it, and he has nothing of the bishop about him, for he only ordains to the sacrificing of the Mass, makes no inquiry at all about how and what is to be preached and what the people need to learn. Therefore, he is satisfied when the priests can hardly read a requiem; he smears them quickly with his chrism and lets them pass on. When these men are preachers, it is God who makes them so, and by them He maintains His Church; it would long since have perished a hundred thousand times if it had depended on the bishops and suffragans.

As for the evil state in which it has been and still is—whose fault is it, except that of the bishops, who sit in the apostles' seat and in the episcopal office, and do none of the things they ought to do, and let everything go to ruin? And yet they cry out that they should be allowed to have the ruling place they used to have, because they seek the salvation of souls. It was a fine government and they seek the salvation of souls! Yes, it was the devil on their heads (for he rides them) and the misfortune of all of us around our necks, as we found out before! It is a question of princely *meum* and *tuum*[8]; the bishop's office will still rest with the pastors and preachers.

They allege further: "We let people study in the universities; they learn to preach ably, and then we have them ordained by the suffragan." That is true—and unfortunate! You let them study; so do the Turks and the Jews! But what help do they give them, and what help do you give them out of your mammon of endowments? And yet this is your serious duty!

Nay, it grieves you that there are universities; you smell a poisonous breath in them. You are rid of the monks or have them in hand; that fruit of the Gospel you have accepted gladly. You would like to be rid of the theologians and scholars too; they are still in your way! If they were out of the way, you would be completely the masters of the parish clergy. Then you could mount again above kings and princes; nay, you could command the pope himself, who cannot do without you, and you bishops would be the only gods and lords on earth. That is what you are after, dear sirs! Is it not true that the secret conference of Mainz, where I could not be present, took a step in this direction? Then we would have a world full of jackasses, and the Church would have no Word and no pastoral office.

Yes, you would them study; but the livings of the chapters, which have been incorporated with the universities, no one gets unless he has first studied by other people's

8 Latin for "what is mine" and "what is thine." Saying someone doesn't know the difference between *meum* and *tuum* is to call that person a thief.

help; and if he is to get them, he must first buy them, and pay for them with a sum of money; and when he has paid for them, is bound to howl and blatt in the chapter, so that his studies and his knowledge bring no benefit to the office of preacher or teacher. That is the way you help the Church!

Granting, however, that you ordain others in your place (which you do not do), who are to preach and be bishops in your stead, you must remember that I am now speaking of bishops and not of men who make appointments. A peasant, a village judge, a town, a prince can also appoint a preacher, but that does not make any of them a bishop. A bishop is one who is himself to feed God's people. For there is Paul's instruction to bishops in the Book of Acts: "Take heed to yourselves and to the whole flock, among whom the Holy Ghost has made you bishops, to feed the community of God, which He has won with His own blood." If you were bishops, as your name and place require you to be, your hair would stand on end at this saying, and you would be as sorry to be bishops as I am to be a preacher and doctor; for you would be little better off than I and men like me. St. Paul also says, "A bishop shall be *didacticus*," that is, "apt to teach," "persistent in teaching." He does not mean prince bishops or castle bishops, but bishops of the Church, who do the work that (praise God!) many of His pastors do, even though they do not wear miters, which blockheads and "Nicholas bishops" can also wear. For that you, as bishops, should supervise what is rightly taught, and do not know yourselves what it is—that is laughable! No, sad to say, it is not laughable! We have had experience of the good that your oversight does, as the subjects above treated show!

Of all this, dear sirs, I have had to remind you and exhort you, because I see that you do not fear God, and seek neither contrition nor repentance for your horribly perverted life, and have not even qualms of conscience over it; for by this God is angered to the uttermost. For since we poor Lutherans have taken wives, you venture to think that you have at last one thing about us to take hold of, because you could find nothing else. You have thought that you would use it, and scourge us with it and press us with it, so that all your shameful, unchaste harlotry, all your robbing of monasteries and stealing of endowments, the whole unsavory mess of your abominations and perverted, unbishoplike abuses, shame, vice, injury, and corruption of the Church—all this would be concealed, covered up, lost in silence, and come to be praised as fair and fine. Thenceforth, you might claim for yourselves all authority, even over the apostles themselves, because you were pure and innocent people who never muddied the water.

A good trip to you, dear sirs! But see that you make no mistakes. Do not say, "Hurrah!" You are not yet over the hill! You have seen how you can dress yourselves up, but you have not yet seen how we can strip the pretty bag off from you and paint you in such colors that you must spit at your very selves. Do not boast and strut; your case is not as good as you think!

Even though you can load us with wives—whom we yet acknowledge before God with a good conscience, and also before the world, as our married wives and not as our harlots—you will never believe in how masterly a fashion we will polish up your mistresses and stolen wives, whom you and we both know that you have with no good conscience, and whom you do not acknowledge before the world except as your harlots.

Thus, you must call yourselves and be judged as whoremaster before both God and the world. Besides, we will paint you Roman Sodom, Italian marriage, Venetian and Turkish brides, and Florentine bridegroom in such wise that you shall see and grasp that our marriage has had sweet revenge on your honorless chastity. And though some of you, perhaps, may not be guilty of all these things, we shall not ask about this. The protector, defender, fellow, and comrade will be on the same footing with those who are themselves guilty, for the reason that they do not rebuke, ban, and avoid these sins (as the Gospel and your own law teach), but help these evildoers, aid them, and join them in raging against us, and by this help, make themselves partakers of all these abominations, and are therefore no better than the guilty.

Never a heathen, never a Turk, never a pope, never an emperor, never a man on earth has made or enforced a law that anyone should be put to death for marrying. Thus, it is a new and unheard-of thing begun by you bishops, who, in your chapters, are the greatest endowment robbers, whoremasters, and hunters of harlots on earth. And you do it not in order to maintain chastity but, because others will not practice harlotry and unchastity as you do, you allow it to go unrebuked. And no one can believe that you mean well by chastity with this penalty, since there are no greater enemies of chastity anywhere than you are, for you persecute it most shamelessly and incessantly in your own persons with all unchastity.

To be sure, this is a very small thing compared with the great common abomination, viz. [namely], that you are the kind of bishops described above and, in time, if you do not improve shall be painted in other colors. For if we are to have godless harlot masters and enemies of God for bishops, we shall honestly show them in what church they belong; this you will certainly discover. For as long as you are unwilling to let our marriage alone, you shall have little honor or joy from your harlotry and anti-Christian bishopry.

If I die because of it, there are others who can do it better! In a word, you and we know that you live without God's Word, but we have God's Word.

Therefore, our supreme request and humble petition is that you will give God the honor, confess your sin, repent, and reform. If not, take this from me: if I live, I shall be your plague; if I die, I shall be your death. For God has set me on you; I must be, as Hosea says, a bear and a lion in the road of Assur; you shall have no rest from my name until you amend your ways or are destroyed!

Therefore, we give you your choice. First, since you cannot and will not perform your episcopal duties, since you and all your scholars verily, verily, are unable to preach and be the comforters and judges of consciences; then leave us your office, which it is your duty to exercise; let us be free to teach the Gospel, and let us serve the poor people, who wish to be godly.

Do not persecute and prevent those who do what you cannot do (though it is your duty), and which others are willing to do for you.

In the second place, we shall make no other request of you, nor will we take any pay from you; but if God supports us otherwise, we will do the work, so that you may be spared both work and pay, trouble and expense. Not that we are so anxious to preach! Speaking for myself, indeed, I can say that there is no message I would hear more gladly than that of my own deposition from the preaching office. I am so tired of it; partly because of the ingratitude of the people, but much more because of the intolerable hardships the devil and the world lay upon me! But though the poor souls do not want my preaching, there is a man who says "No" to my withdrawal. His name is Jesus Christ, and it is right for me to follow Him, for He has earned my service. All of you know (praise God!) that the Lutheran preachers are godly men and do you no harm but are more useful to you than all your and the pope's scholars. You have never had more pious heretics, nor will you ever get them; pray God that they may be spared to you!

In the third place, We will let you remain what you are, and teach—as you have done in the past—that you are to be allowed to be princes and lords, for the sake of peace, and are to be permitted to keep your property.

The Hussites and Wycliffites did not do this, and none of the fanatics or revolutionaries are willing to do it now. Thus, you see that in us you have not enemies but friends, nay, even protectors. For how does it hurt us if you are lords and princes? If you are not willing to do what is right for your class and position, well and good! It is not we but you who must give account. Only keep the peace, and do not persecute us! We ask nothing more, and never have asked anything more, than that the Gospel shall be free. You could help us, and we could help you to peace. If you do it not, then we carry off the honor, and you lose both peace and honor.

In the fourth place, you could set up again the episcopal power, in so far as you left us free to preach the Gospel. For my own part, I shall be ready with help and counsel, so that you may have something of episcopal rank.

You would have two parts of the episcopal office—the one, that in your stead, we and the preachers would teach the Gospel; the other, that with your episcopal power, you would help in the administration of it. Your persons, your life, and your princely ways we would leave to your own conscience and to God's judgment. Heretofore, we never have taken your episcopal authority from you; you yourselves have let it fall. For when you could not maintain with it the indulgences and other intolerable abuses, you let it go altogether, and were not willing to protect our Gospel, or even to tolerate it, but turned this authority against us and against the Gospel. Then it had to strike itself a blow that dulled its edge, for God did not ordain it against His Word but for His Word.

More than this we cannot offer you except the daily prayer, the goodwill, and the service which it is our duty to offer all our enemies. Our offer is this: we will perform the duties of your office; we will support ourselves without cost to you; we will help you to remain what you are and advise that you have authority to see that things go right.

What more should we do? We are carrying a heavy load; we have burdened ourselves with you and the revolutionists and all the world, yes, and all the devils; and nobody helps us. If you, too, will not help, but keep on pressing us down, beware, lest you break our backs in two and try our patience too far. If you are going to suppress the pious heretics who are carrying you along, see what becomes of you. The game is no longer in our hands, as it was before, but the devil has got it away from us; we can help you no more if you do not help yourselves also and have regard, not to yourselves, but to the multitude of common people and to peace. It is high time that you do this, and we too will do our best. If there be among you one pious heart, it can well gather from this whole tract that I am telling the truth, and must tell it, and sincerely mean it well for you and for everyone. More than this I cannot do; your cause is too utterly bad.

But someone may think it a laughable proposal that the bishops shall rule the Church, because it is well known that they cannot and will not learn, and St. Paul says that one who rules his own house badly will never rule the Church well, and it is plain to be seen how the bishops preside over their chapters and maintain discipline by allowing them to be *impunita lupinaria et latrocinia*.[9] My answer is this. I know only too well that it is true; but in order that these wicked people may see that we seek peace and that there is no fault in us, I can suffer it that they provide the parishes and preaching position with spiritual persons, and thus help to administer the Gospel. I would rather that the fault should be theirs than ours, and before now, God has ruled and done good by means of rascals, and He must think that it is now the time when Herod is selling the priestly office in Jerusalem, and the Romans are doing likewise; nevertheless, worship remains, and the Word. But if they wish to quench the Gospel or even to remain unrepentant, let them do it at their own risk; we shall preach what we will. If they are eager for misfortune, God will soon raise up another Müntzer, who will overthrow them entirely. If they will not be bishops in God's name, let them be bathhouse keepers in the devil's name; we are not to blame, nor are we the cause of it. The Lutherans remain masters because Christ is with them and they remain with Christ, though hell, world, devil, princes, and all should go crazy.

To discuss more points now would take too long. God help you at the diet to act in such wise that it may not be necessary for us to go over everything again from the beginning; that is not good for you and we prefer to be spared the trouble. And yet, in order that you may not think that what I am saying is a mere threat, I should here set down the subjects that should be discussed by both sides.

The subjects with which it is necessary to deal in the true Christian Church, and which we discuss:

- What is the Law
- What is the Gospel
- What is sin

9 unpunished prostitution robberies

- What is grace
- What is the gift of the Spirit
- What is true repentance
- How true Confession is made
- What is faith
- What is forgiveness of sins
- What is Christian liberty
- What is free will
- What is love
- What is the cross
- What is hope
- What is Baptism
- What is the Mass
- What is the Church
- What are the Keys
- What is a bishop
- What is a deacon
- What is the preaching office
- The true catechism, that is, the Ten Commandments, the Lord's Prayer, the Creed
- True prayer
- The Litany
- The reading and interpretation of the Scriptures
- What are good works
- The instruction of married folk, children, manservants, and maidservants
- Honoring the government
- Children's schools
- Visitation of the sick
- The care of the poor and of hospitals
- The treatment of the dying

These subjects no bishop has ever dealt with, and they have never been thoroughly understood or taught by your party, and in part have faded out.

You cannot deny this; we were raised in your schools, and your books, which bear witness to it, are still extant; and all the world is witness that these things were never preached before. Now it is certain that everything depends on these things, and that the Christian Church is cared for by means of them and needs none of your unnecessary additions at all.

In this connection, I will not speak of the German hymns, the blessing of the bride, and many good and wholesome books. What great abominations have been put down by them, and rooted out from among us, I shall not here relate; enough has been said to show how many things we would have to speak about, if we wanted to take the time and the space.

The things that have been use and custom in the pretended Church:

1. Indulgences
2. The Sacrifice of the Mass and the innumerable ways of doing it
3. The abuse of the ban
4. Purgatory
5. Ghosts
6. Innumerable pilgrimages
7. Vigils
8. Masses for the dead
9. Anniversary masses for the dead
10. The masses of the four weeks
11. Soul baths
12. The worship of saints, some of whom were never born
13. Saints' days without measure
14. Mary is made a common idol with innumerable services, celebrations, fasts, hymns, and antiphons
15. Butter letters
16. Innumerable relics, with lies
17. Innumerable brotherhoods
18. The celibate life
19. Dedications of churches
20. Dedications of altars
21. Dedications of images with indulgences
22. Baptism of bells, with two hundred godfathers on one rope
23. Distinctions of foods
24. Distinctions of days (regarded as necessary)
25. Distinctions of dress

26. The compulsory seven, or "canonical hours"
27. The Sunday procession, which is a play
28. Extreme Unction for death, not for recovery
29. The sacrament of marriage
30. The sacrament of priesthood
31. The sacrament of confirmation
32. Acolytes

33–34. Tonsurists; lectors (consecration of these not to duties but to liberty)

35. Subdeacons
36. Prayers to Brigitta
37. Other prayers of the same kind, and all sorts of prayer books, full of blasphemous and shameful dishonorings of God

38–41. Tonsures; chasubles; albs; choir vestments (All of these more than is needful and only as special services of God; this is contrary to faith)

42. Cowls
43. Churches
44. Chapels
45. Altars
46. Altar cloths
47. Lights
48. Candlesticks
49. Images
50. Tables

51–54. Crucifixes; candlesticks; banners; censers (all of these beyond what is needful and as special services to God; this is contrary to faith)

55. Fonts
56. Monstrances
57. Pyxes
58. Chalices
59. Organs
60. Bells
61. Holy water
62. Holy salt
63. Incense

64. All kinds of food in Lent
65. Ash Wednesday
66. Hunger cloths
67. Veiling of images
68. Keeping fasts (except the priests)
69. Litany of the saints
70. Hymns to Mary in the evenings
71. The torture of Confession
72. Penance and satisfaction
73. Long preces
74. The palm ass
75. Palm shooting
76. Palm swallowing
77. Palm crosses
78. Compulsory Confession
79. Compulsory Communion
80. Kissing and adoring the cross
81. Burying the cross
82. Half Mass on Quiet Friday
83. Singing psalms at the grave
84. Dark Mass
85. Rattles instead of bells
86. Passion sermons of eight hours
87. Consecrating the fire
88. Easter candles
89. Taking the cross out of the grave and carrying it, playing
90. The consecrating of cakes on Easter Day

91–92. The procession of St. Mark's Day; cross weeks (both good for all unchastity)

93. Ascension at Nones
94. The Holy Ghost on Pentecost
95. Corpus Christi processions
96. The Assumption of the Blessed Virgin
97. Church dedications

98. Festivals of patron saints
99. Community weeks
100. St. Burkart's Day
101. Ember days
102. All Saints' Day
103. All Souls' Day
104. St. Martin's goose
105. Advent, more in honor of Mary than of Christ
106. The Rorate Mass
107. The Conception of the Blessed Virgin
108. The three Christmas masses
109. The apparuit and music
110. The blessing of oats on St. Stephen's Day
111. St. John's draught
112. Candlemas and wax sale
113. St. Agatha's lights
114. St. Blasius's lights

I shall stop here, for who can count up everything in a short space? But if they do not want to have peace, either I or another can keep on counting, so that the dear bishops and canons may not think that the monks are the only sinners, and they are the pure kitten. Not so! For this time, I have wished to point out nothing more than the things that are common usage in the parish churches, though these are the smallest part of your government and have been despised beyond all measure, and you have trodden them underfoot. If, however, I was to take up the chapter churches, cathedrals, official houses, monasteries and preaching places, and then come to the mendicants, the stationaries, and finally the sophists in the universities—God help us! I do not wonder that you forget these abysmal abominations and now seek to adorn yourselves! Did not I myself forget (by the dear God!), and did not I think that you were in the place where I see you to be? Be silent now, for God's sake, and reform, or things will go hard with you!

To be sure, it is a fact that, among the things above mentioned, there are some that are not to be rejected, and some that have fallen out that I did not want to fall but that can easily come back. The best thing of all is that the fine Latin songs *de tempore* have been kept, though they have been almost drowned out by the new sacred songs and count for almost nothing.

To speak my mind briefly, this is the sum of what I think. If these things had been kept as play for the youth and for young pupils so that they would have had a childish game of Christian doctrine and life, in the same way that we must give children dolls and hobbyhorses and other toys—and if the custom had been allowed to stay at that, as we teach the children to fast for the sake of the Christ Child and of St. Nicholas so that they may give them presents on their nights (for it was thus, as we can see, that our ancestors meant it to be)—if it were to be left at that, the palm ass, the ascension, and many things of the kind could be tolerated, for then they would not lead anyone's conscience astray. But for us old fools to go about in miters and clerical finery and take it seriously—so seriously, indeed, that it becomes an article of faith—so that whoever does not adore this child's play must have committed a sin and have his conscience tortured by it—that is the very devil!

It follows, then, that all the things above mentioned, however childish and laughable they may be, do nevertheless fight against and corrupt the Christian faith and the really necessary things, which have also been mentioned above, as though there were no help for one who did not keep them. For, sad to say, it has been our experience heretofore this child's and fools' play has been practiced more, and more seriously, than the things that are really important. This, then, is our opinion: If, for the sake of the young, we can help to retain these childish games that are tolerable, without injury to the really serious and important things, we shall gladly do it. But that we should hold them for articles of faith and even play the fool in bishops' hats—nothing will come of that, no matter who is angry or who laughs!

I have spoken these things to you this time as a kindly and faithful admonition, and I ask with all diligence that you will join us in calling upon God that He may grant you grace and wisdom so to do and to act in these matters that it may be for His honor and the salvation of us all; and also that He may prevent you from self-adornment, and from excusing, defending, or forcibly continuing your former misconduct. For what good is done by making more bad blood among the people? Men's hearts are already too deeply embittered, and not without good cause. It is necessary to sweeten and soften and quiet them with humble confession and open reformation, and not to irritate them further. You know that, even if there were no Gospel, your order is so fallen and corrupt, even when judged by your own laws, that it cannot be endured if you try to brazen things through.

You know, too, that Pope Hadrian himself confessed, through his legate at Nürnberg, that the Roman See was the source of much evil, and that he offered to reform it. Why, then, should you be ashamed to confess the same thing, and obstinately persist in your pride, and grant nothing and yield nothing, but carry things off with force, caring nothing whether the result is better or worse? For you know, or ought to know, that Christian rule or authority has been ordained by God to make things better not to corrupt them, as Paul says, and is not to be a tyranny, but a service. If you were to admit this, we could help to raise you in the opinion of the people.

For I maintain that you cannot do without the Lutherans, those godly heretics, and least of all can you do without their prayers, if you are going to accomplish any permanent results. But if you are going to force your way through this business stiffly and stubbornly (which may God forbid!), then, together with all who believe with me, I hereby call God and all the world to witness that it is no fault of ours if you are dashed to pieces when your pride fails you. Your blood be on your own head! We are and will be guiltless of your blood and your condemnation; for we pointed out to you your offenses, admonished you faithfully to repent, sincerely implored you, and made you every offer that could serve the cause of peace, seeking and desiring nothing else than that sole support and comfort of our souls—the free and pure Gospel. Thus, we can boast with a good conscience that the fault has not been ours.

But may the God of peace and consolation give you His Spirit to guide you and lead you to all truth through our Lord Jesus Christ, to whom be praise and thanks for all His unspeakable grace and gifts forever and ever.

Amen.

John Eck's 404 Theses, 1530
Editor's Introduction

The wording of the Augsburg Confession was, in large part, prepared in response to the vitriolic attack of John Eck against Luther and the Lutheran reformers. John Eck had prepared this attack for the Diet of Augsburg at the command of Emperor Charles V. Eck was Martin Luther's most zealous opponent. Even as Luther and his colleagues believed it to be their duty to speak out against the errors and abuses of the Roman Church of their day, so Eck believed it his duty to defend the Holy Mother Church against Luther and other emerging reformers, such as Zwingli. While Eck attacks as many others as he can think of, it is Luther who is his real target, and, as his cover letter makes clear, it is to Luther that he attributes all the errors of everyone involved in the reforming movement.

These theses are an important insight into the attitudes of the Roman Church and provide important context for understanding the Augsburg Confession. Eck was also the chief author of the Confutation of the Augsburg Confession, to which the Apology of the Augsburg Confession is a reply.

The style of this document is a bit difficult, since what Eck is doing is recounting, with separate paragraphs, the alleged errors of his opponents at different times, in differing circumstances and on a wide variety of topics. Eck's assertions are a mixture or rumor, myth and fact, generally asserted with no citations and nearly always taken completely out of context. This is more a work of propaganda than theology. He pauses to interject comments and then moves on to his next set of assertions, or theses.

Reading through Eck's accusations is an illuminating exercise, since it presents the points at which Rome was disagreeing with Luther and illuminates the depth of the Roman Catholic misunderstanding of the position of the Lutherans.

Also to be noted is how Eck attempts to lump all the reforming movements together, identifying as a group Luther and Zwingli, men who were sharply at odds with each other.

Henry Eyster Jacob's Introduction to Eck's Theses

The Four Hundred and Four Theses of Dr. John Eck, Published in 1530. A Contribution to the History of the Augsburg Confession by Henry Eyster Jacobs, Dean of the Evangelical Lutheran Theological Seminary, Philadelphia, Pennsylvania.

The Presidential Address to the
American Society of Church History.
Read on December 29, 1908.

In fulfilling the duty you have assigned me, I have selected a topic pertaining to the history of the preparation of the earliest and most fundamental Confession of Protestant Christianity, the Augsburg Confession. It is my purpose to estimate the influence, upon its final form, of a document the Lutheran reformers found in circulation on their arrival at Augsburg more than seven weeks before the Confession was presented by the Evangelical princes to Emperor Charles V.

On March 11, 1530, John, the Electoral Duke of Saxony, received at his residence in Torgau an imperial citation, issued from Bologna, January 21, and transmitted by the Imperial Chancellor from Spires, February 20, summoning him to appear at Augsburg, April 8th. The announced purpose was to deliberate concerning war against the Turks and the religious dissensions that were disturbing the peace of the empire. No time was lost. The very next day found the Electoral Council occupied with plans for the journey, the selection of those who were to be asked to accompany the elector, and the providing of the funds necessary for what was to be an expensive undertaking. Saxon Chancellor Dr. George Bruck gave a written opinion concerning topics to be considered, and, two days later, followed this by another, urging the importance of carrying with them to Augsburg a carefully elaborated memorandum concerning the religious questions involved, accompanied with scriptural arguments.

On the same day, March 14, the elector of Saxony wrote to Luther, Justin Jonas, Bugenhagen, and Melanchthon, informing them of the summons he had received, and enjoining them, forsaking all other duties, to apply themselves at once to the preparation of such a memorandum. In this letter, the topics to be comprised are restricted to those concerning where there had been dissensions. The design was to exhibit not the agreements but the points of difference between those whom the elector was to represent and the opponents of the Reformation. The correspondence shows very clearly that the elector was feeling his way and wanted to be prepared for any emergency. For this purpose, he directed Luther, Jonas, and Melanchthon to arrange for their absence from the university, Melanchthon to accompany him to Augsburg, and Luther and Jonas as far on the way as circumstances might advise. They were informed also that other states summoned to the Diet would appoint representatives from their theologians to cooperate. "Since among the subjects to be discussed," he says, "one is with respect to the dissension concerning our Christian religion, it is important that a statement or opinion be first discussed and determined among the states themselves," and this statement is to include "the matters both in faith and in outward Church ceremonies concerning which there is dissent." "In this way, before the Diet begins, a decision may be reached as to how far we and the other states that have received the pure doctrine can, with a good conscience, endure prevalent abuses."

The Wittenberg theologians were instructed to complete their memorandum by March 20, and to hand it on that day to the elector at Torgau. They at once gave all their time to the work committed to them, but it was April 3 before they came to the elector at Torgau, just in time to leave with him next day for Augsburg. The result of their labors up to that time had been no finished document, but a collection of unequally elaborated notes on some points, indicating by mere catchwords matters that might be included. There is a difference of opinion as to whether, with these notes, the Schwabach Articles of 1529 were also included in the material provided for the elector. A long delay occurred at Coburg, where Luther was left on April 23, to remain until after the adjournment of the Diet. Here also the elector received important suggestions as to the contents of the proposed document from a commissioner, Hans von Dolzig, whom he had sent for conference to the Count of Nassau. In his communication, the need of a positive doctrinal statement, beside an elaborate enumeration of abuses, is urged. The stay of a day at Nürnberg doubtless impressed upon them the importance of repudiating certain extremists from whom the churches there had recently suffered.

The Saxons had the honor of being the first participants in the Diet to reach Augsburg. They entered May 2; the emperor did not appear until June 15. The interval gave time for perfecting their plans. Even before the arrival of the other Protestant princes and representatives, Melanchthon resumed the work that had been interrupted by the journey. The revision of the memorandum in accordance with the new conditions he found at Augsburg now occupied all his attention. The preparation of what he calls the "exordium" (i.e., the doctrinal statements preceding the enumeration of abuses complained of) gave him at Augsburg the most concern. The advice of Luther at Coburg was repeatedly sought, and drafts sent to him for his criticism.

When the Saxons had arrived on May 2, they found that, notwithstanding their early appearance, there was one who had anticipated the representatives of the various states, if not in person, nevertheless by his published attacks. The indefatigable opponent of Luther, John Meier von Eck, generally known as Dr. John Eck, professor at Ingolstadt, once on friendly terms with Luther, until the publication of the Ninety-Five Theses, which he answered with his "Obelisks," regarding himself as the chief support of the papacy in its struggle in Germany, was on the scene. He had prepared and published a pamphlet of thirty-four pages in small quarto, which the Protestants found in circulation at Augsburg, under the title *Under the Patronage of the Lord Jesus and Mary: Four hundred and four articles; some pertaining to the disputations at Leipzig, Baden, and Berne; others drawn from the writings of those disturbing the peace of the church; which John Eck, the very least minister of the church, offers to discuss before the Emperor Charles V and the princes of the Empire, as is explained more at large in the program at Augsburg; on a day and hour to be hereafter published by consent of the emperor.* It is an artfully constructed document, written in the most bitter controversial spirit, intended to impose on the credulity of those not well-informed, to excite prejudice, and to announce beforehand that no compromises with Lutheranism could be expected. It is chiefly a collection of statements of Luther and other reformers either torn from their connection and misapplied or else falsely ascribed to them, no reference being made as to the places in which the statements were made. With the statements ascribed to Luther and his associates are others quoted from some whom Luther repudiated as energetically as did Eck, but for whose extravagances the Lutheran reformers are made responsible.

Erasmus wrote with much amusement concerning these articles to Melanchthon, that he found himself quoted, only that Eck had concealed the name of Erasmus and artfully ascribed the statement to *quidam*, "somebody." The articles begin with the Forty-One Propositions of the Bull of Leo X against Luther of December 10, 1520, followed by the Leipzig Theses of Eck against Luther and Carlstadt, and his Eleven Baden Theses against Zwingli and Oecolampadius. Then comes a list of 339 errors ascribed: 203 to Luther, 55 to Zwingli, 48 to Melanchthon, 15 to Bucer, 9 to Oecolampadius, 4 to Bugenhagen, 4 to Osiander. Blaurer, Carlstadt, Pirkheimer, Capito, Rhegias, the Zwickau prophets, the Anabaptists, the Nurnberg preachers, are mingled in one undistinguishable mass, with four "somebodies," acknowledged by Erasmus as his own.

They are gathered under the headings, not arranged in strict logical order, as follows: "Against Christ," "The Holy Spirit," "The Sepulchre of Christ," "God," "The Cross of Christ," "Mary," "The Apostles," "St. Paul," "The Saints," "Relics," "The Council of Nicaea," "Noah," "The Limbus Patrum," "The O.T.," "The N.T.," " The Gospel," "Angels," "The Church," reaching finally, "Sin," "Faith," "Works," "Merits," "Love," "The Sacraments," "Infants," "Confirmation," "The Eucharist," "Both Kinds," "Confession," "Repentance," "The Keys," "Satisfaction," "The Mass," "Canonical Hours," "Marriage," "Divorce," "Celibacy," "Vows," "Purgatory," and so on. Archives at Munich show that Eck was not satisfied with printing and diffusing broadcast at Augsburg these propositions.

There is preserved in that repository a letter addressed to the emperor, a transcript of which has been published by Gustav Plitt in his "Einleitung in die Augustana" (i., 527), in which Eck sets forth, with still greater definiteness than in what he has printed, the purpose of the tract. The printed copy sent with this letter has certain propositions marked to which he desired the emperor to give particular attention and has added in writing occasional annotations. This grandiloquent Latin letter, a translation of which we herewith submit, shows clearly that it is Eck's purpose to hold Luther either directly or indirectly responsible for all the errors contained in his list of heresies.

The second day after his arrival at Augsburg, Melanchthon informed Luther, "Eck has brought together a great heap of conclusions. He asks the princes to arrange for a discussion against the Lutherans." At the same time, he states that he is elaborating "the exordium" of the Confession beyond what had been intended on leaving Coburg. Under the same date, he writes to Veit Dietrich, Luther's companion at Coburg, of his purpose "to run over" within a few days and to bring with him for revision the draft of the Apology he is writing.

A week later, he gives Luther more details: "With this, I am sending you our Apology, or, more properly speaking, Confession. The emperor has no time for extended discussions. Nevertheless, I have said what seemed to be especially profitable or proper. For this purpose, I have embraced about all the articles of faith, because Eck has published against us the most diabolical slanders. Against these, I have decided to oppose a remedy." The doctrinal articles of the Augsburg Confession are, therefore, Melanchthon's "remedy," as he says, against Eck. The self-restraint, the caution, the composure, the concentration of the Augsburg Confession, amidst the many inducements that Eck's Propositions furnished for extended and impassioned treatment, are certainly remarkable.

The object is to meet the misrepresentations with which the mind of the emperor was occupied by brief, calm, objective statements, presenting in exact terms the positive teaching of those attacked in Eck's propositions and combining with this an equally clear and emphatic repudiation of errors and errorists with whom the Lutherans were confused. This declaration thus carefully drawn up by the theologians, when officially approved by the Protestant princes and representatives of states, became a bond between them and a formal contract by which they agreed with each other to stand or to fall. How critical the moment is shown by the intelligence that had reached Augsburg that the emperor was hesitating between condemning them without a hearing and listening to their case. The effect was to declare that, without arguing the justice or injustice of Eck's presentations, whether they were true or false, here is the declaration on the subjects involved, for which alone we are responsible.

The mode in which the articles of the Augsburg Confession were formulated was by following the general outline of the Schwabach Articles, but greatly changing them in view of the changed conditions. "*Subinde enim mutandi sunt atque ad occasiones accommodandi*" (Corpus Reformatorum, ii., 60, Letter to Luther, May 22).

In Article I, treating of God and the Trinity, regard has evidently been taken of Eck's Proposition 82, in which Luther is quoted as saying, "My soul hates the word '*homoousion*,' in other words, the Father and Son of the same essence," and of Proposition 146, in which he is represented as repudiating the Council of Nicaea: "In the Holy Council of Nicaea, faith and the Gospel were lacking, and human traditions gained the upper hand." Hence, the article becomes "Our churches, with common consent, do teach that the decree of the Council of Nicaea, concerning the Unity of the Divine Essence and the Three Persons, is true and to be believed without any doubting; that is to say, there is one Divine Essence which is called, and which is, God; and yet these Three Persons of the same essence and this article is more than a treatment of the doctrine concerning God. In the opening sentences, it places in the foreground the principle of the historical continuity of the Church and declares the reverence with which those who made the Confession dealt, in all their critical work, with historical precedents. It separated them from the ultrasubjectivists who cared nothing for historical considerations.

The second article of the Confession bears a similar relation to Propositions 184, 185, and 186. In the former, Zwingli is referred to as declaring, "Original sin is no sin, but a natural defect like stammering." How nearly true this report concerning Zwingli's doctrine is may be read in *Ratio Fidei*, which he sent to Augsburg, in which his very words are "Original sin is not properly sin." But for this position, the Lutheran representatives at Augsburg were not responsible. Zwingli's view had been one of the subjects of controversy between him and Luther, and at Marburg he had temporarily accepted Luther's position. In order, therefore, to clear the position of those for whom they acted from all suspicions of sympathy with the Zwinglian view, Article II was prepared. In so doing, account was taken also of the circumstances that Proposition 185 charged Melanchthon himself with declaring that Scripture made no difference between original and actual sin. The language of the Augsburg Confession became so explicit on this subject that it repudiated Eck and his colleagues as forcibly as Zwingli and is attacked on this account in the Roman Catholic Confutation of the Confession. The close of the article has in view the misrepresentations made concerning infant Baptism in Propositions 227–33.

Article III covers the ground included in Propositions 66–82, and 83 and 84, concerning Christ and the Holy Spirit, by a paraphrase of the Apostles' Creed, further defining some of its statements. The clause that Christ was "a sacrifice not only for original guilt but for all actual sins of men" answers explicitly the charge brought in Proposition 265 that "no satisfaction is required for sins except the death of Christ" by reaffirming and explaining it.

Article IV is a thoroughly objective and scientifically framed statement of the relation of faith to justification, as over against the one-sided and misleading citations of Propositions 187, 197, 205, and 210.

In Article V, the purpose is to sharply distinguish the teaching of the Lutherans on the work of the Holy Spirit from that of the pure subjectivists of various schools with whom Eck habitually confounds them in his tract. The definition of the Gospel incidentally given as the promise "that God, not for our own, but for Christ's sake, justifieth them that believe," corrects the statement of Proposition 166, in which Luther is quoted as declaring, "The Gospel is nothing but preaching concerning the resurrection of Christ."

Sixteen Propositions of Eck were occupied with various perversions of what those who dissented from Rome taught as to the relation of faith and works (Propositions 152–7, 187, 189, 191, 192, 194, 199–203, and 367). We quote but three:

194: "Faith alone is necessary; all other things are most free, neither commanded, nor prohibited" (Luther).

367: "After one has been justified, no laws or ordinances bind him" (Melanchthon).

162: "The Gospel commands nothing whatever" (Melanchthon); "neither does it prohibit" (Luther).

These are answered by Article VI: "Faith is bound to bring forth good works; and it is necessary to do the good works commanded by God."

The definition of the Church in Articles VII and VIII corrects the inference of any approval of the statement ascribed to Bucer, following Augustine and Wycliff, that "only the predestinated are in the Church; but the wicked or reprobate are not of the Church" (170). "Although the church properly" says Article VIII, "is the congregation of saints or true believers, nevertheless, since in this life many hypocrites and evil men are mingled therewith, it is lawful to use the Sacraments which are administered by evil men in the Church."

Seventeen Propositions of Eck (216–32) are disposed of in two brief sentences of Article IX. The article concerning the Lord's Supper (X) was probably less influenced than any other by Eck's pamphlet. The aim of the Confession is simply to present the doctrine of a generic real presence, in order to disclaim responsibility for what was taught on the subject by those who presented the *Confession of the Four Cities*, the document written by Calvin making clear his position that the body and blood of Christ as far absent from the bread and wine in the Supper "as heaven is from earth." Zwingli published his public statement and presented it to Charles V in his work *Ratio Fidei* at the same time and place.

Article XI is a direct answer to Propositions 255–58, concerning Confession and Absolution; Article XII to 259–66, concerning Repentance, as well as to 190–193, concerning the inadmissibility of grace; Article XIII to 214–54 and 168, concerning the Sacraments in general; Article XIV to 268 and 269, concerning Ordination and the Universal Priesthood of Believers; and Article XV to 300–332, 362–67, concerning Church Authority and Church Ordinances. It was particularly with regard to the topics comprised in Article XVI that the attempt was made to prejudice the emperor and his advisers.

Far more comprehensible to his mind and interesting were the statements concerning civil government than those concerning doctrine. Eck touched the emperor's heart where it was most sensitive, and probably excited his intense indignation by appeals contained in citations like the following:

334. We Christians are free, exempt from all the laws of men, liberated through Baptism (Luther).

335. No laws can be imposed with any right upon Christians, whether by men or by angels, except so far as they themselves be willing (Luther).

336. Subjects neither can, nor will, nor ought to endure your tyranny any longer (Luther to the princes).

339. I regret that I submitted to the emperor at Worms. Whatever tolerance of my doctrine was conceded by my judges is of no account to tyrants (Luther).

340. There is no more excellent secular law than that of the Turk, as he has no canonical or civil law (Luther).

346. Ever since the beginning of the world, a wise prince has been a most rare bird; for, generally, they are either the greatest fools or the very worst rascals; for they are God's policemen and executioners (Luther).

367. To impose law upon Christians is to tempt the devil (Zwingli).

384. There is no hope of a remedy unless, all the laws of men having been once annulled, we judge and rule all things according to the Gospel (Luther).

385. We must not take an oath with respect to temporal things; for he who requires an oath of another, or himself swears, must be of a malicious and trifling mind (Melanchthon).

387. All are heathen who contend in court for property or reputation (Luther).

389. It is a doctrine of devils that it is allowable for a Christian to wage war; for all who go to war are accursed children of Cain (Oecolampadius). To buy and sell are purely heathen matters (Luther).

390. Business contracts even for godly purposes are usurious (Strauss) or at least unjust (Luther).

391. A community of all things is commanded in the New Testament (Melanchthon).

403. It is proper and in accordance with God's Word to excite seditions and tumults; hence, there is no better proof that my doctrine is of God than that it excites discords, seditions, and tumults (Luther). Many of them, therefore, have often publicly testified to the common people: 'The Gospel wants blood' (Zwingli).

404. Among Christians there should be no superiority, no courts, nothing fenced up or closed, no '*meum*' or '*tuum*,'[10] no restraint or excommunication (Anabaptists).

The very phraseology of Article XVI shows that it is an answer to these imputations of communism and anarchy: "Of Civil Affairs, they teach that lawful civil ordinances are good works of God, and that it is right for Christians to bear civil office, to sit as judges, to determine matters by the Imperial and other existing laws, to award just punishments, to engage in just wars, to serve as soldiers, to make legal contracts, to hold property, to make oath when required by the magistrates, to marry, to be given in marriage. They condemn the Anabaptists who forbid these civil offices to Christians. They condemn also those who do not place faith in the perfection of the Gospel, in the fear of God and in faith, but in forsaking civil offices, for the Gospel teaches an eternal righteousness of heart. Meanwhile, it does not destroy the state or the family, but especially requires their preservation as ordinances of God, and in such ordinances the exercise of charity. Therefore, Christians are necessarily bound to obey their own magistrates and laws, save only when commanded to sin." The succeeding article is only an appendix to the sixteenth, repudiating the extravagances of the gross Chiliasts who taught that the time would come when the godly should take forcible possession of the earthly property of those not among their number.

Article XVIII, "On Free Will," is a direct and extended answer to Proposition 332: "It is under the tutelage of Satan that the term Free Will has arisen" (Luther). In Article XIX, Melanchthon repudiates the position he had actually maintained in the first edition of his Loci Communes, (1521), and which Eck had compelled him to face in Proposition 82, that "all things are done by God, both good and evil," to which Eck had appended the note, "in other words, God wills sin."

The last two doctrinal articles, XX and XXI, belong to the material for which provision was made in the Torgau Articles, and, by an afterthought, were transferred from the second to the first section of the Confession. Article XXI, however, directly meets the points made in Propositions 112–27. The influence of Eck's tract may be traced also in the Articles on Abuses, although not to the same extent as in the Doctrinal Articles. In the latter, the Confession is no longer on the defensive, but is aggressive. Compare, however, Article XXII with Propositions 251–54, and 245, 296; XXIII with Propositions 283, 295–99, and 304; XXIV with Propositions 274–78; XXV as on Article XI; XXVI with Propositions 362–67; XXVII with Propositions 300–20. The well-known passage in the final article concerning the relation of the Lord's Day to the Sabbath seems to have been elicited by Propositions 178–80.

Eck's Propositions influenced not only the material of the Confession, but in some parts even the order in which the subjects are treated. The organism of the Confession

10 Latin for "what is mine" and "what is thine." Saying someone doesn't know the difference between *meum* and *tuum* is to call that person a thief.

has greatly troubled some critics, but it is not as confused as it appears. Bearing in mind the fact that the Articles on Abuses were intended as the chief part, and the Doctrinal Articles were only introductory, the order of the latter is logical.

I.	Theology
II.	Anthropology
III.	Christology
IV–VI.	Soteriology
VII–XVI.	Ecclesiology
XVII.	Eschatology
XVIII–XXI.	Answer to various objections and criticisms; it is in the part treating of Ecclesiology that the influence of Eck's Propositions on the order can be traced

Article XI, on "Confession and Absolution," and XII, "On Repentance," appear between the articles concerning the Lord's Supper and the use of the Sacraments in general, because these two articles, from the standpoint of the Roman Church, belong to the discussion of the Sacraments and are so treated in Eck's paper.

This paper of Eck, as time has passed, has almost entirely been lost sight of. It was so thoroughly answered that its influence survives only in the suggestions that it made for the elaboration of the Confession. It was as ephemeral as the issues of the daily press of today, to which, however, historians will turn hereafter to trace influences upon permanent legislation or upon movements of far-reaching importance. The use made by the reformers of Eck's paper also illustrates the conception the Confessors at Augsburg had of their work. They were responding to a particular call. They were meeting a particular emergency and they confined their attention to the issues of that particular hour. "Only those things have been recounted," they say as they close, "whereof we thought it was necessary to speak, so that it might be understood that, in doctrine and ceremonies, nothing has been revived on our part against Scripture or the Church Catholic." As to the question of limiting the testimony of the churches they represent to what is embraced in the Confession, they speak very plainly in the very last sentence: "If anything further be desired, we are ready, God willing, to present ample information according to the Scriptures."

Eck's Cover Letter addressed to Charles V

Most Revered Emperor:

By all Catholics, thou art esteemed as one who has been appointed, elected, and consecrated of God to come to the aid of the wavering Catholic faith, to help the afflicted Church and oppressed churchmen, to maintain the Christian state against the sanguinary Turkish tyrant, the sultan, and, in a word, to save the Christian world.

But since Martin Luther, a domestic enemy of the Church, has not been improved by the former admonition of Thy Imperial Majesty, but having fallen into every Scylla and Charybdis of impiety, calls the pope of Rome Antichrist; the Church a harlot; bishops, masques and idols; universities, synagogues of Satan; cloisters, brothels; theologians, bats; secular princes, fools, drunkards, insane, and worse than Turks; and meanwhile does not withhold himself from attacks also upon Thy Holy Majesty, but teaches the lordship of Christ and maligns and ridicules thy imperial mandates with the most obscene interpretations.

And since, also, he has reached such an extremity of desperation, as a blasphemer of God, impious toward the saints and sacraments, irreverent, reproachful, and rebellious toward all superiors, ecclesiastical as well as secular, an enemy of all good men, that he praises none but heretics, extols schismatics, excites seditions in Germany, prepares for shedding a flood of Christian blood, and is collecting bands of Germans to bathe themselves in the blood of the pope and his cardinals, and is producing a generation of vipers still worse than himself—for to Luther we owe as his children the iconoclasts, Sacramentarians, Capernaites, new Hussites and their progeny the Anabaptists, the new Epicureans who deny the immortality of the soul, and the spiritualists, as well as the new Corinthians who deny the divinity of Christ.

Since also they are rending Germany with these monstrosities and portents, demolishing churches, overthrowing altars, treading underfoot the most holy Eucharist, burning the images of Christ and the saints, abolishing divine worship, casting the images of saints into the rubbish heaps, raging against the gold and silver treasures of the Church, despoiling the revenues of churches and monasteries, voiding the last wills and testaments of the deceased, and, in short, attacking all things pertaining to the Christian religion even worse than Turks, so as by their persecutions and threats to induce virgins consecrated to God to abandon the cloisters; very many of them, amidst crimes so execrable, even dare to announce their readiness to defend themselves according to the Recess of the Diet of Spires, and to respond concerning these things to God and Thy Most August Majesty, as though thou art a patron of their impieties, blasphemies, thefts, sacrileges, and seditions, pretending that the Most Holy Imperial Head of the World, and hoping that the supreme justice of the divine emperor, would defend their supreme injustice.

Notwithstanding the unlawfulness of agitating and discussing anew the things rightly judged and arranged by a council, they excite ancient heresies condemned more than a thousand years ago, follow teachers who have been burned, and men of accursed memory, seducing simple people with the plea that they follow the Gospel, the Bible, the Word of God.

I offer myself, therefore, to Thy Imperial Majesty, prepared, as at Leipzig against Luther, and at Baden against Oecolampadius, to repel their mendacious boasts, to defend all the institutions, practices, doctrines, and observances of the Catholic faith, and to attack their assailants.

Let the Church's enemies, the ministers of ungodliness, the patrons of heresies, the vessels of iniquity, come forth and fulfill that whereof they so insolently boast to the people; let them answer concerning the faith before the power which is of God, the member of God, the Church's advocate, the faith's protector.

Farewell, father of the country, Most August and Victorious Emperor. God protect and guide thee; grant thee victory over the Turk, and mercifully extend thy rule still farther.

Eck's Theses
Ingolstadt, March 14, 1530

Under the patronage of the Lord Jesus and Mary

Four hundred and four articles; some pertaining to the disputations at Leipzig, Baden, and Bern, others drawn from the writings of those disturbing the peace of the church; which John Eck, the very least minister of the church, offers to discuss before the Emperor Charles V and the princes of the Empire, as is explained more at large in the Program at Augsburg; on a day and hour to be hereafter published by consent of the emperor.

Inasmuch as, for a number of years, false prophets have been rising up and attempting to tear away the people from the unity of the Catholic faith, corrupting all Germany with many errors, impieties, and blasphemies, so that what was formerly regarded most Christian has now become the cesspool of all errors, in behalf of the faith and for the Church I have hastily gathered these few out of their infinite errors. And since the enemies of the faith are making a parade of their writings and are offering in secret to dispute concerning them before the people, I offer, according to the judgment and disposition of our Most Glorious Prince and Lord, Charles V, perpetual Emperor of Spain, Germany, Sicily, a Catholic king, and our most clement master, and of that of all the princes of the Roman Empire, especially of our Most Serene Prince and Lord, Ferdinand, King of Hungary and Bavaria, and Archduke of Austria, and of our Most Illustrious Princes of the renowned House of Bavaria, to discuss in public the points below noted against any assailant of the Catholic truth; so as to establish our dogmas and overthrow the false dogmas of the adversaries, to the praise of God, the increase of faith, and the strengthening of the weak.

To God Alone the Glory

While in order that Thy Holy Majesty and the Christian world may see and judge the impieties of the adversaries, I have gathered a very few out of their infinite errors; nevertheless, I have guarded them from head to foot with my assertions, and offer to reply as to all in behalf of the faith and the Church. I assert with entire confidence given by the Holy Spirit that the articles of Luther concerning this shameful matter condemned by Pope Leo X were legitimately condemned as heretical, erroneous, and scandalous. I anathematize and condemn them, and freely declare that they who agree with the bull are Christian men, but that they who oppose it are enemies of the faith who ought to be regarded as heathen and publicans. Hence, we introduce here all these forty-one articles, ready to receive the attacks of any opponent and to take the part of the Church.

1. It is a heretical, but usual statement, that the Sacraments of the New Testament give justifying grace to those who interpose no obstacle.
2. To deny that sin remains in a child after Baptism is to treat both Paul and Christ with contempt.
3. The tinder of sin, even though no actual sin be present, excludes a soul leaving the body from entrance into heaven.
4. The imperfect love of a dying person necessarily carries with it great fear, which is alone sufficient to produce the punishment of purgatory and prevents entrance into the Kingdom.
5. There is no foundation in Holy Scripture or in the ancient Christian teachers for the doctrine that there are three parts of penitence, viz. [namely], contrition, confession, and satisfaction.
6. One is made a hypocrite, aye, a great sinner, by contrition arising from self-examination, and reflection upon and detestation of sins, whereby, in the bitterness of his soul, one reviews his years, by considering the gravity of his sins, their multitude and heinousness, the loss of eternal blessedness, and the penalty of eternal condemnation.
7. Most true is the proverb, and preferable to the doctrine of all hitherto taught concerning contrition, that not to do [penance] is the highest penitence, and a new life the best penitence.
8. Presume in no way to confess venial, or even mortal, sins, because it is impossible to know all mortal sins; hence, in the primitive Church only manifest mortal sins were confessed.
9. In wishing to confess all things absolutely, we only show our unwillingness to leave anything for the mercy of God to forgive.
10. No sins are forgiven unless, when the priest forgives, the person believes that they are forgiven him; aye, sin would remain unless he would believe that it is forgiven; for the remission of sins and the bestowal of grace are insufficient, but one must believe that sin is forgiven.
11. Trust in no way that you are absolved because of your contrition, but because of the word of Christ: "Whatsoever ye shall loose." So I say, trust, if you have obtained Absolution of a priest, and believe firmly that you have been absolved; and without regard to contrition, you will be truly absolved.

12. If it were possible for a person not contrite to confess, or for a priest to absolve not seriously, but in jest, and if one should, nevertheless, believe that he was absolved, he would be absolved.
13. In the sacrament of penance, or remission of guilt, the pope or bishop does no more than the lowest priest; aye, when there is no priest, any Christian, even a woman or a boy, would do equally well.
14. No one should answer the priest that he is contrite, neither should the priest ask it of anyone.
15. Great is the error of those who come to the Sacrament of the Eucharist, relying upon the fact that they have confessed; that they are not conscious of any mortal sins; that they have said their prayers and made their preparations. All these eat and drink judgment to themselves; but if they believe and trust that they will receive grace, this faith alone makes them pure and worthy.
16. It would be well for the Church, in a general council, to resolve that the laity should commune under both forms; and that the Bohemians communing under both forms are not heretics but schismatics.
17. The treasures of the Church, from which the pope gives indulgences, are not the merits of Christ and the saints.
18. Indulgences are pious frauds upon believers, and hindrances to good works, and belong to the number of those things that are lawful, and not to the number of those that are expedient.
19. Indulgences do not avail, where truly received, to remit the punishment that eternal justice demands for actual sins.
20. They are deceived who believe that indulgences bring salvation and a spiritual benefit.
21. Indulgences are necessary only for public crimes and are granted properly only to the hardened and impatient.
22. For six classes of men, indulgences are not necessary or useful: viz., the dead or dying, the sick, those hindered for sufficient reasons, those who have not committed crimes, those who have committed crimes but such as are not public, and those who have reformed.
23. Excommunications are only outward punishments, and do not deprive a man of the common spiritual prayers of the Church.
24. Christians should be taught to love rather than fear excommunication.
25. The Roman pontiff, the successor of Peter, is not the vicar of Christ, appointed by Christ Himself in St. Peter's, over all the churches of the world.

26. The word of Christ to Peter: "Whatsoever thou shalt loose on earth," extends only to those things that Peter himself has bound.
27. It is certain that it is within the power neither of the Church nor of the pope to frame articles of faith or commands concerning morals and good works.
28. Even though the pope, with the great part of the Church, should think so and so, and in thus doing should not err, it is still not a sin or heresy to think the contrary, especially in a matter unnecessary for salvation, until the one were rejected and the other approved by a general council.
29. We have the liberty (literally, "the way has been opened to us") to state the authority of councils and freely contradict their doings and judge their decrees, and confidently confess whatever seems true, whether it have been approved or rejected by any council.
30. Some articles of John Huss condemned in the Council of Constance are most Christian, true, and evangelical, and cannot be condemned by the universal Church.
31. In every good work, the righteous man sins.
32. A good work done in the best way is a venial sin.
33. To burn heretics is against the will of the Spirit.
34. To war against the Turk is to resist God visiting our iniquities upon us through them.
35. No one is sure that he is not always mortally sinning because of the most secret vice of pride.
36. Free will after sin is a thing with the title alone, and in doing what belongs to it, sins mortally.
37. Purgatory cannot be proved from the canonical Scriptures.
38. Souls in purgatory are not secure with respect to their salvation, at least not all; neither can it be proved either by reason or Scripture that they are beyond meriting or increasing love.
39. Souls in purgatory sin without intermission as long as they seek rest and dread punishments.
40. Souls delivered from purgatory by the intercessions of the living have less happiness than if they had made satisfaction of themselves.
41. Ecclesiastical prelates and secular princes would do no wrong if they were to entirely suppress all the mendicant orders.

Eck [here Eck offers comment]:

So horrible are these articles that even Luther, their author, repudiates some, and is unwilling to acknowledge them, and lies when he says that they have been falsely attributed to him. Such are numbers 26, 29, and 41. But there is an old proverb: "One ought to be mindful of a lie," for number 26 he wrote in *De Resolutione Indulgentiarum*, Conclusio V.; number 29 in the "resolution" of the Leipzig Disputation, immediately after the beginning; and number 41 in a popular sermon on "Usury."

I, likewise, undertake to defend the positions invincibly defended by me for nineteen days against Luther and Carlstadt. If either they or their adherents will undertake to present anything new against these positions, I will abundantly satisfy them.

Conclusions of Eck at Leipzig [Articles Eck offered at Leipzig]

42. It is in accordance neither with the declarations of Holy Scripture nor the Holy Fathers, Augustine and others, that our Lord and Master Jesus Christ, when He said, "Repent ye," meant that the entire life of believers should be repentance, and that, therefore, this word could not be understood of sacramental penitence.
43. We deny that even if there are daily venial sins, the righteous nevertheless sins in every good work, even in a holy death. Likewise, we say it is erroneous to say that a righteous one can sin mortally while his righteousness remains, or that after Baptism administered at the will of another, the child retains sin.
44. One declaring in addition that repentance does not properly begin with hatred of sins by reflecting on the gravity of the sin and the punishment, and that this makes one still more of a sinner, a statement contrary to the Gospel and the Holy Fathers, we affirm should not be heard.
45. To say that God, in remitting guilt, remits punishment and does not change it, by means of the canons and the injunction of the priest (declared either entirely or in part) into a temporal satisfactory punishment, we think contrary to Holy Scripture and the usage of the Church.
46. That any priest, to say no prelate, can or ought to remit punishment and guilt to his parishioner seeking it, so that a prelate not fully absolving from guilt and punishment sins, we do not receive, since it is contrary to the Holy Scripture and the use of the Church.
47. That souls in purgatory make no satisfaction for the punishments of sins from whose guilt they have been here absolved, but for which they have not made satisfaction, we account erroneous, just as it is not without error that God requires of one about to die no other punishment than that of death.

48. He errs who, from the fact that man is actively disposed to evil, and only passively to good, denies that man's free will is master of his acts; just as he is not without error who, contrary to the Scholastics, thinks that faith can be corrupted by any crime; neither is he without the greatest error who, without any regard to contrition, boldly asserts that one is absolved by faith alone.

49. Since it is contrary to truth and reason, we do not receive the teaching that from the imperfection of love or faith in the soul of the dead, horror and as it were despair results, with which souls in purgatory are affected, and that they incur this horror from the fear of death, and as it were, die unwillingly.

50. That souls in purgatory merit greater grace, or that, if freed by the merits of others, their rewards are diminished, or that they are not certain of their salvation, or do not wish our prayers, we deny as contrary to our faith and all reason.

51. Since it is contrary to the truth and the apostolical decrees, and as we regard Keys the most imperishable treasure of the Church, we deny the assertion that the merit of the Passion of Christ is not the treasure of the Church from which indulgences are given. We also piously believe that we are aided by the merits of the saints.

52. To say that indulgences do not free is an error; to say further that indulgences are vicious, and thus that one thereby incurs greater guilt, is the very worst error. Hence, we hold that he also errs who says that he is bound to condemn indulgences because the Lord says, "On account of Myself, and not on account of money, I blot out iniquities."

53. That the pope cannot, through indulgences, remit a punishment due on account of sin is an error. Yea, it is erroneous that he cannot absolve from punishment souls existing in purgatory. Moreover, what we repudiate most of all is that those about to die, weak, lawfully impeded, without public crimes, need no indulgences.

54. That the Church of Rome was not superior to other churches prior to the time of Sylvester we deny. But we have always acknowledged him who has the chair and faith of Peter as the successor of Peter and general vicar of Christ.

[Eck continues]:

Luther was subject to the decision of the faculty of Paris, to whom he appealed before the legate of the apostolic chair. Convicted by their opinion, he has defied them with his reproaches. The Conclusions, moreover, which I undertook to defend before the twelve cantons of the Swiss in opposition to Zwingli, Oecolampadius, and their followers, I do not decline to maintain, if Zwingli in his exile should betake himself to Rottenacker.

Conclusions of Eck in Baden

55. That the true body of Christ and His blood are present in the Sacrament of the Altar.
56. They are truly offered in the Office of the Mass for the living and the dead.
57. We ought to invoke Mary and the saints as intercessors.
58. Images of the crucifix and the saints are not to be destroyed.
59. After this life, there is a purgatorial fire.
60. Infants of Christians are born in original sin.
61. The Baptism of Christ, not that of John, removes original sin. Besides these, all other things that Zwingli undertakes to attack in our true and indubitable faith.

Eck

With a black mark, I noted very many godless things of Zwingli. Even the mad author was shocked when he saw them. Such was the following: the frequent making of the sign of the cross terrifies the soul not otherwise than the characters of necromancers terrify the uninformed if they be admitted to them. For this reason, he thinks that the sign of the cross ought to be suppressed in the Mass in the sacramental action. To the Swiss, he writes that this was invented by me against him, but that I said the truth is evident to one reading his Epichiresis concerning the Canon of the Mass (p. 221, p. 2). Zwingli, seeing that his sect had attained much esteem from the disputation at Baden, provided that a disputation should occur at Bern. I refuted his acts with solid writings, and there was no one who responded. But since I now offer myself prepared to defend before the emperor and other princes, contrary Conclusions for the faith and the truth, I propose them as follows:

62. Our Lord Jesus Christ, when about to leave the world, both of Himself and by the Holy Spirit, appointed prelates in the Church as His vicars, having the power of rule, and who are both said to be and are the heads of the Church. He who is rashly rebellious to them departs from Christ and the Church.

63. The Church of Christ and those presiding in it make constitutions and enactments to the glory of God and the reformation of the faithful. If these things be not found in proper form in Holy Scripture, they are nevertheless obligatory in the forum of conscience; so that he who despises these, despises Christ.

64. Christ, our Savior, is our Redeemer and righteousness, of whose Passion and merit we ought to make ourselves partakers through the sacraments and good works. But if one idly thinks that he is saved in the Church without good works and satisfaction, he presumes and sins against the Holy Ghost.
Concerning the truth of the body of Christ in the Eucharist, concerning the sacrifice of the Mass, concerning purgatory and the intercession of saints, against the Bernese I affirm anew and constantly declare my five first Conclusions defended at Baden.

65. To say that marriage is commanded in every estate, even the sacerdotal, for the purpose of avoiding fornication, is the doctrine of Asmodeus; although he treads Christ still more grievously underfoot, and exposes the Christian faith to ridicule throughout the whole world, who thinks that it is the chief virtue of a bishop to have a wife.

In addition to the abovementioned selections of innumerable errors and injurious writings and seditious aberrations, we will note a few more, the contrary to which we will defend in behalf of the faith, the Church, and the Christian Empire.

New and Old Errors Now Stirred Up

Concerning Christ:

66. Christ experienced terrors of soul even to despair (Bugenhagen).

67. Christ in despair cried out, "My God, why hast Thou forsaken Me?" (Premonstratenses, at Magdeburg).

68. The greatest cause of the fear of Christ was the sense of desertion and of divine wrath, by which Christ wavered between hell and life. In this fear, there was a desolation of the divine gifts in Christ. For in this affliction and anguish, there was a despoliation of love; because of the divinity withdrawing itself, love did not glow (Melanchthon).

69. After the death of Christ, His soul ought to suffer in hell, and in martyrdom be attacked by demons (Antoni Zimmerman).

70. Christ complained that He was deserted of God, in other words, that He was bereft of life and blessedness and all good (ibid).

71. Christ is finite according to His humanity; therefore, He truly grew in wisdom and grace (Zwingli).
72. Christ as a man is the adoptive Son of God (Bugenhagen).
73. Christ merited nothing for Himself, but for us (Luther).
74. Christ rose not from a closed sepulcher, neither did He enter into the company of His disciples, while the doors were shut (Bucer).
75. Christ is not Head of the Church according to His human nature (Haller).
76. Christ no longer prays to God for us (Zwingli).
77. Christ did not appear personally to St. Paul, but only through angels (Zwingli).
78. In Christ, the two natures, human and divine, are mixed (Burguer de f. Gallo).
79. Christ did not have an intellectual soul, but in place of His soul had divinity (Luther).
80. Christ Jesus, according to His divine nature, is, properly speaking, the essence of all things (Zwingli).
81. The humanity of Christ is not to be adored; hence, the Eucharist is not to be adored (Zwingli).
82. My soul hates the word *homoousion*, in other words, the Father and the Son are of the same essence (Luther).

Against the Holy Spirit:

83. Since the death of Christ, the Holy Spirit is His Vicar (Bucer).
84. Reason pretends to give Christ honor by reflecting and meditating upon His death, but this is nothing to Christ (Melanchthon).

Against the Sepulcher of Christ:

85. The sepulcher of Christ's body, which the Saracens hold, is no more a matter of care to God than, according to the teaching of Paul, oxen are (Luther).

Against God:

86. The opinion is certain that all things are done by God, both good and evil, not only permissively but properly, as the adultery of David, and

so on. Accordingly, the betrayal of Judas, no less than the call of Paul, is His proper work (Melanchthon), in other words, God wills sins.

87. God wanted Himself regarded foolish by means of folly; a spiritual man by means of folly recognizes God as foolish (Melanchthon).

Against the Cross of Christ:

88. It would be much better were the cross lost than found, humbled than exalted (Luther). And it is an abuse for churches to be built and founded in honor of the wood upon which God hung.

89. It is a silly play and an idolatrous error to enclose a portion of the cross in gold, carry it about the church, and offer it to the people to be kissed; hence, were I to own a portion of the cross, I would burn it to ashes (Luther). In the world, there are so many pieces of the wood of the cross that a house could be built out of them. Would that no crown of thorns, yea, no holy cross had ever come to light.

90. It was a singular and horrible festival that was instituted in honor of the tunic of Christ at Treves.

Against Mary:

91. Christ said to Mary, "What have I to do with thee!" meaning: Because you are a woman, you think that some special favor will be shown you by Me on the ground of a merit of prerogative. Understand, however, that you have no more influence with Me than the woman who was a sinner, or the Syrophenician (Melanchthon).

92. Christ permitted Mary to err (Luther). And Joseph wanted to desert her under the suspicion of adultery (ibid).

93. When Christ preached, the centurion had greater faith than Mary; for while Christ gave His mother great faith at the conception and nativity, afterward it was not, or only rarely, so great, and meanwhile He permitted it to waver (Luther).

94. The contradictory of the statement that the Blessed Virgin was conceived without original sin has not been censured (Luther).

95. We certainly are just as holy as Mary (Luther). On this account, we are unwilling to have her as an advocate.

96. That on the day of the nativity of Mary we use the Epistle concerning the wisdom of God and the Gospel concerning the nativity of Christ is a falsehood and blasphemy (Luther, the Nürnbergers).

97. The "salve regina" and "regina coeli" [two prayers to Mary, "Hail Queen" and "Queen of Heaven"] are improper, and do a wrong to Christ, since they ascribe to a creature what belongs to God (Heathen; the Nürnbergers; Luther).

98. Your prayer, says Luther, is just as precious as that of Mary, because you can aid me just as much as she.

99. Christ was unwilling to comply with the curiosity of Mary, when she asked for a miracle when the wine failed (Zwingli).

100. *Claustra virginitatis Mariae in partu fuerunt aperta et dimota*[11] (Luther).

101. I hate no festival more than that of the Conception of Mary, and that of Corpus Christi (Luther).

Against the Apostles:

102. The Council of the Apostles erred in commanding those converted from the Gentiles to abstain from blood and from what was strangled, and accordingly, they were corrected by Paul to the Colossians: "Let no man judge you."

103. In the time of the apostles, the Gospel was not preached as clearly and purely as by me (Luther). Hence, I was one whom they call Elias, Daniel, and a Man of God.

104. The apostles were not believers when they were baptized. For this reason, Christ willed that the apostles should first baptize men, and then teach what should be done and left undone (Nürnberg preachers).

Against St. Paul:

105. Paul wanted to be damned for his brethren (Melanchthon). So Moses was willing to be led to the devil and to be condemned in soul and body for the people (Luther).

106. Many, with much probability, have asserted that this epistle was not written by the apostle James, and that it is not worthy of an apostolic spirit (Luther).

---

11 Mary lost her virginity when Christ was born.

Against the Gospels:

107. The evangelists wrote contradictions. This is so evident in many passages that they cannot be harmonized. Moreover, we believe that all the apostles could err (Brunsfels).

108. The opinion ought to be abrogated that there are only four Gospels and four evangelists (ibid).

109. We are compelled to assert that there is no Scripture that can be proved to be such, except the Old Testament (ibid).

110. Unless the apostles had explained the Gospel in their writings, we would have nothing but trifles and stupid and lifeless narration. To the apostles Peter, Paul, James, and John, and not to the evangelists, is due the credit of handing down whatever we have that is pure with respect to the use and form of the Gospel (ibid).

111. The New Testament has lost its power as well as the Old. Accordingly, we are to adhere to no Scripture, but only to the Spirit, according to the Eternal Gospel (fanatics and certain persons at Zwickau according to Eraser).

Against the Saints:

112. That those worshiping the saints for temporal advantages are little better than those who for money make a covenant with the devil (Luther).

113. Prayers to the saints for avoiding any temporal evil are to be shunned, since they cannot aid us (Melanchthon).

114. Only through Christ do we have access to God; accordingly, confidence in the saints falls (Luther).

115. Christ alone, and not the saints, has been given as an example of a holy life (Zwingli).

116. The worship of saints has reached such a pass that it were better that there were no festivals of saints and that their names were unknown (Luther).

117. The resorting of men to the churches of saints is a work of the devil (Luther).

118. God cannot suffer that anyone should say: St. Peter is my apostle (Luther).

119. One cannot tell whether it be St. James or a dead dog or horse that is buried at Compostella or Toulouse (Luther).

120. The first Christopher who is portrayed as such was not a saint. A ridiculous story! Every learned man laughs (Pillicanus).

121. Everything is a matter of suspicion that the church of priests reads today concerning Christopher, and not concerning this alone but also concerning two others, Gregory and Margaret (Pillicanus).

122. The Saints are to be honored more on account of their doctrine than on account of their life (Luther).

123. Since the ascension of Christ, no one has gone to heaven or will go until the end of the world (Luther).

124. I have the same access to Christ as Peter and Paul (Luther).

125. Great idolatry has resulted from the worship of saints (Luther, Zileysen, Glaib, Stifelin).

126. I would not give a farthing for the merits of St. Peter, so far as aiding me is concerned. He cannot help himself. Any beggar will be more useful to me than St. Peter, for what can St. Peter have more than you and me? (Luther).

127. The names of the saints ought not to be placed in the Canon of the Mass, but only devils, since they are also devils (Luther). He also calls the Church of all saints the church of devils; and St. Benno he calls the devil of Meissen.

Against Relics:

128. The relics of the saints are nothing but an imposition on the people; on this account, they should be entirely buried in the ground (Luther).

129. The blessed are not members of the Body of Christ (Zwingli).

Against Miracles:

130. Miracles do not prove that saints are to be invoked; the devil assumes masks (Oecolampadius, Zwingli).

131. Miracles have not been given to confirm faith (Zwingli).

Against Jerome:

132. The commentaries of Jerome and Origen are mere trifles and foolishness if compared with those of Melanchthon. They teach their own rather than Pauline and Christian doctrine; but Melanchthon is next to Paul (Luther).

133. Jerome superstitiously extols virginity in opposition to Jovinian. There are in Jerome many such things, superstitious rather than godly (Melanchthon).

134. Jerome did not write in a proper way against Jovinian. He seeks to prevail by assertion rather than by erudition. He also does violence to passages of Scripture, not to say corrupts them. Who knows whether Jerome may not have been one of those of whom it is said in Ezekiel that when a prophet has erred and spoken a falsehood, "I the Lord have deceived that prophet!" (Luther.)

135. If a book of Vigilantius were extant concerning the relics of saints, as there is one of Jerome, I think that the former would have written in a far more Christian way than the latter (Luther). For he is a singular, immodest, vain caviler (Zwingli).

136. Books should be edited by Christians having the sense of Christ. It is on account of this defect that many interpreters of Scripture, even Jerome, have erred in many passages (Luther). Holy Scripture does not admit of several meanings, as they dream of a literal, an allegorical, and so on. But there is one most simple meaning of Scripture (Luther).

Against Gregory:

137. Jerome and Gregory erred when they took from us the right to judge concerning every doctrine (Luther).

138. Jerome erred when he forbade circumcision (Melanchthon). And he is a hundred thousand miles off from the opinion of St. Paul (Luther).

Against Augustine:

139. Augustine thinks that man is the image of God because there are in the soul intelligence, memory, and will; but this figment has been fabricated not only without the authority of Holy Scripture but even without reason.

Against St. Thomas:

140. A dove is painted at the ear of St. Thomas; I think it should have been a young devil in order that he might be adored (Luther).

Against St. Francis:

141. St. Francis erred stupidly and fell, and included himself and his brethren in his poverty; and thus drew the Gospel from without into temporal poverty, against Christ (Luther).

Against Bernard:

142. Bernard, Francis, and Dominic remained in great errors with the godless; for in their ignorance, they worshiped the pope, believing that all that pertains to him is of God and right, which is directly contrary to the Gospel (Luther).
143. Francis, in founding his order, erred as a man. What if all the Fathers erred when they made vows? (Luther). For it was with a pious error that they fell when they vowed; and God tolerated their folly in His elect (Luther).

Against Benedict:

144. Benedict boasts with impious hypocrisy and perverse emulation of men (Luther).

Against the Council of Nicaea:

145. In the Council of Nicaea, certain forms of penance were appointed. I do not declare in what spirit the decree was made by the Fathers. A good part of the Gospel, I see, yea, the true sense of the Gospel was obscured by this tradition (Melanchthon).
146. In the Holy Council of Nicaea, faith and the Gospel were lacking, and human traditions gained the upper hand (Luther).

Against Noah:

147. Although Noah was subject to judgment—and hearing the Word of God and sentence of condemnation, would be judged—nevertheless, he was taken away by the mercy of God (ibid).
148. Noah's flood is the same as that concerning which the heathen have written as the flood of Deucalion (Zwingli).

Against the Limbus Patrum:

149. Christ descended *ad infernos*[12]—not to a *limbus patrum*[13], a term unknown in Holy Scripture—but truly to hell, in order to see all places full of despair. On this account, Christ praises God that He has freed Him from the hell, in whose chains He would have been eternally lost, lowest unless the hand of the Lord had been present (Bugenhagen).

150. That the Fathers in the Old Testament descended to hell is fictitious (Haller).

151. Abraham's bosom is nothing but the Word of God (Luther).

Against the Old Testament:

152. I wish the Mosaic Law to be regarded as belonging to foolish and Gentile laws (i.e., as civil law) (Melanchthon).

153. The part of the Law that has the Decalogue or Moral Precepts has been antiquated in the New Testament (Melanchthon). Of the Decalogue, Luther makes eight and Zwingli eleven commandments.

154. The Old Testament may be observed or omitted today. Hence, Jerome erred asserting that it was abrogated (Luther).

155. They do not sin who are circumcised, or who omit circumcision (Melanchthon).

156. Christ, by His death, confirmed the Old Testament (Melanchthon).

157. The reason why the Mosaic Law was abrogated is that it was impossible for it to be kept (Melanchthon).

158. The Old Testament is not a covenant, but a type of a covenant (Melanchthon).

Against the New Testament:

159. The New Testament is nothing else than a promise of all good things without law, no respect being had to our righteousness, because good things are promised us without condition, since nothing is required in return from us (Melanchthon).

160. Whatever is done under constraint of the Law is sin; hence, in the New Testament there are not precepts that force, but only exhortations and entreaties (Luther).

---

12 to hell

13 temporary resting place of the fathers

161. Christ did not come to make a people or to impose a law (Melanchthon).

Against the Gospel:

162. The Gospel commands nothing whatever (Melanchthon), neither does it prohibit (Luther).
163. The testament of Christ is confirmed by faith by which we believe His death (Eberhard Weidensee.)
164. Christ bore every penalty in the New Testament, and only permitted His Word to act (Luther).
165. [Missing in original.]
166. The Gospel is nothing but a preaching concerning the resurrection of Christ; hence, works here are entirely removed (Luther).
167. Scripture does not distinguish Law and Gospel, so that you would think only that to be Gospel which Matthew, Mark, Luke, and John wrote, and the Books of Moses to be nothing but Law, but the doctrine of the Gospel is scattered through the books of the Old and New Testament (Melanchthon).
168. Just as circumcision is nothing, so also Baptism and the partaking of the Lord's Supper (Melanchthon).

Against Angels:

169. The wicked do not have angels of their own appointed for their guardianship; this pertains only to the elect (Bugenhagen).

Against the Church:

170. Only the predestinated are in the Church, but the wicked or reprobate are not of the Church (Bucer).
171. Whoever is in the Church cannot be damned (Zwingli).

In Regard to Contingency:

172. All things that occur do so according to divine predestination; hence, our will has no freedom. For according to His predestination, all things occur to all creatures necessarily (Melanchthon).
173. All things occur by absolute necessity (Luther).

In Regard to Evangelical Counsels:

174. Between the Commandments and the Evangelical Counsels there is no distinction (Melanchthon).
175. There is but one Evangelical Counsel, viz., virginity (Luther); although this is not praised in Scripture.
176. It is impossible for an Evangelical Counsel to become a commandment (Luther).

Against the Commandments:

177. The Commandments of God are impossible (Melanchthon). You are doing very wrong in denying that our Savior commanded impossibilities (Luther to Silesius) [Faber].

Against the Lord's Day:

178. The Sabbath does not signify the religion of the seventh day; and since the abrogation of the Law, all days are equal (Melanchthon).
179. There are some who think that the Sabbath ought still to be observed, since we have Scripture for this, and not for the Lord's Day.
180. The Lord's Day was instituted only that men might meet to hear the Word of God (Bucer, *non ferianda*; Oscairdg [?], Glaib [?], Carlstadt).

Against Sin:

181. The *fomes*[14] is truly actual sin, an actual privation of that which ought to be present, a thing that is alive and that daily excites to sin (Luther, Rieg) [Urbanus Rhegius (?)].
182. Every sin is ignorance (Melanchthon). And invincible ignorance does not excuse sin (Luther).
183. The distinction made today between venial and mortal sin is wrong, since every affection of concupiscence is mortal sin (Melanchthon). Every sin, according to its nature, is mortal, but it is venial to those who are in Christ (Luther).
184. Original sin is no sin, but a natural defect, like stammering (Zwingli).

14 Latin for "spark" or "fuel." In a theological sense, it refers to original sin.

185. Original sin is an actual wicked desire; hence, Scripture does not distinguish between actual and original sin (Melanchthon).
186. Original sin always remains (Luther).

Against Faith:

187. Faith alone justifies, not works, because faith and works directly antagonize; hence, works cannot be taught without injuring faith (Luther).
188. An error in faith does not hurt, provided one only believes that Christ, our Lord, has saved and redeemed us (Bucer).
189. There are no works so wicked as to be able to accuse and condemn believers in Christ (Luther); where there is faith, no sin injures.
190. He who has once believed that Jesus Christ has redeemed him has the seal of the Holy Spirit and can never sin unto death (Bucer).
191. Christ has ordained that there should be no sin but unbelief and no righteousness but faith (Luther).
192. It is necessary to elevate faith above all virtues; but it is removed by any crime (ibid).
193. We have no doubt whatever that we are saved when we are baptized, since the promise there made is not mutable with respect to any sins. Hence, one baptized, even though he so will, cannot lose salvation, because no sin but unbelief can condemn him. All others are swallowed up by faith in a moment (Luther).
194. Faith alone is necessary; all other things are most free, neither commanded nor prohibited (Luther).
195. Love does not justify, but faith, which is preferred to love (Melanchthon). Moreover, it justifies with respect to no works, whether good or bad.
196. Only unbelievers are wicked (Zwingli), because it is with God, not with men, that they deal by means of works.
197. Faith never respects past, but only future things (Luther).
198. Acquired *fides informis*[15] is a dream, a matter unknown to Holy Scripture, taught by the prostitutes of the pope (Luther); an insanity (Melanchthon).

15 unformed faith

Against Works:

199. All the works of men, however praiseworthy in appearance, are altogether vicious and are sins worthy of death (Melanchthon).
200. Wicked deeds do not make a wicked man (Luther).
201. The Commandments are necessarily fulfilled prior to all works (Luther).
202. We are, we have been, we always remain equals before God (Luther).
203. God cares not for our works; or if they be anything before Him, nevertheless all are equal as to merit.

Against Merits:

204. Paul dissipates the dreams of theologians who, to obtain grace, have invented *meritum congrui et digni*[16] (Luther; Rieger).
205. To say that our works are meritorious is to detract from the honor and merit of Christ (Haller), because there is no merit in man whatsoever (Zwingli).
206. The grace of God is not a quality in us (Melanchthon). He who believes, loves (Nürnberg provosts).

Against Love:

207. All the Commandments of God are to be observed in love; for one sins in not killing if this be not in love (Luther). So one in sin giving alms or doing any other good work, sins (Luther).
208. Love does not abide in the eternal home (Zwingli).
209. The Christian is on his guard lest he ever be uncertain as to whether he be in the grace of God or whether his works please God; for he who doubts as to this sins and loses all his works (Luther).
210. The statement is most certain, that we are always most certain of the remission of sin. The saints know that they are in grace, and their sins are forgiven (Melanchthon).
211. Acts of hope and of faith are not distinguished in Scripture (ibid).
212. I regard it a human fancy that a habit is one thing and an act another. Faith, accordingly, is nothing but a movement of the heart and means "to believe" (Luther).

---

16 Latin for "merit of the fitting and worthy," meaning goodness bestowed on a person because of the actions of Christ.

213. The freedom of the Gospel consists in the fact that all power of accusing has been wrested from the Law, as well as of condemning us; in other words, if you have sinned, you cannot be damned (Melanchthon).

Against the Sacraments:

214. A sacrament is a recent invention (Luther), and there are only three sacraments, viz., Baptism, penitence, and the Holy Supper (Luther); elsewhere, he states but two (Glaib).

215. The Sacraments of the New do not differ from those of the Old Testament, so far as efficacy of significance is concerned (Luther, Bucer).

Against Baptism:

216. Baptism neither justifies nor profits anyone, but it is only faith in the word of promise, to which Baptism is added, that accomplishes this (Luther, Melanchthon).

217. Baptism, even so far as the sign is concerned, is not a momentary, but a permanent matter (Luther).

218. To baptize is incomparably greater than to consecrate bread and wine (Luther).

219. For this reason Baptism cannot be administered except by a priest (Luther).

220. Baptism pertains no less to the second than to the first forgiveness (Melanchthon).

221. Penitence has no other sacramental sign than Baptism (Melanchthon).

222. It is pernicious to believe that, so far as a son of light is concerned, the force of Baptism is lost by sin (Luther).

223. Baptism has respect to the entire course of our life (Luther).

224. The Baptism of Christ and that of John is the same (Zwingli). Accordingly, John the Baptist preached the Gospel before Christ (Zwingli).

225. The form of Baptism is not "in the name of the Father," but "I baptize thee in the names of the Father and of the Son" (Zwingli).

226. The water of Baptism is not to be blessed; neither is exorcism to precede Baptism. But, all ceremonies being excluded, we are to use Baptism in the simplest way, as Christ instituted it (John Landtsperger).

227. Infants are not to be baptized, but when those baptized have attained the use of reason, they are to be rebaptized (Balthasar [Hubmaier] and all the Anabaptists).

228. Baptism does not profit an infant unless it has a faith of its own (Luther, Rieger, Weidensee, Landtsperger). But infused faith is a fictitious thing (Osualdus, Glaib).

229. It is not the laver of Baptism but only the blood of Christ that removes original sin (Luther).

Infants:

230. Infants of Christians, if not prevented, I believe are not condemned (Zwingli).

231. A child must not be hurried to Baptism, for even God cannot give faith to it when it is baptized and is lost, and He can give faith to an unbaptized child who is to be saved (Weidensee).

232. It is not certain, then, that a child departing after Baptism is saved (Weidensee). One, then, is ignorant concerning a child departing without Baptism (Landtsperger).

233. If one would bring up children and know that all are eternally lost, he should not be grieved on this account, nor once lament (Weidensee).

Against the "Indelible Character":

234. The "character" impressed in Baptism or in ordination is a fictitious matter and without scriptural authority (Luther, Melanchthon, Rieger, Zwingli).

Against Confirmation:

235. Confirmation and Extreme Unction are not sacraments instituted by Christ (Luther, Zwingli).

Against the Eucharist:

236. In the Eucharist, the substance of bread and wine remains, because transubstantiation is a figment of sophists and Romanists (Pirkheimer, Melanchthon).

237. I firmly believe not only that the body of Christ is in the bread but also that the bread is the body of Christ (Luther).

238. As the body of Christ is in the bread, where there is neither blood nor soul, so the blood of Christ in the wine is without body and soul (Luther).

239. In the Eucharist, the true body of Christ is not really, but figuratively only and as in a sign (Zwingli, Oecolampadius, Capito, Keller, Retenack).

240. I do not know whether it was a greater abomination to worship the golden calf in Dan or that bread (Zwingli).

241. The Eucharist is the idol of Moazim, which, according to Daniel, we have worshiped in the Holy Place, and is true idolatry (Zwingli).

242. The body of Christ can be only in one place; hence, if it is to be received by us, it must leave the right hand of the Father (Zwingli).

243. The miracles wrought in the Eucharist have Satan as their author (Oecolampadius, from the *Father of Lies*).

244. There is much danger in the adoration of the Eucharist. For this reason, it would be better not to adore it, for such was the practice of the apostles. Neither is Christ there in order to be adored (Luther).

Against Processions:

245. Where the Eucharist enclosed in gold and silver is carried about with pomp and external adoration in a procession, this is nothing else than to make sport of God (Luther, Pirkheimer, Lang, Strauss).

246. Therefore, that the Eucharist should be made a show of or be carried about or be laid aside in an ark are abuses of the Eucharist; but that it should be imprisoned is a sport of demons (Pirkheimer, Glaib, Balthasar [Hubmaier]).

Against Communion:

247. That no one should receive the Eucharist except fasting is a madness madder than any madness; so is it ridiculous that a layman should not handle the Eucharist, the cup, since he can commune himself (Luther). Afterward, however, he prohibited this.

248. They only commune worthily whose consciences are afflicted, confused, erroneous, and burdened with sins (Luther).

249. The greatest sins are committed at Easter on account of the impious requirement of the pope requiring men to commune, even more than at the Carnival (Luther).

250. It is my faithful advice that a Christian, in Lent and at Easter, should neither confess nor come to the Communion, and that he should think, "For this very reason I will not do what that man, the pope, here commands, but I would do it if he had not commanded it" (Luther).

Both Kinds:

251. To deny both kinds to the laity is godless and tyrannical, and bishops sin who give one kind alone (Luther, Osiander).

252. The Greeks and others are not to be accounted heretics or schismatics on account of both kinds, but the Romans are rather to be so accounted (Luther).

253. It would be better to receive neither part than one alone, since it is a snare most harmful to souls to commune once a year under one form (Luther, Zwingli).

254. A layman, without the desire to receive the other form, is godless and denies Christ (Luther).

Against Confession:

255. Confession not made into the ear cannot be approved by divine law; neither was this done originally, but then it was public (Luther, Zwingli, Oecolampadius).

256. That secret sins pertain to sacramental Confession can be proved in no way of reason or from the Scriptures; I suspect that this was an invention either of the avaricious or the curious (Luther, the Psychityranni, Oecolampadius, Rieger, Strauss).

257. A priest ought to absolve a penitent from punishment and guilt, or he sins; a superior likewise sins in reserving cases to himself (Luther).

258. Circumstances are to be entirely disregarded; the observance of places, times, and persons is of no account; and should it be made, it is another superstitious assumption (Luther, Carlstadt).

Penitence:

259. Penitence lacks any sign divinely instituted; accordingly, it is not properly a sacrament, but a way and return to Baptism (Luther, Melanchthon).
260. If St. John had taught that fear is the beginning of penitence, it, nevertheless, would not follow that penitence begins in fear (Luther).
261. It is false and dangerous to think that penance is "the second raft after shipwreck" (Luther, Melanchthon).

Against the Keys:

262. The Keys are not given except to one who is righteous and holy in spirit (Luther, Oecolampadius, Bucer).
263. To bind and to loose is nothing else than to preach the Gospel (Luther, Zwingli).
264. The laws concerning satisfactions, by which we are taught to blot out sins by our works, are impious. Here see that the contrary has been condemned by Christ, viz., all things pertaining to the canonical law and the kingdom of the pope (Luther).

Satisfaction:

265. No satisfaction is required for sins except the death of Christ (Melanchthon, Rieger, Zwingli, Luther).
266. The sacrament of penitence has been abolished by prelates in the Church (Luther).
267. Anyone can absolve anyone; accordingly, the freest authority of hearing confessions is to be conceded to all brethren and sisters (Luther).

Ordination:

268. The Church of Christ ignores the sacrament of ordination (Luther); it is a figment invented by men (Zwingli, Rieger, Amsterdo).
269. As many of us as have been baptized are all equally priests; and any layman can consecrate churches, confirm children, and so on (Luther, Zwingli).

The Mass:

270. The Gospel does not allow the Mass as a sacrifice because to retain the use of masses under the name of sacrifices is to deny Christ (Luther, Rieger).

271. At any hour and as often as one wish, he can celebrate Mass (Luther). Nevertheless, one can no more offer for another than he can drink for him (Zwingli).

272. They lie who say that the Mass of a wicked priest is useful *ex opere operate*[17] (Luther) although the name *Mass* is improperly transferred hither (Zwingli).

273. The office of the Mass is not satisfactory as offered for the dead, the troubled, or as applied for another (Luther).

274. The Mass has been changed into a sacrifice of Satan, and that, too, by a common error—but this is the very worst idolatry and infidelity, and is worse than heathen (Luther, Rieger).

275. We condemn and despise the Canon of the Mass, by the authority of the Gospel (Luther), because it is false and has nothing solid in it (Zwingli, Nürnberg preachers).

276. Today, the celebrants of the Mass are idolaters and commit idolatry as often as they sacrifice (Luther, Oecolampadius).

277. All private masses are to be abrogated; but on every Lord's Day, and then only, the Eucharist alone is to be consecrated (Luther).

278. Nay, all masses, both public and private, are to be abrogated (Zwingli, Bucer, Capito, Haller, Blaurer, Rottenacker).

279. Water is not to be put into the cup in the Mass because it is a wicked and unfavorable sign (Zwingli, Luther, Carlstadt).

Canonical Hours:

280. I believe that they sin more who read the hours coldly than they who omit them, for they are hypocrites. There is scarcely greater sin than that which proceeds from this laborious worship of God, which is rendered by crying out through those canonical hours (Luther). Accordingly, the prelates at Nürnberg have dispensed with Matins and Compline.

---

17 from the work performed

Matrimony:

281. Matrimony is not a sacrament divinely instituted, but one invented by men in the Church (Luther).

282. The conjugal debt is a sin, and, according to Psalm 51, altogether mad (Luther). Yea, it is never paid without sin (ibid).

283. Priests ought to ratify all marriages that have no other impediment than that of the papal, but not of the divine, law (Luther). Every priest—yea, every brother or anyone—can make a dispensation for himself with regard to impediments decreed by the Church (Zwingli).

284. It is lawful to marry the daughter of one's sister, or niece. Likewise, the children of two brothers or sisters may marry; or one may marry the sister of his wife or connection by marriage; also, no spiritual relationship hinders matrimony (Luther, Zwingli).

285. Marriages of children contracted against the will of their parents are invalid; hence, the title "*de clandestina desponsione*"[18] is from Satan (Luther).

286. If those contracting marriage have not completed nineteen years, the marriage is invalid (Thuringian Consistory).

287. If anyone violate a virgin, he will not be obliged to give her anything except a pair of shoes (a new Thuringian law that fell from heaven).

Divorce:

288. When a man is impotent, let the wife seek a divorce; but if he be unwilling, let her, with the consent of her husband, have intercourse with another, or the brother of her husband in secret marriage, and let the offspring be accounted those of the reputed father. The woman is safe in a state of safety (Luther).

289. For I prefer bigamy to divorce (Luther) (as the Lutheran monks have shown effectually).

290. If a wife does not obey her husband when he asks for the conjugal debt, let him call in a servant girl. Yea, on this account, he can ask for a divorce (Luther).

291. Divorce occurs not only on account of adultery but also for other, graver reasons. Suppose a husband be under sentence of death, a madman, quarrelsome, withdrawing from his wife without her consent and long absent! (Thuringians, on Epithal., Luther).

---

18 the secret betrothal

292. When the divorce has been decreed, it is allowable for the innocent party to marry, unless the guilty party should be hindered (Luther, Melanchthon).

293. It is an error to break the marriage if, before it has been consummated, one of the couple enter a monastery or convent (Luther).

294. Former betrothals are not broken if one has afterward known a second spouse (Luther).

Celibacy:

295. Ordination does not hinder marriage or break the contract, but celibacy has been introduced by the devil (Luther).

296. By virtue of the words of Paul, I absolve all priests from celibacy; for between a priest and a true wife, there is a true and inseparable marriage, approved by the commandments of God. This the godless forbid from pure tyranny (Luther, Zwingli, Zell, Blaurer, Stoerer).

297. The Nicene Council concedes marriage to priests (Spengler of Nürnberg, Zwingli, Rieger).

298. In the time of Augustine, no one opposed the marriage of priests (Zwingli).

299. It is allowable for a priest or a bishop not only to marry once but the second, third, and fourth time, whether the bride be a virgin or one who has been corrupted.

Vows:

300. Would that I was able to persuade all persons either to altogether abolish or avoid all vows (Luther, Lambert, Avinio).

301. If a vow be dispensable, any brother can make such dispensation for his neighbor, or he can dispense himself; if a neighbor cannot so dispense, there is then no law by which the pope can do it (Carlstadt, Eberlein).

302. The mode of life proceeding from a vow is without a precedent in the Scriptures (Luther, Blaurer, Ketenbach, Lambert).

303. Parents have the right to remove children from monasteries who have entered without their consent. If the pope says the contrary, he lies (Luther).

304. Religious vows conflict directly with the Gospel of Christ and Baptism, and are opposed to faith and the Word of God (Luther, Lambert).

305. To become a monk is to apostatize from the faith, to deny Christ, and to become a Jew; their vows, accordingly, are worthless (Luther).

306. For a man to be continent is an impossibility; but just as it is necessary for man to eat and drink and to sleep, so also is it to have sexual intercourse. Hence, no man can be without a woman, nor any woman without a man (Luther).

307. The state of virginity is beneath the marriage estate, than which there is none better on earth (Luther). If Jerome had known that marriage would be one of the seven sacraments of a part of the Church, he would have banished virginity and would have spoken more reverently concerning marriage (Some).

308. All vows are temporary and mutable (Luther, Lambert).

309. No monk or priest can be a Christian (Luther, Zwingli).

310. Castigations voluntarily assumed by men, like voluntary fastings, are repudiated by Paul (Bucer).

311. We properly think that all monasteries and cathedral churches and like abominations should be entirely abolished (Luther to the Duke of Savoy).

312. I discourage all from entering any religious order unless he know that the works of the members of these orders, however arduous and holy, in God's eyes, are no better than the works of farmers laboring in the fields (Luther).

313. Whatever is promised men in secular matters is to be fulfilled, but in matters of conscience, if anything be promised God, it is not to be kept (Zwingli).

314. No saint became a saint through monasticism (Luther).

Poverty:

315. Evangelical poverty is exacted of men by divine right; accordingly, no vow should be made (Melanchthon).

316. To establish a mode of life for begging likewise conflicts with the Gospel (Melanchthon, Luther).

317. Monasticism is of the devil (Zwingli, Lambert).

318. Would that all monks and nuns would flee from the cloisters, and that all cloisters throughout the whole world were to be abolished (Luther).

319. All Carthusians, all monks and nuns, depart from that which has been ordained and from liberty when they imagine that they are polluted by eating meat (Luther, Lambert).

320. Put before your eyes the infinite crowd of priests and nuns, with their masses, sacrifices, laws, doctrines, and all their works, and you will see nothing but a theater of Satan, godless people of perdition, reserved for the wrath of God forever (Luther).

321. Church ceremonies always obscure liberty and the force of the Gospel; hence, it is profitable to disregard them (Melanchthon, Nürnberg preachers).

322. Unctions, tonsures, ceremonial vestments, benedictions of water, salt, palms, candles, herbs, consecrations of churches, altars, vases, men and so on are human inventions (Zwingli, Lambert, Bucer, preachers of Nürnberg).

Against Purgatory:

323. There is no purgatory after this life (Zwingli, Osiander, Oecolampadius, Capito, Bucer, Lambert, Rieger, Rottenacker).

324. It would be safer to deny all purgatory than to believe Gregory in his Dialogues (Luther).

325. Here sink anniversaries, vigils for the dead, depositions, the seventh, the thirtieth, fraternities, oblations, and other inventions of men (Zwingli). Chanting, organs, candles, ornaments, vestments, chrism, disappear (Luther, Lambert, Balthasar [Hubmaier]).

326. We have no command to pray for the dead; you may, therefore, pray once or twice for a dead person, but afterward, cease, lest you tempt God or distrust Him (Luther).

327. Moreover, that perpetual masses are founded upon this; and that, every year, the cry ascends as though God had not heard before that year. This is death and the devil, unbelief, making sport of God—such prayer is mere blasphemy (Luther).

328. The office for the dead is of about as much service to deceased Christians as it is to dead cattle (the unhappy provosts of Nürnberg).

329. No Christian implicates himself in masses and prayers for the dead unless he be willing to deny Christ, to repudiate Baptism, and to act in opposition to the whole Bible.

330. If you have in your house a spirit who, when adjured, seeks for aid by means of masses and prayers, account him without any hesitation as the

devil; because from the beginning of the world until now, no soul has appeared, neither does God so permit (Luther).

331. No images are to be kept in the church, but rather to be destroyed and burned; nay, neither publicly nor privately are they to be retained or to be painted or carved, for they are relics of the old idolatry contrary to the Second Commandment (Zwingli, Bucer, Haller, Carlstadt).

332. It is under the tutelage of Satan that the term "free will" has entered, and that with the purpose of seducing men from the way of right; for it is a mere figment, since the will contributes nothing toward its own willing, and that it has any activity in good works is erroneous (Luther, Carlstadt, Rieger).

333. The name *fraternity* forbids one from being superior to another, and especially in spiritual things, from having more right and inheritance than his brother (Luther).

334. We Christians are free, exempt from all the laws of men, liberated through Baptism (Luther).

335. No laws can be imposed with any right upon Christians, whether by men or by angels, unless so far as they be willing (Luther).

336. Subjects neither can, nor will, nor ought to endure your tyranny any longer (Luther to the princes).

337. The emperor and the princes deal in manifest falsehoods and publish contradictory commandments (Luther).

338. That the pope has transferred the power from the Greeks to the Germans is either the chief or greatest mark of Antichrist and is most deceptive (Luther).

339. I regret that I submitted to the emperor at Worms. Whatever tolerance of my doctrine was conceded by my judges is of no account to tyrants (Luther).

340. There is no more excellent secular law than that of the Turk, as he has no canonical and civil law (Luther).

341. The secular princes are stupid, and according to their stupid brain, they want to lead the [saints?] into schools and publish directions, and if the emperor would give a command, they want to appear as though they were seriously doing what was commanded (Luther).

342. The madness of foolish men is directed to the extinction of the faith, because they want to force men to believe (Luther).

343. God has delivered the princes up to a reprobate mind, and He wants to put an end to them, just as to ecclesiastical houses (Luther).

344. The secular government is at just as low a stage as that of the ecclesiastical tyrants, so that the one will not perish without the other (Luther).

345. Princes prohibiting Luther's New Testament act like murderers of Christ, such as Herod; but these tyrants act having more right and inheritance than his brother (Luther). As the secular princes are accustomed to do, in order to satisfy their titles (Luther).

346. Ever since the beginning of the world, a wise prince has been a most rare bird; for generally, they are either the greatest fools or the very worst rascals; for they are God's policemen and executioners (Luther).

347. The common people have now become intelligent and wise; a blow to princes is clearly impending from the side of the people and rabble. I fear that it cannot be prevented (Luther).

348. The Turk is ten times as wise and just as our princes; how then could such fools be prospered against the Turk (Luther).

349. In the halls of princes, the devil sits in the highest place and has there his chief throne (Luther).

350. The kingdom of France, from its impious service to Antichrist, has been impiously called most Christian (Luther). He also has treated the most noble king of England with the greatest insults, wrongs, and reproaches.

351. The sin of robbery is now an honor and title of the nobility (Luther).

352. If the peasants prevail, then the devil is abbot; if the princes prevail, the master will be an abbess (Luther).

353. The kingdom of the pope is nothing but tyranny, the realm of Antichrist with his faces (Luther). Yea, he is Antichrist himself, the son of perdition (Lambert).

354. The name of *Pope* is recent, unheard of in the time of [Pope] Nicholas [I] or of Augusinet (Zwingli).

355. Bishops ought to be grave men, married, laymen, advanced in years (Luther and all).

356. It is not allowable for a bishop to do aught except to teach the Word of God. Preaching the Gospel is so peculiarly the prerogative of a bishop that it is not proper to substitute another for him to teach in his place. If, therefore, he does not teach, he is not a bishop (Melanchthon).

357. There is no ecclesiastical authority over men (Bucer). Hence, the bishops have usurped the jurisdiction that belongs to the secular princes (Luther, Rieger, Zwingli, Blaurer).

358. Ecclesiastical power is not of God (Luther).

359. Christ subjected Himself and His Church to secular power (Haller). This immunity of churches and freedom of the clergy has ceased (Luther).
360. The civil, but not the ecclesiastical power, has the authority to make and ordain laws (Melanchthon).
361. To impose law upon Christians is to tempt the devil (Zwingli).

Constitutions:

362. Neither the constitutions of the Church nor the ordinances of the apostles put the conscience under any obligation (Bucer).
363. We are, therefore, under no obligation to celebrate the festivals of the saints, to fast in Lent and on other days, to abstain from flesh on six festival days, or to obey other human precepts (Luther, Osiander, Rieger, Zwingli).
364. No prelate, but only the Church, can excommunicate (Zwingli, Haller).
365. We confess that the world has been miserably led astray by popes, councils, and decrees of Fathers with these traditions, or more properly, snares of the devil (Luther).
366. No pope or bishop has the right of imposing a single syllable upon any man (Luther).

Against Councils:

367. After one has been justified, no laws or ordinances bind him (Melanchthon).
368. That was an erroneous decision by the Council that essence neither begets nor is begotten; also, that the intellectual soul is man's substantial form (Luther).
369. Ordination is openly heretical and ought to be abolished (Melanchthon).
370. I declare that all the articles of Huss at Constance were most Christian and were condemned by Antichrist and his disciples in a synagogue of Satan collected from the most worthless sophists (Luther).

[Eck interjects:] Here notice, O Emperor, that the calumniator of the most holy and free Council of Constance is now making an appeal to a future Council.

371. Huss and Jerome were burned in violation of faith publicly pledged, because it was concluded in the Council that a safe conduct with heretics ought not to be kept; hence, our Germans have learned from the Romans to break faith and promises (Capito).

372. The princes of Germany once had the highest reputation for their good faith, but they have learned, in obedience to the idol at Rome and to the perpetual ignominy of the nation, to despise nothing more than good faith (Luther).

373. When I was called, I went to Rome, even though I knew that my public faith had been violated by the emperor (Luther).

374. In those things that pertain to faith, every Christian is pope and Church to himself (Luther).

375. Every Christian is allowed to judge concerning every doctrine, for we are not bound to believe councils and popes (Luther, Blaurer).

376. It is only a matter that should be laughed at if a great sedition should arise against bishops and their rule, because those exposing their fortunes and bodies to such an emergency are sons of God, true Christians; and in a short time, matters will come to such a pass that there will be no bishop, no prince under the sun, no cathedral church, no monastery (Luther).

377. Nothing is to be received except what is expressly taught in Holy Scripture (Zwingli, Bucer, Blaurer).

378. I will not permit you to ascribe more than one sense to the Holy Scriptures (Zwingli, Luther). For Scripture does not admit of a number of meanings, "literal, allegorical," and so on.

379. The literal meaning of the creation of the world is hypocrisy and a carnal opinion concerning the condition of nature (Melanchthon).

380. The Apocalypse was not written by John the evangelist (Zwingli). The books of Baruch and Maccabees are not to be received.

381. For the Gospel to share authority with the canon law is an impossibility (Luther).

382. I know that no state is successfully administered by means of laws (Luther).

383. It is impossible at the same time to observe the Gospel and human laws. Accordingly, it is impossible to keep the peace and at the same time the laws (Luther).

384. There is no hope of a remedy unless, all the laws of all men being once annulled, we judge and rule all things according to the Gospel (Luther).

385. We must not swear for temporal things, for he who requires an oath of another, or himself swears, must be of a malicious and trifling mind not regarding the truth (Melanchthon).

386. It is not allowable for a Christian for any cause to take an oath (Anabaptists). For it is unjust and contrary to the Holy Scriptures to make demands on the faith of another (Luther).

387. All are heathen who contend in court for property or reputation (Luther).

388. If anything be taken from us, we ought not to demand it back in court or by war (Luther).

389. It is a doctrine of devils that it is allowable for a Christian to wage war, for all who go to war are accursed children of Cain (Oecolampadius).

390. To buy and sell are purely heathen matters (Luther). Business contracts, even for godly purposes, as churches, benefices, and so on, are usurious (Strauss); or at least unjust (Luther).

391. A community of all things is commanded in the New Testament (Melanchthon).

392. Altars are to be abolished in the New Testament because Christ is there crucified, divided, buried, and bitten with the teeth; for the Supper, a table answers the purpose (Balthasar Hubmaier, Glaib).

393. One should not care to be buried in a cemetery or consecrated place, because it is certain that every place blessed by man is cursed by God (Oswald, Glaib).

394. Wicked spirits will hereafter be saved together with the damned (John Denk).

395. They blaspheme who rave that the Turks or heretics should be attacked not with the Word of God, of which they are ignorant, but with war and worldly tumult, or with the din of censorships (Luther).

396. The word of Christ that many false prophets shall arise and deceive many, I verily think, was spoken with reference to the universities (Melanchthon).

397. The doctrine of all the schools, speculative as well as practical, has been condemned (Luther).

398. All moral virtues and speculative branches of knowledge are not true virtues and sciences, but sins and errors (Luther).

399. I doubt whether the Creed was handed down in writing by the apostles, although I do not doubt that it was composed by apostolic men; and yet, I doubt so far as to wish that it could be proved. Neither, unless I am mistaken, did Augustine believe this. But it was an abuse of the common people, not indeed with a godless opinion, as before. And that good man erred and, in his Christian simplicity, was exceedingly credulous (Some).

400. Pilate was not free to acquit Christ, since his power would have been compelled to serve the madness of the Jews. It is likewise a trifle to affirm that Mary merited by herself to become the mother of God (Some).

401. It is not entirely clear to me whether in the time of Christ's infancy it was clearly revealed to the Virgin Mary that He was God and Man. If Mary and Joseph had known that the child Jesus was God and Man, and would suffer nothing but that which was necessary, why would they have feared and grieved for Him? (Some.)

402. Jesus wished His death not to be mournful, but glorious; not to be deplored, but adored; for He was to be extolled for His victory (Some).

403. It is proper and in accord with God's word to excite seditions and tumults; hence, there is no better proof that my doctrine is of God than that it excites discords, seditions, and tumults (Luther). Many of them, therefore, have often publicly testified to the common people, "The Gospel wants blood" (Zwingli, etc.).

404. Among Christians, there should be no superiority, no courts, nothing fenced up or closed, no *meum* or *tuum*, no restraint or excommunication; and this they want to be frequent (Anabaptists).

Eck's conclusion:

Moreover, who Luther is I will learn; for he wants to be heard. I was the very first whom God put into the field. I never have been false to my trust. Had I been disposed to proceed impulsively, I could have caused great shedding of blood in Germany; aye, I could have begun the game at Worms, if the emperor had not been safe. I am also the one to whom God first revealed this, that I might proclaim these words to you. You know not how much labor it is to contend with the devil; but I know him well, and he knows me well, for I have already eaten with him one or two bits of salt, and I would have perished, had there not been a confession.

All the articles above noted, both those of Luther himself, as clearly a man familiar with the devil, and of those who, being infatuated with his errors, have so degenerated as to become deaf to the truth, we reject and anathematize each of them as heretical, or scandalous, false, and offensive to godly ears, and misleading the simple, or entirely seditious and disturbing the public peace. With respect to this, I am ready to give an account in a public disputation, at the pleasure of the Most Revered Emperor, God aiding me, and the Virgin Mary and all saints supporting me with their intercessions.

To God Alone the Glory

The day and hour of the disputation Eck will publish at the pleasure of the emperor.

INGOLSTADT
Printed 1530.

The Pontifical Confutation

Editor's Introduction to the Roman Confutation

After the Lutherans presented the Augsburg Confession on June 25, 1530, the Roman rulers and leaders met on June 26 and on June 27, presented the emperor with a report that called for a response to the Augsburg Confession. Various options were considered for responding to the Lutherans, and on July 5, the emperor commanded that a confutation be prepared and that the Lutherans submit to his judgment. John Eck, who worked with John Faber, Conrad Wimpina, and John Cochlaeus, led the Roman theologians charged with the preparation of the Confutation. They were ordered to be moderate in their response. The emperor rejected several drafts of a response. They presented 280 pages for the emperor's review, and he rejected all but twelve pages. Finally, after five attempts and six weeks of effort, the emperor accepted a draft and allowed it to be read publicly to the Lutherans, which it was on August 3 by the emperor's secretary, Alexander Schweiss. It was, like the Augsburg Confession, prepared in both Latin and German, but read aloud only in German. Commenting on the preparation of the confutation, John Brenz wrote to Myconius on July 10, "They say they are preparing wagonloads of comments on our Confession. Eck, moreover, that good man, is their chief. Of the rest, there are twenty-three. You might say there is an Iliad of sophists."[19]

The Confutation was regarded as being so bad, even by the Roman Catholics, that they did not allow the Lutherans to have a copy. Fortunately, Lutheran scribes had copied every word down during its reading. It was not published until 1573, in Latin, and did not appear in German until 1808. The Lutherans asked for a copy after it was read and were told by the emperor on August 5 that they would not receive a copy unless they met three conditions: (1) That they do not reply in writing; (2) That they not print anything about it or do anything to publicize it, a demand made specifically by the Roman theologians; and (3) that they join with the emperor and the Roman Catholic estates and concur with the Confutation in every point. These demands were soundly rejected.

A conference between Roman Catholic and Lutheran theologians was convened and met from August 13–21, during which the Confutation was discussed, but neither party was willing to compromise. As a result of the conference, the Lutheran estates

---

19 Johann Brenz, *Anecdota Brentiana*, [*Anecdotes of Brenz: Unprinted Letters and Remembrances*], compiled by Th. Pressel (Tübingen: Verlag von J.J. Heckenhaur, 1868), *Melanchthon's Works*, Corpus Reformatorum 2, edited by Carolus Gottlieb Bretschneider (Berlin: C.A. Schwetschke and Son, 1835), 280. Homer's Illiad has twenty-four books.

agreed that a response to the Confutation should be prepared, and they commissioned Philip Melanchthon to prepare a first draft. Though he was not present when the Confutation was read, Melanchthon worked from the very accurate notes made by Camerarius and others. On September 22, Melanchthon presented his first draft of the Apology of the Augsburg Confession, *apology* meaning "defense." The Apology was offered by Chancellor Brück to the emperor and was received in the name of Emperor Charles V by the count palatinate Frederick but was quickly returned after his brother Ferdinance whispered an order in his ear.

The Pontifical Confutation

In reference to the matters presented to His Imperial Majesty by the elector of Saxony and some princes and states of the Holy Roman Empire, on the subject and concerning causes pertaining to the Christian orthodox faith, the following Christian reply can be given. August 3, 1530.

August 3, 1530

As His Worshipful Imperial Majesty received several days since a Confession of Faith presented by the Electoral Duke of Saxony and several princes and two cities, to which their names were affixed, with his characteristic zeal for the glory of God, the salvation of souls, Christian harmony, and the public peace, he not only himself read the Confession, but also, in order that in a matter of such moment he might proceed the more thoroughly and seasonably, he referred the aforesaid Confession to several learned, mature, approved, and honorable men of different nations for their inspection and examination, and earnestly directed and enjoined them to praise and approve what in the Confession was said aright and in accord with Catholic doctrine, but, on the other hand, to note that wherein it differed from the Catholic Church, and, together with their reply, to present and explain their judgment on each topic. This commission was executed aright and according to order. For those learned men with all care and diligence examined the aforesaid Confession and committed to writing what they thought on each topic, and thus presented a reply to His Imperial Majesty. This reply His Worshipful Imperial Majesty, as becomes a Christian emperor, most accurately read and gave to the other electors, princes, and estates of the Roman Empire for their perusal and examination, which they also approved as orthodox and in every respect harmonious with the Gospel and Holy Scripture. For this reason, after a conference with the electors, princes and states above named, in order that all dissension concerning this, our orthodox holy faith and religion, may be removed, His Imperial Majesty has directed that a declaration be made at present as follows:

In reference to the matters presented to His Imperial Majesty by the Elector of Saxony and some princes and states of the Holy Roman Empire, on the subject and concerning causes pertaining to the Christian orthodox faith, the following Christian reply can be given:

PART I

To Article I

Especially when in the first article they confess the unity of the divine essence in three persons according to the decree of the Council of Nicaea, their Confession must be accepted, since it agrees in all respects with the rule of faith and the Roman Church. For the Council of Nicaea, convened under the emperor Constantine the Great, has always been regarded inviolable, whereat three hundred and eighteen bishops eminent and venerable for holiness of life, martyrdom, and learning, after investigating and diligently examining the Holy Scriptures, set forth this article that they here confess concerning the unity of the essence and the trinity of persons. So, too, their condemnation of all heresies arising contrary to this article must be accepted—viz., the Manichaeans, Arians, Eunomians, Valentinians, and Samosatanes, for the Holy Catholic Church has condemned these of old.

To Article II

In the second article, we approve their confession, in common with the Catholic Church, that the fault of origin is truly sin, condemning and bringing eternal death upon those who are not born again by Baptism and the Holy Ghost. For in this, they properly condemn the Pelagians, both modern and ancient, who have been long since condemned by the Church. But the declaration of the article, that original sin is that men are born without the fear of God and without trust in God, is to be entirely rejected, since it is manifest to every Christian that to be without the fear of God and without trust in God is rather the actual guilt of an adult than the offence of a recently born infant that does not possess as yet the full use of reason, as the Lord says, "Your children which had no knowledge between good and evil," (Deuteronomy 1:39). Moreover, the declaration is also rejected whereby they call the fault of origin concupiscence, if they mean thereby that concupiscence is a sin that remains sin in a child even after Baptism. For the Apostolic See has already condemned two articles of Martin Luther concerning sin remaining in a child after Baptism and concerning the *fomes*[20] of sin hindering a soul from entering the kingdom of heaven. But if, according to the opinion of St. Augustine, they call the vice of origin concupiscence, which in Baptism ceases to be sin, this ought to be accepted, since indeed, according to the declaration of St. Paul, we are all born children of wrath (Ephesians 2:3), and in Adam we all have sinned (Romans 5:12).

To Article III

In the third article, there is nothing to offend, since the entire Confession agrees with the Apostles' Creed and the right rule of faith—viz., the Son of God became incarnate,

20 Latin for "spark" or "fuel." In a theological sense, it refers to original sin.

assumed human nature into the unity of His person, was born of the Virgin Mary, truly suffered, was crucified, died, descended to hell, rose again on the third day, ascended to heaven, and sat down at the right hand of the Father.

To Article IV

In the fourth article, the condemnation of the Pelagians, who thought that man can merit eternal life by his own powers without the grace of God, is accepted as Catholic and in accordance with the ancient councils, for the Holy Scriptures expressly testify to this. John the Baptist says, "A man can receive nothing, except it be given him from heaven" (John 3:27). "Every good gift and every perfect gift is from above and comes down from the Father of lights" (James 1:17). Therefore, "our sufficiency is of God" (2 Corinthians 3:5). And Christ says, "No man can come to Me, except the Father, which hath sent Me, draw him," John 6:44. And Paul, "What hast thou that thou didst not receive?" (1 Corinthians 4:7). For if anyone should intend to disapprove of the merits that men acquire by the assistance of divine grace, he would agree with the Manichaeans rather than with the Catholic Church. For it is entirely contrary to Holy Scripture to deny that our works are meritorious. For St. Paul says, "I have fought a good fight, I have finished my course, I have kept the faith; henceforth there is laid up for me a crown of righteousness, which the Lord, the righteous Judge, shall give me at that day" (2 Timothy 4:7–8). And to the Corinthians, he wrote, "We must all appear before the judgment seat of Christ, that everyone may receive the things done in his body, according to that he hath done, whether it be good or bad" (2 Corinthians 5:10). For where there are wages there is merit. The Lord said to Abraham, "Fear not, Abraham, I am thy shield and thy exceeding great reward" (Genesis 15:1). And Isaiah says, "Behold, His reward is with Him, and His work before Him" (Isaiah 40:10; 58:7–8): "Deal thy bread to the hungry, and thy righteousness shall go before thee; the glory of the Lord shall go before thee; the glory of the Lord shall gather thee up." So, too, the Lord to Cain, "If thou doest well shalt thou not be accepted?" (Genesis 4:7). So the parable in the Gospel declares that we have been hired for the Lord's vineyard, who agrees with us for a penny a day, and says, "Call the laborers and give them their hire" (Matthew 20:8). So Paul, knowing the mysteries of God, says, "Every man shall receive his own reward, according to his own labor" (1 Corinthians 3:8). Nevertheless, all Catholics confess that our works of themselves have no merit, but that God's grace makes them worthy of eternal life. Thus, St. John says, "They shall walk with me in white; for they are worthy" (Revelation 3:4). And St. Paul says in Colossians 1:12, "Giving thanks unto the Father, which hath made us meet to be partakers of the inheritance of the saints in light."

To Article V

In the fifth article, the statement that the Holy Ghost is given by the Word and Sacraments, as by instruments, is approved. For thus it is written, "While Peter yet spoke these words, the Holy Ghost fell on all them which heard the word" (Acts 10:44).

And, “The same is He which baptizeth with the Holy Ghost” (John 1:33). The mention, however, that they here make of faith is approved so far as not faith alone, which some incorrectly teach, but faith which worketh by love, is understood, as the apostle teaches aright in Galatians 5:3. For in Baptism there is an infusion, not of faith alone, but also, at the same time, of hope and love, as Pope Alexander declares in the canon Majores concerning Baptism and its effect, which John the Baptist also taught long before, saying in Luke 3:16, “He shall baptize you with the Holy Ghost and with fire.”

To Article VI

Their confession in the sixth article that faith should bring forth good fruits is acceptable and valid, since “faith without works is dead” (James 2:17), and all Scripture invites us to works. For the wise man says, “Whatsoever thy hand findeth to do, do it with thy might” (Ecclesiastes 9:10). “And the Lord had respect to Abel and to his offering” (Genesis 4:4). He saw that Abraham would “command his children and his household after him to keep the way of the Lord, and to do justice and judgment” (Genesis 18:19). And, “‘By Myself have I sworn,’ saith the Lord, ‘for because thou hast done this thing I will bless thee and multiply thy seed’” (Genesis 22:16). Thus, He regarded the fast of the Ninevites (Jonah 3), and the lamentations and tears of King Hezekiah (2 Kings 20). For this cause, all the faithful should follow the advice of St. Paul: “As we have therefore opportunity, let us do good unto all men, especially unto them who are of the household of faith” (Galatians 6:10). For Christ says, “The night cometh when no man can work” (John 9:4). But in the same article, their ascription of justification to faith alone is diametrically opposite the truth of the Gospel, by which works are not excluded, “because glory, honor and peace to every man that worketh good” (Romans 2:10). Why? Because David (Psalm 62:12), Christ (Matthew 16:27), and Paul (Romans 2:6) testify that God will render to every one according to his works. Besides, Christ says, “Not everyone that saith unto Me, ‘Lord, Lord’ shall enter into the kingdom of heaven; but he that doeth the will of My Father” (Matthew 7:21). Hence, however much one may believe, if he works not what is good, he is not a friend of God. “Ye are My friends,” says Christ, “if ye do whatsoever I command you” (John 15:14). On this account, their frequent ascription of justification to faith is not admitted, since it pertains to grace and love. For St. Paul says, “Though I have all faith so that I could remove mountains and have not charity, I am nothing” (1 Corinthians 13:2). Here, St. Paul certifies to the princes and the entire Church that faith alone does not justify. Accordingly, he teaches that love is the chief virtue: “Above all these things put on charity, which is the bond of perfectness” (Colossians 3:14). Neither are they supported by the word of Christ: “When ye shall have done all these things, say, ‘We are unprofitable servants’” (Luke 17:10). For if the doors ought to be called unprofitable, how much more fitting is it to say to those who only believe, “When ye shall have believed all things say, ‘We are unprofitable servants!’” This word of Christ, therefore, does not extol faith without works, but teaches that our works bring no profit to God; that no one can be puffed up by our works; that, when contrasted with the divine reward, our works are of no account and nothing. Thus St. Paul says, "I reckon that the sufferings of this present time are not worthy to be compared to the glory which shall be revealed in us" (Romans 8:18). For faith and good works are gifts of God whereby, through God's mercy, eternal life is given. So, too, the citation at this point from Ambrose is in no way pertinent, since St. Ambrose is here expressly declaring his opinion concerning legal works. For he says, "Without the law," but, "Without the law of the Sabbath, and of circumcision, and of revenge." And this he declares the more clearly on Romans 4, citing St. James concerning the justification of Abraham without legal works before circumcision. For how could Ambrose speak differently in his comments from St. Paul in the text when he says, "Therefore, by the deeds of the law, there shall no flesh be justified in his sight?" Therefore, finally, he does not exclude faith absolutely, but says, "We conclude that a man is justified by faith without the deeds of the law."

To Article VII

The seventh article of the Confession, wherein it is affirmed that the Church is the congregation of saints, cannot be admitted without prejudice to faith if by this definition the wicked and sinners be separated from the Church. For, in the Council of Constance, this article was condemned among the articles of John Huss of cursed memory, and it plainly contradicts the Gospel. For there we read that John the Baptist compared the Church to a threshing floor that Christ will cleanse with His fan and will gather the wheat into His garner but will burn the chaff with unquenchable fire (Matthew 3:12). Wherefore this article of the Confession is in no way accepted, although we read in it their Confession that the Church is perpetual, since here the promise of Christ has its place, who promises that the Spirit of truth will abide with it forever (John 14:16). And Christ Himself promises that He will be with the Church always unto the end of the world. They are praised also in that they do not regard variety of rites as separating unity of faith, if they speak of special rites. For, to this effect, Jerome says, "Every province abounds in its own sense" (of propriety). But if they extend this part of the Confession to universal Church rites, this also must be utterly rejected, and we must say with St. Paul, "We have no such custom" (1 Corinthians 11:16). "For by all believers universal rites must be observed," St. Augustine, whose testimony they also use, well taught of Januarius; for we must presume that such rites were transmitted from the apostles.

To Article VIII

The eighth article of the Confession, concerning wicked ministers of the Church and hypocrites—viz. [namely], that their wickedness does not injure the Sacraments and the Word—is accepted with the Holy Roman Church, and the princes commend it, condemning on this topic the Donatists and the ancient Origenists, who maintained that it was unlawful to use the ministry of the wicked in the Church—a heresy that the Waldenses and the Poor of Lyons revived. Afterward, John Wycliff in England and John Huss in Bohemia adopted this.

To Article IX

The ninth article, concerning Baptism—viz., that it is necessary to salvation, and that children ought to be baptized—is approved and accepted, and they are right in condemning the Anabaptists, a most seditious class of men who ought to be banished far from the boundaries of the Roman Empire in order that illustrious Germany may not suffer again such a destructive and sanguinary commotion as she experienced five years ago in the slaughter of so many thousands.

To Article X

The tenth article gives no offense in its words, because they confess that in the Eucharist, after the consecration is lawfully made, the body and blood of Christ are substantially and truly present—if only they believe that the entire Christ is present under each form, so that the blood of Christ is no less present under the form of bread by concomitance than it is under the form of the wine, and the reverse. Otherwise in the Eucharist, the body of Christ is dead and bloodless, contrary to St. Paul, because "Christ, being raised from the dead, dieth no more" (Romans 6:9). One matter is added as very necessary to the article of the Confession—viz., that they believe the Church, rather than some teaching otherwise and incorrectly, that by the almighty Word of God in the consecration of the Eucharist, the substance of the bread is changed into the body of Christ. For thus, in a general council, it has been determined concerning the exalted Trinity and the Catholic faith. They are praised therefore, for condemning the Capernaites, who deny the truth of the body and blood of our Lord Jesus Christ in the Eucharist.

To Article XI

The eleventh article—their acknowledgment that private Absolution with Confession should be retained in the Church—is accepted as Catholic and in harmony with our faith because Absolution is supported by the word of Christ. For Christ says to His apostles in John 20:23, "Whosoever sins ye remit, they are remitted unto them." Nevertheless, two things must here be required of them: one, that they compel an annual Confession to be observed by their subjects, according to the constitution, canon Omnis Utriusque, concerning penance and remission and the custom of the Church universal. Another, that through their preachers they cause their subjects to be faithfully admonished when they are about to confess, that although they cannot state all their sins individually, nevertheless, a diligent examination of their conscience having been made, they make an entire confession of their offences—viz., of all that occur to their memory in such investigation. But in regard to the rest that have been forgotten and have escaped our mind, it is lawful to make a general confession, and to say with the psalmist (Psalm 19:17), "Cleanse me, Lord, from secret faults."

To Article XII

In the twelfth article, their confession that such as have fallen may find remission of sins at the time when they are converted, and that the Church should give Absolution unto such as return to repentance, is commended, since they most justly condemn the Novatians who deny that repentance can be repeated, in opposition both to the prophet who promises grace to the sinner at whatever hour he shall mourn (Ezekiel 18:21) and to the merciful declaration of Christ, our Savior, who replied to St. Peter that not until seven times but until seventy times seven in one day he should forgive his brother for sinning against him (Matthew 18:22). But the second part of this article is utterly rejected. For when they ascribe only two parts to repentance, they antagonize the entire Church, which from the time of the apostles has held and believed that there are three parts of repentance—contrition, confession, and satisfaction. Thus the ancient doctors Origen, Cyprian, Chrysostom, Gregory, and Augustine taught in attestation of the Holy Scriptures, especially from 2 Kings 12, concerning David; 2 Chronicles 3:1, concerning Manasseh; Psalms 31, 37, 50, 101, and so on. Therefore, Pope Leo X of happy memory justly condemned this article of Luther, who taught: "That there are three parts of repentance—viz., confession, contrition, and satisfaction—has no foundation in Scripture or in Holy Christian doctors."

This part of the article, therefore, can in no way be admitted. So, too, neither can that which asserts that faith is the second part of repentance, since it is known to all that faith precedes repentance; for unless one believes, he will not repent. Neither is that part admitted that makes light of pontifical satisfactions, for it is contrary to the Gospel, contrary to the apostles, contrary to the Fathers, contrary to the councils, and contrary to the universal Catholic Church. John the Baptist cries, "Bring forth fruits meet for repentance" (Matthew 3:8). St. Paul teaches, "As ye have yielded your members as servants to uncleanness, even so now yield your members as servants to righteousness unto holiness" (Romans 6:19). He likewise preached to the Gentiles that they should repent and be converted to God, bringing forth fruits meet for repentance (Acts 20:21). So Christ Himself also began to teach and preach repentance: "Repent, for the kingdom of heaven is at hand" (Matthew 4:17). Afterward, He commanded the apostles to pursue this mode of preaching and teaching (Luke 24:47), and St. Peter faithfully obeyed Him in his first sermon (Acts 2:38). So Augustine also exhorts that "everyone exercise toward himself severity, so that, being judged of himself, he shall not be judged of the Lord," as St. Paul says (1 Corinthians 11:31). Pope Leo, surnamed the Great, said, "The Mediator between God and men, the man Christ Jesus, gave to those set over the churches the authority to assign to those who confess the doing of penance, and through the door of reconciliation to admit to the communion of the sacraments those who have been cleansed by a salutary satisfaction." Ambrose says, "The amount of the penance must be adapted to the trouble of the conscience." Hence, diverse penitential canons were appointed in the holy Synod of Nicaea, in accordance with the diversity of satisfactions. Jovinian the heretic, thought, however, that all sins are equal, and accordingly, did not admit a diversity of satisfactions. Moreover, satisfactions should not be abolished in the Church contrary to the express Gospel and the decrees of councils and Fathers, but those absolved by the priest ought to perform the penance enjoined, following the declaration of St. Paul: He "gave Himself for us, to redeem us from all iniquity, and purify unto Himself a peculiar people, zealous of good works" (Titus 2:14). Christ thus made satisfaction for us, that we might be zealous of good works, fulfilling the satisfaction enjoined.

To Article XIII

The thirteenth article gives no offence, but is accepted, while they say that the Sacraments were instituted not only to be marks of profession among men but rather to be signs and testimonies of God's will toward us; nevertheless, we must request them that what they here ascribe to the Sacraments in general they confess also specifically concerning the seven sacraments of the Church and take measures for the observance of them by their subjects.

To Article XIV

When, in the fourteenth article, they confess that no one ought to administer in the Church the Word of God and the Sacraments unless he be rightly called, it ought to be understood that he is rightly called who is called in accordance with the form of law and the ecclesiastical ordinances and decrees hitherto observed everywhere in the Christian world, and not according to a Jeroboitic (cf. 1 Kings 12:20) call or a tumult or any other irregular intrusion of the people. Aaron was not thus called. Therefore, in this sense, the confession is received; nevertheless, they should be admonished to persevere therein, and to admit in their realms no one either as pastor or as preacher unless he be rightly called.

To Article XV

In the fifteenth article, their confession that such ecclesiastical rites are to be observed as may be observed without sin and are profitable for tranquility and good order in the Church is accepted, and they must be admonished that the princes and cities see to it that the ecclesiastical rites of the Church universal be observed in their dominions and districts as well as those that have been kept devoutly and religiously in every province even to us, and if any of these have been intermitted, that they restore them, and arrange, determine, and effectually enjoin upon their subjects that all things be done in their churches according to the ancient form. Nevertheless, the appendix to this article must be entirely removed, since it is false that human ordinances instituted to propitiate God and make satisfactions for sins are opposed to the Gospel, as will be more amply declared hereafter concerning vows, the choice of food, and the like.

To Article XVI

The sixteenth article, concerning civil magistrates, is received with pleasure, as in harmony not only with civil law but also with canonical law, the Gospel, the Holy Scriptures, and the universal norm of faith, since the apostle enjoins that "every soul be subject unto the higher powers. For there is no power but of God: the powers that be are ordained of God. Whosoever, therefore, resisteth the power, resisteth the ordinance of God, and they that resist shall receive to themselves damnation" (Romans 13:1). And the princes are praised for condemning the Anabaptists, who overthrow all civil ordinances and prohibit Christians the use of the magistracy and other civil offices, without which no state is successfully administered.

To Article XVII

The confession of the seventeenth article is received, since from the Apostles' Creed and the Holy Scripture, the entire Catholic Church knows that Christ will come at the Last Day to judge the quick and the dead. Therefore, they justly condemn here the Anabaptists, who think there will be an end of punishments to condemned men and devils and imagine certain Jewish kingdoms of the godly before the resurrection of the dead, in this present world, the wicked being everywhere suppressed.

To Article XVIII

In the eighteenth article, they confess the power of the free will—viz., that it has the power to work a civil righteousness, but that it has not, without the Holy Ghost, the virtue to work the righteousness of God. This confession is received and approved. For it thus becomes Catholics to pursue the middle way, so as not, with the Pelagians, to ascribe too much to the free will, nor, with the godless Manichaeans, to deny it all liberty; for both are not without fault. Thus Augustine says, "With sure faith we believe, and without doubt we preach, that a free will exists in men. For it is an inhuman error to deny the free will in man, which everyone experiences in himself, and is so often asserted in the Holy Scriptures." St. Paul says, "Having power over his own will" (1 Corinthians 7:37). Of the righteous, the wise man says, "Who might offend, and hath not offended? or done evil, and hath not done it?" (Ecclesiastes 31:10). God said to Cain, "If thou doest well, shalt thou not be accepted? And if thou doest not well, sin lieth at the door. And unto thee shall be his desire, and thou shalt rule over him" (Genesis 4:7). Through the prophet Isaiah, He says, "If ye be willing and obedient, ye shall eat the good of the land. But if ye refuse and rebel, ye shall be devoured with the sword." This also Jeremiah has briefly expressed: "Behold, thou hast spoken and done evil, as thou couldest" (Jeremiah 3:5). We add also Ezekiel 18:31–32: "Cast away from you all your transgressions whereby ye have transgressed, and make ye a new heart and a new spirit; for why will ye die, O house of Israel? For I have no pleasure in the death of him that dieth, saith the Lord God; wherefore turn yourselves and live." Also St. Paul: "The spirits of the prophets are subject to the prophets" (1 Corinthians 14:32).

Likewise 2 Corinthians 9:7: "Every man according as he purposeth in his heart; not grudgingly or of necessity." Finally, Christ overthrew all the Manichaeans with one word when He said, "Ye have the poor with you always, and whensoever ye will ye may do them good" (Mark 14:7). To Jerusalem, Christ says, "How often would I have gathered thy children together, even as a hen gathered her chickens under her wings, and ye would not!" (Matthew 23:37).

To Article XIX

The nineteenth article is likewise approved and accepted. For God, the supremely good, is not the author of evils, but the rational and defectible will is the cause of sin; wherefore let no one impute his misdeeds and crimes to God, but to himself, according to Jeremiah 2:19: "Thine own wickedness shall correct thee and thy backslidings shall reprove thee;" and Hosea 13:9: "O Israel, thou hast destroyed thyself; but in Me is thy help." And David, in the spirit, acknowledged that God is not one that hath pleasure in wickedness (Psalm 5:4).

To Article XX

In the twentieth article, which does not contain so much the confession of the princes and cities as the defense of the preachers, there is only one thing that pertains to the princes and cities—viz., concerning good works, that they do not merit the remission of sins, which, as it has been rejected and disapproved before, is also rejected and disapproved now. For the passage in Daniel is very familiar: "Redeem thy sins with alms" (Daniel 4:27); and the address of Tobit to his son: "Alms do deliver from death and suffereth not to come into darkness" (Tobit 4:10); and that of Christ: "Give alms of such things as ye have, and behold all things are clean unto you" (Luke 11:41). If works were not meritorious, why would the wise man say, "God will render a reward of the labors of His saints" (The Wisdom of Solomon 10:17)? Why would St. Peter so earnestly exhort to doing good works, saying, "Wherefore the rather, brethren, give diligence by good works to make your calling and election sure" (2 Peter 1:19)? Why would St. Paul have said, "God is not unrighteous to forget your work and labor of love, which ye have showed toward His name" (Hebrews 6:10)? Nor by this do we reject Christ's merit, but we know that our works are nothing and of no merit unless by virtue of Christ's Passion. We know that Christ is "the way, the truth and the life" (John 14:6). But Christ, as the Good Shepherd, who "began to do and teach" (Acts 1:1), has given us an example that as He has done we also should do (John 13:15). He also went through the desert by the way of good works, which all Christians ought to pursue, and according to His command, bear the cross and follow Him (Matthew 10:38; 16:24). He who bears not the cross neither is nor can be Christ's disciple. It is also true what John says, "He that saith he abideth in Him ought himself also so to walk, even as He walked" (1 John 2:6). Moreover, this opinion concerning good works was condemned and rejected more than a thousand years ago in the time of Augustine.

To Article XXI

In the last place, they present the twenty-first article, wherein they admit that the memory of saints may be set before us, that we may follow their faith and good works, but not that they be invoked and aid be sought of them. It is certainly wonderful that the princes especially and the cities have allowed this error to be agitated in their dominions, which has been condemned so often before in the Church, since eleven hundred years ago, St. Jerome vanquished in this area the heretic Vigilantius. Long after him arose the Albigenses, the Poor Men of Lyons, the Picards, the Cathari old and new—all of whom were condemned legitimately long ago. Wherefore this article of the Confession, so frequently condemned, must be utterly rejected, and in harmony with the entire universal Church, be condemned; for in favor of the invocation of saints, we have not only the authority of the Church universal but also the agreement of the Holy Fathers Augustine, Bernard, Jerome, Cyprian, Chrysostom, Basil, and this class of other Church teachers. Neither is the authority of Holy Scripture absent from this Catholic assertion, for Christ taught that the saints should be honored: "If any man serve Me, him will My Father honor" (John 12:26). If, therefore, God honors saints, why do not we, insignificant men, honor them? Besides, the Lord was turned to repentance by Job when he prayed for his friends (Job 42:8). Why, therefore, would not God, the most pious, who gave assent to Job, do the same to the blessed Virgin when she intercedes? We read also in Baruch 3:4, "O Lord Almighty, Thou God of Israel, hear now the prayers of the dead Israelites." Therefore, the dead also pray for us. Thus did Onias and Jeremiah in the Old Testament. For Onias the high priest was seen by Judas Maccabaeus holding up his hands and praying for the whole body of the Jews. Afterward, another man appeared, remarkable both for his age and majesty, and of great beauty about him, concerning whom Onias replied, "This is a love of the brethren and of the people Israel, who prayeth much for the people and for the Holy City—to wit, Jeremiah the prophet" (2 Maccabees 15:12–14). Besides, we know from the Holy Scriptures that the angels pray for us. Why, then, would we deny this of the saints? "'O Lord of hosts,' said the angels, 'how long wilt Thou not have mercy on Jerusalem and on the cities of Judah, against which Thou hast had indignation?' And the Lord answered the angel that talked with me comfortable words" (Zechariah 1:12–13).

Job likewise testifies, "If there be an angel with him speaking, one among a thousand, to show unto man His uprightness, He will pity him and say, 'Deliver him from going down to the pit'" (Job 33:23–24). This is clear besides from the words of that holy soul John the evangelist, when he says, "The four beasts and the four and twenty elders fell down before the Lamb, having each one of them harps and golden vials, full of odors that are the prayers of saints" (Revelation 5:8); and afterward, "An angel stood at the altar, having a golden censer, and there was given unto him much incense, that he should offer it with the prayers of all saints upon the golden altar that was before the throne. And the smoke of the incense, which came up with the prayers of the saints, ascended up before God out of the angel's hand." Lastly, St. Cyprian the martyr, more than twelve hundred and fifty years ago, wrote to Pope Cornelius (Book I, Letter 1), asking that "if any depart first, his prayer for our brethren and sisters may not cease." For if this holy man had not ascertained that after this life the saints pray for the living, he would have given exhortation to no purpose. Neither is their Confession strengthened by the fact that there is one Mediator between God and men (1 Timothy 2:5; 1 John 2:1). For although His Imperial Majesty, with the entire Church, confesses that there is one Mediator of redemption, nevertheless the mediators of intercession are many. Thus Moses was both mediator and agent between God and men (Deuteronomy 5:31), for he prayed for the children of Israel (Exodus 17:11; 32:11–12). Thus, St. Paul prayed for those with whom he was sailing (Acts 27); so, too, he asked that he be prayed for by the Romans (Romans 15:30), by the Corinthians (2 Corinthians 1:11), and by the Colossians (Colossians 4:3). So while Peter was kept in prison, prayer was made without ceasing of the Church unto God for him (Acts 12:5). Christ, therefore, is our chief Advocate, and indeed the greatest; but since the saints are members of Christ (1 Corinthians 12:27; Ephesians 5:30), and conform their will to that of Christ, and see that their Head, Christ, prays for us, who can doubt that the saints do the very same thing they see Christ doing? With all these things carefully considered, we must ask the princes and the cities adhering to them that they reject this part of the Confession and agree with the holy universal and orthodox Church and believe and confess concerning the worship and intercession of saints what the entire Christian world believes and confesses—and what was observed in all the churches in the time of Augustine: "A Christian people," he says, "celebrates the memories of martyrs with religious observance, that it share in their merits and be aided by their prayers."

PART II
REPLY TO THE SECOND PART OF THE CONFESSION

To Article XXII

Of Lay Communion under One Form

As in the confessions of the princes and cities, they enumerate among the abuses that laymen commune only under one form, and as, therefore, in their dominions both forms are administered to laymen, we must reply, according to the custom of the Holy Church, that this is incorrectly enumerated among the abuses, but that, according to the sanctions and statutes of the same Church, it is rather an abuse and disobedience to administer to laymen both forms. For under the one form of bread the saints communed in the primitive Church, of whom Luke says, "They continued steadfastly in the apostles' doctrine and fellowship, and in breaking of bread" (Acts 2:42). Here, Luke mentions bread alone. Likewise, (Acts 20:7) says, "Upon the first day of the week, when the disciples came together to break bread." Yea, Christ, the institutor of this most holy Sacrament, rising again from the dead, administered the Eucharist only under one form to the disciples going to Emmaus, where He took bread and blessed it, and brake and gave to them, and they recognized Him in the breaking of bread (Luke 24:30–31), where indeed Augustine, Chrysostom, Theophylact, and Bede, some of whom many ages ago and not long after the times of the apostles, affirm that it was the Eucharist. Christ also (John 6) very frequently mentions bread alone. St. Ignatius, a disciple of St. John the evangelist, in his Epistle to the Ephesians, mentions the bread alone in the communion of the Eucharist. Ambrose does likewise in his books concerning the sacraments, speaking of the Communion of laymen. In the Council of Rheims, laymen were forbidden from bearing the Sacrament of the body to the sick, and no mention is there made of the form of wine. Hence, it is understood that the viaticum was given the sick under only one form. The ancient penitential canons approve of this. For the Council of Agde put a guilty priest into a monastery and granted him only lay Communion. In the Council of Sardica, Hosius prohibits certain indiscreet persons from receiving even lay Communion unless they finally repent.

There has always been a distinction in the Church between lay Communion under one form and priestly Communion under both forms. This was beautifully predicted in the Old Testament concerning the descendants of Eli: "'It shall come to pass,' says God" (1 Kings 2; 1 Samuel 2:36) "'that everyone who is left in thine house shall come and crouch to him for a piece of silver and a morsel of bread, and shall say, "Put me, I pray thee, into one of the priests' office (Vulgate reads, "Ad unam partem sacerdotalem."), Oh that I may eat a piece of bread."'" Here, Holy Scripture clearly shows that the posterity of Eli, when removed from the office of the priesthood, will seek to be admitted to one sacerdotal part, to a piece of bread. So our laymen also ought, therefore, to be content with one sacerdotal part, the one form. For both the Roman pontiffs and cardinals, and all bishops and priests, save in the Mass and in the extreme hour of life for a viaticum, as it is called in the Council of Nicaea, are content with taking one form, which they would not do if they thought that both forms would be necessary for salvation. Although, however, both forms were of old administered in many churches to laymen (for then it was free to commune under one or under both forms), yet on account of many dangers, the custom of administering both forms has ceased. For when the multitude of the people is considered—where there are old and young, tremulous and weak and inept—if great care be not employed, injury is done the Sacrament by the spilling of the liquid. Because of the great multitude, there would be difficulty also in giving the chalice cautiously (for the form of wine, which also, when kept for a long time, would sour and cause nausea or vomition to those who would receive it); neither could it be readily taken to the sick without danger of spilling.

For these reasons and others, the churches in which the custom had been to give both forms to laymen were induced, undoubtedly by impulse of the Holy Ghost, to give thereafter but one form, from the consideration chiefly that the entire Christ is under each form, and is received no less under one form than under two. In the Council of Constance, of such honorable renown, a decree to this effect appeared, and so, too, the Synod of Basel legitimately decreed. And although it was formerly a matter of freedom to use either one or both forms in the Eucharist, nevertheless, when the heresy arose that taught that both forms were necessary, the Holy Church, which is directed by the Holy Ghost, forbade both forms to laymen. For thus the Church is sometimes wont to extinguish heresies by contrary institutions; as when some arose who maintained that the Eucharist is properly celebrated only when unleavened bread is used, the Church for a while commanded that it be administered with leavened bread; and when Nestorius wished to establish that the perpetual Virgin Mary was mother only of Christ, not of God, the Church for a time forbade her to be called Christotokos, mother of Christ. Wherefore we must entreat the princes and cities not to permit this schism to be introduced into Germany or the Roman Empire, or themselves to be separated from the custom of the Church universal. Neither do the arguments adduced in this article avail, for while Christ indeed instituted both forms of the Sacrament, yet it is nowhere found in the Gospel that He enjoined that both forms be received by the laity. For what is said in Matthew 26:27, "Drink ye all of it," was said to the twelve apostles, who were priests, as is manifest from Mark 14:23, where it is said, "And they all drank of it." This certainly was not fulfilled hitherto with respect to laymen; whence the custom never existed throughout the entire Church that both forms were given to laymen, although it existed perhaps among the Corinthians and Carthaginians and some other churches.

As to their reference to Gelasius, Canon *Comperimus* ("of Consecration," district 2), if they examine the document, they will find that Gelasius speaks of priests and not of laymen. Hence, their declaration that the custom of administering but one form is contrary to divine law must be rejected. But most of all, the appendix to the article must be rejected, that the procession with the Eucharist must be neglected or omitted, because the Sacrament is thus divided. For they themselves know, or at least ought to know, that by the Christian faith, Christ has not been divided but that the entire Christ is under both forms and that the Gospel nowhere forbids the division of the sacramental forms as is done on Parasceve (Holy or Maundy Thursday) by the entire Church of the Catholics, although the consecration is made by the celebrant in both forms, who also ought to receive both. Therefore, the princes and cities should be admonished to pay customary reverence and due honor to Christ the Son of the living God, our Savior and Glorifier, the Lord of heaven and earth, since they believe and acknowledge that He is truly present—a matter which they know has been most religiously observed by their ancestors, most Christian princes.

To Article XXIII

II. Of the Marriage of Priests

Their enumeration among abuses, in the second place, of the celibacy of the clergy and the manner in which their priests marry and persuade others to marry, are verily matters worthy of astonishment, since they call sacerdotal celibacy an abuse when that which is directly contrary, the violation of celibacy and the illicit transition to marriage, deserves to be called the worst abuse in priests. For that priests ought never to marry, Aurelius testifies in the second Council of Carthage, where he says, "Because the apostles taught thus by example, and antiquity itself has preserved it, let us also maintain it." And a little before, a canon to this effect is read, "Resolved, that the bishops, presbyters, and deacons, or those who administer the sacraments, abstain, as guardians of chastity, from wives." From these words, it is clear that this tradition has been received from the apostles and not recently devised by the Church. Augustine, following Aurelius in the last question concerning the Old and New Testaments, writes upon these words and asks, "If perhaps it be said, if it is lawful and good to marry, why are not priests permitted to have wives?" Pope Caliztus, a holy man and a martyr, decided thirteen hundred years ago that priests should not marry. The like is read also in the holy councils of Caesarea, Neocaesarea, Africa, Agde, Gironne, Meaux, and Orléans. Thus, the custom has been observed from the time of the Gospel and the apostles that one who has been put into the office of priests has never been permitted, according to law, to marry.

It is indeed true that, on account of lack of ministers of God in the primitive Church, married men were admitted to the priesthood, as is clear from the Apostolic Canons and the reply of Paphnutius in the Council of Nicaea; nevertheless, those who wished to contract marriage were compelled to do so before receiving the subdiaconate, as we read in the Canon *Si quis corum*, Distinct. 32. This custom of the primitive Church, the Greek Church, has preserved and retained to this day. But when, by the grace of God, the Church has increased so that there was no lack of ministers in the

Church, Pope Siricius, eleven hundred and forty years ago, undoubtedly not without the Holy Ghost, enjoined absolute continence upon the priests, Canon *Plurimus*, Distinct. 82—an injunction that Popes Innocent I, Leo the Great, and Gregory the Great approved and ratified, and that the Latin Church has everywhere observed to this day. From these facts, it is regarded sufficiently clear that the celibacy of the clergy is not an abuse and that it was approved by Fathers so holy at such a remote time and was received by the entire Latin Church. Besides, the priests of the old law, as in the case of Zacharias, were separated from their wives at times when they discharged their office and ministered in the temple. But since the priest of the new law ought always to be engaged in the ministry, it follows that he ought always to be continent. Furthermore, married persons should not defraud one the other of conjugal duties except for a time that they may give themselves to prayer (1 Corinthians 7:5). But since a priest ought always to pray, he ought always to be continent. Besides, St. Paul says, "But I would have you without carefulness. He that is unmarried careth for the things that belong to the Lord, that he may please the Lord. But he that is married careth for the things that are of the world, how he may please His wife" (1 Corinthians 7:32–33).

Therefore, let the priest who should please God continually flee from anxiety for a wife, and not look back with Lot's wife (Genesis 19:26). Moreover, sacerdotal continence was foreshadowed also in the Old Testament, for Moses commanded those who were to receive the law not to approach their wives until the third day (Exodus 19:15). Much less, therefore, should the priests, who are about to receive Christ as our Legislator, Lord, and Savior, approach wives. Priests were commanded likewise to wear linen thigh bandages, to cover the shame of the flesh (Exodus 28:42); which, says Beda, was a symbol of future continence among priests. Also, when Ahimelech was about to give the blessed bread to the servants of David, he asked first if they had kept themselves from women, and David replied that they had for three days (1 Samuel 21:4–5). Therefore, they who take the living bread that came down from heaven (John 6:32–33), should always be pure with respect to them. They who ate the Passover had their loins girded (Exodus 12:11). Wherefore the priests, who frequently eat Christ our Passover, ought to gird their loins by continence and cleanliness, as the Lord commands them, "Be ye clean," He says, "that bear the vessels of the Lord" (Isaiah 52:11). "Ye shall be holy, for I am holy" (Leviticus 19:2). Therefore, let priests serve God "in holiness and righteousness all their days" (Luke 1:75). Hence, the holy martyr Cyprian testifies that it was revealed to him by the Lord, and he was most solemnly enjoined, to earnestly admonish the clergy not to occupy a domicile in common with women. Hence, since sacerdotal continence has been commanded by the pontiffs and revealed by God and promised to God by the priest in a special vow, it must not be rejected. For this is required by the excellency of the sacrifice they offer, the frequency of prayer, and liberty and purity of spirit, that they care how to please God, according to the teaching of St. Paul. And because this is manifestly the ancient heresy of Jovinian, which the Roman Church condemned and Jerome refuted in his writings and St. Augustine said that this heresy was immediately extinguished and did not attain to the corruption and abuse of priests, the princes ought not to tolerate it to the perpetual shame and disgrace of the Roman Empire, but should rather conform themselves to the Church universal, and not be influenced by those things that are suggested to them. For as to what Paul says (1 Corinthians 7:2) "To avoid fornication, let every man have his own wife," Jerome replies that St. Paul is speaking of one who has not made a vow. As Athanasius and Vulgarius understand the declaration of St. Paul, "If a virgin marry, she hath not sinned" (1 Corinthians 7:28), that here a virgin is meant who has not been consecrated to God. So, in reference to "It is better to marry than to burn" (1 Corinthians 7:9), the pointed reply of Jerome against Jovinian is extant. For the same St. Paul says (1 Corinthians 7:1), "It is good for a man not to touch a woman." For a priest has the intermediate position of neither marrying nor burning, but of restraining himself by the grace of God, which he obtains of God by devout prayer and chastising of the flesh, by fasting and vigils. Furthermore, when they say that Christ taught that all men are not fit for celibacy, it is indeed true, and on this account, not all are fit for the priesthood; but let the priest pray, and he will be able to receive Christ's word concerning continence, as St. Paul says, "I can do all things through Christ which strengtheneth me" (Philippians 4:13). For continence is a gift of God, (The Wisdom of Solomon 8:21). Besides, when they allege that this is God's ordinance and command (Genesis 1:28), Jerome replied concerning these words a thousand years ago: "It was necessary first to plant the forest, and that it grow, in order that that might be which could afterward be cut down." Then the command was given concerning the procreation of offspring, that the earth should be replenished, but since it has been replenished so that there is a pressure of nations, the commandment does not pertain in like manner upon those able to be continent.

In vain, too, do they boast of God's express order. Let them show, if they can, where God has enjoined priests to marry. Besides, we find in the divine law that vows once offered should be paid (Psalm 49; 75; Ecclesiastes 5; Psalm 50:14; 76:11; Ecclesiastes 5:4). Why, therefore, do they not observe this express divine law? They also pervert St. Paul, as though he teaches that one who is to be chosen bishop should be married when he says, "Let a bishop be the husband of one wife" which is not to be understood as though he ought to be married, for then Martin, Nicolaus, Titus, John the evangelist, and yea, even Christ, would not have been bishops. Hence, Jerome explains the words of St. Paul, "that a bishop be the husband of one wife," as meaning that he be not a bigamist. The truth of this exposition is clear not only from the authority of Jerome, which ought to be great with every Catholic, but also from St. Paul, who writes concerning the selection of widows, "Let not a widow be taken into the number under three score years, having been the wife of one man" (1 Timothy 5:9). Lastly, the citation of what was done among the Germans is the statement of a fact, but not of a law, for while there was a contention between Emperor Henry IV and the Roman pontiff, and also between his son and the nobles of the empire, both divine and human laws were equally confused, so that at the time the laity rashly attempted to administer sacred things, to use filth instead of holy oil, to baptize, and to do much else foreign to the Christian religion. The clergy likewise went beyond their sphere—a precedent that cannot be cited as law. Neither was it regarded unjust to dissolve sacrilegious marriages that had been contracted to no effect in opposition to vows and the sanction of Fathers and councils; as even today the marriages of priests with their so-called wives are not valid.

In vain, therefore, do they complain that the world is growing old, and that, as a remedy for infirmity, rigor should be relaxed, for those who are consecrated to God have other remedies of infirmities; as, for instance, let them avoid the society of women, shun idleness, macerate the flesh by fasting and vigils, keep the outward senses, especially sight and hearing, from things forbidden, turn away their eyes from beholding vanity, and finally dash their little ones—in other words, their carnal thoughts—upon a rock (and Christ is the rock), suppress their passions, and frequently and devoutly resort to God in prayer. These are undoubtedly the most effectual remedies for incontinence in ecclesiastics and servants of God. St. Paul said aright that the doctrine of those who forbid marriage is a doctrine of demons. Such was the doctrine of Tatian and Marcion, whom Augustine and Jerome have mentioned. But the Church does not thus forbid marriage, as she even enumerates marriage among the seven sacraments; with which, however, it is consistent that on account of their superior ministry, she should enjoin upon ecclesiastics' superior purity. For it is false that there is an express charge concerning contracting marriage, for then John the evangelist, St. James, Laurentius, Titus, Martin, Catharine, Barbara, and so on, would have sinned. Nor is Cyprian influenced by these considerations to speak of a virgin who had made a solemn vow, but of one who had determined to live continently, as the beginning of Letter XI, Book I sufficiently shows. For the judgment of St. Augustine is very explicit: "It is damnable for virgins who make a vow not only to marry but even to wish to marry." Hence, the abuse of marriage and the breaking of vows in the clergy are not to be tolerated.

To Article XXIV

III. Of the Mass

Whatever in this article is stated concerning the most holy office of the Mass that agrees with the Holy Roman and Apostolic Church is approved, but whatever is added that is contrary to the observance of the general and universal orthodox Church is rejected, because it grievously offends God, injures Christian unity, and occasions dissensions, tumults, and seditions in the Holy Roman Empire. Now, as to these things that they state in the article: first, it is displeasing that, in opposition to the usage of the entire Roman Church, they perform ecclesiastical rites not in the Roman but in the German language, and this they pretend that they do upon the authority of St. Paul, who taught that, in the Church, a language should be used that is understood by the people (1 Corinthians 14:19). But if this were the meaning of the words of St.

Paul, it would compel them to perform the entire Mass in German, which even they do not do. But since the priest is a person belonging to the entire Church, and not only to his surroundings, it is not wonderful that the priest celebrates the Mass in the Latin language in a Latin church. It is profitable to the hearer, however, if he hear the Mass in faith of the Church; and experience teaches that, among the Germans, there has been greater devotion at Mass in Christ's believers who do not understand the Latin language than in those who today hear the Mass in German. And if the words of the apostle be pondered, it is sufficient that the one replying occupy the place of the unlearned to say amen, the very thing that the canons prescribe. Neither is it necessary that he hear or understand all the words of the Mass, and even attend to it intelligently; for it is better to understand and to attend to its end, because the Mass is celebrated in order that the Eucharist may be offered in memory of Christ's Passion.

And it is an argument in favor of this that, according to the general opinion of the Fathers, the apostles and their successors until the times of the Emperor Hadrian celebrated the Mass in the Hebrew language alone, which was indeed unknown to the Christians, especially the converted heathen. But even if the Mass had been celebrated in the primitive Church in a tongue understood by the people, nevertheless this would not be necessary now, for many were daily converted who were ignorant of the ceremonies and unacquainted with the mysteries; and hence, it was of advantage for them to understand the words of the office; but now Catholics imbibe from their cradles the manners and customs of the Church, whence they readily know what should be done at every time in the Church. Moreover, as to their complaints concerning the abuse of masses, there is none of those who think aright but does not earnestly desire that the abuses be corrected. But that they who wait at the altar live of the altar is not an abuse but pertains equally to both divine and human law. "Who goeth a warfare any time at his own charge?" says Paul. "Do ye not know that they who minister about holy things live of the things of the temple? and they who wait at the altar are partakers with the altar?" (1 Corinthians 9:7, 13). Christ says, "The laborer is worthy of his hire" (Luke 10:7). But worthy of censure, above all things, is the discontinuance of the private Mass in certain places, as though those having fixed and prescribed returns are sought no less than the public masses on account of gain. But by this abrogation of masses the worship of God is diminished, honor is withdrawn from the saints, the ultimate will of the founder is overthrown and defeated, the dead deprived of the rights due them, and the devotion of the living withdrawn and chilled. Therefore, the abrogation of private masses cannot be conceded and tolerated. Neither can their assumption be sufficiently understood that Christ, by His Passion, has made satisfaction for original sin and has instituted the Mass for actual sin; for this has never been heard by Catholics, and very many who are now asked most constantly deny that they have so taught. For the Mass does not abolish sins, which are destroyed by repentance as their peculiar medicine, but abolishes the punishment due sin, supplies satisfactions, and confers increase of grace and salutary protection of the living, and, lastly, brings the hope of divine consolation and aid to all our wants and necessities.

Again, their insinuations that, in the Mass, Christ is not offered must be altogether rejected, as condemned of old and excluded by the faithful. For Augustine says this was a very ancient heresy of the Arians, who denied that in the Mass an oblation was made for the living and the dead. For this is opposed both to the Holy Scriptures and the entire Church. For through Malachi, the Lord predicted the rejection of the Jews, the call of the Gentiles, and the sacrifice of the evangelical law: "'I have no pleasure in you,' He saith, 'neither will I accept an offering at your hand. For from the rising of the sun, even unto the going down of the same, My name shall be great among the Gentiles, and in every place, incense shall be offered unto My name and a pure offering'" (Malachi 1:10–11). But no pure offering has already been offered to God in every place, except in the sacrifice of the altar of the most pure Eucharist. This authority St. Augustine and other Catholics have used in favor of the Mass against faithless Jews, and certainly with Catholic princes it should have greater influence than all objections of the adversaries. Besides, in speaking of the advent of the Messiah the same prophet says, "And He shall purify the sons of Levi, and purge them as gold and silver, that they may offer unto the Lord an offering in righteousness. Then shall the offering of Judah and Jerusalem be pleasant unto the Lord, as in the days of old and as in former years" (Malachi 3:3–4). Here, in the spirit, the prophet foresaw the sons of Levi—in other words, evangelical priests, says Jerome—about to offer sacrifices, not in the blood of goats but in righteousness, as in the days of old. Hence, these words are repeated by the Church in the Canon of the Mass under the influence of the same Spirit under whose influence they were written by the prophet. The angel also said to Daniel, "Many shall be purified and made white and tried; but the wicked shall do wickedly, and none of the wicked shall understand." And again, "The wise shall understand; and from the time that the daily sacrifices shall be taken away and the abomination that maketh desolate set up, there shall be a thousand two hundred and ninety days" (Daniel 12:10–11). Christ testifies that this prophecy is to be fulfilled but that it has not been as yet fulfilled (Matthew 24:15). Therefore, the daily sacrifice of Christ will cease universally at the advent of the abomination (i.e., of Antichrist) just as it has already ceased, particularly in some churches, and thus will be unemployed in the place of desolation—viz., when the churches will be desolated, in which the canonical hours will not be chanted or the masses celebrated or the sacraments administered, and there will be no altars, no images of saints, no candles, no furniture. Therefore, all princes and faithful subjects of the Roman Empire ought to be encouraged never to admit or pass over anything that may aid the preparers of Antichrist in attaining such a degree of wickedness, when the woman (i.e., the Catholic Church) as St. John saw in the Spirit, will flee into the wilderness, where she will have a place prepared of God, that she may be nourished there twelve hundred and sixty days (Revelation 12:6). Finally, St. Paul says in Hebrews 5:1, "Every high priest taken from among men is ordained for men in things pertaining to God, that he may offer both gifts and sacrifices for sins." But since the external priesthood has not ceased in the new law, but has been changed to a better, therefore, even today, the high priest and the entire priesthood offer in the Church an external sacrifice, which is only one, the Eucharist.

To this topic, that also is applicable which is read, according to the new translation, in Acts 13:1–2: Barnabas, Simeon, Lucius of Cyrene, Manaen, and Saul sacrificed—in other words, they offered an oblation, which can and ought justly to be understood not of an oblation made to idols but of the Mass, since it is called by the Greeks *liturgy*. And that in the primitive Church, the Mass was a sacrifice the Holy Fathers copiously testify, and they support this opinion. For Ignatius, a pupil of St. John the apostle, says, "It is not allowable without a bishop either to offer a sacrifice or to celebrate masses." And Irenaeus, a pupil of John, clearly testifies that "Christ taught the new oblation of the New Testament, which the Church, receiving from the apostles, offers to God throughout the entire world." This bishop, bordering upon the times of the apostles, testifies that the new evangelical sacrifice was offered throughout the entire world. Origen, Cyprian, Jerome, Chrysostom, Augustine, Basil, Hilary, and so on, teach and testify the same, whose words, for brevity's sake, are omitted. Since, therefore, the Catholic Church throughout the entire Christian world has always taught, held, and observed as it today holds and observes, the same ought today to be held and observed inviolably. Nor does St. Paul in Hebrews oppose the oblation of the Mass when he says that by one offering we have once been justified through Christ. For St. Paul is speaking of the offering of a victim (i.e., of a bloody sacrifice, of a lamb slain, viz., upon the cross) which offering was indeed once made whereby all sacraments, and even the sacrifice of the Mass, have their efficacy. Therefore, He was offered but once with the shedding of blood—viz., upon the cross; today He is offered in the Mass as a peace-making and sacramental victim. Then, He was offered in a visible form capable of suffering; today, He is offered in the Mass veiled in mysteries, incapable of suffering, just as in the Old Testament He was sacrificed typically and under a figure. Finally, the force of the word shows that the Mass is a sacrifice, since *mass* is nothing but *oblation*, and has received its name from the Hebrew word *misbeach*, "altar"—in Greek, *thysiasterion*—on account of the oblation. It has been sufficiently declared above that we are justified not properly by faith, but by love. But if any such statement be found in the Holy Scriptures, Catholics know that it is declared concerning *fides formata*, which works by love (Galatians 5), and because justification is begun by faith, because it is the substance of things hoped for (Hebrews 11:1). Neither is it denied that the Mass is a memorial of Christ's Passion and God's benefits, since this is approved by the figure of the Paschal Lamb, which was at the same time a victim and a memorial (Exodus 12:13–14), and is represented not only by the Word and Sacraments, but also by holy postures and vestments in the Catholic Church; but to the memory of the victim, the Church offers anew the Eucharist in the mysteries to God the Father Almighty. Therefore, the princes and cities are not censured for retaining one common Mass in the Church, provided they do this according to the sacred canon, as observed by all Catholics. But in abrogating all other masses, they have done what the Christian profession does not allow. Nor does anyone censure the declaration that, of old, all who were present communed. Would that all were so disposed as to be prepared to partake of this bread worthily every day! But if they regard one Mass advantageous, how much more advantageous would be a number of masses, of which they nevertheless have unjustly disapproved. When all these things are properly considered, we must ask them to altogether annul and repudiate this new form of celebrating the Mass that has been devised and has been already so frequently changed and to resume the primitive form for celebrating it according to the ancient rite and custom of the churches of Germany and all Christendom—and to restore the abrogated masses according to the ultimate will of their founders, whereby they would gain advantage and honor for themselves and peace and tranquility for all Germany.

To Article XXV

IV. Of Confession

As to Confession, we must adhere to the reply and judgment given above in Article XI. For the support they claim from Chrysostom is false, since they pervert to sacramental and sacerdotal Confession what he says concerning public Confession, as his words clearly indicate when in the beginning he says, "I do not tell thee to disclose thyself to the public or to accuse thyself before others." Thus Gratian and Peter Lombard replied three hundred years ago. And the explanation becomes still more manifest from other passages of Chrysostom. For in his twenty-ninth sermon, he says of the penitent, "In his heart is contrition; in his mouth, confession; in his entire work, humility. This is perfect and fruitful repentance." Does not this most exactly display the three parts of repentance? So, in his tenth homily on Matthew, Chrysostom teaches of a fixed time for Confession, and that after the wounds of crimes have been opened, they should be healed, penance intervening. But how will crimes lie open if they are not disclosed to the priest by Confession? Thus, in several passages, Chrysostom himself refutes this opinion, which Jerome also overthrows, saying, "If the serpent, the devil, have secretly bitten anyone, and without the knowledge of another have infected him with the poison of sin, if he who has been struck be silent and do not repent, and be unwilling to confess his wound to his brother and instructor, the instructor, who has a tongue wherewith to cure him, will not readily be able to profit him. For if the sick man be ashamed to confess to the physician, the medicine is not adapted to that of which he is ignorant." Let the princes and cities, therefore, believe these authors rather than a single gloss upon a decree questioned and rejected by those who are skilled in divine law. Wherefore, since a full confession is, not to say, necessary for salvation, but becomes the nerve of Christian discipline and the entire obedience, they must be admonished to conform to the orthodox Church. For, according to the testimony of Jerome, this was the heresy of the Montanists, who were condemned over twelve hundred years ago because they were ashamed to confess their sins. It is not becoming, therefore, to adopt the error of the wicked Montanus, but rather the rite of the Holy Fathers and the entire Church—viz., that each one teach, according to the norm of the orthodox faith, that Confession, the chief treasure in the Church, be made in conformity to the rite kept among them also in the Church.

To Article XXVI

V. Of the Distinction of Meats

What they afterward assert concerning the distinction of meats and like traditions, of which they seem to make no account, must be rejected. For we know from the apostle that all power is of God, and especially that ecclesiastical power has been given by God for edification. For this reason, from the Christian and devout heart of the Holy Church, the constitutions of the same Holy, Catholic and Apostolic Church should be received as are useful to the Church, as well for promoting divine worship as for restraining the lust of the flesh while they enable us the more readily to keep the divine commands, and when well considered are found in the Holy Scriptures. And he who despises or rashly resists them grievously offends God, according to Christ's word: "He that heareth you, heareth Me; and he that despiseth you, despiseth Me; and he that despiseth Me, despiseth Him that sent Me" (Luke 10:16). A prelate, however, is despised when his statutes are despised, according to St. Paul, not only when he says, "He that despiseth, despiseth not man, but God, who hath also given unto us His Holy Spirit" (1 Thessalonians 4:8) but also to the bishops: "Take heed, therefore, unto yourselves and to all the flock over which the Holy Ghost hath made you overseers, to rule (Vulgate) the Church of God" (Acts 20:28). If prelates, therefore, have the power to rule, they will have the power also to make statutes for the salutary government of the Church and the growth of subjects. For the same apostle enjoined upon the Corinthians that among them, all things should be done in order (1 Corinthians 14:40); but this cannot be done without laws. On that account, he said to the Hebrews, "Obey them that have the rule over you, and submit yourselves; for they watch for your souls, as they that must give an account" (Hebrews 13:17). Here, St. Paul reckons not only obedience but also the reason for obedience. We see that St. Paul exercised this power, as, in addition to the Gospel, he prescribed so many laws concerning the choice of a bishop, concerning widows, concerning women—that they have their heads veiled, that they be silent in the church—concerning even secular matters (1 Thessalonians 4:1, 2, 6) and concerning civil courts (1 Corinthians 6:1–11). And he says to the Corinthians very clearly, "But to the rest speak I, not the Lord" (1 Corinthians 7:12). And again he says elsewhere, "Stand fast and hold the traditions which ye have been taught, whether by word or our epistle" (2 Thessalonians 2:15).

Wherefore, the princes and cities must be admonished to render obedience to ecclesiastical statutes and constitutions, lest when they withdraw obedience that is due God, obedience may be withdrawn also from them by their subjects, as their subjects attempted in the recent civil insurrection not to allow themselves to be seduced by false doctrines. Most false, also, is their declaration that the righteousness of faith is obscured by such ordinances; nay, he is rather mad and insane who would observe them without faith. For they are given to believers, and not to Turks or Ishmaelites. "For what have I to do to judge them that are without?" (1 Corinthians 5:12). Moreover, in extolling here faith above all things, they antagonize St. Paul, as we have said above, and do violence to St. Paul, whom they pervert to evangelical works when he speaks of legal works, as all these errors have been above refuted. False, also, is it that ecclesiastical ordinances obscure God's commands, since they prepare man for these, as fasts suppress the lust of the flesh and help him from falling into luxury. False, also, is it that it is impossible to observe ordinances, for the Church is not a cruel mother who makes no exceptions in the celebration of festivals and in fasting and the like.

Furthermore, they falsely quote Augustine in reply to the inquiries of Januarius, who is diametrically opposed to them. For in this place, he most clearly states that what has been universally delivered by the Church be also universally observed. But in indifferent things, and those whose observance and nonobservance are free, the Holy Father Augustine states that, according to the authority of St. Ambrose, the custom of each church should be observed. "When I come back to Rome," he says, "I fast on the Sabbath; but when here, I do not fast." Besides, they do violence to the Scriptures while they endeavor to support their errors. For Christ (Matthew 15) does not absolutely disapprove of human ordinances, but of those only that were opposed to the law of God, as is clearly acknowledged in Mark 7:8–9. Here also, Matthew 15:3 says, "Why do ye also transgress the commandment of God by your tradition?" So Paul (Colossians 2) forbids that anyone be judged in meat or in drink, or in respect to the Sabbath, after the Jewish manner; for when the Church forbids meats, it does not judge them to be unclean, as the Jews in the synagogue thought. So the declaration of Christ concerning what goes into the mouth (Matthew 15:11) is cited here without a sure and true understanding of it, since its intention was to remove the error of the Jews, who thought that food touched by unwashed hands becomes unclean and rendered one eating it unclean, as is manifest from the context. Nor does the Church bring back to these observances Moses with his heavy hands.

In like manner, they do violence to St. Paul, for in 1 Timothy 4:1–4, he calls that a doctrine of demons that forbids meats, as the Tatianites, Marcionites, and Manichaeans thought that meats were unclean, as is clear from the words that follow, when St. Paul adds, "Every creature of God is good." But the Church does not forbid meats on the ground that they are evil or unclean, but as an easier way to keep God's commandments; therefore, the opposite arguments fail. If they would preach the cross and bodily discipline and fasts, that in this way the body be reduced to subjection, their doctrine would be commendable; but their desire that these be free is condemned and rejected as alien to the faith and discipline of the Church. Nor does the diversity of rites support them, for this is properly allowed in regard to particular matters, in order that each individual province may have its own taste satisfied, as Jerome says. But individual ecclesiastical rites should be universally observed, and special rites should be observed each in their own province. Also, they make no mention of Easter, for the Roman pontiffs reduced the Asiatics to a uniform observance of Easter with the universal Church. In this way Irenaeus must be understood, for without the loss of faith, some vigils of the apostles were not celebrated with fasting throughout Gaul, which Germany nevertheless observes in fasts. The princes and cities must also be admonished to follow the decision of Pope Gregory, for he enjoins that the custom of each province be observed if it employs nothing contrary to the Catholic faith (Canon *Quoniam*, Distinct. 12). Hence, we are not ignorant that there is a various observance of dissimilar rites in unity of faith, which should be observed in every province as it has been delivered and received from the ancients, without injury, however, to the universal rites of the entire Catholic Church.

To Article XXVII

VI. Of Monastic Vows

Although many and various matters have been introduced in this article by the suggestion of certain persons (another text, *Codice Pflugiano*, reads "preachers"), nevertheless, when all are taken into consideration with mature thought—since monastic vows have their foundation in the Holy Scriptures of the Old and New Testaments, and most holy men, renowned and admirable by miracles, have lived in these religious orders with many thousand thousands, and for so many centuries, their ordinances and rules of living have been received and approved throughout the entire Christian world by the Catholic Church—it is in no way to be tolerated that vows are licentiously broken without any fear of God. For, in the Old Testament, God approved the vows of the Nazirites (Numbers 6:2–21), and the vows of the Rechabites, who neither drank wine or ate grapes (Jeremiah 36:6, 19); while He strictly requires that the vow once made be paid (Deuteronomy 23:21–23). "It is ruin to a man after vows to retract" (Proverbs 20:25). "The vows of the just are acceptable" (Proverbs 15:8). God also teaches specifically through the prophet that monastic vows please Him. For in Isaiah 56:4–5, it is read as follows: "Thus saith the Lord, 'Unto the eunuchs that keep My Sabbath and choose the things that please Me and take hold of My covenant, even unto them will I give in Mine house and within My walls a place and a name better than that of sons and of daughters. I will give them an everlasting name that shall not be cut off.'" But to what eunuchs does God make these promises? To those, undoubtedly, whom Christ praises, "which have made themselves eunuchs for the kingdom of heaven's sake" (Matthew 19:12). To those, undoubtedly, who, denying their own, come after Christ and deny themselves and follow Him (Luke 9:23), so that they are governed no longer by their own will but by that of their rule and superior. In like manner, according to the testimony of the apostle, those virgins do better who, contemning the world and spurning its enticements, vow and maintain virginity in monasteries than those who place their necks beneath the matrimonial burden. For thus St. Paul says in 1 Corinthians 7:28, “He that giveth her in marriage doeth well; but he that giveth her not in marriage doeth better.” Also, concerning a widow, he continues, “She is happier if she so abides, after my judgment.”

No one is ignorant of the holiness of the hermit Paul, of Basil, Anthony, Benedict, Bernard, Dominic, Francis, William, Augustine, Clara, Bridget, and similar hermits, who indeed despised the entire realm of the world and all the splendor of the age on account of love to our Lord Jesus Christ. Moreover, the heresy of the Lampetians was condemned in most ancient times, which the heretic Jovinian attempted in vain to revive at Rome. Therefore, all things must be rejected that in this article have been produced against monasticism—viz., that monasteries succeeded vows. Of the nunneries, it is sufficiently ascertained that, though pertaining to the weaker sex, how in most cloisters the holy nuns persevered far more constantly to vows once uttered, even under these princes and cities, than the majority of monks; even to this day it has been impossible to move them from their holy purpose by any prayers, blandishments, threats, terrors, difficulties or distresses. Wherefore, those matters are not to be admitted that are interpreted unfavorably, since it has been expressly declared in the Holy Scriptures that the monastic life, when kept with proper observance, as may by the grace of God be rendered by any monks, merits eternal life; and indeed, Christ has promised to them a much more bountiful reward, saying, “Everyone that hath forsaken houses or brethren or sisters or father or mother or wife or children or lands for My name's sake shall receive a hundredfold, and shall inherit everlasting life” (Matthew 19:29).

That monasteries, as they show, were formerly literary schools is not denied; nevertheless, there is no ignorance of the fact that these were at first schools of virtues and discipline to which literature was afterward added. But since no one putting his hand to the plough and looking back is fit for the kingdom of heaven (Luke 9:62), all marriages and breaking of vows by monks and nuns should be regarded as condemned, according to the tenor not only of the Holy Scriptures but also of the laws and canons, “having damnation, because they have cast off their first faith,” as St. Paul says (1 Timothy 5:12). Moreover, that vows are not contrary to the ordinance of God has been declared with reference to the second article of the alleged abuses. That they attempt to defend themselves by dispensations of the pope is of no effect. For although the pope has perhaps made a dispensation for the king of Aragon, who, we read, returned to the monastery after having had offspring, or for any other prince on account of the peace of the entire kingdom or province, to prevent the exposure of the entire kingdom or province to wars, carnage, pillage, debauchery, conflagrations, and murders—nevertheless, in private persons who abandon vows in apostasy such grounds for dispensations cannot be urged. For the assumption is repelled that the vow concerns a matter that is impossible. For continence, which so many thousands of men and virgins have maintained, is not impossible. For although the wise man says (The Wisdom of Solomon 8:21), “I knew that I could not otherwise be continent, unless God gave it me,” nevertheless Christ promised to give it. “Seek,” He says, “and ye shall find" (Luke 11:9; Matthew 18:28). And St. Paul says, "God is faithful, who will not suffer you to be tempted above that ye are able, but will with the temptation also make a way to escape, that ye may be able to bear it" (1 Corinthians 10:13).

They are also poor defenders of their cause when they admit that the violation of a vow is irreprehensible, and it must be declared that by law such marriages are censured and should be dissolved, C. Ut. Continentiae, xxvii. Q. 1, as also by the ancient statutes of emperors. But when they allege in their favor *convivae nuptiarum*,[21] they accomplish nothing, for it speaks of a simple—not of a religious vow—which the Church observes also to this day. The marriages of monks, nuns, or priests have therefore never been ratified. Futile, also, is their statement that a votive life is an invention of men, for it has been founded upon the Holy Scriptures, inspired into the most Holy Fathers by the Holy Ghost. Nor does it deny honor to Christ, since monks observe all things for Christ's sake and imitate Christ. False, therefore, is the judgment whereby they condemn monastic service as godless, whereas it is most Christian. For the monks have not fallen from God's grace, as the Jews of whom St. Paul speaks in Galatians 5:4, when they still sought justification by the Law of Moses; but the monks endeavor to live more nearly to the Gospel, that they may merit eternal life. Therefore, the allegations here made against monasticism are impious. Moreover, the malicious charge that is still further added, that those in religious orders claim to be in a state of perfection, has never been heard of by them; for those in these orders claim not for themselves a state of perfection but only a state in which to acquire perfection—because their regulations are instruments of perfection and not perfection itself. In this manner, Gerson must be received, who does not deny that religious orders are states wherein to acquire perfection as he declares in his treatises "Against the Proprietors of the Rule of St. Augustine," "Of Evangelical Counsels," "Of Perfection of Heart," and in other places. For this reason, the princes and cities should be admonished to strive rather for the reformation of the monasteries by their legitimate superiors than for their subversion—rather for the godly improvement of the monks than that they be abolished—as their most religious ancestors, most Christian princes, have done. But if they will not believe holy and most religious Fathers defending monastic vows, let them hear at least His Imperial Highness, the Emperor Justinian, in *Authentica*, "De Monachis," Coll. 2.

To Article XXVIII

VII. Of Ecclesiastical Power

Although many things are introduced here in the topic of ecclesiastical power, with greater bitterness than is just, yet it must be declared that to most reverend bishops and priests and to the entire clergy, all ecclesiastical power is freely conceded that belongs

21 the bridal chamber [the marriage bed]

to them by law or custom. Besides, it is proper to preserve for them all immunities, privileges, preferments, and prerogatives granted them by Roman emperors and kings. Nor can those things that have been granted ecclesiastics by imperial munificence or gift be allowed to be infringed by any princes or any other subject of the Roman Empire. For it is most abundantly proved that ecclesiastical power in spiritual things has been founded upon divine right, of which St. Paul indeed says, "For though I should boast somewhat more of our authority, which the Lord hath given us for edification, and not for your destruction" (2 Corinthians 10:8), and afterward, "Therefore, I write these things being absent, lest being present I should use sharpness, according to the power that the Lord hath given me to edification, and not to destruction (2 Corinthians 13:10). Paul also displays his coercitive disposition when he says, "What will ye? Shall I come unto you with a rod, or in love and in the spirit of meekness?" (1 Corinthians 4:21). And of judicial matters he writes to Timothy, "Against an elder receive not an accusation but before two or three witnesses" (1 Timothy 5:19). From these passages, it is very clearly discerned that bishops have the power not only of the ministry of the Word of God but also of ruling and coercitive correction in order to direct subjects to the goal of eternal blessedness. But for the power of ruling, there is required the power to judge, to define, to discriminate, and to decide what is expedient or conducive to the aforesaid goal.

In vain, therefore, and futile is all that is inserted in the present article in opposition to the immunity of churches and schools. Accordingly, all subjects of the Roman Empire must be forbidden from bringing the clergy before a civil tribunal, contrary to imperial privileges that have been conceded. For Pope Clement the Martyr says, "If any of the presbyters have trouble with one another, let whatever it be adjusted before the presbyters of the Church." Hence, Constantine the Great, the most Christian emperor, was unwilling in the holy Council of Nicaea to give judgment even in secular cases. "Ye are gods," he says, "appointed by the true God. Go, settle the case among yourselves, because it is not proper that we judge gods." As to what is further repeated concerning Church regulations has been sufficiently replied to above. Nor does Christian liberty, which they bring forth as an argument, avail them, since this is not liberty but prodigious license, which, inculcated on the people, excites them to fatal and most dangerous sedition. For Christian liberty is not opposed to ecclesiastical usages since they promote what is good, but it is opposed to the servitude of the Mosaic Law and the servitude of sin. "Whosoever committeth sin is the servant of sin," says Christ (John 8:34). Hence their breaking fasts, their free partaking of meats, their neglect of canonical hours, their omission of Confession (viz., at Easter) and their commission and omission of similar things are not a use of liberty but an abuse thereof, contrary to the warnings of St. Paul, who earnestly warned them, saying, "Brethren, ye have been called unto liberty; only use not liberty for an occasion to the flesh, but by love serve one another" (Galatians 5:13). Hence, no one ought to conceal his crimes under the pretext of Gospel liberty, which St. Peter also forbade: "As free, and not using your liberty for a cloak of maliciousness, but as the servant of God" (1 Peter 2:16). As to what they have added concerning abuses, all the princes and estates of the empire undoubtedly know that not even the least is approved either by His Imperial Majesty or by any princes or any Christian man, but that both the princes and the estates of the empire desire to strive with a common purpose and agreement in order that, the abuses being removed and reformed, the excesses of both estates may be either utterly abolished or reformed for the better, and that the ecclesiastical estate, which has been weakened in many ways and the Christian religion, which has grown cold and relaxed in some, may be restored and renewed to its pristine glory and distinction. To this, as is evident to all, His Imperial Majesty has thus far devoted the greatest care and labor, and kindly promises in the future to employ for this cause all his means and zeal.

Conclusion

From the foregoing—viz., the Confession and its reply—since His Imperial Majesty perceives that the elector, the princes, and the cities agree on many points with the Catholic and Roman Church and dissent from the godless dogmas that are disseminated all over Germany and the pamphlets circulated everywhere and that they disapprove of and condemn them, His Holy Imperial Majesty is fully convinced and hopes that the result will be that when the elector, princes, and cities have heard and understood this reply, they will agree with united minds in regard to those matters also in which they perhaps have not agreed hitherto with the Roman Catholic Church, and that in all other things above mentioned they will obediently conform to the Catholic and Roman Church and the Christian faith and religion. For such conduct on their part His Imperial Majesty will be peculiarly grateful and will bestow his special favor upon them all in common, and also, as opportunity offers, upon them individually. For (which may God forbid) if this admonition, so Christian and indulgent, be unheeded, the elector, princes, and cities can judge that a necessary cause is afforded His Imperial Majesty that, as becometh a Roman emperor and Christian caesar and a defender and advocate of the Catholic and Christian Church, he must care for such matters as the nature of the charge committed to him and his integrity of conscience require.